Plotinus and the Presocratics

SUNY series in Ancient Greek Philosophy

Anthony Preus, editor

Plotinus and the Presocratics

A Philosophical Study of Presocratic Influences in Plotinus' Enneads

Giannis Stamatellos

State University of New York Press

Published by
State University of New York Press, Albany

Printed in the United States of America

For information, address State University of New York Press,
194 Washington Avenue, Suite 305, Albany, NY 12210-2384

Production by Judith Block
Marketing by Michael Campochiaro

Library of Congress Cataloging-in-Publication Data

Stamatellos, Giannis, 1970–
Plotinus and the presocratics : a philosophical study of presocratic influences in Plotinus' *Enneads* / Giannis Stamatellos.
p. cm. — (SUNY series in ancient Greek philosophy)
Includes bibliographical references and index.
ISBN-13: 978-0-7914-7061-9 (hardcover : alk. paper)
ISBN-13: 978-0-7914-7062-6 (pbk. : alk. paper)
1. Plotinus. 2. Philosophy, Ancient. 3. Pre-Socratic philosophers. 4. Plotinus. Enneads. 5. Soul. 6. Intellect. 7. One (The One in philosophy) I. Title. II. Series.
B693.E63S73 2007
186'.4—dc22 2006017562

10 9 8 7 6 5 4 3 2 1

To my grandparents

Nikos and Elpinike Tetradi

Contents

Acknowledgments

Gratefully, I would like to acknowledge all those who have assisted me in this work. First and foremost, I would like to thank Professor Rosemary Wright for her constant encouragement, insightful instruction, and philosophical inspiration throughout this project. Her help was invaluable and I owe her gratitude for her unconditional support.

I would like to express my special thanks to Professor Andrew Smith and Professor David Cockburn for their invaluable comments. I am also thankful to the Blegen Library of the American School of Classical Studies at Athens and the Library of the American College of Greece for offering me all the necessary facilities to accomplish my research project. In addition, I would like to acknowledge Dr. Paul Kalligas and Dr. Evangellos Roussos for providing me with important bibliographical sources and notes not only on the particular subject, but also generally on Plotinus.

I am also grateful to my wife Alexandra, my daughter Antonia, my son Aristoteles, and my mother Antonia for their care and support. Without their perennial patience and encouragement, I would not have completed this book.

Finally, I wish to thank my friends Kostas Andreou, Kostantinos Andronis, Fotis Terzakis, David Lewis, Dr. Spyridon Rangos, and Dr. Dionysis Metzeniotis for their support and the creative inspiration during our philosophical discussions.

Introduction

Plotinus (AD 204–205) and the Presocratic thinkers (AD *c.* 6th–5th c.) designate the historical boundaries of ancient Greek philosophy. Whereas the Presocratics determine the beginning of Greek philosophy, Plotinus initiates the last period of Greek intellection which is usually marked by the closure of Plato's Academy in Athens by the emperor Justinian (AD 529). Plotinus' philosophy is a clear innovation in the development of Platonism and for this reason his work is regarded as the beginning of the Neoplatonic movement. His thought assimilates nearly eight centuries of philosophy and intellectual history, and the attentive reader of the *Enneads* is able to detect various direct and indirect citations of ancient authors from the Presocratic, Classical and Hellenistic periods. Plotinus mentions by name leading Greek philosophers spanning these centuries such as Pherecydes, Pythagoras and the Pythagoreans, Heraclitus, Empedocles, Anaxagoras, Socrates, Plato, Aristotle, the Stoics, and the Epicureans. It is noteworthy that Plotinus never refers by name to any philosopher later than Epicurus.

Despite the fact that the Presocratic philosophers are present in the *Enneads*, in modern scholarship on Plotinus, scant attention has been paid to the Presocratic origins of his thought. As well as the lack of consideration of Presocratics in the *Enneads*, the general attitude is deflationary, but a detailed study of the text points in the opposite direction. Plotinus' references to the Presocratics are not without purpose and significance. In many cases, he refers directly to eminent Presocratic thinkers along with Plato and sometimes Aristotle in the same respectful manner and without making any distinction regarding their philosophical ability and authority. Particularly, throughout the *Enneads*, Plotinus refers by name four times to Heraclitus, five times to Empedocles, twice to Parmenides and Anaxagoras, four times to Pythagoras and the early Pythagorean School and once to Pherecydes. In addition, there are a large number of indirect allusions to other important Presocratics such as Anaximander, Philolaus, and the early Atomists.

These direct and indirect references show the Presocratics appearing in different areas of Plotinus' philosophy. Plotinus returns to Presocratic accounts in his discussions of (1) the One and the unity of Being; (2) the structure of the living Intellect and the predicates of Being; (3) the nature of eternity and time; and (4) the life of the ensouled bodies and the formation of the material world.

Within this framework, Plotinus' One, the First Hypostasis of Being, is to some extent foreshadowed by the concept of the Presocratic first principle found in Heraclitus' One, Empedocles' *Philia*, the Pythagorean Monad and Anaxagoras' Mind. Plotinus' self-thinking Intellect, the Second Hypostasis of Being, reflects the predicates of Parmenides' Being, the fundamental ontological connection between thinking and being and Anaxagoras' self-inclusiveness principle. The non-durational nature of eternity is strongly influenced by Parmenides' timelessness of Being and the association of eternity with the life of Intellect may be traced back to Heraclitus' concept of ever-living fire and Empedocles' eternal life. With regard to the Soul, the Third Hypostasis of Being, the descent of living bodies reflects Heraclitus' cosmic alterations of soul and Empedocles' cycles of the *daimōn*. Furthermore, Presocratic self-knowledge is for Plotinus the goal of the Soul's ascent to the One, and the unity of Plotinus' universe echoes the unity of the Presocratic cosmos. Finally, Plotinus interacts with Presocratic concepts of matter found in Anaximander's *apeiron*, Empedocles' theory of the four roots, Anaxagoras' primordial mixture and early Atomic materialism.

In the detailed analysis of these topics, the aim of this monograph is threefold: (1) to reinstate the significance of the Presocratic tradition for Plotinus; (2) to offer a comparative philosophical study between fundamental Presocratic and Plotinian concepts; and (3) to suggest possible new references to Presocratic fragments within the *Enneads*, beyond those mentioned in modern studies and commentaries. In pursuit of this aim, the thesis will focus mainly on the following *Enneads*, since they include the most striking references to the Presocratics: II.1 [40] *On Heaven*; II.4 [12] *On Matter*; III.7 [45] *On Eternity and Time*; IV.8 [6] *On the Descent of the Soul into the Bodies*; V.1 [10] *On the Three Primary Hypostases*; and VI.6 [34] *On Numbers.* A study of these treatises forms the kernel of the book, although the research extends to relevant passages throughout the *Enneads*. The main Presocratics involved are Heraclitus, Parmenides, Empedocles, Anaxagoras, the early Pythagoreans, and the early Atomists, since Plotinus refers directly to them and their theories are fundamental to his thought. The study will not, however, be limited to these Presocratics but aims to present the wider Presocratic tradition in the *Enneads*.

Within this framework and after an introductory chapter on the origins of Plotinus' philosophy, the four main sections of the book, showing the significance of Presocratic tradition in Plotinus' philosophy, follow the main ontological levels of Plotinus' system of the Three Hypostases: One and Unity in chapter 2, Intellect and Being in chapter 3, Eternity and Time in chapter 4, and Matter and Soul in chapter 5. The book is also supplemented by an appendix with the text of the Presocratic fragments in Plotinus' *Enneads* as well as an *Index Fontium* with the references of the Presocratic fragments and testimonies in the *Enneads*.

Chapter 1

The Origins of Plotinus' Philosophy

1.1 PLOTINUS' PREDECESSORS

A comparative study of the origins of Plotinus' philosophy presupposes, first, an investigation into his philosophical sources and, second, an analysis of his philosophical method. Modern scholarship recognizes the importance of both. In the last fifteen years many studies on Plotinus focus on his philosophical sources as well as the manner in which these sources are treated in the *Enneads*.[1] This new attitude towards Plotinus and Neoplatonism aims to illuminate not only the importance of this later period of Greek philosophy, but also the development of Greek thought within the history of ideas.[2]

Plotinus belongs to the later Greek philosophical tradition (AD 3rd c.) where Greek thought is characterized by mature intellection and divergent elaboration. The *Enneads* accordingly is an invaluable source material for philosophical argument and criticism.[3] The philosophy of Plotinus' predecessors is incorporated and discussed within the flow of the text as a unified synthesis of thought that is underlined by inspired and sometimes obscure speculations. Plotinus' prose style includes a unique poetic rhythm of philosophizing with the arguments presented elaborately, but without an obvious systematic and organized structure. However, Plotinus was neither a historian of philosophy, nor did he aim to act in such a way as to present and preserve a literal account of the preceding sources.

Consequently, the modern scholar of the *Enneads* will often find it difficult to identify in Plotinus the hidden references to his predecessors. As M. L. Gatti observes, Plotinus' citations and allusions "are far more numerous than direct references, and these, along with biographical material, permit us both to deepen and to broaden significantly our knowledge of Plotinus' sources by tracing the trajectory of speculation through Plotinus' predecessors."[4] Hence, the reader has to focus, as Plotinus himself did, more on the philosophical meaning of the text. Therefore, with suitable caution we may explore two interrelated parameters of Plotinus' philosophy: first, his philosophical method of inquiry, which incorporates his language, teaching, and writing practice, and second, his general attitude towards his philosophical sources.

1.2 PLOTINUS' PHILOSOPHICAL METHOD

The most important ancient testimony regarding Plotinus' philosophical method derives from Porphyry. According to Porphyry (*Life* 3.33 ff., and 14.14–16), Plotinus based his method of lecturing on the teaching method of his master Ammonius. When Plotinus, at the age of twenty-eight, felt a strong impulse to study philosophy, he was disappointed with the lectures of the Alexandrian philosophers until he attended the lectures of Ammonius (*Life* 3.6–19). Plotinus was so enthusiastic after hearing Ammonius lecture that he exclaimed approvingly: "this is the one I was looking for" and he stayed with Ammonius from AD 232 to 243 (*Life* 3.13). Among Plotinus' own students were Erennius, Olympius, the Platonic Origen,[5] and Longinus. Erennius, Origen, and Plotinus had made an agreement to keep silent on the doctrines of Ammonius, but none of them kept their promise (*Life* 3.24 ff.).

Ammonius (AD c. 175–242) was an enigmatic but influential philosopher, a self-taught Platonist who wrote nothing.[6] He founded a school in Alexandria probably at the beginning of the third century AD and, although his philosophy is regarded as a link between Middle-Platonism and Neoplatonism, in fact, we know very little about his thought. According to Hierocles and Nemesius, Ammonius held the view that "every reality derives from God," and he seemed to distinguish reality in three different but successive levels of existence: (1) the supreme reality of God, the gods and the celestial realities; (2) the intermediate reality of the ethereal nature and the good spirits; (3) the lowest reality of humans and the terrestrial beings.[7]

Ammonius was a philosopher with a free and independent mind. If we interpret correctly Plotinus' reaction to Ammonius' lectures, his teaching probably revealed a unique and inspired way of philosophizing. This way seems to have been extremely influential and it was inherited by Plotinus. In an illuminating passage, Porphyry stresses the fact that his master based his distinctive line of investigation on the theoretical course of his teacher Ammonius. Porphyry testifies that, during his lectures, Plotinus did not speak directly from books or notes but adopted a distinctive personal approach, following Ammonius' 'mind' (νοῦς) (*Life* 14.14–16). But what exactly was the 'mind' of Ammonius? Gatti maintains that Porphyry refers to Ammonius' method of reconciliation between Plato and Aristotle.[8] This claim is justified by Photius' testimony in the *Bibliotheca* (461a35–8) that Ammonius had tried to harmonize the doctrines of Plato and Aristotle, for the confrontation between Platonic and Aristotelian doctrines was a debatable matter in the Platonic and the Neoplatonic tradition.

But, *pace* Gatti, in Porphyry's passage, the 'mind' of Ammonius implies something more specific and technical in the lectures of Plotinus. As Porphyry continues in the next lines of his biographical work (*Life* 14.17 ff.), Plotinus was not interested in the philological or textual implications of the sources but in the philosophical ideas to be derived from them. Plotinus, following Ammonius' method of teaching, referenced his sources quickly and then gave a short but profound account of the text before passing on to his own interpretation. In a previous chapter (*Life* 3.33–39), Porphyry informs us that Plotinus, during his prewriting period, followed in his oral lectures the lively discussions of Ammonius' seminars. In the spirit of these discussions, Plotinus encouraged the participants during the lectures to ask him questions freely, which resulted in "complete lack of order" and a "great deal of pointless chatter" (*Life* 3.37). This teaching method seems to be the 'mind' of Ammonius shown in a free, independent, inspired, and profound philosophical discussion, and it is this method of philosophizing that appears both in Plotinus' lectures and writings.

1.2.1 Lectures and Writings

Plotinus' oral teaching and writings were unique for their unsystematic way of philosophical investigation. The *Enneads* present a philosopher who seems to be more interested in the philosophical exegesis of a text than its philological analysis. Plotinus was more of an original thinker than a philosopher-commentator such as Proclus, Iamblichus, and Damascius, or a systematic scholar writing introductions like Albinus. That is why Plotinus disparagingly regarded Longinus as a scholar and not a philosopher (*Life* 14.20). Plotinus, like his master Ammonius, clearly preferred free-ranging philosophical discussion of a topic to the scholarly analytical observations of the philologists. This unsystematic attitude is probably a reaction to the scholastic interpretations of the ancient texts found especially in the scholars of the period. Plotinus' decision to study in Alexandria with Ammonius and then establish his school in Rome, far away from Athens, the center of Platonism, implies that he literally wanted to distance himself from the traditional Platonism of the Academy. He seems to have in mind a new approach to the study of Platonic philosophy, an approach which could not be developed freely in the Academy. In all probability, this was the reason for Plotinus choosing Ammonius' free and lively seminars and adopting his method. A comprehensive style of thinking characterizes the *Enneads*, so that the reader shares the experience of free and lively philosophical argument, and may well feel that reading the *Enneads* comes close to hearing Plotinus' lectures.

Indeed Porphyry informs us that in his lectures Plotinus used to focus on his own thoughts, being interested not so much in the formal and systematic interpretations of a philosophical question, but more on his own inspiration and philosophical originality (*Life* 8). Hence, in his writings, as Porphyry testifies, he was concise, full of thought and brief in philosophical expression, concentrating more on the meaning of the words than the words themselves (*Life* 14.1–4). He was not concerned with the calligraphy of the letters, the correct spelling or the correct division of his text (*Life* 8.4–8 and 18.10 ff.). Plotinus preferred to be completely immersed in his train of thought, writing down his ideas continuously and spontaneously as if he were copying them from a book (*Life* 8.8–12). But, because of his problematic eyesight, reading and revision were difficult, and so his language appears complicated and obscure, with many grammatical and spelling errors (*Life* 8.1–6). This is probably the main reason why Plotinus entrusted Porphyry both with the editing and the arrangement of his writings (*Life* 7.50–52; 24.1–5).

Furthermore, Porphyry stresses Plotinus' remarkable ability to combine inner meditation with external activity; this ability was clearly shown not only in his writings, but also in his oral teachings (*Life* 8.19–23; 9.16–22). On this issue, R. T. Wallis mentions three major points common to Plotinus' lectures and writings: first, his preference to deal more with individual philosophical problems than to expound his thought in a formal system; second, his usual practice of starting his investigations from the traditional interpretation of a Platonic or Aristotelian passage and then trying to deny, correct, or develop this interpretation into his own interpretative line; third, his unique style of philosophical narrative in the form of a vivid dialogue with an imaginary interlocutor, using a rapid interchange between questioner and responder.[9] From Plotinus' style of lecturing and writing, it is important to focus attention on his unique philosophical discourse and demonstrate how this discourse develops from his philosophical language.

1.2.2 Language, Simile, and Metaphor

Plotinus' philosophical language is fashioned upon the theoretical background of his metaphysics. His metaphysical thought moves either upwards following the resemblance of the perceptible image to the intelligible archetype, or downwards following the procession of the intelligible archetype to the perceptible image. Plotinus applies this process to the development of his writings. Frequently, his method is to start from his own experience and to proceed inductively to the self-justification of this experience in theoretical terms. An excellent example of this method appears in the opening lines of *Ennead* IV.8 where Plotinus describes his own autobiographical metaphysical experience and then proceeds to the explanation and evaluation of this experience through a theoretical analysis.

Plotinus' inductive way of reasoning is not a mathematical induction, but primarily associated with the evaluation of a dialectic inference. He collects empirical instances with metaphysical value and tries to harmonize the results of this experience with the inherent structure of the intelligible world; he then proceeds to some general metaphysical conclusions. Hence, Plotinus' philosophical language serves as verbal representation of the intelligible world. As F. M. Schroeder comments, "the model of representation departs from the perceptible world and attempts to account for intelligible reality in such a way that the two realms will not be confused with each other."[10]

This is the reason why Plotinus' language, despite its prose style, manifests a poetic rhythm with complex linguistic schemata. In V.1.2.17–23, for instance, Plotinus stresses the need for the Soul to recollect the whole universe, to free itself from illusion and attain true quietude. At this higher level, the individual soul will be able to see the greater soul illuminating, animating, and ordering the world in divine quietness. Likewise, in *Ennead* VI.4.7, Plotinus, in order to express the simultaneous presence of the intelligible order throughout every part of the perceptible world, uses the illustrations of a "hand controlling a plank and a small body illumining a large sphere." In *Ennead* III.8.10, in order to describe the unending and unified power of the One, Plotinus uses similes, first, of the "spring" which spreads out its power to the rivers while itself remaining unexhausted and in unity and, second, of a "huge tree" which spreads out its life to the branches while its origins remain firmly settled in its roots. In *Ennead* VI.5.5, Plotinus uses his favorite metaphor of the "circle and the radii" in order to illustrate the expansion of the intelligible world from the undifferentiated center of the circle (the One) radiating into the multiplicity of the intelligible universe.[11] Moreover, Plotinus, in order to show through his language the "presence of being everywhere", provides as an analogy the example of the all-united-centers (or the one-center) radiating their lines to the next realities. But besides this extension the center remains one as the only source of all the lines. According to A. H. Armstrong, this metaphor "can be used at any level of the hierarchy to describe the combination of immanent presence and transcendent separateness which Plotinus sees when he is trying to describe the relationship of a relatively complex and multiple derived reality to its simpler and more unified one."[12]

From the above examples, it can be concluded that Plotinus recognizes the limitations of abstract expression and often turns to the construction of similes and metaphoric images which represent, as much as they can, his spiritual experience. Plotinus uses his philosophical language as a dynamic medium of expression and not as a strict formalistic system of justification. His linguistic expression represents a lively paradigm of his own metaphysical understanding of the world and focuses more on the meanings revealed through the words than the words themselves. Mindful of these considerations, we can now turn to the way in which Plotinus' quotes his predecessors throughout the *Enneads*.

1.2.3 Quoting Predecessors

Plotinus' modus operandi with his sources is based upon his philosophical dialectical method. According to Steven Strange, Plotinus' proper philosophical method could be regarded as a dialectical method of philosophy with a threefold structure:[13] (1) stating the arguments—the position of the many; (2) analyzing and evaluating the arguments—agreements and disagreements; (3) resolving the arguments—minimizing contradictions in one position. In assessing these stages, Strange concludes that Plotinus' method adapts Aristotle's philosophical practice in the *Topics* (101a35–b4), the *Nicomachean Ethics* (1145b6–8), and the *Metaphysics* (995a28–31).[14] Plotinus begins from the views of his predecessors by stating briefly their theories on a philosophical problem and proceeds to the evaluation of the problem itself. In this case, Plotinus uses the views of the ancients in the same way as Aristotle uses the "opinions of the wise" (ἔνδοξα). First, Plotinus compares and contrasts these opinions, summarizing their inherent agreements and disagreements. Second, based on his own philosophical expertise, he develops dialectically the philosophical questions arising from the subject-matter. Third, he answers the questions by reconciling the various views and minimizing their contradiction and difficulties in a new Plotinian theory.

An excellent example of the above methodological practice can be found in *Ennead* III.7. This treatise presents a careful and critical demonstration of preceding accounts of the philosophical problem of eternity and time. In the first chapter of the treatise (1.8–17), Plotinus stresses the need to investigate the subject-matter in question with regard to the "ancient philosophers" (οἱ παλαιοί) before proceeding to his own interpretation and evaluation. Plotinus finds it unhelpful to construct a theory on a philosophical problem or to present a solution to an enquiry without previously analyzing the philosophical background of the subject-matter. The "statements" (ἀποφάσεις) of the ancient philosophers form the philosophical background of the philosophical question, but they do not resolve the problem immediately.

On the other hand, the ancient philosophers may have found the truth but not in its absolute purity—they are not unquestionable authorities of truth. Plotinus, while he fully recognizes the opinions of the ancients, is not willing to follow this uncritical method. Since there is no definite and immediate answer to a serious philosophical problem, the problem still remains debatable. Just "parroting" the views of the ancients is a sterile and unacceptable attitude for a philosopher, for it is not in the nature of philosophy to reply to a question by just presenting the earlier answers. On this basis, in III.7.7.10–17, Plotinus stresses again the need to examine the earlier theories of the ancients. Since there has been a thorough investigation by them, then the initial consideration of their account is absolutely necessary. The philosopher should be aware of the philosophical background of his subject-matter and not proceed unwarily to new arbitrary theoretical conceptions. The philosopher has to maintain a balance between critical thinking and theoretical awareness.

As in *Ennead* III.7, Plotinus follows this attitude towards his predecessors frequently throughout the other treatises of the *Enneads*. He refers to the ancient philosophers both in relation to their "accounts"[15] and to the "ancients"[16] themselves. In all cases, Plotinus speaks of his predecessors with admiration and respect. Actually, in the early Platonic tradition, the expression "the ancient philosophers" (οἱ παλαιοί φιλόσοφοι) usually denotes a specific group of philosophers, especially the early Platonists. For instance, Antiochus of Ascalon (1st century BC) indicates with this expression Plato and Aristotle as well as their contemporary philosophers of the Old Academy (Cicero *De finibus* 5.23). In the *Enneads*, the use of the "ancients" (παλαιοί) indicates something much more extensive. Plotinus' expression is not only limited to Plato and Aristotle, but also includes the Presocratics and the early Pythagoreans, and in some cases the Stoics and the Epicureans.

Prima facie Plotinus' approach is almost the same as that of Aristotle. Yet, according to Strange, it is likely that Plotinus recognized in Aristotle's methodology the shadow cast by Plato's practice in the Academy, so that he regarded Aristotle's method more as that of an Academic student than an autonomous philosopher.[17] Because of this, Plotinus' mode of investigation needs to be placed in the wider context of Platonic dialectic and not restricted to the Aristotelian version. In addition, it should be noted that there are fundamental differences between Aristotle and Plotinus in their method of reference. First, for Plotinus, the ancient philosophers were ex hypothesi wise and with the right approach in their observations and initial considerations. For instance, as we have seen, Plotinus significantly calls the earlier thinkers "godlike men" (θείοι ἄνδρες), using a similar expression for Plato (ὁ θεῖος Πλάτων).[18] Second, Plotinus stresses the authority of the ancients in order to prove the continuation of Greek thought and to justify his own theoretical background. Third, Plotinus, as is his philosophical method, refers to his predecessors without presenting a literal account of their ideas; he gives us only fragments of their theoretical vocabulary and the main lines of their accounts. In contrast, Aristotle sometimes gives lengthy accounts of his predecessors' views but without affirming any special reverence or respect. Aristotle tends to see his predecessors as taking faltering steps towards the goal he has now reached, and to interpret their ideas in terms of his own philosophy and terminology. In Plotinus' case, this arrogant attitude is clearly missing from the *Enneads*; his criticism is more a return to his philosophical roots than a radical abolition or replacement of the earlier views. This difference in attitude between Aristotle and Plotinus is mainly seen in the treatment of philosophical sources.

1.3 PLOTINUS' PHILOSOPHICAL SOURCES

Plotinus' philosophy is characterized by the following fundamental principle: *reality exists in a successive triadic hierarchy of Being*. The structure of his system is founded on two axes: (1) the Three Hypostases of Being, named the One (ἕν), the Intellect (νοῦς), and the Soul (ψυχή), and (2) the dual productive phases of each Hypostasis, named the phases of Procession (πρόοδος) and Return (ἐπιστροφή). Whereas the former has its origins partly in Plato's ontological distinction between being and becoming, intelligible and perceptible world, the latter derives from Aristotle's dynamic interrelation between actuality and potentiality, priority, and the posterior.

Plotinus demonstrates the outline of his metaphysics in *Ennead* V.1 *On The Three Primary Hypostases*. According to this treatise, any higher Hypostasis of Being participates in a purer degree of ontological perfection, unity, and intellection; any lower Hypostasis is generated by contemplating the higher Hypostasis in itself. At the highest level of purity, unity and simplicity resides the One, the primary causal principle of every existence.

The Plotinian One (comparable to the Platonic Good) is absolutely ineffable and transcendent; it is the simplest non-composite and unified prior principle that generates all composite and multiple posteriors. Since the existence of the One is more unified and simple, every posterior depends on, aims at, and refers to the One. The Intellect, the Second Hypostasis, a synthesis of Plato's world of Forms and Aristotle's self-thinking Intellect, derives from the One by a timeless self-contemplation. The Intellect is for Plotinus the Indefinite Dyad, the divine level of Being where all the Platonic Forms are self-included in the most perfect and truest condition. The Intellect possesses perfect self-knowledge and infinite eternal life. The Soul, the Third Hypostasis, is a by-product of the Intellect. The Soul restlessly produces, animates, formulates, and governs the perceptible world by shedding its intelligible light on the insubstantial impassability of matter.

The perfection and purity of the three levels of being are designated by the everlasting illumination of the One. The outflowing illumination of each Hypostasis is accompanied almost simultaneously by an ascending contemplative attendance to its higher Hypostasis. This organic order of being underlies Plotinus' concept of the Hypostases and signifies his philosophical originality. His scheme of ontological hierarchies underpins the fundamental principle of Neoplatonism: *that reality consists in a hierarchy of degrees of unity*.

But the idea of unity is not unique to Plotinus. As R. T. Wallis observes, the scheme is a "systematization of the Pythagorean-Platonic tradition's identification of goodness and order with form, measure, and limit, which in their turn imply number and mathematical ratio and hence, ultimately the presence of an organizing unity."[19] On this basis, relating Plotinus' metaphysics to the Greek philosophical tradition, H. Dörrie characterizes Plotinus as both "traditionalist" and "innovator."[20] Every innovation in Plotinus' system has its roots in the tradition, and traditional accounts can be clearly observed in the *Enneads*. The criteria that Plotinus used to criticize or evaluate the ancient theories were also the criteria of his originality.[21] In fact, Plotinus' fundamental objective was to harmonize, systematize, and primarily subsume his metaphysical thought in the context of Greek philosophical tradition. Plotinus was not able to realize this aim by following an uncritical and eclectic way of philosophizing. As with his predecessors, Plotinus set out to search for the truth and not just reiterate, parrot-fashion, the opinions of others. From a historical point of view, the truth for Plotinus was known initially by the ancients, and, since the ancients had found the truth, he needed initially to speculate on them and their theories.

In order to understand the relationship of Plotinus' philosophy to the Greek philosophical tradition, it is essential to observe briefly the influences of his predecessors in the *Enneads*. These influences cannot be reduced merely to Platonic/Middle-Platonic metaphysics or the Pythagorean/Neopythagorean mathematical mysticism. It is also important to draw attention to Aristotelian psychology and metaphysics and to Stoic psychology and cosmology as well as to Plotinus' general attitude to the contemporary movements of the third century AD.

1.3.1 Plato

Among Plotinus' predecessors, Plato is undoubtedly the leading philosophical authority—he is the one who above all attained the truth. Plato is the philosopher whose work underlies the fundamental theoretical principles of Plotinus' metaphysical, psychological, and cosmological investigations. Throughout the *Enneads*, Plotinus refers to Plato by name fifty-six times.[22] In all these cases, Plotinus, like the later Neoplatonists, uses Plato's work as his principal source, and most of his theories are a deep and original insights into Platonic theories. For instance in V.1.8.11–14, Plotinus states clearly that his accounts are depended on Plato's writings. Plotinus actually defines himself as an "interpreter" (ἐξηγητής) of Plato and his philosophy as an exegesis of Plato's accounts (τοῦ Πλάτωνος γράμμασιν).[23] Plotinus clearly states that his own accounts are neither new nor of the present time but rather that his philosophical views are old, belonging to the Platonic teaching.[24]

Plotinus systematizes Plato's metaphysical theories, especially those found in the *Parmenides*, the *Republic*, the *Sophist*, and the *Second Platonic Epistle*.[25] In the *Parmenides*, Plato's Parmenides develops a series of hypotheses concerning the nature of the 'one' and its relation to the 'many'. The first two hypotheses were of central importance to Plotinus' account of the three Hypostases.[26] In the first hypothesis at 137c–142a, where Parmenides states in negative terms that "if there is one in absolute unity then nothing can be predicated of it," Plotinus discovers the absolute ineffability of his own transcendent One, the First Hypostasis.[27] In the first part of the second hypothesis (142b–155e), where Parmenides states in affirmative terms that "if one exists all predicates can be ascribed to it," Plotinus finds the nature of Intellect, his Second Hypostasis. Finally, in the last part of the third hypothesis (155e–157b), where Parmenides deals with the idea of temporal becoming, Plotinus formulates a distinct hypothesis which is related to the Soul, his Third Hypostasis.[28]

As a result of this, it would seem that Plotinus considers the *Parmenides* to be a crucially important dialogue in Plato's metaphysics. However, the purpose of this particular dialogue was not clear during the history of Platonism. For some Platonists such as Albinus (*Isagoge*, 3) it was only a "logical exercise" (γυμνάσιον λογικόν), while for others it was a manifestation of Plato's metaphysical teaching.[29] After Plotinus, later Neoplatonists focused on the latter interpretation and considered the *Parmenides* to be one of the most important metaphysical dialogues in Plato's works. According to Proclus' testimony (*in Timaeum* I.13.14–17), Iamblichus regarded the *Parmenides* along with the *Timaeus* as the only dialogues which contained Plato's original metaphysical teaching, while Proclus himself considered the *Parmenides* to be the dialogue that included the "truth on gods" and, by extension, the complete system of Platonic theology (*Platonic Theology* I.2.4–6).[30]

However, the *Parmenides* is not the only Platonic work where Plotinus sees an appropriate reference for the systematization of the three Hypostases. In an obscure passage of the *Second Platonic Letter* (312d–313a), Plotinus discovers the triadic reality of being, while in the *Republic* (509b), he finds the prime nature of the One identified with the Good 'beyond being' (ἐπέκεινα τῆς οὐσίας).[31] From a consideration of the *Timaeus* (30c ff.) and the *Sophist* (248e–49d), he interprets the nature of the Intellect as intelligible living being, eternal perfect life, and true being. Plotinus therefore inherits from the *Sophist* (244b–45c) the five Genera of Being, Rest, Motion, Sameness, and Otherness, and uses them instead of the ten Aristotelian Categories (VI.1.1–24), or the Stoic Genus (VI.1.23–29) as more appropriate to the nature of the intelligible world (VI.2.2). Finally, with regard to the perceptible world, Plotinus' cosmos reflects the structure of the Platonic cosmos, the world of becoming set against the world of being.

In addition to the central importance of the Platonic dialogues for Plotinus' philosophy, another aspect of Plato's teaching, the famous "unwritten doctrines,"[32] seems to play a considerable role in the *Enneads*. Plotinus and especially the later Neoplatonists accepted Aristotle's testimony for the existence of unwritten doctrines and reached the conclusion that Plato's philosophy was propounded within the dialogues but also elsewhere. H. J. Krämer presents serious evidence for the influence of the unwritten doctrines in Plotinus.[33] According to his research, the unwritten doctrines are especially relevant to Plotinus' doctrines of the One beyond being and the multilevel plurality of being. In a similar context, and putting in one and the same framework the whole Neoplatonic tradition, L. P. Gerson states that the unwritten doctrines were part of Neoplatonism's Plato and since, he continues, "the interpretation of Plato is so much a part of Neoplatonism, it is extremely useful to have available an understanding of the material outside the dialogues that led the Neoplatonists to read the dialogues as they did."[34]

However, despite the above evidences, the exact contribution of Plato to the *Enneads* remains a debatable manner for modern scholars. Whereas some regard Plotinus merely as a disciple or uncritical interpreter of Plato, others regard him as an autonomous thinker with respect to Plato and his predecessors, an original representative of a long tradition of Greek metaphysical thought who was aware of his own innovations and arguments.[35] But there is no doubt that Plotinus was fully aware of Plato's dialogues and, as G. Faggin observes, no one can deny his original philosophical creativity.[36] On this interpretive line, R. Arnou and P. R. Blum observe that Plotinus' philosophy is Platonism in process—a process which underlies a new progress in the development of Platonic teaching.[37] Indeed, Plotinus' thought derives fundamentally from a systematic and careful reading of Plato. As J–M. Charrue maintains, Plotinus' work is a synthetic representation of the ancient texts, a careful elaboration of his sources and a mature reconsideration of Plato's dialogues that leads to a new perspective of Platonic philosophy.[38]

On the other hand, Plotinus is not, like Plato, a careful writer who refines the linguistic quality of his text, nor a faithful disciple who follows his master in all the aspects of his thought. Plotinus is more interested in metaphysics than mathematics, ethics, or politics, and, even though Plotinus had a competent knowledge of geometry, arithmetic, mechanics, optics, and music, his main concern was the metaphysical dimension of these disciplines and not the disciplines themselves (*Life* 14. 7–10). In addition, Plotinus was not completely uncritical of Plato. In some cases he seems to question Plato's account (as for example at *Ennead* II.1.2). In other cases he does not hesitate to point out contradictory accounts in Platonic dialogues. For example, in *Ennead* IV.8, where the problem of the descent of the soul into the bodies is discussed, Plotinus notes that two contradictory positions are taken by Plato: on the one hand, the negative or pessimistic view given in the soul's descent in the *Phaedo*, the image of the cave in the *Republic*, and the *Phaedrus'* myth and, on the other, the positive or optimistic view of soul and cosmos in the *Timaeus*.[39]

Consequently, Plotinus should not be understood as an eclectic or a mere interpreter of Plato. The originality of Plotinus is confirmed by the testimonies of his contemporaries and later Neoplatonists. Proclus, for instance, was impressed by his originality and names his philosophy as a "divine revelation to men" (*Platonic Theology* I.6.16ff), and St. Augustine characterized Plotinus as the "man in whom Plato lived again" (*Contra Academicos* 3.18).[40] Thus, Plotinus' philosophy cannot be reduced to a mosaic of Platonic or other earlier ideas. He must be regarded both as a devoted Platonist and as an original philosopher who contributed with his radical thought to a new perception of Platonism, that of Neoplatonism.

1.3.2 Aristotle

Aristotle is also an important influence in Plotinus' thought, although not to the same degree as he was for the later Neoplatonists, and Plotinus refers to Aristotle by name only four times (II.1.2.12, 4.11; II.5.3.18; V.1.9.7). On the other hand, Porphyry testifies to the presence of concealed Peripatetic doctrines in the *Enneads* and in particular to the extensive use of Aristotle's *Metaphysics* (*Life* 14.5–6).[41] Yet, whereas Plotinus seems to prefer Plato's dialectic ontology to Aristotle's logic, later Neoplatonists tended to construct their system on both Aristotelian logic and Platonic ontology, fusing, as far as they could, Plato and Aristotle into one unified account.[42] But Plotinus followed a middle course of interpretation. In many cases, he used Aristotelian terminology to defend Plato's doctrines and the validity of his ideas. This practice presupposes a sound knowledge of Aristotelian philosophy, which is clearly manifest throughout the *Enneads*.

Furthermore, whereas Plotinus accepts the Aristotelian doctrines of Intellect and Intelligible Matter as well as Aristotle's psychological vocabulary and the dynamic philosophical antitheses of "matter-form," "potentiality-actuality," and "prior-posterior," he criticizes Aristotle's psychology in identifying inseparably the soul with the body (IV.7.8[5]); his ethics in making happiness dependent on external prosperity (I.4.5); and his theology in denying a supreme principle beyond Intellect (V.6.2–6, VI.7.37–42). He also disagrees with Aristotle's theory in both metaphysics and physics in applying wrongly the Categories to both the intelligible (VI.1.1–24) and the perceptible world (VI.3.3). As we mentioned before, the ten Aristotelian Categories could be easily reduced to the five Platonic Genera.[43]

1.3.3 Stoics and Epicureans

With regard to the Stoics and Epicureans, the former are of greater significance for Plotinus than the latter. A. Graeser offers an invaluable comparison between Plotinus' philosophy and the Stoic tradition.[44] According to his study, Plotinus seems to be aware of the Old Stoa, Poseidonius and Epictetus as well as other major Stoic philosophers. Porphyry testifies to the appearance of concealed Stoic writings, along with the Peripatetic ones, in the *Enneads* (*Life* 14.5). Indeed, Plotinus accepts the Stoic accounts of cosmology, human nature, and *logos,* and especially their theories of the seed-principles, cosmic sympathy, theodicy, the vitalistic conception of the intelligible world, and the forms of individuals. On the other hand, Plotinus is completely opposed to the Stoic accounts of the world soul as highest deity, the soul as a material entity being spatially present in body, God as a mode of matter, and Fate governing the cosmos.[45] Finally, of great interest is Plotinus' adaptation of the Platonizing Stoicism of Poseidonius, especially concerning the notion of the cosmos as a spiritual continuum extending through a definite series of ontological media from God to matter.[46] The main difference between the theory of Poseidonius and that of Plotinus can be located in the theory of divinity as "spirit incorporeal and fiery." For Plotinus, Poseidonius' definition implies a materialistic and unstable notion of divinity incompatible with the nature of Intellect (Stobaeus, *Eclogae* I.2.29).[47]

1.3.4 Middle-Platonists, Aristotelians, and Neopythagoreans

According to the testimony of Porphyry (*Life* 14.10–14),[48] Plotinus seems to be aware of the works of several contemporary Platonic and Aristotelian commentators. Among Platonists were the second-century Middle-Platonists Severus, Cronius, Numenius of Apamea, and Atticus,[49] and among the Peripatetics, the second-century Aristotelian commentators Aspasius, Adrastus, and Alexander of Aphrodisias (the latter was the head of the Athenian Peripatetic School at the beginning of the third-century AD). Cronius and Numenius of Apamea were two central Platonic figures whose work was an amalgamation of Middle-Platonic and Neopythagorean doctrines. However, due to the lack of Middle-Platonic sources, an adequate comparison between Plotinus and these Platonists is extremely difficult.[50] Nothing survives from the work of Gaius and any information on his philosophy derives only from the works *Epitome* and *Didaskalikos* of his pupil Albinus (AD c. 153) who taught at Smyrna. In these works we find a strong Aristotelian influence.[51] Albinus' main doctrines seem to be: the identification of the Supreme Deity with the Aristotelian Intellect, the consideration of the Platonic Forms as thoughts of God, the characterization of the Supreme Deity as ineffable, the denial of the temporal beginning of the world, and the denial of the production of matter and the word soul by God.[52] The second doctrine, which originally derives from Philo of Alexandria (*De Opificio Mundi*, 5), prefigures Plotinus' synthesis in his Intellect of the Platonic Forms and the Aristotelian Intellect (*Epitome* IX), while the third doctrine anticipates Plotinus' doctrine of the One (*Epitome* X). On the other hand, Atticus was the chief anti-Aristotelian Middle-Platonist. Some of his criticisms involve Aristotle's denial of virtue's self-sufficiency for happiness, his doctrines denying the soul's immortality, his theory of the heavens as composed of the fifth element, and his denial of a temporal beginning for the cosmos. These criticisms seem to have been followed by Plotinus, especially in the Aristotelian polemics of his middle period.

Numenius of Apameia was also a strong influence on Plotinus' thought. He prefigures Plotinus on the following topics: in considering the absolute incorporeality of being, in articulating the structure of being in a hierarchical triad of gods, in positing the presence of everything in everything, in enhancing the mystical union of human with God, and in suggesting the idea of contemplation as creation.[53] In fact there were so many similarities between the doctrines of Plotinus and Numenius that the former was accused of plagiarism. For this reason, Plotinus asked his pupil Amelius to write a defense with the title *The Doctrinal Differences between Plotinus and Numenius* in order to reinstate Plotinus' originality (*Life* 17.1–6).

Apart from the Middle-Platonic Neopythagoreans, another influential Neopythagorean figure who anticipates Plotinus' philosophy is Moderatus of Gades (AD 1st century).[54] As Porphyry describes his system in his work *On Matter* (quoted by Simplicius *in Physica* 230.34 ff.),[55] the three main lines in Moderatus' philosophy which prefigure Plotinus are: Matter as produced by God, the theory of three divine Hypostases, named, as in Plotinus, as the One, the Intelligible World, and the Soul, and the interpretation of Plato's *Parmenides*.

With regard to the Neopythagorean influence in Plotinus, it should be noted that the Neoplatonist lived in one of the most disturbed periods of the Roman Empire, between the death of Marcus Aurelius (AD 180) and the accession of Diocletian (AD 284)—the imperial period that E. R. Dodds characterizes as the "age of anxiety."[56] It was in this period that there appears to have been a genuine rebirth and rethinking of the Pythagorean tradition, which was embodied in the movement known as Neopythagoreanism. The characteristics of this movement were a reaffirmation of the soul's immortality, a reconsideration of universal immateriality and incorporeality, and the mystical union with the God.[57] The fundamental doctrine underlying Neopythagoreanism was based on a hierarchical successive system of the Monad, the Indefinite Dyad, and Numbers. Nicomachus of Gerasa (AD c. 150) was one of the most influential Neopythagoreans who played a central role in the development of the later Neoplatonic mathematical mysticism, especially that of Proclus and Iamblichus.[58] Nicomachus' *Theological Arithmetic* (preserved in Photius *Bibliotheca*, 187), a peculiar work in which there is a metaphysical identification of numbers with the traditional gods, could be regarded as the initial and maybe the most influential starting point for this Neopythagorean rebirth.

Finally, with regard to the Aristotelians who appear to have been read in Plotinus' school, Adrastus, Aspasius, and Alexander of Aphrodisias were three of the most important commentators of the period. Adrastus was the commentator of the *Categories* and Plato's *Timaeus* as well as the author of some lexigraphical and historical studies of the Aristotelian *corpus*. Aspacius, the earliest of the commentators (AD second century), who wrote on the *Nicomachean Ethics*, was also the commentator of Aristotle's *Categories*, *Metaphysics*, and *De Caelo*. Alexander of Aphrodisias, perhaps the most significant Aristotelian commentator, was the author of commentaries on the *Metaphysics*, *Prior Analytics*, and *Topics* (among others), as well as a series of shorter philosophical works, including *On Fate* and *On Mixture*.[59] Plotinus seems to be deeply influenced by Alexander's interpretation of Aristotelian psychology and metaphysics.[60] In the field of metaphysics, Plotinus follows especially Alexander's unification of God with the Pure Thinker in *Metaphysics* XII and the Active Intellect in *De Anima* III,[61] as well as Alexander's development of Aristotle's identification of Intellect with its thoughts. In the field of psychology, Plotinus agrees with Alexander's fundamental denial of the spatial presence of the soul in the body (*Ennead* IV.3.20 and *De Anima* 13.9 ff.).

1.3.5 Gnostics, Christians, the Orient, and Other Contemporary Movements

Equally important is the relationship between Plotinus and some of the philosophical and religious movements of his time. Porphyry testifies (*Life*, 16) that at Plotinus' lectures there were many Christians and other heretics of the old philosophy, probably belonging to the movement of Gnosticism.[62] These people seemed to have caused difficulties in Plotinus' school. According to Porphyry, they used to compose revelations based on Zoroaster, Zostrianus, Nicotheus, Allogenes, and Messus, and then re-interpret Platonic teaching accordingly (*Life* 16.1–9). For this reason, Amelius wrote a book against Zostrianus, and Porphyry similarly against Zoroaster (*Life* 16.12–18). But the most important polemic against the movement of Gnosticism derives from Plotinus' *Ennead* II.9, *Against the Gnostics*.[63] Plotinus strongly attacks the Gnostics for taking the doctrines of Plato and other Greek philosophers and misinterpreting them according to their own deceptive doctrines. For Plotinus (II.9.6), the Gnostics are lying when they speak of the divine creator as an ignorant or evil Demiurge who produced an imperfect material world. They are also completely false when they regard the creative activities of the Demiurge as the result of a spiritual fall in the intelligible hierarchy (II.9.10–12). They are melodramatic and wrong when they speak about the influence of the cosmic spheres (II.9.13); they are blasphemous when they lay claim to the higher powers of magic (II.9.14); and completely misleading when they believe in immortality achievable through the complete rejection of and abstention from the material world. Even worse are their denial of the divinity of the Word Soul and the heavenly bodies, the rejection of salvation through true virtue and wisdom, the unphilosophical support of their arguments, and the arrogant view of themselves as saved by nature, that is as privileged beings in whom alone God is interested.[64]

Concerning the Christians, Plotinus never refers to them directly. In contrast to the well-known polemic by Porphyry, *Against the Christians*, Plotinus keeps silent about the Christian movement. In all probability Christians and Gnostics appeared to belong to the same group of heretics who infiltrated his school, and his anti-Gnostic treatise perhaps is also addressed to some Christians.

The Oriental influence in Plotinus' thought is extremely obscure and difficult to evaluate. Apparently Plotinus wanted to become acquainted with the philosophy of the Persians and the Indians, and so joined the expedition of the Emperor Gordian (*Life*, 3).[65] But Gordian's expedition was unsuccessful and Plotinus escaped with difficulty to Antioch. It is not known if Plotinus then delayed there to foster his interest in Oriental thought, but in any case the *Enneads* follow the traditional Greek ways of thought and argumentation without any clear reference to Oriental philosophical systems.

On the other hand, it is indisputable that Greek philosophy, from the earlier days of its development, had links with some Oriental doctrines. Here M. L. West's influential work, *Early Greek Philosophy and the Orient*, is an invaluable guide,[66] and Wallis' argument on the subject follows his line of interpretation: "from their earliest days Greek philosophy and science had drawn freely on the ideas of the Near East, to which they had habitually given new meaning by organizing them in a conceptual system hitherto lacking, and it is therefore to be expected that the Neoplatonists should have done the same."[67] In addition it should not be forgotten that Plotinus' family originated in all probability from Lycopolis in Upper Egypt, and many other Neoplatonists had their roots in Eastern regions: Porphyry was a Phoenician from Tyre, Iamblichus and Damascius probably had Syrian origins, and Proclus was a Lycian. And there is the well-known story of the Greek philosophers who went to Persia after the closure of the Platonic Academy (AD 529) as preserved in Agathias' *History* (II.30–1).[68]

Finally, Plotinus' philosophy seems to stand outside the influence of the *Chaldean Oracles*. Although Michael Psellus (*Patrologia Graeca* CXXII.1125 C–D) finds a Chaldean influence in the beginning of *Ennead* I.9, Plotinus seems to pay scant attention to the *Chaldean Oracles*. Whereas the later Neoplatonists regarded the *Chaldean Oracles* as divine revelation applicable to their theurgic practice, Plotinus appears to ignore them, although he was aware of some related Orphic and Pythagorean doctrines.

1.4 PLOTINUS AND THE PRESOCRATICS

The philosophical importance of the Presocratics in the *Enneads* has been generally overlooked by modern scholarship.[69] Apart from the lack of consideration of the Presocratic sources in the *Enneads*, the general attitude of some eminent modern scholars also seems to be deflationary. For instance, A. H. Armstrong, the translator of Plotinus' *Enneads* in the *Loeb* series, considers the Presocratic references in the *Enneads* as mere citations of little importance and less interest. According to this scholar, Plotinus recognizes the Presocratics as thinkers who do not require any independent study and in most cases appear only as indirect citations through the testimony of Aristotle.[70] Similarly, J. M. Rist only briefly reviews the Presocratics and suggests that, even if Plotinus regarded the most important of them, they are "at best props, and sometimes mere names traditionally listed when a new doctrine comes up for discussion."[71] Following a similar line of interpretation, C. Kahn, commenting on Heraclitus' fragment 84a–b (preserved only by Plotinus), surmises that the Neoplatonic philosopher quotes from memory and so "we have no way of telling how far his memory reflects his own reading of Heraclitus or some more traditional account."[72] Furthermore, this negative attitude towards Presocratic sources in Plotinus has led most contemporary Presocratic commentators to exclude the *Enneads* from their studies. It is worth noting that H. Diels, for instance, includes only limited citations from Plotinus' *Enneads*, and omits apparent references to the Presocratics which could easily serve as later testimonies to these philosophers.

But, in contrast to these judgments, the text of the *Enneads* leads us in the opposite direction. As J. Mansfeld observes, Plotinus gives a positive account of the early Greek philosophers and "some of his quotations may point to a reading of the originals."[73] Indeed a careful and objective reader is able to recognize that Plotinus' references to the Presocratics are not without purpose and significance. In many cases, Plotinus refers to the Presocratics by name along with Plato and sometimes with Aristotle with the same respect and without making any special distinction.[74] As T. Gelzer observes, Plotinus quotes the Presocratics either referring to them by name individually (as for instance IV.8.1 and V.1.8–9), or in a group as "the ancients" (as for instance II.9.6 and III.7.1, and 7).[75] In the latter case, there is also a unique but important reference to the Presocratics as "natural philosophers" (περὶ φύσεως εἰρηκότες) at *Ennead* II.1.2.6–9. Plotinus' references to the Presocratics can therefore be divided into direct and indirect: direct when Plotinus refers to an individual Presocratic by name and indirect when he refers to a Presocratic quotation or account.

Plotinus refers directly four times to Heraclitus (II.1.2.11, IV.8.1.12, IV.8.5.6, V.1.9.3), five times to Empedocles (II.4.7.1, IV.8.1.19–20, IV.8.1.34,

IV.8.5.5, V.1.9.5), twice to Parmenides (V.1.8.15, VI.6.18.42), and Anaxagoras (II.4.7.2, V.1.9.1), four times to Pythagoras and the early Pythagoreans (IV.7.8[4].3, IV.8.1.21, V.1.9.28, V.5.6.27), and once to Pherecydes (V.1.9.29) alongside Pythagoras. In addition to the above direct references, the *Index Fontium* of Henry-Schwyzer and E. N. Roussos (1974) notes that in the *Enneads* Plotinus refers indirectly or alludes thirty-seven times to Anaxagoras,[76] three times to Anaximander,[77] eleven times to Democritus,[78] fourteen times to Empedocles,[79] thirty-five to Heraclitus,[80] once to Leucippus,[81] twenty-six times to Parmenides,[82] twice to Philolaus,[83] four times to Pherecydes,[84] fourteen times to the Pythagoreans as a group,[85] and once each to Thales,[86] and Xenophanes.[87]

These references should still be treated with caution; the Presocratic list of references is neither complete nor undisputed. For instance, some references such as that to Xenophanes fr. 25 in *Ennead* V.8.7.25–31 can hardly be accepted as an indirect allusion to the Presocratic; the passage is more a Platonic one. In addition, while Presocratic terminology appears in the background of Plotinus' thought, some terms had already become technical and popular in the philosophers before Plotinus. An excellent example is that of Anaxagoras' *dictum* ὁμοῦ πάντα, an expression which is frequently used by Plotinus to express the "all-togetherness" of the intelligibles within Intellect. Whenever this expression appears in the *Enneads*, it should be treated carefully, whether it reflects Anaxagoras or is just another case of the commonly used term. Finally, some other Presocratic references are defective; for instance, reference to Heraclitus at *Ennead* IV.8.1.11–17 includes also an indirect reference to Heraclitus' fr. 101 which remains unnoticed, as well as the citation of Pythagoras at *Ennead* IV.8.1.20–22.

In general, concerning the Presocratic sources of the *Enneads*, the issue is obscure and controversial. On this problem, there are three possible alternatives: (1) Plotinus has direct contact with the original copy of some leading Presocratics; (2) Plotinus collects his information from secondary sources such as philosophical anthologies or handbooks of the period; (3) Plotinus derives his Presocratic material intermediately from the Aristotelian *corpus*.

The clearest example of the first case is the passage on Parmenides in *Ennead* V.1. The accuracy of Parmenides' fr. 3 in 8.14–23, unique as regards any other Presocratic fragment in the *Enneads*, is strong evidence for this position. It has to be mentioned that Plotinus in this passage refers clearly to Parmenides' "own writings" (ἐν τοῖς ἑαυτοῦ συγγράμμασιν), using the same expression again in *Ennead* III.7.13.1–18 when he criticizes the Peripatetic theory of Time and stresses the obscurity of some Aristotelian "writings." Unfortunately, Plotinus never refers to the "writings" of any other Presocratic. Can we suppose that Plotinus had a copy only of Parmenides' poem in his library? It is difficult to give a definite answer.

With regard to the second case, Rist states that Plotinus' general usage of the Presocratics implies that the Neoplatonist "is going to a handbook rather than bothering with the original texts."[88] Similarly M. Atkinson maintains that Plotinus "was familiar with a handbook rather than with the original text."[89] But this case cannot be justified either from the *Enneads*, or any biographical sources.

Concerning the third case, the position seems to be much more hypothetical. With regard to the Presocratic sources, the main position of some leading modern scholars is that Plotinus' information derives directly from Aristotle or other Peripatetic sources and the doxographical tradition.[90] According to Armstrong, Plotinus does not indicate any independent study of the Presocratics but bases his account on Aristotle in an entirely Peripatetic spirit.[91] Again this position is unjustified. Aristotle occasionally seems to be the main source for Plotinus, as in the case of Anaxagoras in *Ennead* V.1.9.1–2, but not always. In fact, Plotinus never gives us clear evidence for using Aristotle or any other Peripatetic author intermediately as a secondary source but rather refers to the Presocratics by name as individual philosophers with knowledge of their theories. Thus, no certain conclusion can be drawn, but the first option, that Plotinus did have direct access to Presocratic texts, is closer to the available evidence and so preferable.

Finally, it has to be mentioned that Presocratic texts to a considerable extent derive from the fragments preserved in the Neoplatonists and especially in Simplicius, who is, of course, later than Plotinus. But, as Roussos observes, since Plotinus is the most important later contributor to the Greek philosophical tradition, the investigation of the earlier sources in the *Enneads* would be extremely interesting.[92] Neoplatonic quotations from the Presocratics undermine Eusebius' testimony that books of philosophers before Plato were "rare to find" (*Praeparatio Evangelica* X.3.468).[93]

On the one hand, a possible objection concerning the study of the Presocratics in Plotinus might stem from the fact that the Neoplatonists developed their doctrines within a different philosophical framework from that of the Presocratics, but, on the other hand, it is clear that the Neoplatonists were aware of Presocratic theories. If we allow some uniform progress to the history of Greek philosophy, then the Presocratic origins have a right to be studied in the light of Neoplatonism, and, since Neoplatonism begins with Plotinus, the need of a comparative study between Plotinus and the Presocratics is even more pressing. We can begin our research by exposing and analyzing the Presocratic references in Plotinus' theory of the One; the ultimate principle of his metaphysics.

Chapter 2

One and Unity

2.1 THE ONE IN PLOTINUS

The One is the fundamental principle in Plotinus' philosophy; it is the transcendent source of being, intelligence, life beyond substance, and form.[1] The One is the First Hypostasis of Being, the supreme non-composite metaphysical principle prior to any plurality, multiplicity, and opposition. It is the ultimate cause of every subsequent reality, the supreme incorporeal element of all existences, and the ineffable object of desire for every spiritual life. The Plotinian One is everywhere and nowhere, everything and nothing, omnipresent to all existences without being any of them. Plotinus himself points out that the true nature of the One is extremely difficult to be apprehended through thought and therefore defined or expressed through language. Nevertheless, it is named "the One" (τὸ ἕν) as the derivative and unitary principle of everything and "the Good" (τὸ ἀγαθόν) as the perfect goal of all aspirations and spiritual ascent. The former is related to the Phase of Procession where the One produces the Intellect and then through Intellect the Soul, while the latter to the Phase of Reversion where the Good inspires the Intellect and the Soul to return to their primary source.

Plotinus' theory of the One is mainly presented in his early but influential treatise VI.9 [9], *On the Good or the One*.[2] This treatise may be supplemented by the two preceding *Enneads*: VI.7 [38], *How the Multitude of the Forms came into Being, and on the Good*, and VI.8 [39] *On Free Will and the Will of the One*. Porphyry places these treatises at the very end of the *Enneads* to emphasize the importance of the One as the ultimate goal of the human mind and the "end of the journey" for every philosophical ascent. In fact all the treatises which are included in *Ennead* VI refer, according to the thematic classification of Porphyry (*Life*, 24–26), to the nature of the One. Furthermore, an introduction to the One and its causal relationship to the other Hypostases can be found in *Ennead* V.1.4–7, and there are other important comments in *Enneads* V.2.1 and V.5.6–11.

According to J. R. Bussanich, the Plotinian One is represented (1) as the transcendental absolute unity beyond being and all predication, and (2) as omnipresent.[3] These two aspects correspond respectively to the negative and positive concepts of the One. Fundamentally, Plotinus' understanding of the One derives from two major Platonic dialogues: the *Republic*, and the *Parmenides*. The Plotinian One is, on the one hand, identified with the absolute supra-transcendent nature of the Platonic Good "beyond being" in the *Republic* (509b), and, on the other, defined according to the negations of the "one" in the first hypothesis of the *Parmenides* (137c–142a).[4] In the latter dialogue, Plato poses a metaphysical question that seems to be of great importance in Plotinus' conception of the One (133b–134b):[5] *is it possible through the perceptible realm to have knowledge of the transcendent intelligible realm and finally succeed in our ultimate ascent to the divine world of the Forms?* Plotinus' One is an attempt to answer this Platonic question and has its origins in the Presocratic One as first principle of unity (V.1.9), and the Pythagorean One as negation of plurality (V.5.6.26–8), as well as the early Platonic theories of Speusippus and Xenocrates.[6] On this basis, Plotinus places the One beyond being, life, intelligence, beauty, form, and substance as the unique principle of all things (V.2.1.1–5), the principle that exists at every ontological level and makes the ascent to the Forms possible (VI.7.32–40; VI.8.12).

Fundamentally, Plotinus' theoretical innovation is to be found in the concept that the supreme principle transcends being: the "marvel of the One, which is not being" (VI.9.5.30) (θαῦμα τοῦ ἕν, ὅ μὴ ὂν ἐστιν); being is just a "trace" (ἴχνος) of the One (V.5.5.12). Within this framework, Plotinus justifies the supra-transcendence of the One with the following argument: since multiplicity is always inferior to unity and the producer superior to its product, there must be an ultimate, unified, non-composite principle prior to any multiple posterior which is the productive cause of all composite and complex realities.[7]

Thus, the One is the supreme universal source, unified and unifying, which connects and makes coherent all the Hypostases of Being from the highest level of Intellect to the lowest level of Soul. It is the "principle of everything" (ἡ πάντων ἀρχή) (VI.9.5.23; VI.7.15.15; V.5.10.13–15) as well as "cause of the cause" (αἰτία τοῦ αἰτίου) (VI.8.18.38), "source" (πηγή) and "root" (ῥίζα) of the whole intelligible universe. It is termed the "simple" (τὸ ἁπλοῦν), the supreme "non-composite" (οὐ μεμιγμένον) prior to multiplicity, the ultimate "first" (τὸ πρῶτον) before all existences, the "one alone" (ἓν μόνον), and the absolute "transcendent" (τὸ χωριστόν) (VI.9.9; V.4.1.1–17). As Plotinus argues, the One, as a principle of everything, has to be *simple*, since *duality* entails *complexity* which is a priori inferior to *simplicity* and therefore has no place in his metaphysical system (V.1.7.20 ff.). Since the Platonic Forms are originally multiple, they cannot be the principle that we are seeking. Dominic O'Meara names this idea the "Principle of Prior Simplicity."[8]

As the productive source of everything, the One has to be "perfect" (τέλειον) and "superabundant" (ὑπερπλῆρες) (V.2.1). It is the generative cause of everything, the "seminal power of all things" (δύναμις τῶν πάντων) (III.8.10.1; V.1.7.9–10; V.3.15.33; V.4.1.36), due to the fact that all subsequent realities are derived from its perfection and plenitude (V.1.6.38 ff.). The One is "omnipotent," sometimes in the sense of its power implying "potency" and sometimes "actual activity" (VI.8.1.1–14). Its power is "limitless" (ἄπειρον) (VI.9.6.10–12; V.5.6.15 ff.), not, however, in size, number or measure but in its inexhaustible productive force which eternally produces in plenitude the whole intelligible universe.[9] The Plotinian One spreads out its inexhaustible power to every single being that comes after it (V.5.5.1–2; V.2.1.7–10). It is like an inexhaustible spring of life which gives a plenitude of existence to all (III 8.10.5–14). Arthur Lovejoy names this idea the "Principle of Plenitude."[10]

Life is the unbounded activity of the One (VI.7.21.1–6). As the productive power of all, the One is "all things and none of them" (V.2.1.1–3; VI.7.32.12–14)—"all things" to the extent that the One is the absolute source of everything, "none" to the extent that it is completely distinguished from everything (V.2.1.1–10). The One is "all things" in a transcendent mode: that is, in a unified, unextended, and unfragmented form. Hence, while all things derive from the One and depend on it, the One itself is "self-sufficient" (αὐταρκέστατον) and "independent" (ἀνενδεέστατον) (VI.9.6.16–42; V.4.1). The One is "self-determined" (αὐτεξούσιον) (VI.8.7.47–50), being "what it is," altogether self-directed and self-related (VI.8.17.22–27). However, self-determination is not an attribute of the One, but an indication of its being "itself by itself," containing no opposing factor (VI.8.8.1–13); it remains in itself by itself, and it is the cause of itself in itself (VI.8.14.29 ff.). The One is not limited in relation to others, or in relation to itself (V.5.11.4 ff.). Since everything derives from the One, all things have a trace of it in the way in which a product always has a trace of its producer (VI.7.18). Consequently, the *universality* and *commonality* of the One in all posterior existences establish a metaphysical "link" not only between the One and all its derivative realities, but also between these realities themselves.

The One transcends multiplicity and all types of thinking (V.3.12–17), and the intelligible Forms are only images of the One (VI.7.17; V.5.5). The One is beyond thought and reason since it exists before the thought of it (VI.7.38.21–25); it is an absolute self-sufficient source in perfect contemplation of itself, alone by itself (VI.7.40.11–27), and, moreover, it does not need to have knowledge of itself, intellection of itself, or consciousness of itself, being beyond substance, life, and intelligence (VI.8.16–38: ὑπερνόησις). The One, being therefore beyond intelligence and thought, is absolutely transcendent, without oppositions or contradictions, and so incapable of absolute definitions. There is no definition for the One because the One is the defining principle of all (VI.8.9.43–50). For this reason the One is conceived and expressed more accurately through negative statements, and so is described in negative terms as *the lifeless source of life, the formless source of form, the hyper-intelligent source of intelligence, the unmeasured and infinite source of measure and limit* (V.5.4–11; VI.7.17). The One is not life but life is a trace of the One (VI.6.7.17), which is the source of beauty beyond beauty as it is beyond being and existence (VI.7.32.33 ff.).

The One itself is partless and for this reason it is identified with the Platonic Good (VI.7.18.40). Remaining loyal to Plato, Plotinus identifies the One with the "light of the Good" in the *Republic* (VI.7.22–3); the transparent "light" of the One "colors" the succeeding realities, giving them grace and love (VI.7.31). The One is like a light dispersed far and wide from some entity translucent in itself (VI.8.18.35). It is the active presence of light in the form of Good beyond intelligence (VI.8.15.19–20). This inner light leads the ascent of the human soul to the One where true freedom and independence belong. For this reason, freedom is the power in the human soul to ascend to the Good without hindrance (VI.8.4). Plotinus describes the ascent to the ultimate One through a "scale" of goods throughout the Hypostases (VI.7.25–30).[11] According to this scale, form is the good for Matter, Soul is the good for Body, Intellect the good for Soul, and the One is the good for Intellect (VI.7.28). Thus, for Plotinus, everything derives from and aims at the Good, but the Good is not a predicate of the One (VI.7.38; V.3.10). Our desire to return to the One is explained by the immanent goodness of the One in every existence (VI.7.22.18–20).

2.2 THE PRESOCRATIC ONE IN THE *ENNEADS*

E. R. Dodds (1928) in his influential article "The Parmenides of Plato and the Origin of the Neoplatonic One" argues that Plotinus' One originates from Plato's *Parmenides* and the *Republic*. But a careful reading of the *Enneads* shows that Plotinus' One is not only related to Plato's teaching, but also has connections with the Presocratic One in early Greek philosophical thought.

Plotinus' passage on the "number of beings" in VI.1.1.1–4 shows his knowledge of Presocratic thought and may be used as an introduction to the subject:

> The extremely ancient philosophers investigated beings, how many there were and what they were; some said there was one being, some a definite number, and some an infinite number; and in each of these groups some said the one being was one thing and some another, and the same applies to those who said it was infinite.

The passage, translated by Armstrong, is an indirect reference to the Presocratics, "the extremely ancient philosophers" (οἱ πάνυ παλαιοί) who speak on the number of beings. It is noteworthy that the passage opens the influential discussion of *Enneads* VI.1–3, *On the Kinds of Being I–III*. Armstrong says of this passage that Plotinus as usual is taking his information from Aristotle's *Metaphysics* 984a and summarily dismisses the Presocratics.[12] But while the Aristotelian source is relevant the assumed dismissal of the Presocratics is not apparent in the text. The subject-matter of the Aristotelian text is the Presocratic *archē*, and not the kinds of being. In addition, the fact that Plotinus begins such an important discussion with the Presocratics shows their influence on the subject and their significance as original authorities and authentic thinkers.

Particularly, in the above passage, Plotinus distinguishes between the Presocratics who speak of "one being" and the Presocratics who speak of "many beings." If being is one it has to be either "one in itself" or "one in plurality." If there are many beings, they have to be either definite or indefinite in number. In all probability, with regard to the "one in itself" Plotinus refers to Thales, Anaximenes, Heraclitus, and the Ionian monists generally; with "one in many," he seems to refer to Parmenides and the Eleatics; with "definite number of beings" to Empedocles and the Pythagoreans, and with "indefinite number of beings" to Anaxagoras, Democritus, and the early Atomists.

Moreover, in other passages of the *Enneads*, Plotinus admits that his theory of the One as well as some aspects of the other Hypostases are rooted in Presocratic philosophy. He mentions directly the Presocratic One specifically in V.1.8.22–23, V.1.9.1–7, V.1.9.27–32, VI.6.18.42–43, and V.5.6.26–30. In V.1.9.1–7, Plotinus refers to the Presocratic One as the first and unique originative principle of all; V.1.8.22–23 is a criticism of Parmenides' monism; VI.6.18.42–43 ascribes the Parmenidean One to the unity of being; V.5.6.26–30, and V.1.9.27–32 relate the Pythagorean Monad to the One's ineffability and singularity. In V.1.9.1–7, the Presocratics under discussion are mainly Anaxagoras, Heraclitus, and Empedocles; in V.1.8.22–23 and VI.6.18.42–43 Parmenides; in V.5.6.26–30 and V.1.9.27–32, Pherecydes, and the Pythagoreans are taken as a group.

Particularly, in *Ennead* V.1,[13] Plotinus introduces the Presocratic discussion in chapters 8 and 9. His aim is to justify the metaphysical principles of his system through the authority of the ancients. Both chapters provide us with striking evidence that for Plotinus the theory of the Three Hypostases is not a radical innovation in Greek philosophy but has its origins in antiquity and especially in Platonic and Presocratic thought. Plotinus refers by name to leading Presocratic figures such as Parmenides, Anaxagoras, Empedocles, and Heraclitus, as well as to Plato and Aristotle. Plato is of course the main authority for Plotinus; his wisdom is acknowledged in this passage, but the Presocratics are undoubtedly foreshadowing Plato.

According to M. Atkinson, Plotinus' reasons for including such a doxography in *Ennead* V.1 are the following: (1) like all of his age he wished to show that he was in the tradition of scholastic orthodoxy;[14] (2) he wished to rebut any suggestion of innovation; and (3) he aimed to justify the validity of his theories through the wisdom and antiquity of the ancient philosophical accounts.[15] Concerning the importance of the Presocratic citations in *Ennead* V.1, Armstrong states that Plotinus does not regard the Presocratics as traditional authorities on a level with Plato and often thinks that they are wrong, confused, or obscure.[16] But Armstrong's claim cannot be justified by the text. A careful reading of V.1.8–9 show clearly that Plotinus treats the Presocratics as original and individual thinkers and not merely as Plato's predecessors of no philosophical interest. The importance of the Presocratics in Plotinus' thought can be also justified by the fact that reference to them and a discussion of them appears in a basic treatise of Plotinus' philosophy.

However, there is no doubt that Plato is the main authority for Plotinus and evidently his philosophical theories rely on and are developed through the Platonic perspective.[17] But with the "old opinions" (παλαιαὶ δόξαι) in V.1.8.13, Plotinus refers not only to Plato, but also to the ancient philosophers before Plato. As P. A. Meijer states, Plotinus announces his accounts as explaining "what was implicit in Plato and the Preplatonici'.[18] Indeed, in *Ennead* II.9, the ancient philosophers are for Plotinus the "godlike men" (6.36) (οἱ θεῖοι ἄνδρες), the philosophers who, along with Plato, present the true teaching of Greek philosophy.[19] On this basis, the intention of Plotinus in V.1.8 is to stress the validity and the continuation of his accounts not only through the diachronic value of Plato's teaching, but also through the philosophical background of Plato himself. This does not mean that Plotinus regards the Presocratics as just a Preplatonic group. As emerges from the text, he treats them individually, with a sound knowledge of their central theories.

On the other hand, Meijer interprets chapters 8 and 9 as an *apologia* of Plotinus, a conscious effort by the Neoplatonist to refute any modernity of his system.[20] Likewise, Graeser observes that whereas Aristotle marks the definite step to the development of Greek philosophy "Plotinus intended nothing more than a reaffirmation of that truth which—as it seemed to him and other Neoplatonists—was almost definitely revealed by Plato six centuries before."[21] However, for Plotinus, philosophy did not end with Plato or Aristotle. He was, for example, ready to criticize Aristotle throughout the *Enneads* and introduce his own radical ideas, especially that concerning the nature of the One (VI.7.37.3 ff.).[22] Plotinus' main reason for using this doxographical material in V.1.8–9 is just his intention to show that his philosophical system is not a mere "modernity" (καινοτομία) but an essential "continuation" (συνέχεια) of Greek philosophy. As Atkinson observes, Plotinus "wanted to show that his own beliefs were not inconsistent with their stated doctrines, in so far as these were true."[23] Plotinus aims to prove that the fundamental principles of his metaphysical system were rooted in Greek philosophical tradition and the teaching of the ancients.

Thus, chapters 8 and 9 of *Ennead* V.1 are an invaluable source for Presocratic philosophy and doxography. In particular, the subject-matter of chapter 8 comprises the philosophical origins of Plotinus' theory of Intellect and Being in Parmenides (8.14.23), and Plato's *Timaeus* (8.1–14 and 23–27), while in chapter 9 the origins of Plotinus' theory of the One includes references to: Anaxagoras (9.1–3), Heraclitus (9.3–5), Empedocles (9.5–7), Pherecydes, and the Pythagoreans (9.28–32). This discussion of the Presocratics in chapter 9 is interrupted by a long reference to Aristotle (9.7–27) where Plotinus criticizes him for the priority of the self-thinking Mind rather than the One in *Metaphysics* 1071b2 ff., and for the plurality of the Unmoved Mover(s) in *Metaphysics* Λ.[24]

Furthermore, *Ennead* VI.6 deals with the nature of numbers and especially the ideal numbers worked on in Platonic Academy.[25] In this particular treatise, Plotinus focuses not so much on the nature of the ideal numbers but rather on their metaphysical connection with the One. The problem again for Plotinus, as with many others cases through the *Enneads*, is the nature of the One as the derivative source of all realities with the means whereby the human soul can return to this source and participate in the absolute unity of One. With regard to the Presocratics, Plotinus recognizes Parmenides as the philosopher who maintained the oneness and unity of Being. Particularly, in passage VI.6.18.42–43, Plotinus fully recognizes and accepts Parmenides as the philosopher who correctly asserted the uniqueness, impassability, and self-existence of Being. It is noteworthy that VI.6.18.42–43 and V.1.8.22–23 are the only direct references to Parmenides in the *Enneads*.

Finally, *Ennead* V.5, as R. Harder maintained, is the third part of a greater Plotinian work including *Enneads* III.8, V.8, V.5, and II.2.[26] The subject matter of this important treatise is the inner structure of Intellect and its relationship to the One. Plotinus maintains the perfect self-identity between intelligible object and intelligible subject at the level of Intellect and the One's transcendence and ineffability beyond Intellect and Form.[27] In chapter six, Plotinus asserts that the One is beyond form and substance since it is *not* any particular thing but rather the indefinite, ineffable, unknowable, and unthinkable originative principle of all things. In V.5.6.26–30, Plotinus refers to the Pythagorean One and recognizes its etymological connection with the figure of Apollo as symbolizing negation of plurality. On this basis, V.5.6.26–30 is connected to V.1.9.27–32, where Plotinus favorably mentions the Pythagoreans and Pherecydes on the supreme nature of the One.

Keeping in mind the aforementioned observations, we can now proceed to a detailed analysis of the above passages in relation to the Presocratic theories.

2.3 PARMENIDES' MONISM

Prima facie passages V.1.8.22–23 and VI.6.18.42–43 seems to be contradictory.

> Ἓν δὲ λέγων [ὁ Παρμενίδης] ἐν τοῖς ἑαυτοῦ συγγράμμασιν αἰτίαν εἶχεν ὡς τοῦ ἑνὸς τούτου πολλὰ εὑρισκομένου
> But although he [Parmenides] speaks of "one" in his own writings, he was criticized, since this one is found to be many. [V.1.8.22–23; trans. Atkinson modified]

> ὥστε ταύτῃ Παρμενίδης ὀρθῶς *ἓν* εἰπὼν τὸ ὄν· καὶ οὐ δι' ἐρημίαν ἄλλου ἀπαθές, ἀλλ' ὅτι ὄν· μόνῳ γὰρ οὕτῳ παρ' αὐτοῦ ἐστιν εἶναι.
> Therefore Parmenides was right in saying that being was one; and it is not unaffected because of the absence of anything else, but because *it really is*; for only being can be by itself. [VI.6.18.42–44; trans. Armstrong modified]

Whereas Plotinus in the former passage criticizes Parmenides for speaking about the ἕν as one of the many predicates of Being, in the latter he commends Parmenides for saying that Being is ἕν. But a careful comparative reading of these passages removes the contradiction.

In *Ennead* V.1, passage 8.22–23 is part of a longer passage in the same chapter (8.14–23) devoted to the Presocratic Parmenides and especially to: (1) the connection between thinking and being in fr. 3 (8.14–20); (2) the immobility of Being in fr. 8.26 (8.20–22); (3) the completeness of Being in fr. 8.42–44 (8.20–22); and (4) the ἕν as predicate of Being in fr. 8.6 (8.22–23).[28] In particular in lines 22 to 23, Plotinus criticizes Parmenides for speaking about the One not as first principle but as a predicate of Being. In this criticism, Plotinus has in mind Parmenides' description of the "signs" (σήματα) or predicates of Being in fr. 8.1–6 where the ἕν as a "sign" of Being is found in fr. 8.6.[29] For Plotinus, while Parmenides speaks of "one being," this Being appears in fr. 8.3 to be "many." On this basis, the Parmenidean One *could not* be identified with the Plotinian One since the latter transcends any form of plurality and difference. Plotinus aims to show that the Parmenidean One has rather to be identified with the unity-in-plurality of Forms in the reality of Intellect.

Plotinus' criticism of Parmenides' view of the ἕν as predicate of Being here is Platonic in origin, appearing first in Plato (*Sophist* 244a–245e), and then Aristotle (*Physics* I–II). Plato criticizes Parmenides in the *Sophist* for not clarifying the distinction between perfect unity and the unity predicated by the sum of parts. Since Parmenides' One could mean either "unity," or "the one substance," Palmer calls Plato's critique in this dialogue the first critique of Eleaticism and, according to the same scholar, Plato preserves the uniqueness of Parmenides' Being only as an attribute of each Form,[30] and it is precisely this plurality of the Forms that is a departure from Parmenides' monism. On this basis, Parmenides can be equally a predicational monist in terms of the singularity of each predicate and a numerical pluralist due to the plurality of predicates.

Plotinus in V.1.8.22–23 is aware of the above discussion, and, because of the inferred inaccuracy of Parmenides on these two grounds, returns to Plato's *Parmenides*:

> But Parmenides in Plato speaks more accurately, and distinguishes from each other the first One, which is more properly called One, and the second which he calls "One-Many" and the "One and Many." In this way he too agrees with the doctrine of the three natures. [V.1.8.23–27; trans. Armstrong]

This passage is a clear reference to Plato's *Parmenides* 137c–142a, 144e5, and 155e5. It is the concluding passage of chapter eight which encompasses the whole spirit of Plotinus' understanding of Plato and Parmenides and is the only passage where Plotinus claims that the three Hypostases, including the Soul, can be found in the *Parmenides*. Thus, for Plotinus, Plato's Parmenides (ὁ δὲ παρὰ Πλάτωνι Παρμενίδης) is "more accurate" (ἀκριβέστερος) than the Presocratic Parmenides in distinguishing "the first One" (τὸ πρῶτον ἕν),[31] from the "One-Many" of Intellect (ἓν πολλά),[32] and the "One *and* Many" of Soul (ἓν καὶ πολλά),[33] namely, the Three Hypostases.[34]

The fact that Plato's *Parmenides* is for Plotinus more accurate than the Presocratic Parmenides does not mean that the Eleatic philosopher is wrong. As the text clearly shows, the Presocratic Parmenides is for Plotinus only less accurate in distinguishing the first One from the one Being. Parmenides spoke of the One but he did not distinguish in his writings between the "supreme one" (IV.2.2.54–5: τὸ ὑπέρτατον ἕν), the ἕν which corresponds to the unity-in-plurality of Intellect, and the ἕν which corresponds to unity-and-plurality of Soul. This clarification was the work of Plato's *Parmenides*, a dialogue which rightly took the name of the Presocratic Parmenides as the pioneer of the unity of Being.

In fact, the original Parmenides is primarily criticized because, as we mentioned before, on the one hand he characterizes Being as One in fr. 8.6, but, on the other, he attributes to this One "many signs," or "many predicates" in fr. 8.2–3. Then, with regard to Parmenides, since his Being has "many signs" it cannot be Plotinus' One; the First Hypostasis. It would be better related to the unity-in-plurality of the Intellect; the Second Hypostasis. As

Atkinson correctly notes, Plotinus never applies Parmenides' predicates of Being to the One, and this is a "further proof that he took Parmenides' One to refer to Intellect."[35] For Atkinson, moreover, there is additional evidence that Plotinus took Parmenides' One to refer to Intellect in the fact that the negative adjectives of fr. 8 such as "ungenerated," "indestructible," and "imperturbable" are always applied to Intellect and never to the One.[36] Here lies the radical reading by Plotinus of Parmenides' Being. Due to Being's plurality, Plotinus identifies the one Being of Parmenides with his Intellect and not with his One. On this basis, as A. H. Coxon claims, Plotinus distinguishes Parmenides' Being from the Platonic One and associates it with the eternal nature of Intellect.[37]

Thus, Plotinus' discussion of Parmenides' ἕν is important for his understanding of the Presocratic, and this leads us to *Ennead* VI.6.18.42–44 where Plotinus refers again to Parmenides by name, and provides evidence for the unity of Being. It has to be noted that in this passage Armstrong does not recognize Plotinus' reference to the Presocratic Parmenides but identifies it as an allusion to Plato's *Parmenides* at the beginning of 142b.[38] But the *Index Fontium* of Henry and Schwyzer, Roussos[39] and Atkinson[40] reinstate the correct reference of the passage to the Presocratic Parmenides. This can also be justified by the fact that throughout the *Enneads* Plotinus always makes it clear whether he is referring to a Platonic dialogue or to an individual philosopher. For instance, as we have seen in *Ennead* V.1, Plotinus draws a sharp distinction between the Presocratic Parmenides and the Platonic Parmenides, so there is no doubt that Parmenides in VI.6.18.42–43 is the Presocratic philosopher and not the Platonic one.

With regard to the text of VI.6.18.42–43, the conclusive "therefore" (ὥστε) at the beginning of the passage refers to the whole discussion of chapter 18. This chapter focuses on the intelligible reality and the perfection of the eternal living Intellect. Parmenides' name in the chapter comes immediately after Plotinus' discussion of the nature of the intelligible substance. For Plotinus, the intelligible substance underlies the eternal life, stability and purity of the intelligibles (18.31–36). Due to this substance, life abides and intellect abides, and the real beings stand still in eternity. Hence, the intelligible being is unaffected and self-existing with nothing contrary to its unified nature, and for these reasons the intelligible being would be for Parmenides what Plotinus describes as "one being" in his philosophy (18.38–42).

Moreover, with the word "rightly" (ὀρθῶς) Plotinus stresses his recognition and appreciation of Parmenides' thesis. It is noteworthy that Plotinus uses the same expression again at V.9.5.29.30 when he quotes Parmenides' fr. 3. In both passages the word ὀρθῶς shows validity and approval, and, if we compare these passages with V.1.8.24, it becomes clear that Plotinus accepts the validity of the Eleatic words with no intention of ascribing falsity to the

Presocratic. Furthermore, Plotinus' respect for Parmenides seems to derive not only from his radical theory on Being, but also from Plato's well-known recognition of Parmenides' authority and originality.[41]

The explicit reference of VI.6.18.42–43 to the Presocratic Parmenides is again good evidence for Plotinus' knowledge of the philosophical terminology of Parmenides, and especially the description of Being as given in fragment 8.1–49. With the "one" (ἕν) in line 42 we have a direct reference to Parmenides' ἕν in fr. 8.6. The same reference in fr. 8.5–6 was noted at the beginning of the chapter (18.7): "being one and all together and whole." Apart from these references to fr. 8.5–6 no other allusion has been observed in this passage either by Henry, and Schwyzer, or Roussos, but a closer look at the passage and some technical words of the whole chapter reveals several indirect allusions to Parmenides.

More precisely, with the term "unaffected" (ἀπαθές) in line 43, and previously in line 39, Plotinus perhaps echoes Parmenides' "indestructible" (ἀνώλεθρον) in fr. 8.3 and in general the stated "indestructibility of Being" in frs 8.21 and 8.27. The phrase "for only being can be by itself" (μόνῳ γὰρ τούτῳ παρ' αὑτοῦ ἐστιν εἶναι) in lines 43–4 probably alludes to Parmenides' statement "remaining the same and in the same it abides by itself" (ταὐτόν τ' ἐν ταὐτῶι τε μένον καθ' ἑαυτό τε κεῖται) in fr. 8.29. And, with the word "unchanging" (ἀκίνητον) in line 32, Plotinus gives forewarning of Parmenides' quotation in the present passage.

Thus, Plotinus' criticism of Parmenides in V.1.8.22–23 is not against the Presocratic for speaking on the unity of Being; rather it is a criticism directed to the "one" as a predicate of the supreme principle. According to Plotinus this principle cannot be described in language, nor grasped in thinking since it is ineffable and beyond intelligence. To find the connection between Plotinus' first principle and the Presocratic One, we now turn our attention to the ineffability of the One.

2.4 THE INEFFABLE ONE

Plotinus' One is beyond intelligence and language. Since it is impossible to comprehend a boundless nature such as the One (V.5.6.14–15), it is "before intelligence" (ἀνόητον) and "ineffable" (ἄρρητον) (V.3.10–14; VI.9.5.31–33). On this account, Plotinus maintains that since the One is "beyond intelligence" (ἐπέκεινα νοῦ), therefore it is "beyond knowledge" (ἐπέκεινα γνώσεως) and, since there is no way of thinking or knowing it, therefore there is no way of speaking of it, and we can only make signs about it.[42] Strictly speaking, even the terms "one" or "good" should not be attributed to it.[43] Since the One is fundamentally unthinkable, unknowable, and ineffable it is "false even to say that it is One" (V.4.1.9).

For Plotinus, language will never disclose the essence of the One. If language can tell us anything this cannot be *what the One is*, only *what it is not*. The One is what it is, absolute and free of definitions and internal limitations, independent of external relations and complexities (VI.8.10.15–20). Hence, the One is above all predicates, definitions, or statements. Any plurality of predicates ascribes additions to the One, which mark a diminution of its excellence.[44] The One is beyond everything and so we need a particular form of language that will be able to manifest the One's supra-transcendence beyond any definite formula. Indeed it is impossible to speak properly about the One (VI.8.18.53–54). In our descriptions of the One, we should assume "as if" for every term or word for it (VI.8.13). More properly, the One should be conceived only in silence and complete abstraction (VI.8.21.26) without enquiries and questions (VI.8.11). Consequently, it would be better if the One remained unexpressed.

However, a serious cognitive and linguistic problem arises from the One's ineffability: *how can we speak or learn about a nature which is fundamentally unknowable and ineffable?* In V.3.14.1–7, Plotinus maintains that the only statements that are able to indicate the nature of the One without depriving it of its true essence are negative predications.[45] Only negations can denote linguistically what the "One is not." As F. M. Schroeder states: "Plotinus uses negation to avoid confusion of an incorporeal reality accessible only to the mind or spirit with the corporeal reality perceived by our senses."[46]

According to the positive aspect of the One, even if the term "the One" is inappropriate, it is the only "name" that denotes negation of plurality and implies absolute unity and indivisibility (VI.9.5.31–33) Likewise, the term "the Good" would also mark an unnecessary deficiency as a positive addition to the One's nature (III.8.11.12–15). As R. T. Wallis puts it, the term "good" does not denote any particular form or quality, but connotes that "it is just because it is unrestricted by any form that the One is Good."[47] The One is Good for all the other things and not for itself (VI.7.24.13–16; VI.9.6.39–42). When we say that "the One is Good," we are not predicating that Good belongs to the One, but denoting its absolute perfection (VI.7.38.1 ff.). As Plotinus himself puts it, when we refer to the first principle of all, which is originally ineffable, with the name "the One" or "the Good," we must realize that these names are not predicates but only explanatory terms (II.9.1.7). Hence, the One is called in other positive terms "the first" in the sense that it is "the simplest" and "self-sufficient" in the sense that it is "non-composite."[48]

On the other hand, the negative aspect of the One is more important and appropriate for Plotinus' thought.[49] For this reason, Plotinus names the One as "ineffable" (ἄρρητον);[50] "formless" (ἄμορφον / ἀνείδεον);[51] "without intelligence" (ἀνόητον);[52] "non-being" (μή ὄν / μηδέν);[53] "without dimensions" (ἀδιάστατον),[54] and "without limits" (ἄπειρον).[55] The One is ineffable insofar as it is inexpressible in language; formless to the extent that it is beyond any duality; without intelligence in terms of transcending thought and knowledge; without limits since it is boundless and indefinite in power and comprehension; without dimensions in so far as it is before extension; non-being insofar as the One is beyond Being. Plotinus summarizes the negative nature of the One in VI.9.3.41–45:

> For since the nature of the One is generative of all things it is not any one of them. It is not therefore something or qualified or quantitative or intellect or soul; it is not in movement or at rest; not in place, not in time, but "itself by itself" of single, or rather formless, being, before all form, before movement and before rest; for these pertain to being and are what make it many. [trans. Armstrong]

In this passage, Plotinus describes the One with the following negations: the One is "*not* particular" (οὔτε τι); "*not* qualified" (οὔτε ποιόν); "*not* quantitative" (οὔτε ποσόν); "*not* intellect" (οὔτε νοῦν); "*not* soul" (οὔτε ψυχήν); "*not* in movement" (οὐδὲ κινούμενον); "*not* at rest" (οὐδ' ἑστώς); "*not* in place" (οὐκ ἐν τόπῳ); "*not* in time" (οὐκ ἐν χρόνῳ). Plotinus' argument is that since the One, as the generative cause of everything has to be before all things, then it has to be a nature "beyond being" and therefore beyond form and plurality. The One remains super-transcendent, at the apex of the metaphysical hierarchy, "itself by itself" in absolute unity and singularity.

Plotinus' apophatic treatment of the One had a great influence on later Neoplatonic thought, but more importantly on the Negative Theology developed by such early Christian authors as Dionysius Aeropagita and Johannes Chrisostomus.[56] But the negative nature of a first principle such as the One is not new in Plotinus, for it had already been established in the Platonic-Pythagorean interpretation of the first hypothesis of Plato's *Parmenides*, but more significantly in the Presocratic tradition. The origins of apophatism can be found in the negative apprehension of the first principle in Anaximander, Xenophanes, Parmenides, and Empedocles, as well as in the mysticism of the Pythagorean Monad.

2.4.1 The Apophatism of the First Principle

Plotinus' apophatism of the One echoes Anaximander's negative predication of the *apeiron*.[57] Like the Plotinian principle, Anaximander's originative principle is characterized by the following negations at the level of time, space, quantity, and quality: the ἄπειρον is (1) "without temporal limits," for it is "unborn," "ageless," "deathless," and "indestructible" (fr. 3: ἀθάνατον ἀνώλεθρον; fr. 2: ἀγήρω);[58] (2) "without spatial limits," for it is without πέρας (fr. 1); (3) "without quantitative limits," for it is "inexhaustible"; (4) "without qualitive limits," for it is the indefinite source of the material elements of the cosmos but not to be identified with any of them (fr. 1). Similarly, in Xenophanes the "one god" (fr. 23: εἷς θεός) *is not* like mortals in body and thought. It is an unmoving single god (fr. 26), separate from all things and yet effortlessly the cause of their movement (fr. 25). Again in Eleatic philosophy the nature of Being is also described in negative terms. For Parmenides, Being is "ungenerated" (ἀγ ένητον), "indestructible" (ἀνώλεθρον); "imperturbable" (ἀτρεμές), and "timeless" (fr. 8.3–5). For Melissus, it is also "without limits" in space and time (frs 2–4). In Empedocles, the principles of Love, Strife, and the four "roots" are "deathless" (fr. 35.31: ἀθάνατα) while the "holy mind" (φρὴν ἱερή) is "incorporeal" and "inexpressible" (fr. 134).

2.4.2 The Pythagorean Apophatism of the Monad

The Pythagorean apophatism of the Monad appears to be even more significant for Plotinus.[59] In the sixth chapter of *Ennead* V.5, Plotinus recognizes that the symbolic representation of the Pythagorean One in the name of Apollo manifests the apophatic nature of the Plotinian One as a transcendent and single principle (V.5.6.26–30). As Plotinus puts it, the etymology of the name Apollo implies a denial of plurality (*a* = not, *polla* = many):[60]

> Τάχα δὲ καὶ τὸ 'ἓν' ὄνομα τοῦτο ἄρσιν ἔχει πρὸς τὰ πολλά. Ὅθεν καὶ Ἀπόλλωνα οἱ Πυθαγορικοὶ συμβολικῶς πρὸς ἀλλήλους ἐσήμαινον ἀποφάσει τῶν πολλῶν. Εἰ δὲ θέσις τις τὸ ἕν, τό τε ὄνομα τό τε δηλούμενον, ἀσαφέστερον ἂν γίνοιτο τοῦ εἰ μή τις ὄνομα ἔλεγεν αὐτοῦ.
> But perhaps this name "one" contains a denial of plurality. This is why the Pythagoreans symbolically signified it to each other by the name of Apollo, in negation of the multiple. But if the One—name and reality expressed—was to be taken positively it would be less clear than if we did not give it a name at all. [V.5.6.26–30; trans. Armstrong]

The above passage is crucial for Plotinus' knowledge of the Pythagoreans and especially their mystical approach of the One or the Monad.

Beside this passage, Plotinus refers three more times to the Pythagoreans as a group in IV.7.8[4].3–5 (οἱ ἀμφὶ Πυθαγόραν); IV.8.1.20–22 (Πυθαγόρας καὶ οἱ ἀπ' ἐκείνου); V.1.9.27–32 (οἱ συντασσόμενοι τοῖς Πυθαγόρου).[61] It is noteworthy that according to Longinus (in Porphyry's *Life* 20.71–72) Plotinus expounded the principles of the Pythagorean philosophy and offered the clearest exegesis of them. As P. Kalligas comments on passage V.5.6.26–30, Plotinus' deviation from Platonic orthodoxy is probably the reason behind Longinus' claim.[62] In all probability, Longinus interpreted Plotinus' conceptions as influenced by the doctrines of the Neopythagorean movement. Wallis seems to follow Longinus' claim by regarding Plotinus' philosophy as a systematization of Pythagorean-Platonic teaching.[63] This view can be justified by the fact that the works of several important Neopythagorean authors were read in Plotinus' school (*Life* 14.11–12).[64]

But, apart from the above evidence, a definite conclusion on the influence of the Pythagoreans or the Neopythagoreans in the *Enneads* cannot be made. Even if Plotinus speaks in favor of the Pythagoreans in V.5.6.26–30 and V.1.9.27–32, he criticizes them in IV.7.8[4].3–28 for their doctrine of the soul as harmony and in IV.8.1.17–26 for their riddling statements on the ensouled body. What can be said for sure is that Plotinus in V.5.6.26–30, and V.1.9.27–32 seems to accept the supremacy and singularity of the Pythagorean Monad. The passage on the etymology of Apollo and the identification with the One justifies this claim.

In fact, the reference to Apollo in V.5.6.26–30 is unique in the *Enneads*. Plotinus states that the name Ἀπόλλων appeared in Pythagorean mystical thought with a symbolic meaning of the One in terms of manifesting a negation of plurality and the symbolic meaning of this passage echoes the symbolism of the One in V.3.13.5. The mystical connotation of the passage can also be justified by the last lines of the chapter where Plotinus speaks of the One as a name for unifying the mind of the seer by indicating simplicity beyond any quantitive or qualitative plurality, or perceptual or spiritual multiplicity. For Plotinus the true nature of the One can be revealed only in the mystical union (VI.7.36). Since the One is ineffable, the mystical union happens in silence where the unity with the "unspoken first" diminishes duality and opposition, like the mystical experience of the initiator in the mysteries (VI.9.10–11).[65]

Plotinus' etymology of Apollo as "negation of plurality" clearly echoes Plutarch's identification of the Pythagorean One with Apollo in *Isis and Osiris*. As Plutarch testifies, the Pythagoreans embellished numbers and figures with the appellations of the gods. The Monad was identified with Apollo (354F2–3: τὴν μονάδα ὀνομάζειν Ἀπόλλωνα), first because of its rejection of plurality and, second, because of the singleness and simplicity of unity (381E9–F3: τὸ δ' ἓν Ἀπόλλωνα πλήθους ἀποφάσει καὶ δι' ἁπλότητα τῆς μονάδος). Plato in the *Cratylus* (405c–d) connects also Apollo with "the simple" (τὸ ἁπλοῦν) and "the truth" (τὸ ἀληθές), and Macrobius in *Saturnalia* I.XVII.7 identifies etymologically Apollo in Latin with "sol solus" = (sun alone).

The figure of Apollo, the Sun God, plays a central role in the Pythagorean tradition. It is significant that Pythagoras himself had the name "Hyperborean Apollo" (Aelianus *Varia Historia* II.26). This is also testified by Iamblichus in *De Vita Pythagorica* (91; 135; 140), who reports that Pythagoras was given the name of the Hyperborean Apollo by the people of Croton.[67]

Apollo was well known in Greek mythology for his connection to and identification with the sun. For the Pythagoreans the One was also equated with the element of fire: the central fire of the universe.[68] This makes the analogy between the One and Apollo even more evident. Furthermore, the figure of Apollo is in some cases related to Empedocles, who seems to be influenced by some Pythagorean doctrines. Diogenes Laertius (*Vitae Philosophorum* 8.57) testifies that, according to Aristotle, Empedocles wrote a *Hymn to Apollo*. However, a separate work on Apollo by Empedocles is questionable.[69] It is reported by Ammonius that Empedocles rejected the anthropomorphic mythical accounts of the gods, and especially that of Apollo, for more suitable demythologizing accounts based on *logos* (*in De Interpretatione*, 249). This is further supported by Menander Rhetor who states that a hymn to Apollo was actually an account about "the nature of the sun."[70] Menander also relates this issue to the Orphics. Ammonius' testimony includes Empedocles' extant fragment 134 on the non-anthropomorphic nature of god:[71]

> He is not equipped with a human head on a body, two branches do not spring from his back, he has no feet, no swift knees, no shaggy genitals, but he is mind alone, holy and inexpressible, darting through the whole cosmos with swift thoughts. [trans. M. R. Wright]

Prima facie the denial of anthropomorphism is clearly presented in the text and echoes Xenophanes' rejection of the traditional gods[72] in favor of a single non-anthropomorphic deity.[73] Empedocles' God, like that of Xenophanes, is an incorporeal "holy mind" which affects the whole cosmos (frs 24 and 25).

Empedocles' fr. 134 presents some interesting analogies with Plotinus' apophatism of the One: first, God is expressed in a series of negations, and second, it is defined as "inexpressible" (ἀθέσφατος) and "alone" (μοῦνον). The latter attributes anticipate Plotinus' ineffability and supra-transcendence of the One. He speaks in a similar way to Empedocles in fr. 134 when in *Ennead* III.8.2.1–4 Nature personified denies anthropomorphic attributes. The "work of nature" is not a matter of artistic creation (*technē*) but rather of contemplation (*theoria*). The similarity of wording in Empedocles' fr. 134, and *Ennead* III.8.2.1–4 is striking and has not been noted in the *Index Fontium* of Henry and Schwyzer or mentioned elsewhere in ancient or modern commentaries.

In addition, Ammonius' reference to Apollo in Empedocles' fr. 134 is most probably to be explained as representing the intelligent source of heavenly fire. On this basis, Hippolytus (*RH* 1.3, DK31A31) states that Empedocles identified God with intelligent fire.[74] The reference to the Monad and intelligent fire again suggests that the divine being may be understood as Apollo. Likewise, Plotinus, as a devoted Platonist, uses the image of the sun for the

One. However, Plotinus is aware that the sun-image is not altogether appropriate to describe the negative nature of the One since the sun has a physical body with particular properties and with definite spatial dimensions.[75] For this reason, Plotinus insists that the image of the sun needs to be dematerialized and taken out of space. The sun therefore should not be conceived as a material body but rather as a substantial incorporeal power (IV.5.6–7),[76] then the inexhaustible productive power of the One can be compared to the vital radiation of the sun everlastingly spreading out its "light" (φῶς), or energy to all beings and realities (V.1.7.1–4).[77]

Thus, the One as the source of intelligible life/light is the cause both for existence and contemplation (VI.7.16.24–31). On this basis, the mystical unification with the One as the final object of contemplation is again exemplified by the seer who patiently waits in silence for the rising of the sun (V.5.8.1–8). The evidence therefore points to a connection between Plotinus and the Pythagoreans on the One, the divine figure of Apollo, and the simile of the sun found initially in Plato's *Republic* VI.

Furthermore, the concept of the One was fundamental to Pythagorean number-mysticism. According to Aristotle, the Pythagoreans regarded number both as the matter of things and as properties and states (*Metaphysics* 968a). But for the Pythagoreans, the One (or the Monad) was not the first in a series of number, nor even a number itself, but the generator of numbers, the "principle" or "origin" of all numbers.[78] As Aristotle puts it, "number proceeds from the One" (*Metaphysics* 968a20–21). Numerical duality or opposition such as "even" and "odd," "unlimited," and "limited," remains undifferentiated within the unity of the Monad.[79] For this reason, the unity of the One is contrasted with the plurality of the Many in the Pythagorean table of opposites reported by Aristotle in *Metaphysics* 986a22. More significantly, on the authority of Iamblichus *in Nic.* 77.8, the Pythagorean Philolaus conceived the One as "the first principle of all things" (fr. 8: ἓν ἀρχὰ πάντων).[80] Moreover, in the cosmology of the same Pythagorean, the One is the unified principle in the center of the sphere identified with the central fire: the hearth (fr. 7).[81]

For Plotinus there is a further sense in which his supreme One is anticipated by the Pythagorean Monad. Plotinus uses, in some particular cases, Monad as synonymous with the One and Dyad as synonymous with the Intellect (V.5.4.20–25). His aim is again to show the singularity and unity of the first principle, so that the One can be conceived of as a unification of "monad" and "point" (VI.9.6.2–3).[82] Particularly in V.1.9.27–32, the Neoplatonist again shows himself aware of the Pythagorean One:

> Ὥστε τῶν ἀρχαίων οἱ μάλιστα συντασσόμενοι αὖ τοῖς Πυθαγόρου καὶ τῶν μετ᾽ αὐτὸν καὶ Φερεκύδους δὲ περὶ ταύτην μὲν ἔσχον τὴν φύσιν [ν.τοῦ ἑνὸς]· ἀλλ᾽ οἱ μὲν ἐξειργάσαντο ἐν

> αὐτοῖς αὐτῶν λόγοις, οἱ δὲ οὐκ ἐν λόγοις, ἀλλ' ἐν ἀγράφοις ἐδείκνυον συνουσίαις ἢ ὅλως ἀφεῖσαν.
> So, of the ancients, it is those who sided most with the doctrines of Pythagoras and his successors and Pherecydes who busied themselves with this nature [*sc.* the One]. But whereas some of them dealt with the One fully in their own writings, others worked orally in unrecorded group discussions, or failed to elaborate on the One at all. [trans. M. Atkinson modified]

In this passage, Plotinus recognizes the originality of the Pythagorean One, but, in contrast with V.5.6.26–30, he has a more careful approach to the Pythagorean sources since some of the Pythagorean doctrines were based on oral discussions and not fully elaborated in written argument.

According to Atkinson, Plotinus in V.1.9.27–32 makes a distinction between (1) the ancients who have given a full written explanation of the doctrine of the One, and (2) those who have not written down their ideas in treatises, but he then concludes that the philosophers who failed to elaborate their theories might be some unmentioned monists such as Thales or Anaximander, or even the seven sages.[83] But Plotinus' reference in V.1.9.27–32 is clearly to the followers of Pythagoras and not to the Ionian monists.

Plotinus divides the Pythagoreans who dealt with the nature of the One into two categories: (1) those who expounded their doctrines in treatises, and (2) those who worked orally in group philosophical discussions; some of the latter Pythagoreans failed completely to elaborate their ideas on the One. As the text shows, that the distinction is between groups of Pythagoreans is clearly highlighted by the οἱ μὲν and οἱ δὲ antithesis in lines 30 and 31 respectively: one group used written arguments, the other did not.

Concerning the Pythagoreans who worked in oral group discussions, the interpretations vary. Whereas Atkinson suggests that Plotinus is probably thinking of the "unwritten doctrines" of Plato in terms of Plato's Pythagoreanism,[84] Armstrong believes that Plotinus' refers to his master Ammonius.[85] In my view, neither interpretation can be justified. Whatever the position of Plotinus is with regard to the Platonic "unwritten doctrines," he never links Plato to the Pythagoreans. Furthermore, Plotinus' reference cannot be to Ammonius since he refers to the earlier Pythagoreans and not to the later Neopythagoreans, which include Ammonius. The problem can be solved if we simply assume that Plotinus' reference to the "unwritten group discussion" refers to Pythagoras himself and his close circle of philosophers.

On this, Plotinus seems to follow the common position, already widespread from ancient times, that Pythagoras did not leave any written work. Pythagoras preferred to record his teachings in the minds of his disciplines.[86] Josephus in *Contra Apionem* (I.163) states clearly that "there is no book generally agreed to be the work of Pythagoras." This view is also justified by Plutarch in *De Alexandri Magne Fortuna aut Virtute* (328A8–10), who places Pythagoras along with Socrates and other philosophers who wrote nothing, as well as by Galen (*De Placitis Hippocratis et Platonis* V.6.43.4), and Posidonius, who claims that there is no serious evidence for any work of Pythagoras surviving.[87] This position was later also held by Porphyry (*Vita Pythagorae*, 57), and Iamblichus (*De Vita Pythagorica*, 252). On the other hand, Diogenes Laertius (*Vitae Philosophorum* 8.6) testifies that, although some insist that Pythagoras left no writings at all, he actually wrote three books: *On Education*, *On Statesman*, and *On Nature*. But the genuineness of these three books is doubtful; in all probability, they are *pseudepigraphaī*: forgeries devised to defend the authenticity of Pythagoras' teaching.[88] Thus, Plotinus in V.1.9.27–32 are supporting the long-established position that Pythagoras did not write anything.

Plotinus' reference in V.1.9.27–32 to the Pythagoreans who developed in treatises their theories of the One, probably goes to the written doctrines of some immediate followers of Pythagoras such as Philolaus and Archytas (Diogenes Laertius, *Vitae Philosophorum* 8.80 and 85). But the more striking point in V.1.9.27–32 is the direct reference to Pherecydes' name alongside Pythagoras, recognized by Diels as a testimony of Pherecydes from Plotinus.[89] The Pherecydes' reference is also verified by Henry and Schwyzer's *Index Fontium* who further connect DK7A7a to an earlier chapter of the same treatise (V.1.6.5):[90]

> How, then, does it see, and whom, and how in any case did it become an independent entity and has arisen from the One so that it can see at all? The soul now accepts the necessity that these Forms exist, but yearns to know in addition *the answer to this question much asked by ancient philosophers* too, how from unity such as we say the One is did anything become an independent entity, whether a multiplicity, a dyad or a number. [V.1.6.1–8; trans. M. Atkinson]

In this passage, Plotinus' phrase about the ancients anticipates the doxographical discussion of chapter 9 including the Presocratic monism of Heraclitus, Empedocles, and Anaxagoras, and the discussion of the One as derivative source as well as the nature of the Pythagorean One. But it is hard to see any reference to Pherecydes behind the "ancient wise" in V.1.6.5. The only possible conclusion is that Pherecydes, following V.1.9.27–32, is to be included in Plotinus' list of Pythagorean philosophers who speak of the One. This claim appears in Aristotle's *Metaphysics* 1091b (=DK7A7) where Aristotle places Pherecydes among the ancient philosophers who agree with primary sovereignty. According to Aristotle, Pherecydes, along with Empedocles and Anaxagoras, is a philosopher who "blends" the mythical with the non-mythical.[91] If Aristotle's reference is correct then Plotinus' ascription of the One to Pherecydes is also acceptable.

On the other hand, Plotinus' testimony in V.1.9.27–32 is not universally accepted. Whereas some scholars such as R. Harder and H. S. Schibli delete Pherecydes' name from the passage either as irrelevant or as a learned gloss,[92] others such as Henry-Schwyzer, Atkinson and Armstrong[93] keep the name of Pherecydes in the text as relevant to its context.[94] And the name of Pythagoras is indeed related to that of Pherecydes.[95] In Diogenes Laertius (*Vitae Philosophorum* 1.119), according to the testimony of Aristoxenus, Pherecydes died and was buried by Pythagoras in Delos. More importantly, it is generally regarded and justified from various ancient sources that Pherecydes was the teacher of Pythagoras.[96] Plotinus' testimony is another source in favor of this position.

From a philosophical point of view, the reference to Pherecydes within Plotinus' discussion about the Pythagorean One is significant, and echoes Aristotle's testimony at *Metaphysics* 1091b. As Atkinson observes, the context of the passage requires that any philosopher mentioned should, like Pythagoras, have believed in the One.[97] Schibli criticizes Plotinus on the grounds that "the inclusion of Pherecydes with ancient thinkers such as Pythagoras and his followers, who derive existence from the One, is obviously mistaken, given Pherecydes' clear triadic statement . . . he [sc. Plotinus] would be therefore quite capable of forcing Pherecydes into his schema, perhaps surmising for Pherecydes' triad an original unity as for his own three Hypostases of One-Nous-Soul."[98] But Shibli's criticism is not well-grounded. Plotinus never identifies in V.1.9.27–32, or in any other *Ennead*, his three primary Hypostases of Being with Pherecydes' everlasting trinity of Zas, Chronos, and Cthonie (fr. 1). Plotinus' theory of the Three Hypostases is actually a monistic theory where the One is the first principle of all, the First Hypostasis which produces successively Intellect and Soul, while Pherecydes' principle is primarily triadic and thus pluralistic. Furthermore, the subject matter of V.1.9.27–32 is the One and not the Three Hypostases. Again, as Atkinson comments, the later Neoplatonic references to Pherecydes such as that of Porphyry (*De Antro Nympharum*, 31) are not relevant.

It can be therefore concluded that Plotinus' reference in V.1.9.27–32 to Pherecydes serves only to justify the historical relationship between Pherecydes and Pythagoras, and to suggest that Pherecydes probably spoke about the One.[99]

2.5 THE ONE AS FIRST PRINCIPLE

The most striking evidence of Plotinus' use of the Presocratic One as first principle appears in the opening lines of *Ennead* V.1.9. In the first seven lines of this chapter, Plotinus refers to three Presocratics: Anaxagoras, Heraclitus, and Empedocles. For Plotinus, these philosophers speak more appropriately than Parmenides on the true nature of the One. The Plotinian One should be understood as closer to the first principle of Anaxagoras, Heraclitus, and Empedocles than as a predicate of Parmenides' Being. This distinction between the One as "principle" and the One as "predicate" leads to the conclusion that Plotinus was fully aware of the antagonism between Eleatic and Ionian monism.

> Ἀναξαγόρας δὲ νοῦν καθαρὸν καὶ ἀμιγῆ λέγων ἁπλοῦν καὶ αὐτὸς τίθεται τὸ πρῶτον καὶ χωριστὸν *τὸ ἕν*, τὸ δ' ἀκριβὲς δι'ἀρχαιότηταπαρῆκε. Καὶ Ἡράκλειτος δὲ *τὸ ἕν* οἶδεν ἀίδιον καὶ νοητόν· τὰ γὰρσώματα γίγνεται ἀεὶ καὶ ῥέοντα. Τῷ δὲ Ἐμπεδοκ–λεῖ τὸ νεῖκος μὲνδιαιρεῖ, ἡ δὲ φιλία *τὸ ἕν*-ἀσώματον δὲ καὶ αὐτὸς τοῦτο-τὰ δὲ στοιχεῖα ὡς ὕλη.
> Again, Anaxagoras, in calling Nous pure and unmixed, is affirming the Primary as simple and the One as transcendent, but because of his antiquity he has neglected to be precise. Heraclitus also knows that the One is eternal and intelligible, since bodies are always coming to be, and are in flux. For Empedocles, Strife divides, Philia is the One—he too makes this incorporeal—and the elements serve as matter. [V.1.9.1–7; trans. Atkinson modified]

The above passage begins with Anaxagoras' Nous, relevant since chapter 9 continues the discussion of Intellect in chapter 8. Atkinson states that the Presocratics in V.1.9.1–7 are to be understood "according to the interpretation of Aristotle and the doxographical tradition."[100] But, except for Anaxagoras, Plotinus' source cannot be justified as Peripatetic or doxographical.

The important issue in V.1.9.1–7 is not so much its textual origins but its philosophical influence and significance. In this passage, the Presocratics under discussion anticipate Plotinus' One in different ways: it echoes Anaxagoras' Nous as the pure controlling principle, Heraclitus' One as the substantial inner-principle of the universal unity and Empedocles' Love as a unifying principle and motive power of the cosmos. More precisely, Plotinus refers clearly to: (1) Heraclitus' monism mainly in frs 10 and 50; (2) Empedocles' theory of Philia and Strife in frs 17 and 26; and (3) the nature of Anaxagoras' Mind in fr. 12. Based on these allusions, a further analysis shows the connection between Plotinus and these three Presocratics in V.1.9 and some other *Enneads* where Plotinus refers directly or indirectly to these fragments about the concept of unity and the One.

2.5.1 Heraclitus' One

In V.1.9.3–5, Plotinus recognizes Heraclitus as one of the Presocratics who spoke about the One, as Aristotle, in *Metaphysics* 984a, included Heraclitus in the list of material monists along with the Milesian philosophers. Plotinus accepts the Heraclitean monism of the one principle, but interprets it in metaphysical terms. Despite the importance of V.1.9.3–5, Plotinus' reference to Heraclitus is not included in the studies of H. Diels, M. Marchovich or C. Kahn.

Plotinus' reference to Heraclitus can be divided in two parts: (i) Heraclitus also knows that the One is eternal and intelligible; (ii) since bodies are always coming to be, and are in flux. In (i), Plotinus describes the Heraclitean One as "eternal" (ἀίδιον) and "intelligible" (νοητόν). In (ii), Plotinus refers to the material world of Heraclitus and the "everlasting flux of becoming" (γίγνεται ἀεὶ καὶ ῥέοντα). The aim of the above passage is clearly to highlight Heraclitus' distinction between the One and the world of becoming as well as the incorporeality and immateriality of the One. The antithesis that Plotinus points out is that between the One (τὸ ἕν) and "the bodies" (τὰ σώματα); the distinction between "one" and "many"; "eternity" and "everlastingness"; "intelligible stability" and "perceptible flux". However, Plotinus' One is never described as "eternal" or "intelligible"; these are properties of Intellect and not of the One. So Plotinus' intention is not to identify his One with Heraclitus' One, but to highlight the apparent distinction in Heraclitean monism between a single, incorporeal, and transcendent principle and the material world of becoming.

According to Armstrong,[101] Roussos,[102] Atkinson,[103] and the *Index Fontium*,[104] Plotinus' source of V.1.9.3–5 is the general account of Heraclitus' teaching in Diogenes Laertius (*Vitae Philosophorum* 9.8). Atkinson further notes that the reference goes back to the doxographical tradition and especially to Aristotle's *Metaphysics* 987a33–34, 1078b12 ff., and *De Caelo* 298b29–33, as well as to the Platonic distinction in the *Timaeus* between the world of intelligible Being and the world of perceptible Becoming. But Plotinus' reference to the Heraclitean One in V.1.9.3–5 goes beyond the testimony of Diogenes Laertius. Diogenes' summary does not include any reference to Heraclitus' One as "intelligible" or "everlasting," nor any clear analysis of the everlasting flux of becoming. Most probably, on the flux of becoming Plotinus' source is Plato's *Cratylus* 402a8–10, and the Heraclitean frs 12 and 91. The reference to Heraclitus by name in II.1.2.1–13 on the everlasting flux of the heavenly bodies is striking and supports the assumption of Plotinus' more direct knowledge of Heraclitus, perhaps *via* Platonic or Aristotelian sources, but he may well have been acquainted with some of Heraclitus' original sayings. In particular, with the term "everlasting" (ἀίδιον), Plotinus refers to

Heraclitus' One Principle, the "ever-living fire" (πῦρ ἀείζωον) of fragment 30. Again, with the term "intelligible" (νοητόν) Plotinus refers to the "one wise" (ἓν σοφόν) in Heraclitus' frs 32, 41, 50 and 108.

Within this framework, V.1.9.3–5 echoes the Heraclitean dictum "all things are one" (ἓν πάντα) of fragments 10 and 50. In these fragments unity (ἕν) and plurality (πάντα) are interrelated; plurality derives from unity and unity emerges from plurality. Through logical ambiguity and the phenomenal antithesis between the unity of the One and the plurality of the cosmos, all things are claimed to be one in their totality. Heraclitus' argument seems to be as follows: since the one is the source of all things and all things in their totality are one (fr. 10), therefore all things are in unity (fr. 50). In other words, while fragment 10 implies the derivative process of cosmic generation *from one to many* or *from unity to plurality*, fragment 50 entails the underlying universal state of being: *everything is in unity*.

These fragments express Heraclitus' monism. C. H. Kahn indeed regards Heraclitus' fragment 50 as the earliest extant statement of systematic monism, denying Aristotle's interpretation of Milesian monism in *Metaphysics* A3 where a material element (water, air, unlimited) is the one derivative source or the single *archē* of all things.[105] The Milesian concept of a single material source of all things provides the basis for Heraclitus' thought to formulate his monism as follows: (1) all things are derived from a single *archē*; (2) all things are organized within a single cosmos; (3) the initial principle encompasses, steers, and governs the whole cosmos by imposing a rational structure on it.[106] The Milesian *archē* is to be recognized as the first step towards the idea of monism that was further elaborated in Presocratic philosophy and was crucial to the Eleatic denial of plurality.

M. Marcovich states that fragment 50 expresses the consequence of apprehending the *logos* in the cosmic process as it is described in fragment 10.[107] The apprehension of *logos* establishes the ontological connection between apparent plurality and underlying unity, for *logos* is the common unifying principle behind the phenomenal complexity (fr. 2). On this basis, *logos* is identified with the "one divine law" that nourishes the "laws" for all humans (fr. 114); the divine law that all have to listen to and understand (fr. 50). Then those who are truly aware of the universality of *logos* are able to recognize that "cosmos is *one* and *common* for all" (fr. 89).

Moreover, for Heraclitus, the understanding of *logos* is the prerequisite of wisdom. For this reason, the "one" is also related to the "wise" (fr. 32) which "governs all things through all" (fr. 41), and "is set apart from all things" (fr. 108). The "one wise" represents the divine *logos* which is both present to all and apart from all, the principle of all things within all things but not to be identified with any one particular thing. The "one" is then connected with the universal exchange of fire in fr. 90: "All things are an equal exchange for fire and fire for all things, as goods are for gold and gold for goods." In this case, the "one" and "many" of frs 10 and 50 correspond to the "fire" and the "turnings of fire" of fr. 31, "kindling and quenching" according to the alternations of the cosmic cycle.

Within this framework, Heraclitus' cosmic paradigm is that of unity-in-opposition: *the one principle of all things perfectly self-includes and unifies two opposite forces in one single pattern.* This unitary pattern is realized in the conjunction of opposite pairs (fr. 88): "living" and "dead," "waking" and "sleeping," "young" and "old" as well as in the conception of a "single god" as "day" and "night," "winter" and "summer," "war" and "peace," "satiety" and "hunger" (fr. 67). The pattern is a harmony of opposite tensions (fr. 51), the unseen harmony which is better and stronger than the apparent one (fr. 54). Thus, the "one" is connected to and differentiated from the "many" in terms of being the connecting principle that unifies the many in one single form and totality without being identified with any of them. On this account, all things embrace in unity the following opposites in terms of "connexions" (fr. 10). Thus, since all things derive from the "one," all things depend on, and are governed by the "one." The "one" is the source and cause of unity. It is this monistic conception of the "one" in Heraclitus that is closely related to the One in Plotinus.

In particular, Plotinus frequently uses throughout the *Enneads* the Heraclitean dictum ἕν πάντα.[108] The most striking cases are in *Enneads* II.3.16.53–54; II.6.1.8–9; III.1.4.17–20; III.3.1.9–12; III.8.9.45; IV.4.38.17–19; V.2.1.1–3; VI.5.1.24–26. A comparison of these passages shows that Plotinus' language in most cases reflects Heraclitus' terminology. The discussion on *logos* and the "opposites" (ἐναντία) in *Enneads* II.3.16.53–54, III.3.1.9–12, and IV.4.38.17–19 is significant and in all probability denotes Heraclitus' presence in the background of Plotinus' thought. From a philosophical point of view, it can be clearly observed that Plotinus uses the Heraclitean tenet ἓν πάντα to express either the universal unity of Being; or the transcendent One as the single derivative source of all things. As Roussos observes, Plotinus accepts the Heraclitean influence not only in reducing all things to the One source, but also particularly in the productive process from unity to plurality and from plurality to unity.[109] More precisely, Heraclitus' monism corresponds to Plotinus' monism, in the expression "the one is all things but no single one of them" (τὸ ἓν πάντα καὶ οὐδὲ ἕν) in V.2.1.1–3.[110]

Plotinus' One is "all things" for it is universally omnipresent as the derivative principle of "all existence," "but no single one of them," for it is a transcendent principle beyond anything multiple or composite:

> The One is all things but no single one of them: it is the principle of all things, not all things, but all things have that other kind of transcendent

existence; for in a way they do occur in the One; or rather they are not there yet, but they will be. How then do all things come from the One, which is simple and has no diverse variety, or any sort of doubleness? It is because there is nothing in it that all things come from it: in order that being may exist, the One is not being but the generator of being. This, we may say, is the first act of generation: the One, perfect because it seeks nothing, has nothing, and needs nothing, overflows as it were, and its superabundance makes something other than itself. [V.2.1.1–10; trans. Armstrong, adapted]

For this reason, the omnipresence of Plotinus' One is indistinguishable from its transcendence. As first principle the One contains everything in a transcendental mode.[111]

The One is at the same time "everywhere and nowhere"; "everywhere" because it is the productive cause of "all things," "nowhere" because it is the transcendent source before all things.[112] Being everywhere and nowhere, and, since multiplicity necessarily implies prior simplicity, the One must be at the same time one principle alone by itself and the omnipresent element in all other things (V.6.3.10–15), yet the omnipresence of the One should not be interpreted as immanence in its derivatives.[113] Hence, "all things are the One and not the One" (V.2.2.24–29), and the principality of the One provides the grounds both for its omnipresence and for its functioning as efficient causality.[114]

In order to illustrate this idea Plotinus uses the analogy of the seed (τὸ σπέρμα) and its parts (τὰ μέρη) which are always one in absolute unity.[115] Plotinus identifies the seed with the *logos* of the Soul which is one and many simultaneously (VI.4.11). Within this framework, Plotinus justifies two basic principles of his metaphysics: (1) that the One can be the ultimate source of plurality, and (2) that plurality entails a fundamental unity. Thus, in Plotinus' intelligible universe as in Heraclitus' cosmos, since *all things derive from unity*, then *all things are in unity and all things strive towards the One*.[116] As Plotinus puts it in a passage strongly influenced by Heraclitean monism:

> For all things sprung from a unity come together into a unity by natural necessity, so that, though they grow out different and come into being as opposites they are, all the same, drawn together into a single common order by the fact that they come from a unity. [III.3.1.9–12; trans. Armstrong]

Due to the perfection of the One, everything in the universe is placed in the appropriate place and the harmony in the world comes from the unity of the opposites.[117] The wisdom in nature is not to produce one out of many but rather to resolve the many out of the One (V.8.5.6–8).

In the light of the above analysis, the revival of Heraclitean monism can be found in Plotinus' system in (1) the theory of the Three Hypostases, (2) the structure of the cosmos, (3) the nature of Intellect, (4) the unity of the Soul, and (5) the unity of God.[118] As was shown earlier, all these levels derive from the concept of "unity in plurality." Through Plotinus the Heraclitean concept of ἓν πάντα was transmitted to later Neoplatonists such as Porphyry and Syrianus who endorsed Plotinus' idea of the One's transcendent causality and omnipresent universality.[119] Heraclitus' principle was also important earlier for the Stoics and Philo.[120] And it is worth noting that Marius Victorinus, the Latin Christian Neoplatonist of the fourth century AD, in *Adversus Arium* IV.22.6–10 quotes almost literally the Plotinus' words of V.2.1.1–3; through this source Plotinus' model of the One's transcendent causality was transmitted to the Latin West and especially to the Christianity of St. Augustine.[121] Within this framework, Plotinus gives Heraclitus' ἓν πάντα a metaphysical context. Whereas for Plotinus the context is metaphysical and the term explains the unity of Being by the transcendent supremacy of the One, in Heraclitus the context is natural and the term explains the unity of the cosmos by the inner commonality and universality of *logos*. Within this framework, Plotinus interprets Heraclitus' pantheistic monism through a Platonic perspective, which leads eventually to the Neoplatonic metaphysical monism of the One.

2.5.2 *Empedocles'* Philia

In the last two lines of V.1.9.1–7, Plotinus refers to Empedocles' Love and Strife as well as the four material elements. Plotinus interprets the Empedoclean *Philia* as the One in terms of being immaterial and incorporeal contrasted with the materiality of the four elements. Plotinus' passage can be divided in two parts: (i) For Empedocles, Strife divides, Philia is the One—he too makes this incorporeal; (ii) and the elements serve as matter. In (i) Plotinus refers directly to Empedocles' frs 17.7–8 and 26.5–6 on the motive forces Love (ἡ Φιλία) and Strife (τὸ Νεῖκος).[122] In (ii) he refers to Empedocles' four material elements or "roots" (ῥιζώματα), namely fire, air, water, and earth.[123] Plotinus' reference to Empedocles frs 17.7–8 and 26.5–6 in V.1.9.6–7 here has been recognized by Armstrong,[124] Atkinson,[125] and the *Index Fontium*, but it is not mentioned in Diels/Kranz nor any other modern study or commentary on Empedocles.

As with Anaxagoras and Heraclitus, Plotinus' aim in the case of Empedocles is to highlight the difference between the incorporeality of the supreme One and the materiality of the perceptible world, rather than adopting the traditional interpretation of Empedocles as a pluralist.[126] In V.1.9.6–7, Plotinus recognizes Empedocles' duality in the principles of Philia and Strife, but he focuses on and identifies the One with the Empedoclean Philia since Philia is the motive principle that brings plurality into unity.[127]

In particular, Empedocles' natural philosophy follows a middle path between Heraclitus' pluralism and Parmenides' monism. Empedocles' thought runs upon two theoretical axes: (1) the immortal, unchangeable and imperishable four elemental material roots, and (2) the motive forces of Love and Strife.[128] For Empedocles, all the above principles are eternal natures: the Four Roots are indestructible, imperishable, and immortal *material* elements; Love and Strife are the *incorporeal* creative forces of the cosmos that act upon the four roots. Within this framework, the creative process of the cosmos is a continuous production that happens in two phases, one corresponding to the increasing dominance of Philia and the other to the increasing dominance of Strife (frs 8 and 23). On this basis, Empedocles follows Parmenides' denial of ex nihilo creation as well as the elimination of generation and destruction from nonbeing (fr. 12) but allows for so-called birth and death. Since generation cannot be creation from nothing nor destruction complete separation into nothing, so-called generation is the mixture (μίξις) of the elements by the act of Philia and destruction their separation (διάλλαξις) under the act of Strife (fr. 8). Mortals are in a continual cyclical exchange: from "many" to "one" and from "one" to "many" (fr. 17.1–8).

During the phase of Philia mortals become united under one generation (fr. 17.7), during the phase of Strife mortals are divided and return again to multiplicity (fr. 17.8 and 26.5–6).[129] With this passage, as well as with the relevant one in fr. 26, Empedocles outlines clearly the difference between the life of "immortals" (ἀθάνατα) and the life of "mortals" (θνητά) (frs 20 and 22). And in fr. 17.7 the phrase ἓν ἅπαντα echoes Heraclitus' principle, establishing a connection between Heraclitus and Empedocles on the conception of "unity in plurality," confirmed by the fact that Plotinus follows Empedocles' passage immediately after Heraclitus in V.1.9.3–5.

Based on the immortal and incorporeal connective motive power of *Philia*, Plotinus interprets Empedocles' Love as his own First Principle and a forerunner of the Neoplatonic One. But, according to Atkinson, Plotinus remains unclear in V.1.9.6–7 on how Strife fits into his philosophy, because he does not make any identification with the divisive principle.[130] Atkinson's comment can be answered by analyzing the other three occurrences of Empedocles' frs 17.7–8 and 26.5–6 in *Enneads* III.2.2.1–7, IV.4.40.1–9, and VI.7.14.18–23.

In III.2.2.1–7, Plotinus states that Love and Strife are the inherent opposite and creative forces within the cosmos. The perceptible universe is not truly one but one in multiplicity since it is divided into different and necessarily conflicting parts. Whereas *Philia* keeps the cosmos as one unified universe, *Neikos* divides the universe into multiple parts:

> For from that true cosmos which is one this cosmos comes into existence, which is not truly one; for it is many and divided into a multiplicity, and

> one part stands away from another and is alien to it, and there is not only Philia but also Enmity because of the separation, and in their deficiency one part is of necessity at war with another. [III.2.2.1–7; trans. Armstrong modified]

In this passage, Plotinus uses Empedocles' Love and Strife in order to express the natural antithesis between unity and plurality, cohesiveness and separation, concordance and discordance at the level of the perceptible world. It is significant that Plotinus refers to Empedocles' Strife with the term "enmity" (ἔχθρα: III.2.2.5), which echoes Empedocles' fr. 22 where enmity is synonymous with "strife" (νεῖκος). In this fragment, Empedocles, like Plotinus, stresses the connection between what can be mixed and is brought together in unity by Philia, and what is kept apart in multiplicity and enmity by Strife.[131] The conflicting enmity of Strife is also justified in Empedocles by Theophrastus in *De sensu et sensibilibus* 16 (=DK 31A86). Again Plato at the *Sophist* 242e speaks ironically of the Ionian and the Sicilian muses who believed that being is one and many, bound by both sympathy and enmity (*Sophist* 242e1–2).

Plotinus also speaks about Strife in terms of separation and division in VI.7.14.18–23; here the subject matter is not the cosmos but Intellect. For Plotinus, Intellect is one-many in perfection without conflict, confusion, or material separation contrasted with the imperfect unity of the perceptible realm. The intelligible realm poses "true unity" (ἀληθὴς φιλία) closer to the supra-transcendent unity of the One:

> But the division which is in Intellect is not of things confused, though of things existing in unity, but this is what is called the Philia in the All, not the Philia in this All; for this is an imitation, since it is a loving of things which are separate; but the true Philia is all things being one and never separated. But [Empedocles] says that what is within this our sky is separated. [VI.7.14.18–23; trans. Armstrong]

For Plotinus true *Philia* is the unity of the One. From a Platonic perspective, the *Philia* of the perceptible realm is just an image of the intelligible one and so an imperfect copy of it. On this basis, true *Philia* for Plotinus has to be closer to the absolute unity of all things beyond any form or separation (VI.7.14.22).

Moreover, at IV.4.40.1–9, Plotinus vividly states that *Philia* and *Neikos* constitute the true magic of the universe (ἡ ἀληθινὴ μαγεία ἡ ἐν τῷ παντὶ φιλία καὶ τὸ νεῖκος αὖ):

> But how do magic spells work? By sympathy and by the fact that there is a natural concord of things that are alike and opposition of things that are different, and by the rich variety of the many powers which go to

> make up the life of the one living creature. For many things are drawn and enchanted without anyone else's magical contrivance: and the true magic is the Philia and also the Strife in the All. And this is the primary wizard and enchanter, from observing whom men came to use his philtres and spells on each other. [trans. Armstrong]

The above passage opens the influential Plotinian discussion on "magic" in chapters IV.4.40–45. This discussion has attracted the interest of eminent scholars.[132] P. Kingsley (1995), for example, refers explicitly to *Ennead* IV.4.40.1–9, and reads Plotinus' account on the "primary wizard" (ὁ γόης ὁ πρῶτος καὶ φαρμακεὺς οὗτός ἐστιν) to Empedocles as a wizard.[133] But it is not evident that for Plotinus the "wizard" in the particular passage is indeed Empedocles himself—Plotinus may refer in general to the figure of the magician or the wizard who combines the cosmic forces of Love and Strife in order to exercise his magical art.

Plotinus, throughout these chapters, shows a sound knowledge of magical practices and their cosmic consequences. As Armstrong notes, Plotinus makes clear that magic is a "manipulation of natural forces, attractions and sympathies resulting from the living organic unity of the physical universe."[134] On this basis, Plotinus seems to be influenced by the Stoic idea of "cosmic sympathy" (συμπάθεια).[135] For Plotinus, the "magic spells" (τὰς γοητείας) work because of the natural organic interconnection of opposing forces within the universe (IV.4.40.1). While the positive force of *concordance* "brings together things that are alike" (συμφωνίαν εἶναι ὁμοίων), the negative force of *division* "separates things that are different" (ἐναντίωσιν ἀνομοίων) (IV.4.40.2–3). The former force corresponds to Empedocles' Love, the latter to Strife. The key concept in this issue is again "unity." A living organism keeps its parts in unity because of the equilibrium between the two opposing forces, and the unity of the universe as a great living organism is maintained by the same cosmic law. Plotinus' argument is that *since the universe is a living organism, whatever happens in one part of it can produce a sympathetic reaction in another* (II.3.7).[136] Therefore, the magicians produce their effects by studying and applying the relevant cosmic forces at that level.

Similarly in IV.9.3.3 (εἰς τὸ φιλεῖν ἑλκομένους κατὰ φύσιν), Plotinus speaks again about the forces of magic where the cosmic sympathy is again related to Empedocles' Philia. The wizard's magic spells work because of the unity and cosmic sympathy of the Soul.[137] Since the Soul is one, the magician can exercise his practice at a distance by using the power of cosmic sympathy via the continuum of the universal soul medium (IV.4.26.1–4).[138] Thus, because one part of the world is in sympathetic connection with another, the magician is able to make use of this organic unity to affect someone in one place from another. To explain it, Plotinus offers the analogy of the one tense string (IV.4.41.3: μιᾷ νευρᾷ τεταμένῃ)—when the string is plucked at the lower end it has a vibration at the upper, and when one string is plucked another has a kind of sense of it and by this concord is tuned to the same scale. Likewise, cosmic sympathy works for magicians in terms of the single universal harmony in the cosmos composed of opposite parts.

Here it has to be noted that this simile in IV.4.41 echoes Heraclitus' use in fragment 51 of the bow and the lyre: "there is a harmony of opposite tensions, as in the bow and lyre."[139] If we look closely at the terminology of IV.4.41, it can be seen that Plotinus' language clearly echoes that of Heraclitus. The expression on the vibration of the string "up and down movement" in line 4 reflects Heraclitus' unity of opposites in fr. 60; likewise the phrases "one harmony deriving from the opposites" in line 8 mirrors Heraclitus' concept of the harmonious unity of the opposites, so Plotinus is likely here to have Heraclitus' unity of the opposites in the background of his thought.[140]

On the other hand, even if Plotinus shows a sound knowledge of magic, his interest in the forces of magic seems to be more philosophical than practical. As R. T. Wallis says, while for Plotinus magic is a real force, it is "yet of limited application and has no place in the philosopher's training."[141] Indeed, since magic is used and applied only at the lower of the perceptible cosmos, the magicians can affect only the lower part of the human soul that is related to the body.[142] For Plotinus, the "wise man" cannot be affected by magic spells (IV.4.43), and he will not be involved in evil actions (I.4.7.45–47). The inner light of the wise man is like the "light in a lantern when it is blowing hard outside with a great fury of wind and storm" (I.4.8.4–5). The latter Plotinian metaphor clearly echoes again Empedocles and his image of the storm-lantern in fr. 84:

> As when a man who intends to make a journey prepares a light for himself, a flame of fire burning through a wintry night; he fits linen screens against all the winds which break the blast of the winds as they blow, but the light that is more diffuse leaps through, and shines across the threshold with unfailing beams.[143] [trans. Wright]

For Armstrong, the context of Plotinus' text is quite different form that of Empedocles where the storm-lantern is an analogy for the structure of the eye.[144] But in all probability Plotinus wants to apply the physical aspect of Empedocles' storm-lantern to the metaphysical analogy of the Soul.[145]

Hence, magic as an external force cannot affect the higher souls either of the philosopher or of the gods (II.9.14). The philosopher focuses on the higher rational and unaffected part of the soul and not on the lower bodily part where magic applies (IV.4.43.1–11). For this reason, the philosopher is even able to resist magical attacks through counterspells of his own, as Plotinus himself did according to Porphyry's testimony (*Life* 10.1–13). In this apocalyptic testimony, it is clear that Plotinus was acquainted with magical practices, and the extract undoubtedly connects with IV.4.43.1–11. In fact, Plotinus uses magic as self-defense and not as a common practice.[146]

Plotinus clearly believed that magic worked. This is evident in IV.3.11 where he speaks in favor of ancient theurgic practices in animating a divine statue. But he is interested in the sympathetic reactions of the organic unity of the Soul from a philosophical perspective and not for a magico-practical one. For Plotinus, magic is unnecessary for the philosopher and on this basis he wanted to turn the interest of his pupils from magic, theurgic practice, and popular religion to philosophical inspiration and higher contemplation (*Life* 10.33–8). The scene in the temple of Isis (*Life* 10.15–33) where an Egyptian priest named Plotinus' guardian spirit to be a god and not merely a daemon is deceptive. According to Porphyry, Plotinus was inspired by this incident to write the early treatise III.4 *On our Allotted Guardian Spirit*. In this *Ennead*, Plotinus makes clear that our allotted personal spirit is not an anthropomorphic God but a transcendent psychological principle beyond the conscious state of life, and placed at the level of the higher Soul close to the intelligible realm. The philosopher has to ascend to the higher realm of Intellect through pure contemplation, which is real purification for the Soul (I.2.3.10–20). By focusing on the higher intelligible realm, the Soul transcends the limits of the perceptible realm and therefore remains unaffected by the practice of magic which is directed only at the bodily level of the Soul. Here, as Wallis notes, Plotinus posed a challenge for later Neoplatonists and especially Iamblichus who fully recognized the importance of theurgy in philosophy.[147]

On this basis, J. Edwards (1990) finds some parallels between Empedocles' Philia and the *Oracle on Plotinus* preserved in Porphyry's *Life* 22, in which Plotinus' spirit appears to be enjoying celestial bliss along with the gods and ancient philosophers such as Pythagoras, Socrates, and Plato; Edwards claims that there is an echo of Empedocles' Philia in the word φιλότης of the verse of line 48.[148] But Edwards' hypothesis cannot be further justified.

Thus, it can be concluded from the above that Plotinus recognizes Empedocles not as a magician but rather as a philosopher who introduced firstly the incorporeality and immateriality of the first principle, and secondly *Philia* and *Neikos* as fundamental creative forces for both cosmic equilibrium and unity of Soul and Cosmos.[149] Within this framework, Empedocles plays an important role in Plotinus' psychology, a subject to be discussed later.[150]

2.5.3 Anaxagoras' Mind

In the first three lines of V.1.9.1–7, Plotinus refers to Anaxagoras' account of Nous given in fragment 12.[151] The reference to fragment 12 is recognized by

Atkinson,[152] Armstrong,[153] and the *Index Fontium*, and, in addition, Henry and Schwyzer in the *Index Fontium* find further allusions to fragment 12 at *Enneads* I.8.2.19; II.1.6.23–4; V.1.8.4–5; V.3.3.21–2, 3.45, 6.11–12, 14.14; V.8.3.25–6; VI.2.8.6; VI.8.5.2, and VI.9.3.26. But despite the importance of Plotinus' reference to Anaxagoras in *Ennead* V.1.9.1–3, the citation is not included in Diels/Kranz or in D. Sider's commentary of Anaxagoras, or in any other relevant study about the Presocratic.

Plotinus' reference to Anaxagoras can be divided into three parts: (i) Again, Anaxagoras, in calling Nous pure and unmixed; (ii) is affirming the Primary as simple and the One as transcendent; (iii) but because of his antiquity he has neglected to be precise. In (i) Plotinus alludes to Anaxagoras' fragment 12 by describing his Νοῦς as "pure" (καθαρόν) and "unmixed" (ἀμιγῆ)—this can be named as the doxographical part. In (ii) Plotinus interprets, in the light of (i), the Anaxagorean First or Primary Principle (τὸ πρῶτον) as "simple" (ἁπλοῦν) and "transcendent" (χωριστὸν)[154]—this can be named as the interpretative part. In (iii) Plotinus explains that Anaxagoras' terminology was not accurate because of his early philosophical thinking—this can be named as the concluding part.

Plotinus interprets Anaxagoras' theory of Nous in the following way: *since the first principle is pure and unmixed, then it has to be simple and transcendent.* Plotinus explains the simplicity of the First Principle in terms of Nous' purity and the transcendence of the One in terms of being unmixed, beyond anything material. For this reason, Anaxagoras' Nous and Plotinus' One are related, for Anaxagoras' Nous as a First Principle can be linked to Plotinus' One in terms of being (1) simple beyond any multiplicity, and (2) transcendently incorporeal beyond anything material. This can also be observed in the next lines devoted to Heraclitus and Empedocles where Plotinus highlights the difference between the incorporeality of the first principle and the materiality of the world of becoming. Consequently, Plotinus recognizes Anaxagoras, along with Heraclitus and Empedocles, as a monist—a philosopher who came close to the true concept of the One as a transcendent, simple, and first principle beyond natural phenomena.

However, Anaxagoras' monism has been debated since antiquity. Theophrastus regarded Anaxagoras as dualist and not a monist (*Physicorum Opiniones* fr. 4 *ap.* Simplicius *in Physica* 27.17 = DK 59A41). Theophrastus' testimony has led some modern scholars to maintain that Anaxagoras was really a dualist in the sense of a positing a dualism of Mind and Matter.[155] However, Theophrastus offers a testimony which is basically a Peripatetic interpretation of Anaxagoras—although he recognizes that Anaxagoras spoke originally about Nous as a single cause, he proceeds to apply to him an Aristotelian distinction between Mind or Form and Matter.[156] But Plotinus clearly denies any dualism for Anaxagoras and regards the Presocratic originally as a monist, interpreted in the context of the Neoplatonic monism of the One as the supreme principle and matter as the unsubstantial nonbeing.

Anaxagoras indeed speaks of the monistic nature of Nous as unique principle in both fragments 11 and 12. In fragment 11, Nous is described as completely separate, the only exception to the universal criterion "everything in everything" (ἐν παντὶ παντὸς μοῖρα).[157] In fragment 12, Nous is described as "unlimited" (fr. 12.1: ἄπειρος), "self-controlling" (fr. 12.2: αὐτοκρατές), "unmixed" (fr. 12.2: μέμεικται οὐδενί), "alone in itself and by itself" (fr. 12.2–3: μόνος αὐτὸς ἐπ' ἑωυτοῦ), "the finest" (fr. 12.8: λεπτότατον), "the purest" (fr. 12.8: καθαρώτατον), "with complete knowledge" (fr. 12.9: γνώμην περὶ παντὸς πᾶσαν ἴσχει), "supreme in power" (fr. 12.9–10: ἰσχύει μέγιστον), "the controller of everything alive" (fr. 12.10–12: ὅσα ψυχὴν ἔχει).[158]

Furthermore, according to Anaxagoras' fragments 1 and 2, Nous is the unlimited force that *initiates* the original rotation of matter, *controls* the consequent separatings, and *arranges* the whole in an ordered cosmos. The revolutionary formation of the cosmos started when the all that was together began to separate out by the motive power of Nous. Nous initiated the rotation of the "stuffs," which resulted in the predominantly heavy parts coming to the center of the vortex and the predominantly lighter parts moving outwards.[159] But on the intelligibility of Nous Anaxagoras remains silent.[160] It is well known that Socrates earlier had complained that Anaxagoras did not explain whether or how Mind was an intelligent nature arranging everything for the best.[161] Aristotle in *Metaphysics* 985a18 also criticized Anaxagoras for the arbitrary use of Nous as Mind and Force.

By comparing V.1.9.1–3 with fr. 12, we can observe that Plotinus refers with the term "pure" (καθαρόν) to "the purest" (καθαρώτατον) in Anaxagoras fr. 12.8; with "unmixed" (ἀμιγῆ) to "mixed with nothing" (μέμεικται οὐδενί) in fr. 12.2. The terms "simple" (ἁπλοῦν) and "first" (πρῶτον) are not present in the extant fragments of Anaxagoras and actually belong to the interpretative part (ii) of V.1.9.1–3. The word "simple" can be found in Aristotle' criticism of Anaxagoras' Nous in *Metaphysics* 989b14–21,[162] where the Aristotelian text is in all probability the source of Plotinus' V.1.9.1–7. As Atkinson observes, the verbal parallels between Plotinus and Aristotle are clearly evident.[163]

Indeed Plotinus and Aristotle both agree in the above passages that, since Anaxagoras' Nous is "pure" and "unmixed," therefore it is "simple" and "one." They also agree in the concluding lines of both passages (and this is the most striking evidence for Plotinus' knowledge of Aristotle's criticism) that Anaxagoras is inaccurate on the exact nature of Nous because of his antiquity. But Plotinus, in contrast to Aristotle, does not criticize Anaxagoras for his theory of Nous. On the contrary, he recommends the Presocratic for putting a simple and unmixed principle beyond everything multiple and composite.

With the concluding phrase "because of his antiquity he has neglected to be precise," Plotinus has doubts not so much about the soundness of Anaxagoras' philosophy but the clarity of expression from so long ago. Plotinus' attitude towards Anaxagoras is similar to his attitude towards Parmenides in comparing the Eleatic with Plato in V.1.8.23. Plotinus is puzzled by Anaxagoras' thought in that there appear to be some contradictory characteristics of Nous as a First Principle.

Certainly, within the context of Plotinus' philosophy of the One, the supreme principle cannot entail intelligence. Anaxagoras' Nous is usually translated as Mind or Intelligence, but, for Plotinus, intelligence implies multiplicity and not simplicity (V.3.11.1). Throughout the *Enneads* terms such as "simple," "first," and "transcendent" are usually attributed to the One and not to the Intellect. For instance, in V.4.1.1–17, Plotinus describes the One exactly in terms of V.1.9.1–7 as "the first," "the simple," and "non-composite," "being one alone." However, the Anaxagorean terms καθαρός and ἀμιγής are also attributed by Plotinus to Intellect in order to manifest the perfect unity-in-plurality of the Second Hypostasis.[164]

In addition, Plotinus frequently uses another famous Anaxagorean principle to describe Intellect's all-togetherness: ὁμοῦ πάντα in frs 1.1; fr. 4.13; fr. 6.7 along with Parmenides' ὁμοῦ πᾶν in fr. 8.5;[165] ὁμοῦ πάντα in Anaxagoras frs 1.1, 4.13 and 6.7 is clearly a reply to Parmenides' ὁμοῦ πᾶν in fr. 8.5.[166] Anaxagoras' πάντα in comparison with Parmenides' πᾶν shows the difference between the pluralistic approach of the Ionian School and the monistic one of the Eleatics. Plotinus uses both ὁμοῦ πᾶν and ὁμοῦ πάντα to denote the inner all-togetherness of the intelligibles in the intelligible world as well as the complete unity and totality of intelligible being. The more striking reference to Parmenides' ὁμοῦ πᾶν appears at VI.4.4.24–6 where Plotinus speaks of the unity and completeness of intelligible being. This clear reference to ὁμοῦ πᾶν in Parmenides' fr. 8.5 includes in its context an exact quotation from 8.25. And this also shows that Plotinus was aware of Parmenides' program at the beginning of fr. 8 and its subsequent elaboration.

On the other hand, since Intellect is for Plotinus unity-in-plurality the ὁμοῦ πάντα of Anaxagoras appears more suitable for his philosophical purposes than Parmenides in this context, and hence it is used more than thirty times throughout the *Enneads*. In particular, Plotinus uses ὁμοῦ πάντα (1) to denote the complete unity-in-plurality and altogetherness of the intelligibles within Intellect;[167] (2) to contrast the One with the plurality of intelligibles;[168] (3) to express the unity of eternal life in the intelligible realm;[169] (4) to show how the Soul contemplates the real beings in unity within its higher intelligible self;[170] (5) to draw the analogy between the One and the seed;[171] (6) to illustrate the nature of Matter.[172] From these references it can be seen that the expression ὁμοῦ πάντα appears to be a favorite technical term for Plotinus, but it has to be admitted that this was a popular term by the time of Plotinus, and we cannot assume that Plotinus traces back to Anaxagoras in the above passages; indeed, if we exclude cases 5 and 6, Plotinus has taken the term out of its context in Anaxagoras' philosophy and adapted it to his own purposes.

However, Plotinus does follow Anaxagoras in the purity and simplicity of Nous. Nous for Plotinus is also pure and simple in terms of being the finest of the things in the precreative state of cosmos and independent of them.[173] In particular, the Anaxagorean term καθαρός appears in *Enneads* V.3.6.10–12; V.3.14.14–15; V.8.3.24–28; VI.2.8.5–6; VI.8.5.2; VI.9.3.22–27; V.3.2.20–22.[174] In these passages, Plotinus uses Anaxagoras' term καθαρός to express the simplicity and purity of the intelligible unity. The Plotinian Intellect is "pure" due to the perfect composition of the intelligibles. At this level, Intellect is actually unmixed and remains closer to the absolute unity of the transcendent One. The One is the simplest object of contemplation and thus Intellect is the first manifestation of the One's purity at the intelligible level of the Second Hypostasis. It is significant that Plotinus in V.3.2.20–22 refers to Intellect as ἄκρατος, an epithet that echoes Plutarch's testimony of Anaxagoras in *Pericles* 4 (=DK 59A15). The term does not appear as such in Anaxagoras' extant fragment, but on the authority of Plutarch and Plotinus it may well be that ἄκρατος was used originally by Anaxagoras as an epithet of Nous.

From all the available evidence it is clear that Plotinus reads Anaxagoras from a metaphysical perspective. He interprets Anaxagoras' Nous not as Intelligence or Mind, but as transcendent principle which is like the One even before intelligence and Being. For this reason, Plotinus adds the terms "simple," "first," and "transcendent" to highlight the identification of Anaxagoras' Nous with the "pure" One. Thus, Plotinus correctly understands Anaxagoras' Nous as First Principle rather than Mind, and it is on Plotinus' theory of Intellect that we are going to turn now our attention in the next section.

Chapter 3

Intellect and Being

3.1 PLOTINUS' THEORY OF INTELLECT

Plotinus' theory of Intellect (Νοῦς) is one of the most original concepts of Greek philosophy.[1] It links Plotinus' Neoplatonic philosophy not only with the philosophy of Middle-Platonism and especially with Numenius and Albinus,[2] but also with the original Presocratic, Platonic, and Aristotelian tradition. As Armstrong states: "It is the fullest expression in his system of the universal later Hellenic belief in a totally unified cosmic order."[3] Plotinus' innovation lies in integrating into one concept (1) Plato's world of Forms, (2) the Middle Platonic idea of the Forms as thoughts of God, (3) the Aristotelian theory of the self-thinking God, and (4) Parmenides' theory of Being.[4] Fundamentally, it is a synthesis of Plato's theory of the Forms in the *Phaedo,* the *Timaeus,* the *Parmenides*, the *Sophist*, and especially the middle books of the *Republic* with Aristotle's account of the divine mind as a pure thinker in *Metaphysics* and of the active intellect in *De Anima*. In this framework, Plotinus' Intellect is a unified organism of intelligibles, a revealing unity-in-plurality of the Forms self-produced through the eternal generation of the One. As H. J. Blumenthal puts it, Intellect's thinking is 'a thinking of proper intellectual objects, namely, its own contents, thereby amalgamating the highest principles of both Plato and Aristotle in the highest form of existence in Plotinus' system."[5]

With regard to Plato, Plotinus accepts the Forms as true and eternal living intelligences with their own substantial content. In the light of Plato's teaching, Plotinus connects his Νοῦς with the "all-complete ever-living being" of the *Timaeus* (29d7–47e2), with the "true being" endowed with life and intelligence of the *Sophist* (248e–249a), and with the second hypothesis in the second part of the *Parmenides* (137c–142a, 144e5; 155e5).[6] Following Plato's *Sophist*, Plotinus regards the Forms not as self-subsistent universals but as living intelligible beings. This is due to the identification of Intellect with its Being in the Forms (V.1.4.26–9), and of individual Forms with individual intellects (V.9.8.3–7); each Form is both the object and the subject of intellection.[7] On this basis, Intellect becomes a self-contained all-complete world of active intelligibles where every intelligible is not only "actually itself," but also "potentially" all the others (VI.2.20; III.8.8.40 ff.).

With regard to Aristotle, Plotinus' theory of Intellect seems to be influenced by the Aristotelian thesis of the "self-thinking" divine activity in *Metaphysics* (1074b34: νόησις νοήσεως). At the divine level, the object of intelligence is identified with the intellectualizing subject and this self-intellectualization is the essence of God's perfect life; and since life is the actuality of thought, and God is that actuality, then God's eternal, self-dependent actuality is the best life (1072b26–29). The attributes of the Aristotelian God in *Metaphysics* then are eternity, immutability, indivisibility, imperceptibility, and self-sufficiency, constituting a divine nature that is supreme, pure actuality in thinking-itself (1072b18–21). The divine identity of thought and its object appears again in *De Anima* 431a1: "actual knowledge is identical with its object." For Aristotle, this identity is the purest form of thought, appearing only at the level of the immaterial intelligibles. As he explains at 430a3–4: "in the case of the immaterial objects [the intelligibles], that which thinks and that which is being thought are the same."[8]

Based on these considerations, Plotinus' theory of Intellect has to be regarded as a departure from Plato's original theory: the Platonic Forms now become substantially active forces which constitute the divine Intellect "boiling over with life" (VI.5.12.9: ὑπερζέουσα ζωή).[9] And at this point, we have in Plotinus the influence of Aristotle's self-thinking God. Whereas Aristotle's God thinks himself but not by thinking the Forms (which Aristotle does not accept as separate entities), Plotinus' God thinks himself by thinking essentially the Forms. In Plotinus, self-thinking activity is actually conflated with the activity of the Aristotelian Unmoved Mover, which in turn is treated in the *Timaeus* as the self-thinking activity of the Demiurge.[10] Thus, Aristotle's God becomes a Neoplatonic version of the Platonic Demiurge: *a divine Intellect thinking the Forms in itself.*

Within the system of Plotinus' Hypostases, the Intellect is the first by-product of the One; it is the realm of True Being, Intelligence and Life, the first duality after the One. Intellect is self-generated in two phases: (1) the phase of Procession in which an infinite and formless stream of life overflows from the One; and (2) the phase of Reversion in which Intellect returns upon the One and receives order and form from it. At the phase of Procession Intellect remains Indefinite (ἀόριστος) until, at the phase of Reversion, it delimits itself (ὁρίζεται) by returning upon the One:

> This, we may say, is the first act of generation: the One, perfect because it seeks nothing, has nothing, and needs nothing, overflows as it were, and its superabundance makes something other than itself. This, when it has been generated, turns back upon the One and is filled, and becomes Intellect by looking towards it. Its halting and turning towards the One constitutes Being, its contemplation upon the One, Intellect. Since it

halts and turns towards the One that it may see, it becomes at once Intellect and Being. [V.2.1.7–13; trans. Armstrong modified]

Plotinus illustrates the above generative process of Intellect with the metaphor of sight (V.3.11.1 ff.). While at the phase of Procession the Intellect remains unformed in potentiality, like "sight searching for vision" (ἀτύπωτος ὄψις), at the phase of Reversion the Intellect contemplates the One in actuality and becomes a complete "actualized vision" (ἰδοῦσα ὄψις). In the metaphysical context, while at the stage of Procession, Intellect receives an immediate apprehension of the One; it actually becomes Intellect only in the phase of Reversion.

In the light of this assumption, Plotinus identifies Intellect's Procession with the controversial but fundamental concept of Indefinite Dyad (V.1.5.14: ἀόριστος δυάς), or Intelligible Matter (II.4.5: νοητὴ ὕλη).[11] This concept of Indefinite Dyad has its roots both in Plato's *Philebus* (23c1 ff.), and in Aristotle's *Metaphysics Z* (1035a9, 1037a4), and *H* (1045a34, 36). But, as Armstrong observes, Plotinus' concept is not strictly Platonic, since for Plato the two principles are independent correlatives.[12] In Plotinus we have again an amalgamation of the Platonic Indefinite Dyad and the Aristotelian Intelligible Matter. Within the system of the Hypostases, the Indefinite Dyad appears at the phase Procession, that of the first effluence from the One. At this moment of generation, Intellect remains in potentiality. When Intellect returns upon the One, the Indefinite Dyad becomes defined, contemplating the One not in simplicity but rather in multiplicity. This multiplicity constitutes the world of Forms. Thus, while the cause of Intellect is the One itself, Intellect's existence is delimited and formulated by the Forms, the first multiple manifestation of the One and Intellect's substantial object of intellection. On this basis, the Indefinite Dyad is again described as "indefinite sight" (V.4.2.6: ἀόριστος ὄψις), indefinite until it is defined and delimited by contemplation upon the One (VI.7.16–17; V.3.11.1–12), and then it becomes sight in actuality (V.1.5.19). Thus, as J. M. Rist observes, Plotinus' Indefinite Dyad can be understood from two complementary viewpoints: on the one hand, it is the first effluence from the One proceeding in "otherness" and then returning to the unity and "sameness" of its source, on the other, it is the basis for the world of Forms constructed as a complex of Forms and Intelligible Matter.

Intellect exercises intellection in order to conceive the infinite perfection of the One. But since Intellect could not apprehend a full vision of the One and it was unable to hold the One's received power, Intellect fragmented this power and transformed the "one" power to "many."[13] In this way, Intellect became a unity in plurality, a multiple living organism containing in unity the plurality of the intelligibles (τὰ νοητά). As such, the intelligibles are the byproducts of its self-thinking activity (VI.2.22.26–7):

> For when Intellect contemplates the One, it does not contemplate it as one, otherwise it would not become Intellect. But, beginning as one, it did not stay as it began, but, without noticing it, became many, as if heavy with drunken sleep, and unrolled itself because it wanted to possess everything . . . and it became like a circle unrolling itself in shape and surface and circumference and center and radii, some parts above and some below. [III.8.8.32–39; trans. Armstrong modified]

Plotinus' Intellect therefore is not the Nous of one intelligible but a universal Intellect of many intelligibles (III.8.8.41–2). Universal intellect is the "one" universal intelligible whole of the "many" individual intelligibles. While, on the one hand, Intellect potentially self-includes all the intelligibles like a "great living animal," on the other, the intelligibles actualize a potentiality which the universal Intellect includes (IV.8.3.6–16).

On this basis, Intellect is the first image of the One, "one" and "many" simultaneously (ἓν πολλά)—πολλά due to the "many" intelligibles, ἕν because of its perfect inner-identity between Intellect and intelligibles in one unified and undivided intelligible whole.[14] Every intelligible is perfect and contemplates all intelligibles in every other intelligible. All the intelligibles are everywhere in the intelligible realm and thus each intelligible embraces all: "All the intelligibles are transparent to the other intelligibles as light is transparent to light" (V.8.4.1–11). In other words, every intelligible within the realm of Intellect is actually itself, but "potentially all the others" like the Euclidean theorems which each contains not only its own mathematical truth, but also by implication the truth of geometry (III.9.2).[15]

Due to Intellect's perfect self-identity, Plotinus frequently attributes to Intellect the prefix "self-" (αὐτο-), so that Intellect is described as "self-determined" (VI.8.4.2: αὐτεξούσιος); as "life in its own right," absolute and unqualified (III.8.813: αὐτοζωή); as "self-intelligence" (V.9.13.3: αὐτονοῦς), and as absolute "self-knowledge" (V.8.4.40: αὐτοεπιστήμη). Only self-intellection and self-knowledge are able to manifest the absolute perfection and unity of intelligible reality. Truth can only be attained when thought is self-reflexive, achieving a self-referential coherence between intelligible object and intelligible subject. Since for Plotinus the intelligible object is not outside Intellect and Intellect's object is the Forms, the eternal "true being" itself, then the infallibility of Intellect is firmly established, and with it the absolute perfection of the intelligible eternal life.

Working from this conclusion, Plotinus proceeds to the crucial metaphysical thesis of the *Enneads*, that "every life is intelligence" (πᾶσα ζωὴ νόησις) (III.8.817). Within the system of the Three Hypostases, the principle of "life" (ζωή) signifies the nature both of Intellect and Soul. At the level of the Second Hypostasis, ζωή signifies the eternity of the intelligible realm:

Intellect's nondiscursive self-intellection towards Being (III.7.3), at the level of Soul, ζωή signifies time: Soul's discursive thinking towards Intellect (III.7.11). The principle of ζωή, however, does not have a clear position within the system but can be obscure and the subject of controversy. Whereas in some cases it appears as the third lower principle of the intelligible world after Being and Intelligence (VI.6.8, and 17), in other cases life is equated both with the phase of Procession, where Intellect receives life from the One, and with the stage of Reversion, where Intellect is self-formulated (VI.7.17.14–26, and 21.2–6).[16] The latter case seems to be closely related to the later Neoplatonic interpretation of ζωή as a principle intermediate between Being and Intelligence, but this is not made explicit in the *Enneads*.[17]

It can be observed that in the context of the three Hypostases, ζωή for Plotinus becomes a metaphysical principle underlying all the ontological levels of Being, including human and perceptible life. All forms of ζωή, even at the lower levels of Being, are *logoi*, and thus exercise in their own way "intelligence" (νόησις). On this basis, we have "growth intelligence" (φυτικὴ νόησις), "sense intelligence" (αἰσθητικὴ νόησις), and "soul intelligence" (ψυχικὴ νόησις) (III.8.8.14–16). But these forms of life are dimmer than the real intelligible life of Intellect and so have less clarity and strength. The eternity of Being is best manifested at the level of Intellect where the identity between intelligible subject and object is substantial and infallible. Since Intellect is the "first form of intelligence" (πρῶτος νοῦς), and "every life is intelligence" (πᾶσα ζωὴ νόησις), then the life of Intellect is the "first and most perfect form of life" (πρώτη ζωή).[18]

In this account of life as intelligence, Plotinus distinguishes two forms of cognitive thinking corresponding to different ontological levels: (1) the discursive thinking activity of the Soul (διάνοια), moving progressively from one concept to another,[19] and (2) the nondiscursive contemplative self-thinking activity of Intellect (νόησις).[20] Whereas Intellect's self-thinking activity is a nondiscursive contemplative intellection, Soul's thinking activity is a transitory discursive thinking towards either the intelligibles at the higher level or the perceptibles at a lower one.[21] Plotinus associates discursive thinking with two modes of alterity: (1) conceptual alterity (transition from one concept to another), and (2) ontological alterity (distinction between the thinking subject and the thinking object).[22] Discursive thinking is actually exercised only by the Soul, and it is exactly this transitory form of thinking activity that constitutes "time" (III.7.11.44). Soul's discursive thinking is absolutely external, combining and dividing in two directions, either the mental images derived from the senses (V.3.2.7–8), or the imprinted images shining from Intellect (V.3.2.9–10).[23]

On the other hand, with regard to Intellect's nondiscursive thinking, Intellect is not subject to any mode of alterity or to any form of transitory thinking.

Intellect's thinking is "timeless" (ἄχρονος), "unextended" (οὐδὲ διέξοδος), "non-transitory" (οὐδὲ μετάβασις), "undivided" (οὐκ διαίρεσις), not involving memory of any kind (ἀδύνατον μνήμην) (IV.4.1.12–15). Intellect encompasses all immortal and intelligible beings in a stable and perfect condition. Intellect thinks not by seeking but by having (V.1.4.16). At the level of the Second Hypostasis, Intellect and Being are just two aspects of the same nature (V.9.8.15–16). When the Intellect thinks, it actually thinks itself; when the Intellect knows, it actually knows itself (V.3.5.45–6; V.9.5.14–6). Intellect's self-thinking activity is internal. Self-intellection and self-knowledge underlie the real nature of Intellect's nondiscursive contemplative thinking where intelligible object and intelligible subject are identical.[24]

With regard to Intellect's nondiscursive thinking, there is a long debate in modern scholarship on whether Intellect's nondiscursive self-thinking activity is propositional or not. While, on the one hand, A. C. Lloyd maintains that Intellect's thinking is noncomplex, nonpropositional, not self-direct and tactual,[25] on the other, R. Sorabji claims that since Intellect's object of thought (the intelligible Forms) are complex then its thought can only be propositional. My intention is to follow from a slightly different viewpoint the former interpretation for the following reasons.[26] First, it is beyond any doubt that propositional thinking presupposes memory for the construction of the logical propositional transition from premise A to B and from B to C in order for a conclusion to be established. But Plotinus constantly mentions that Intellect's self-thinking does not involve either memory or transition; it is the eternal contemplation of the intelligibles (IV.4.1).[27] Second, a proposition can be either true or false, but Intellect's object of thought (what Intellect thinks) are the Forms themselves, and these are intelligibles which are a priori infallible. Third, the propositions are linguistic representations of things and not the things themselves. For Plotinus, Intellect's thoughts are not representations of the intelligibles but the intelligibles themselves; *the intelligibles are not propositions*.[28] As Plotinus clearly states in V.5.1, the intelligibles are complete with intelligence and life, primary intelligibles which are certainly not "propositions" (προτάσεις), or "axioms" (ἀξιώματα), or "expressions" (λεκτά); "for then they would only say something about other things and would not be the things themselves" (32–39). For these reasons, Intellect's self-thinking activity has to be regarded not as discursive or propositional but more appropriately as contemplative. Contemplation is a special form of thinking which brings the many intelligibles into one unified intelligible actualisation.

3.2 ELEATIC BEING IN THE *ENNEADS*

Despite the recognized Platonic and Aristotelian influences on Plotinus' theory of Intellect scant attention has been paid to the Presocratic context of his theory. From a careful reading of the *Enneads* a series of direct and indirect references emerges not only of some fundamental Presocratic concepts, but also of Presocratic terminology. It is most striking that Parmenides' influential ontology of Being is clearly in the background of Plotinus' metaphysics. In particular, Plotinus regards Parmenides as one of the ancient philosophers who introduced the true nature of Being, and the interrelationship between thinking and being. Consequently, this section is devoted to the influence of Parmenides' Being on Plotinus' intelligible Being.

The most striking evidence of Parmenides' theory of Being in Plotinus' *Enneads* appears in V.1.8.14–23. As shown in the previous chapter, this passage is part of a long discussion by Plotinus of Parmenides' theory of Being, and it can be supplemented with the relevant discussion at *Ennead* VI.6 where Plotinus recognizes Parmenides as the philosopher who correctly maintained the unity and the uniqueness of Being (VI.6.18.40).[29] On the other hand, even if Parmenides is the most important Presocratic in the development of Plotinus' theory of Intellect, he also shows knowledge of Anaxagoras' theory of Nous in passage V.1.9.1–7. But Nous it is not interpreted by Plotinus as Intelligence or Mind, but as a transcendent principle which is, like the One, even before Intelligence and Being.[30] Indeed, as was also shown, Plotinus describes the intelligible realm with Anaxagoras' ὁμοῦ πάντα instead of Parmenides' ὁμοῦ πᾶν to express the complete unity-in-plurality and altogetherness of the intelligibles within Intellect. However, it is significant that Plotinus quotes Parmenides' all-togetherness of Being in fr. 8.5 as well as verse 8.25 "for Being is adjacent to Being" (ἐὸν γὰρ ἐόντι πελάζει), but without naming the Presocratic, in *Ennead* VI.4.4.25–27. In this passage, the discussion involves the justification of the unity of Being in the complete all-togetherness of Intellect despite the plurality of the intelligibles. To some extent the passage should be regarded as a response to Parmenides' immobile non-plural unity of Being and hence it can be connected to the criticism of passage *Ennead* V.1.8.14–22. Let us look in detail at the above passages on the nature of Being to both Parmenides and Plotinus.

3.3 THE NATURE OF BEING

Parmenides is for Plotinus the philosopher of Being (τὸ ὄν). All the discussions in the *Enneads* that involve the Eleatic are based on and influenced by his radical ontology of Being (τὸ ἐόν).[31] In particular, Parmenides' ontology and terminology are in the background of Plotinus' metaphysics of Intellect, the Second Hypostasis of Being, and Plotinus acknowledges Parmenides as the Presocratic philosopher who introduced the intelligibility, oneness, unity, indestructibility, uniqueness, impassability, and eternal timelessness of Being. Plotinus is not only aware of and uses Parmenides' terminology and concepts, but also interprets, systematizes, and develops his Eleatic philosophy within the context of his own Neoplatonic system. It is significant that Plotinus departs from the traditional philosophical line of Parmenides and the post-Parmenidean thinkers on the priority of Being and the denial of its creation from non-Being. Within Plotinus' system of the three Hypostases, Being is secondarily produced from the One, which is frequently expressed as non-Being in terms of its supra-transcendence beyond Being and Intelligence.

Thus, in the light of Plotinus' Parmenides, we can observe from a historical perspective the development of the Greek philosophical concept of Being, starting initially with the Eleatic movement and proceeding through the teaching of Plato and Aristotle to Neoplatonic metaphysics. Plotinus' philosophical testimony of Parmenides, therefore, is an invaluable source for the development and impact of the Eleatic on Greek philosophical tradition and especially on the tradition of Platonism.

3.3.1 Parmenides' Theory of Being

The core of Parmenides' philosophy can be summarized in a single ontological question: *what is the nature of Being?* Parmenides' work was written in the form of Homeric hexameters and is usually divided into three interrelated sections: (1) the allegorical prologue in which Parmenides describes the journey of a youth driven in a chariot by the daughters of Helios to an unnamed goddess who reveals to him the only two conceivable ways of enquiry: the way of Truth and the way of Opinion (fr. 1.1–32); (2) the exposition of the arguments in favor of "truth" (ἀλήθεια) (frs 2–8.49); and (3) the account of "human opinions" (βροτῶν δόξαι) (frs 8.50–19).

In particular, the nature of Parmenides' Being is argued in detail in fragment 8.1–49. In the first six lines of this fragment the goddess summarizes the true "signs" (σήματα) or predicates of Being:

> One way only is left to speak of, namely, that it is. Along this way are many signs: that Being is ungenerated and indestructible, unique, unmoved and complete; it never was nor will be, since it is now, all together, one, continuous. (fr. 8.1–6; trans. Wright modified)

According to the above account, Parmenides' Being is (i) "ungenerated" (8.3: ἀγένητον) and "indestructible" (8.3: ἀνώλεθρον); (ii) "unique" (8.4: οὖλον), "the only one of its kind" (8.4: μουνογενές);[32] (iii) "immutable" (8.4: ἀτρεμές) and "complete" (8.4: ἠδέ τελεῖον);[33] (iv) "timeless" (8.5: οὐδέ ποτ' ἦν οὐδ' ἔσται, ἐπεὶ νῦν ἔστιν); "all together" (8.5: ὁμοῦ πᾶν); "one" (8.6: ἕν) and "continuous" (8.6: συνεχές).[34] Parmenides then argues for these predicates in the main body of the fragment. According to the argument,

Parmenides shows that (i) since nonbeing is rejected, there is no temporal beginning or end to what-is (8.6–21); (ii) what-is remains undivided, without internal differentiation or contradiction (8.22–25); (iii) it is unchangeable, immobile, and complete, recognized only by thinking (8.26–41); (iv) it is equal to itself from every direction, outside any spatial application, equally balanced and uniformly complete (8.42–9).[35]

With regard to the meaning of Parmenides' Being there is a long and controversial discussion. According to C. E. L. Owen, the subject of Parmenides' philosophy is nothing more than the participle of ἔστι (it is).[36] Owen's interpretation is that ἔστι here is primarily existential ("what there is to think and speak of"); thinking and speaking requires an existing entity as object of thought and speech.[37] J. Barnes follows the existential reading of ἔστι and claims that whatever is the object of study exists.[38] But, on the other hand, Barnes anachronistically claims further that Parmenides' existential approach of Being was echoed later in Berkeley's thesis *esse est percipi*.[39] D. Gallop rejects Barnes' view and maintains that since for Parmenides reality is not mind-dependent we cannot assume that whatever is thought exists.[40] On this basis, Gallop seems to follow a more Cartesian viewpoint. But the Cartesian *cogito* focuses on the importance of the subject and not the priority of the object, which is Parmenides' aim. Whereas Parmenides' reality is objective (established only through the cognitive recognition of the thinking subject), Descartes' reality is primarily subjective (established by a self-thinking existential reflection of the subject upon the object).

Parmenides' ἐόν is without any division or extension in time and space, any expansion or destruction in becoming, and, most of all, any generation, alteration, mobility, otherness, or discontinuity in its real essence. It is universally equal with itself and uniformly determined.[41] To some extent, Parmenides' ἐόν seems to follow the nontraditional newly established conception of Being linked both to Xenophanes' unique, intelligent, and unmoving god (frs 23–26), and Heraclitus' wise and divine one (frs 32, 41, 50). For Xenophanes, the traditional anthropomorphic gods have to be abandoned and the old theology of Homer and Hesiod rejected (frs 11, 14, 15, 16, 32). The new theology speaks of only "one god" (εἷς θεός), superior to any anthropomorphic god or human mortal in appearance and intelligence; a God who thinks, hears, and sees as a whole; a God who is separate from all things, unmoved, always staying in the same place; a divine power who causes effortlessly the movement of the cosmos by the thinking of his divine mind (frs 23–26).[42] Thus, for Xenophanes, God constitutes the divine and intelligible principle of the cosmos. But Parmenides' account of ἐόν expresses a new vision of a transcendent monistic existence where what exists is timeless, changeless, and indestructible.[43] Parmenides' Being is unqualified, remaining continually in a timeless present, and this startling conception of Being marks a new direction in Greek thinking. His ontology extends the Presocratic borders and moves forward, not only to Platonic and Aristotelian thought, but also to the philosophy of later Hellenistic metaphysics.

For Plato, Parmenides' monistic idea of Being seems to be multiplied in the realm of the Forms. A. H. Coxon has shown that even if Plato never makes a direct reference to the Eleatic in the development of his theory, he clearly inherits and uses Parmenides' language as the theoretical basis of his own conception of True Being.[44] In Plato's theory of the Forms, Being is not an unconditional and unqualified but a dynamically ever-living organism which receives its stability and everlastingness from the unified perfection of each Form.[45]

But the influence of Parmenides' ontology does not stop with Plato. Aristotle in *Metaphysics* (1028b3–4) testifies that the question of Being has uninterruptedly engaged philosophers in a continuous investigation of "What is it which is?" For Aristotle this leads on to the further question "What is substance?" (1028b4). But for Parmenides the question of Being implies another kind of enquiry. What is the nature of Being and how can this Being be conceived by the human mind? How can there *be* anything which is nonexistent? Can we really understand and know something which is not? Is there any true way to find Being? To what extent can the reality of Being be related to human experience and understanding?

Parmenides' goddess provides some answers to these questions. She offers two paths of knowledge: one way [P], the way of truth, is "that there is something and it is not possible for it not to be," and the second [Q] is "that there is nothing and it is necessary for it not to be" (fr. 2). In the former case [P], the way is that of Being (ἔστι), in the latter [Q] the way is that of non-Being (οὐκ ἔστι). But from these two assumptions there might arise a possible third assumption: a synthetic case [S] for the same thing "to exist and not."[46] After an analysis of these three ways, the goddess concludes that only one of the three can lead to genuine and unalterable knowledge of truth.

[Case Q]:
For Parmenides the way of non-Being is not the way of Truth;[47] non-Being or "what is not" is not only inconceivable, but also nameless (fr. 8.17), since it is not possible to know what is not nor indicate it in speech (fr. 2.7–8).[48] Since only what-is is and nothing is not, then what is spoken of and thought about must necessarily exist as what there is to speak and think (fr. 6.1–2). According to A. P. D. Mourelatos, the negative meaning of non-Being, which in Parmenides' poem is also expressed as μηδέν (frs 6.9, 8.10, 9.7) and οὐκ ἐόν (8.46); it is not a rejection of the possibility of negative predication in general; "it is rather a rejection of negative attributes in answer to speculative, cosmological questions."[49] Parmenides does not actually exclude negative thought as a contingent way of thinking, but he rejects all negative thought from the

appropriate cognitive recognition of the true nature of Being. The aim of the goddess' discourse is not a logical exposition or analysis of things as such but the true nature of what there is.[50] In an additional move, he asks, even granted that Being could come from the (denied) non-Being, what necessity would cause it to arise later rather than earlier, that is, at one time rather than another. Arguing from what later became known as the Principle of Sufficient Reason, Parmenides states that anything which becomes presupposes necessarily a principle sufficient to explain its generation at a particular time. But how can such a generative principle be a part of what is not? For Parmenides ex nihilo creation is impossible: something cannot begin from nothing (fr. 8.7–10), and, conversely, what there is cannot cease to be and end in (the rejected) nothing; Being exists entirely in the timeless present, fettered by the powers of Justice (fr. 8.14). It is impossible for Being to have begun from nothing and to become in time. In the same way as Being does not have a temporal beginning in becoming because that would imply a previous state of non-Being, so it will never be extinguished or perish since a future state of non-Being is similarly discounted (fr. 8.20–21).

[Case S]:
Parmenides maintains that the two ontological conditions Being and non-Being cannot be true of the same subject simultaneously, yet humans generally accept Being and non-Being at different times or circumstances or from different points of view because they depend for their judgements on perception rather than reason. If something can possibly be and not be at the same time then it is also possible for it to be the same and not be the same simultaneously, but this leads us to a logical absurdity (fr. 6.8–9). As Simplicius states (*in Physica*116.6), quoting this fragment, Parmenides' assumption is clearly the first "denial of contradiction," the initial conception of the Law of Contradiction which was subsequently used and developed by Aristotle and the Peripatetics.[51] Case S therefore, since it applies contradictory predicates, cannot stand; it will be reinstated in the way of belief but with a caveat on its failure to meet the strict criterion of truth.

[Case P]:
Consequently, the only reasonable conclusion that remains for ἐόν is an unqualified premise: "to be." The acceptable way of truth is "that there is being and it is not possible for there to be not-being" (fr. 2.3). Parmenides' final justification is based upon an axiom that will be of central influence for the relationship between "being" and "thinking" in subsequent philosophy. Since it is impossible to recognize or name "what is not" (fr. 2.13–14) and what can be spoken and thought needs necessarily "to be" (fr. 6.1–2), then it follows that everything which can be thought presupposes necessarily that something has

firstly to be in order to be thought, spoken, recognized, and named. That means that only essential being can be apprehended by reason and thinking and not non-Being. Based on this premise, Parmenides concludes that "the same thing is for thinking and for being" (fr. 3: τὸ γὰρ αὐτὸ νοεῖν ἐστίν τε καὶ εἶναι); only Being can be truly thought and be.

> What is there to be thought of is the same as what is thought, for you will not find thinking apart from what-is, which is what is referred to. [fr. 8.34–6; trans. Wright]

Since what can be thought is the same as the object of thought and there is nothing else apart from what there is, then the conclusion which arises is that it is impossible to find thinking without Being. Therefore, Being is not only that which *is* and that which *is thought*, but also the place where true existence and genuine knowledge belong. Parmenides' theory of Being may now be correlated to Plotinus' theory of Intellect in the *Enneads*.

3.3.2 Plotinus on Parmenides' Being

Henry and Schwyzer, in their *Index Fontium*, give twenty references of Plotinus to Parmenides. In all these references, Parmenides is used exclusively to support the true nature and structure of Plotinus' Intellect. However, despite the undoubted importance of these references, most of them are not included in modern editions of Parmenides, nor is there any complete study in modern scholarship. Plotinus throughout the *Enneads* refers to Parmenides twice by name: in V.1 *On the Three Primary Hypostases* and VI.6 *On Numbers*.[52] In both *Enneads* the subject-matter of Plotinus is the nature of Intellect, and in this context Plotinus uses the terminology of the Eleatic and systematizes his thought in accordance with his own metaphysical system.

In *Ennead* V.1.8.1–10, Plotinus finds his Three Primary Hypostases in the dubious Platonic *Second Platonic Epistle* (312e1–4); he identifies Intellect with the Platonic Craftsman in the *Timaeus* (34b3); he relates the Soul to the creation of the "mixing bowl" in the same dialogue (41d4; 35a3); he recognizes the One in Plato's Good "beyond being" of the *Republic* 509b7–8, and understands the Platonic Idea as a synthesis of Being and Intellect.[53] Working on this interpretation, Plotinus concludes that Plato "was aware that Intellect derives from the Good, and the Soul from Intellect" and thus he was aware of the triadic nature of Being. Based on the relation between Being and Intellect in the Platonic theory of the Forms, Plotinus immediately testifies that Parmenides was the pioneer of this theory (8.14–23). Parmenides is the Presocratic who first "touched" on this kind of thought and for this reason must be acknowledged as introducing the theory:

῞Ηπτετο μὲν οὖν καὶ Παρμενίδης πρότερον τῆς τοιαύτης δόξης καθόσον εἰς ταὐτὸ συνῆγεν ὂν καὶ νοῦν, καὶ τὸ ὂν οὐκ ἐν τοῖς αἰσθητοῖς ἐτίθετο *τὸ γὰρ αὐτὸ νοεῖν ἐστί τε καὶ εἶναι* λέγων. Καὶ *ἀκίνητον* δὲ λέγει τοῦτο-καίτοι προστιθεὶς τὸ νοεῖν-σωματικὴν πᾶσαν κίνησιν ἐξαίρων ἀπ' αὐτοῦ, ἵνα μένῃ ὡσαύτως, καὶ *ὄγκῳ σφαίρας* ἀπεικάζων, ὅτι πάντα ἔχει περιειλημμένα καὶ ὅτι τὸ νοεῖν οὐκ ἔξω, ἀλλ' ἐν ἑαυτῷ. ῞Εν δὲ λέγων ἐν τοῖς ἑαυτοῦ συγγράμμασιν αἰτίαν εἶχεν ὡς τοῦ ἑνὸς τούτου πολλὰ εὑρισκομένου.
. . . and Parmenides, before Plato, was touching on a view like this, in so far as he was bringing together Being and Intellect, and was not placing Being among perceptible things, saying "because the same thing is for thinking and for being." And he says it is "unmoved"—even if he adds thinking to it—excluding all physical movement from it, so that it remains always in the same condition, resembling the "mass of a sphere," since it contains all things in its circumference and since thinking is not outside Being, but in itself. But even if he says, in his own works, that this Being is "one," this "one" appears to be found as "many." [V.1.8.14–23; my translation]

In a further textual analysis, Plotinus begins the passage with a prospective μέν which seems to correlate with the δέ in line 18. This divides the passage in two sections: (1) Plotinus attributes to Parmenides the idea of "bringing together," "thinking," and "being" (14–18); (2) Plotinus criticizes the Presocratic for the immobility and the alleged oneness of the Parmenidean Being (18–23).

Without doubt the whole passage clearly shows Plotinus' knowledge of Parmenides' poem and philosophy. For Plotinus, Parmenides is the one who made the first step towards the intelligibility of Being, a theory further developed by Plato in his theory of the Forms. Parmenides is regarded as a forerunner of Plato and for this reason must be credited with independent authority. In particular, Plotinus uses in this passage: (1) an exact reference to Parmenides' fr. 3 at lines 17–18 "for the same is for thinking and for being" (τὸ γὰρ αὐτὸ νοεῖν ἐστί τε καὶ εἶναι); (2) a segmental reference to fr. 8.26 "it [the Being] is immobile in the bonds of great chains" (αὐτὰρ ἀκίνητον μεγάλων ἐν πείρασι δεσμῶν), and fr. 8.38 "whole unmoved" (οὖλον ἀκίνητον) with the key word "unmoved" (ἀκίνητον) repeated from line 18; (3) the comparison from fr. 8.43 "like the bulk of a well-rounded sphere" (εὐκύκλου σφαίρης ἐναλίγκιον ὄγκῳ) picked up with "mass of a sphere" (ὄγκῳ σφαίρας) at line 20, and (4) an indirect reference to fr. 8.29 "remaining the same and in the same it abides by itself" (ταὐτόν τ' ἐν ταὐτῷ τε μένον καθ' ἑαυτό τε κεῖται) at line 20 "remaining always in the same condition" (ἵνα μένῃ ὡσαύτως). Finally, Plotinus' lines 22–23 on the ἕν refer to the ἕν of Parmenides' "signs" (σήματα) of Being at fr. 8.6 and begin the critique of the plurality of the Eleatic One. Thus, being well aware of Parmenides' terminology and philosophy, using Parmenides' fr. 3 and fr. 8.1–49, Plotinus maintains and justifies his own theory of the structure of the intelligible world and the intelligibles. He offers us invaluable data on fr. 3 and fr. 8.1–49 in V.1.8.14–22 as he directs the discussion of the references to the intelligible world and, on this basis, interprets Parmenides' Being as denoting the Plotinian Intellect.

3.3.3 Thinking and Being

As has been previously shown, Parmenides' fragment 3 is the kernel of the Eleatic conception of Being and the cognitive apprehension of its essential nature through thinking. It is noteworthy that in Parmenides' poem the verb νοεῖν "to think,"[54] as well as the derivative words "thinkable" (νοητόν) (fr. 8.8), and "unthinkable" (ἀνόητον) (fr. 8.17), implies the knowing activity of the thinking subject towards the cognitive establishment of the thinking object.[55] Likewise, the words νόημα (thought),[56] and νόος (mind)[57] are used to express the act or the content of thinking and the highest mental faculty.[58] Both terms are used to present the intelligible understanding of *what is* and never *what is not*. As M. R. Wright further explains, "it is impossible to think a blank or converse about nothing, and, since reasoning and intelligent speech therefore require an object, whatever it is that can be thought (is there for thinking) can be (is there for being)."[59] This argument gives the starting point for Parmenides' entailments regarding Being (what there is), proving the presupposition of an object of thought and the essential priority of Being over thinking; once that is established, the attributes of Being follow logically from it.

The exact translation, interpretation, and reconstruction of fragment 3, however, have been the subject of lengthy discussions and controversy.[60] D. Gallop quotes Sparshott: "a certain crankiness in Parmenides' venerable syntax, perhaps even in his venerable character, prevents us from ever being quite sure."[61] With regard to the textual position of the argument, H. Diels places fragment 3 immediately after fragment 2, suggesting a related textual and conceptual continuation between the two fragments. This position has been followed by most scholars based, first, on the explanatory usage of the word γάρ in fr. 3, and, second, on the similar linguistic use of dative or purpose infinitives in the two fragments;[62] fragment 3 has therefore usually been taken as the completion of fr. 2.[63] In contrast to this position, L. Tarán claims that fragment 3 does not imply the inconceivability and inexpressibility of fr. 2 and thus the word γάρ cannot lead us to its completion.[64]

With regard to the translation and interpretation of fr. 3, the issue appears to be more complicated and controversial. Diels translates the fragment:

"denn dasseble ist Denken und Sein." The most literal translation of the fragment is: "for the same is to think and to be" and is followed by B. Bauch and G. Vlastos.[65] According to Tarán, this literal interpretation of the fragment derives from an identification of 'being' and 'thought'; although, since the identification in Parmenides' text has different meanings, it is inappropriate and unhelpful to keep to this literal interpretation.[66] Thus, based both on the linguistic form of the Greek text and the philosophical analysis of the parallel fragments 2.7–8, 6.1–2, 8.34–36, the most natural translation of fr. 3 would be that "the same thing is for thinking and for being," implying that "what can be thought can be," or, more clearly, "for what can be thought of is the same as what can be." This form of translation and interpretation was first proposed by E. Zeller: "den dasselbe kann gedacht werden und sein." He maintains that instead of ἐστίν, we should read ἔστιν and take the infinitives with the value of datives as εἰσι νοῆσαι in fr. 2.2.[67] A similar construction was adopted by Gallop (1984: "because the same thing is there for thinking and for being"), and Coxon (1986: "for the same thing is for conceiving and for being"). But the above translations, even if they follow Zeller's form of interpretation, diminish his initial idea of "possible"; Gallop understands the steady presence of Parmenides' Being and adds the expression "is there", while Coxon understands and interprets τὸ νοεῖν as "conceiving."[68] Finally, M. Conche departs more from the above translations and offers: ". . . car le même est à la fois penser et être."[69]

On the other hand, some scholars suggest that the fragment implies a more fundamental and essential identification of the predicates of "thinking" and "being." Following an existential interpretation, W. J. Verdenius (1942) adopts the translation "knowing is the same as being," asserting that thought is something that exists. But Gallop reasonably rejects this interpretation as "untenable because Parmenides recognizes only unqualified being and denies the reality of different existents."[70] According to other interpretations, fragment 3 is translated as "to think and to be is the same," asserting a tautological form of relationship between the two terms. B. Snell (1924) maintains the identity of subject and object of thought based on the fundamental principle that "the same is recognized by the same," while P. Friedländer interprets the fragment as meaning that since 'being' exists and 'thought' exists, then both are one and the same.[71] On this basis, W. A. Heidel (1913) translates: "for it is one and the same thing to think and to think that it is."[72] In addition, P. Aubenque (1987) offers an even more exaggerated analysis by discovering behind fragment 3 echoes of the fundamental Aristotelian self-thinking divine principle, that of the identity of the act of thinking and the object of thought, concluding that the direction of fragment 3 is that "intelligence coincides with being what it thinks, at the moment when it thinks it." But, as M. Conche concludes in his discussion these subsequent interpretations, they are far from Parmenides' original and have nothing to do with the composition of the text.[73]

On the former interpretation then, Parmenides' link between 'thinking' and 'being' leads us to the initial conclusion that something to be thought has necessarily to be, and what can be thought (intelligently) is the same as what has to be (essentially). The latter (unwarranted) identification of 'thinking' and 'being' is usually attributed to an alleged misinterpretation of Plotinus in the *Enneads*. For instance, E. D. Phillips defends his thesis identifying 'thinking' and 'being' as based on Plotinus.[74] Moreover, Atkinson and Coxon claim that the Neoplatonist ascribes the identification of Intellect and Being back to Parmenides' fragment 3, while Gallop, within the same framework, mentions that Plotinus and Clement of Alexandria are the first to offer the misinterpretation that identifies 'thinking' and 'being' in Parmenides. But a closer and more careful reading of Plotinus' text, as well as the other two sources of the fragment, leads to the conclusion that, whereas Plotinus was aware of Parmenides' meaning in fragment 3, influenced by Platonic and Aristotelian theory, he proceeded to the development and systematization of Parmenides' account in the context of the three Hypostases, especially in that of the fundamental principle of Intellect, his Second Hypostasis of Being.

In fact, Plotinus along with Clement and Proclus—authors who all belong to late antiquity—are the sole ancient sources of Parmenides' fragment 3. According to these authors, fragment 3 asserts a fundamental connection or identity between what can be thought and what possesses essential being, and, in the more metaphysical interpretation of Proclus, there is an identification between Intelligence and Being as far as the two terms signify the real structure of the divine intelligible nature. Coxon erroneously maintains that all these authors understood Parmenides' fragment 3 "as asserting the identity of conceiving or knowing with being,"[75] but, from a closer look at the sources, this assumption becomes untenable.

Clement of Alexandria, in the sixth book of his work *Stromateis* (VI.2.23), preserves Parmenides' fragment 3 within the framework of a lengthy polemic against the Greeks. In the second chapter of this book, he criticizes the Greeks for plagiarizing one another and giving different meanings to the words of their predecessors. Clement offers a series of examples taken from the whole spectrum of Greek literature, including the mythical, historical, and philosophical tradition. In the case of Parmenides' fragment 3, Clement quotes it arbitrarily in association, first, with a Pythian discourse about Glaucus the Spartan given by Herodotus ("in the case of God to say and to do are equivalent") and, second, with Aristophanes' fragment 691K ("for to think and to do are equivalent"). In this passage, even if Clement does not provide us with a philosophical exegesis of the fragment, we can suppose, based on the parallel quotation of Aristophanes and Herodotus and the usage of the "equal" (ἶσον), that the Christian author interprets his quotation from Parmenides as denoting a connection between 'thinking' and 'being' and not a tautological one. Thus, the translation of the fragment in Clement as "the same thing is for thinking and for being" seems to be the most probable and reasonable.

On the other hand, Proclus interprets fragment 3 clearly in a Platonic context, applying to Parmenides' words a metaphysical identification of the concepts of Intelligence and Being. Proclus *in Parmenidem* 1152.24–37 quotes and interprets Parmenides' fragment along with some verses from fr. 8 and 4,[76] interpreting them as connoting the intelligibility of Being.[77] In this passage, Proclus offers an amalgamation of some central fragments of Parmenides on the nature of Intelligence and Being. He allies Intelligence to Being, concluding with its immanent and essential intelligibility. According to Proclus' interpretation, since Parmenides in the above fragments situates 'thinking' and 'being', then he accepts that Being has to possess a certain type of motion therein, that of intellectual motion (1152.38–39). This conclusion is based upon a connection that Proclus makes between fragments 3 and 8.35–6. For Proclus, since "it is the same for thinking and for being" (fr. 3), and "it is impossible to find thinking without being" (fr. 8.35–6), then Being has to be essentially intelligible. In fact, the paraphrase of Parmenides' original theory derives from the Neoplatonic background of Proclus. By taking ταὐτόν as implying the intelligible co-identity of 'thinking' and 'being', and adding ἐκεῖ to denote that this identification exists at the level of the intelligible world, Proclus is clearly systematizing Parmenides' fragment within the Neoplatonic framework. Proclus understands Parmenides' νοεῖν as "intelligence." This can be also verified by the second allusion to Parmenides' fragment 3 in the *Platonic Theology* (I.66.3–5).[78] In this passage, Proclus again uses Parmenides' fragment to establish not only the fundamental intelligibility of Being for Neoplatonism, but also the identification of Intelligence and Being as the true essence of Intellect.

Plotinus is the first who establishes this identification between Intelligence and Being at the level of Intellect—the living internal unity between Platonic True Being (the Forms) as the object of intelligence and Intellect as its subject. In the context of this essential identification of the intelligible object, the Being, and the intelligible subject, Intellect, Plotinus takes a middle position of interpretation between Clement and Proclus, understanding, on the one hand, the original meaning of Parmenides' words, but developing, on the other, Parmenides' words through a new Platonic perspective. This is obvious from the way in which the fragment is treated in the relevant *Enneads*.

Ennead V.1.8.14–18 is usually regarded as Plotinus' misinterpretation of Parmenides' fragment 3, tracing back to Parmenides an alleged *identification* between thinking and 'being'.[79] But a closer look at the text shows that this consideration is groundless. Based on the textual analysis of the passage, Plotinus begins his quotation with the word ἥπτετο, the imperfect tense of the word ἅπτομαι, usually translated as "touch on" or "handle."[80] The use of the imperfect tense in the text implies a lack of completion in Parmenides' thought. As the imperfect tense denotes, Parmenides seems to be touching for a long time in the past on the connection between the concepts of 'thinking' and 'being' but not reaching an identification.[81] The meaning here is supported by a passage from *Ethica Eudemia* (1227a1–2) where Aristotle speaks of the legislators who, even if they are not thoroughly accurate in their account, approximate in some way to the truth.[82] Plotinus is extremely careful in his quotation of the fragment, for example, even though the particle γάρ is not logically needed in line 17, he uses it in order to be exactly true to the original;[83] throughout he is aware of and makes an exact use of the original meaning of the Eleatic words.

For Plotinus, despite the fact that Parmenides was the pioneer of the intelligibility of Being, the Eleatic did not give a complete theory; this was the work of Plato in his study of Forms and the nature of True Being. In V.1.8.15, Plotinus maintains correctly that Parmenides "brought together" or "connected" 'thinking' and 'being', and not that the Presocratic identified the two terms. This is also clear from the usage of the verb συνάγω, which is also in the imperfect tense. Again in lines 18–19 Plotinus says that Parmenides "added thinking" to Being (προστιθεὶς τὸ νοεῖν), but not that he identified the two. It can be concluded that Plotinus' aim in this passage was not so much to recognize an alleged identification in Parmenides between 'thinking' and 'being' but rather to mark Parmenides' innovation in asserting the intelligibility and immateriality of Being.

A previous passage of chapter four (V.1.4.31–32) seems to prefigure his discussion of Parmenides' fr. 3. Despite the fact that E. N. Roussos recognizes this passage as an allusion to Parmenides, Henry and Schwyzer do not include it in their *Index Fontium*. Atkinson recognizes that Plotinus has traces of Parmenides' fr. 3 at 4.26–27.[84] In my view, the whole passage 4.26–33 can be seen as an allusion to Parmenides fr. 3. This is the text where Plotinus uses Parmenides' terminology and offers his own interpretation on the metaphysical integration between Intellect and Being:

> Each of them [the intelligibles] is Intellect and Being, and the whole is the sum of Intellect and the sum of Being, Intellect with its thinking establishing Being, and Being, by being thought, giving to Intellect its thinking and its Being. The cause of the thinking is something else [the One], which is also the cause for Being; so something else is the cause of both, since they are together and exist inseparably and do not abandon each other, although two, forming this integrated unity Intellect and Being, the thinker and what is thought, Intellect ranged with the thinker, Being with what is thought. [V.1.4.26–33; trans. Armstrong]

This illuminating passage, probably unique for its completeness and clarity, shows vividly how for Plotinus Intellect and Being are established integrated and identified by the following argument: *since Intellect establishes Being by thinking it and Being gives thinking to Intellect by being thought, then Intellect and Being form an integrated intelligible unity, Intellect as the thinker (the subject) and Being as what is thought (the object).*

Moreover, apart from passage 8.14–22 in *Ennead* V.1, Plotinus uses Parmenides' connection of 'thinking' and 'being' frequently in the *Enneads*. As mentioned before, according to the *Index Fontium* of Henry-Schwyzer and Roussos,[85] Plotinus refers directly or indirectly to Parmenides' fr. 3 fourteen times in the *Enneads*.[86] However, a careful study of these passages shows that only four cases, along with *Ennead* V.1.8.14–22, belong without doubt to Parmenides' fr.3: these are in *Enneads* I.4, III.8, and V.9. In passages I.4.10.5–6, III.8.8.6–8, and V.9.5.26–32, Plotinus quotes Parmenides' fr. 3 almost verbatim. Unfortunately, these passages are not included in Diels' edition. On the other hand, Conche[87] and Coxon[88] restore in their edition V.9.5.26–32 as a recognized reference to Parmenides' fr.3. With regard to I.4.10.5–6 and III.8.8.6–8, only Coxon includes them in his edition, adding VI.7.41.18 as a direct allusion to the fragment. Only Atkinson[89] recognizes all the above references. All the other references to Parmenides in the *Enneads* mentioned by Henry-Schwyzer and Roussos are not included in modern editions of Parmenides and no contemporary philosophical discussion linking the two philosophers is to be found.

In addition to the four direct quotations of Parmenides' fr. 3, it has been recognized that Plotinus echoes or paraphrases fr. 3 without either naming Parmenides or giving the exact words of the Eleatic in the passages.[90] Most of these passages derive from the fifth *Ennead* which, according to Porphyry (*Life* 25.30–35), includes the main treatises on the nature of Intellect. The subject of the passages highlights some fundamental aspects of Plotinus' theory of Intellect and especially its internal identification of Intelligence and Being. Yet the above passages reflect more Plotinus' own theory of Intellect's self-identification between intelligible object and intelligible subject and not Parmenides' fr. 3. We can only assume that the repetitive use of the terms ὁμοῦ and ἕν could be regarded as a distant echo of Parmenides' theory of Being, but this consideration can hardly be derived from the text. However, from the direct references of Parmenides' fr. 3 in I.4.10.5–6, III.8.8.6–8, and V.9.5.26–32, as well as in V.1.8.17–18, there is a firm basis for asserting the presence of Parmenides in these texts.

Ennead V.9.5.26–32 is a unique amalgamation of Parmenides' fr. 3, Heraclitus' fr. 101, Plato's theory of Recollection[91] and Aristotle's theory of knowledge of the incorporeals.[92] It is the second exact quotation of Parmenides' fr. 3 along with that of V.1.8.14–22. Heraclitus' fr. 101 is also alluded to at

IV.8.1.17–18.[93] Moreover, Plotinus' statement on the indestructibility and inalterability of Intellect (5.35–36) probably goes back to Parmenides' fr. 8. It is significant that while Parmenides' and Heraclitus' quotations are verbatim, the reference to Plato and Aristotle are brief allusions to their theories:

> Intellect therefore really thinks the real beings, not as if they were somewhere else: for they are neither before it nor after it; but it is like the primary lawgiver, or rather is itself the law of Being. So they are correctly the statements "the same is for thinking and for being" and "knowledge of immaterial is the same as its object" and "I searched myself"; so are also "the recollections"; for none of the real beings is outside, or in place, but they remain always in themselves and undergo no alteration or destruction: that is why they are truly real. [V.9.5.26–34; trans. Armstrong modified]

According to Armstrong, this passage is "an excellent example of how Plotinus collects texts form earlier philosophers of very varied significance in their original context to support his own doctrine,"[94] but in my view, for Plotinus these earlier philosophers are, in contrast to Armstrong's comment, of equal significance. This can be justified by the word ὀρθῶς at the beginning of the passage that clearly stresses Plotinus' acceptance of the following accounts.[95] Moreover, it is noteworthy that Plotinus reconciles in one paragraph philosophers that are traditionally in philosophical contradiction such as Parmenides and Heraclitus, Plato and Aristotle.

On the other hand, the historical line of Plotinus' quotation is undoubtedly odd. He starts from Parmenides' connection of 'thinking' and 'being', he proceeds to an Aristotelian identity of subject and object within the self-thinking Intellect, then to Heraclitus' self-knowledge, and ends with Plato's theory of recollection. In all probability, Plotinus wants to mention two different philosophical lines: (1) the internal self-identified structure of Intellect, and (2) the self-thinking activity of Intellect. Here it is noteworthy that it is not the first time that Plotinus considers Heraclitus in the same light as Plato.[96] Likewise, in *Ennead* II.1 *On Heaven*, Plotinus strikingly reconciles Plato's view in the *Republic* 530b2–3 on the unchangeable nature of the visible heavenly bodies with the views of the "natural philosophers," and especially with Heraclitus' fragment 6.[97] Above all, with V.9.5.26–32 Plotinus recognizes himself as the philosopher who systematizes earlier ideas in one concept, that of Intellect.

Moreover, V.9.5.26–32 comes in the fifth chapter of a treatise where Plotinus discusses Intellect and explains its internal structure and intelligible activity. Intellect's intelligence is not external or in potentiality; it is a self-thinking activity towards its own intelligible contents (the Forms) (V.9.5.1–10).

Intellect "thinks itself and in itself" (5.14–15). Intellect thinks in itself the Forms (the real beings) and establishes them in Being (5.12–13). For this reason, Intellect is the first and perfect lawgiver of the intelligibles (5.28: νομοθέτης πρῶτος),[98] that is the law of Being (5.28–29: νόμος τοῦ εἶναι), the higher intelligible nature which contains totally in itself all real beings. This perfect self-inclusive nature of Intellect is the cause of its perfect knowledge.

For Plotinus, it is exactly this self-identification in Intellect between Being and Intelligence that echoes the earlier accounts of Parmenides and Heraclitus as well as Plato and Aristotle. Thus, since at the level of Intellect, self-knowledge is the supreme activity of Intelligence directed towards Being, so at the level of human soul, self-knowledge is the only inward thinking activity for the Soul's ascent to the intelligible world. Self-knowledge has to be the goal for the individual soul in order to remove its attention from the perceptibles to the intelligibles by exercizing contemplation.

For Plotinus, contemplation is that immanent transcendent power in all beings which enables them to ascend to a higher ontological realm. From the lowest level of Nature to the highest level of Intellect, contemplation is related to the process of Reversion. Through contemplation a being transcends the limits of its existence and becomes unified with the higher existence which is its source. On this basis, Plotinus states his central thesis: "all things are from contemplation and are contemplation":

> But, as contemplation ascends from nature to soul, and soul to intellect, and the contemplations become always more intimate and united to the contemplators, and in the soul of the good and wise man the objects known tend to become identical with the knowing subject, since they are pressing on towards intellect, it is clear that in intellect both are one, not by becoming akin, as in the best soul, but substantially, and because "thinking and being are the same." [III.8.8.1–8; trans. Armstrong]

Here Plotinus explains the unity of the whole intelligible universe and the possibility of contemplation in all entities because of the originative perfect unity of Intellect. Since every life is intelligence and the highest form of life is that of Intellect, Intellect exercises the perfect form of intelligence—that of identity of contemplation and object contemplated (III.8.8.17), the perfect unity of Intellect and Being. Plotinus expresses this identity by recalling Parmenides' fr. 3 in line 8 (ταὐτὸν τὸ εἶναι καὶ τὸ νοεῖν). In fact, Plotinus' allusion to fr. 3 is a paraphrase of the original. Armstrong recognizes the allusion to fr. 3 and notes that Plotinus uses it implicitly to support his doctrine that the intelligibles are not outside Intellect.[99] Plotinus stresses the theory that Intellect's object of contemplation is actually itself. Hence, at the level of Intellect intelligible subject and intelligible object are one, not discursively akin as at the level of Soul but substantially in a perfect living contemplative unity (III.8.8.10).

Another allusion to Parmenides' fr. 3 appears in Plotinus' late treatise *Ennead* I.4 *On Well-Being*. This treatise deals with the practical problem of how we as humans can achieve well-being in our lives and finally attain "true good." In fact, this treatise is not only an exposition of Plotinus' own views, but also a critical examination of the Platonic, Aristotelian, Stoic, and Epicurean accounts of the "good life." In the steps of Plato, Plotinus establishes his own position that well-being is the life of Intellect, the highest form of life that originates in purity from the One/Good, beyond any material, sensible or emotional satisfactions (chs. 1–4).

Particularly, Plotinus' allusion to Parmenides' fr. 3 appears in the tenth chapter of the treatise. The subject-matter of this chapter, as well as of the next one, is the relationship between well-being and awareness. Plotinus' position is that awareness is a secondary activity; it is the reflection of the intelligible life at the level of Soul. By using the simile of the mirror-reflection, he states that awareness is not the primary intelligible activity of Intellect, but a secondary activity reflected in the Soul. Because of this, awareness, or any sort of consciousness, is not the good life, since "good life" and "well-being" exist only at the level of Intellect where the living interaction between intelligence and being is always present as a steady and unified condition: "there must be an activity prior to awareness" if "thinking and being are the same" (I.4.10.5–6).

Finally, in I.4.10.5–6, Plotinus paraphrases Parmenides' fr. 3 in line 6 (τὸ αὐτὸ τὸ νοεῖν καὶ εἶναι) to express the unity of Intelligence and Being at the level of Intellect and, by extension, to justify the purest form of intelligible life beyond awareness. This citation has been observed by A. H. Armstrong[100] and P. Kalligas,[101] who agree that Plotinus here misinterprets Parmenides' words in the context of his own theory of Intellect's internal unity of Intelligence and Being. Even so, on this fundamental concept regarding Intellect, Plotinus immediately recalls Parmenides' fr. 3.

Having shown therefore that Parmenides' fr. 3 is continuously in the background of Plotinus' thought in his discussions of the internal unity of Intelligence and Being at the level of Intellect, we can now proceed to an analysis of Parmenides' predicates of Being in the *Enneads*.

3.4 THE PREDICATES OF BEING

Plotinus' criticism of Parmenides' immobility of Being in *Ennead* V.1.8.14–22 depends on the principles of his philosophical system. Despite the fact that Plotinus recognizes Parmenides as a forerunner of his theory of Being, he criticizes him because, regardless of the assertion of the intelligibility of Being, this Being remains "unmoved" (ἀκίνητον). For Plotinus, intelligence at the level of Intellect involves an *active* contemplative κίνησις towards the One. This intelligible κίνησις is related to the Motion of the five genera of Plato's *Sophist* (254d–e) and fundamentally underlies the Life (ζωή) of the intelligible world. For Plotinus the five Platonic categories from the *Sophist* represent different facets of Intellect's eternal life; Motion (κίνησις) and Otherness (ἑτερότης) are connected to the phase of Procession (πρόοδος), in which Being descends from unity to plurality, while Rest (στάσις) and Sameness (ταυτότης) are connected to the phase of Reversion (ἐπιστροφή), in which being ascends from plurality to unity.[102] The five Genera are also the condition of Intellect's "unity-in-plurality," the status of plurality in the intelligible world.[103] The 'one' Intellect self-includes the 'many' intelligibles in a unified living whole.[104] As Plotinus puts it in V.1.4.34–41 (a significant passage on the relationship of Intellect and Being to the Platonic genera), Motion is related to Intellect's act of thought, Otherness to the difference between intelligible subject and intelligible object, Rest to Intellect's self-thinking, and Sameness to Intellect's self-unity and universal self-likeness.[105] Accordingly, self-thinking at the level of Intellect will be impossible without both Otherness and Sameness: Otherness due to the necessary presupposition of subject and object, Sameness due to inherent self-identity. Since therefore Intellect exercises intelligence and intelligence presupposes intellectual movement, then Intellect cannot be immobile as Parmenides asserts in his poem.

It has been shown how Plotinus recognizes Parmenides' One (ἕν) at fr. 8.6 as one of the predicates of Being.[106] We have also shown why Plotinus rejects Parmenides' "all-togetherness" in ὁμοῦ πᾶν in favor of Anaxagoras' ὁμοῦ πάντα, since the latter is more appropriate to denote the plurality of Intellect. But Plotinus' description of Being reflects more predicates or signs from Parmenides' Being. Throughout the *Enneads*, Plotinus' intelligible Being, like the Eleatic Being, is indestructible, ungenerated, imperturbable, changeless, timeless, complete, indivisible, one, and continuous in existence, self-identical and all-together in its plurality and unity of the intelligibles. These predicates from Parmenides, appearing in Plotinus' text and discourse, repay further analysis.

3.4.1 Ungenerated and Indestructible

Parmenides' Being is ungenerated and indestructible (fr. 8.3). The subject of the fragment is the ἐόν which is significantly described with two negative terms: *without* generation (ἀγένητον)[107] and *without* destruction (ἀνώλεθρον).[108] As well as having no generation Parmenides justifies the indestructibility of Being in fr. 8.6–21. The argument of the Eleatic is based on the rejection of non-Being; Being can have no beginning in time since this implies (the rejected) non-Being when it did not exist, and no end as this would imply non-Being after its termination. Thus, since there is no temporal beginning or end for Being there is no generation, nor destruction for it (fr. 8.19–21).[109] This conclusion is the basis for the justification for the immobility of Being in fr. 8.26–33. Since generation and destruction have been rejected (8.27–8) all change (as multiple generations and destructions) is rejected, and Being is without change or movement. Given then that Being is immobile and utterly unchanging (fr. 8.34–41), it is complete temporally and also spatially, comparable to the bulk of a well-rounded sphere, equally balanced about the center in every direction (fr. 8.42–49). It is on this point that Plotinus directs his critique against Parmenides in V.1.8.18–22.

With regard to the indestructibility of Being, Plotinus seems to allude to Parmenides' terminology twice in the *Enneads* IV.7.9.9–19, and IV.3.5.5–8. Both references are mentioned by Henry and Schwyzer in the *Index Fontium*. *Ennead* IV.7.9.17 (ἥν ἀνώλεθρον καὶ ἀθάνατον) is recognized as an indirect reference to Parmenides' ἀνώλεθρον in fr. 8.3, while the question (πόθεν γὰρ ἂν καὶ γένοιτο, ἢ εἰς τί ἀπόλοιτο); in lines 16–17 is a direct allusion to Parmenides' *aporia* (πῶς δ' ἂν ἔπειτ' ἀπόλοιτο ἐόν; πῶς δ' ἄν κε γένοιτο); in fr. 8.19.[110] *Ennead* IV.3.5.5–8 is also regarded as an indirect reference to this fragment.

Indeed IV.7.9.9–19 is the most important allusion to Parmenides' indestructibility of Being. Here Plotinus supports the superiority of the intelligible Being and the whole chapter reflects Parmenides' thought. Intellect is "primarily alive," an intelligible existence steadily focused on itself, complete, indestructible, and immortal:

> For certainly all things cannot have a borrowed life: or it will go on to infinity; but there must be some nature which is primarily alive, which must be indestructible and immortal of necessity since it is also the origin of life to the others. Here, assuredly, all that is divine and blessed must be situated, living of itself and existing of itself, existing primarily and living primarily, without any part in essential change, neither coming to be nor perishing. For where could it come into being from, or into what could it change when it perished? And if we are to apply the name "being" to it truly, then being itself ought not to exist at one time, but not at another. [trans. Armstrong]

This passage is a straight allusion to Parmenides' philosophy. It is not only Plotinus' language that reveals the Parmenidean context, but also the philosophical meaning of his words. The Neoplatonist speaks of Intellect's perfection and superiority in terms of Eleatic Being. Like the Being of Parmenides, the Being of Plotinus is indestructible, changeless, self-same, and timeless in its self-existence. Because of these characteristics, Plotinus' Being is the immortal and divine origin of life in all subsequent beings. As he puts it in the first lines of the chapter, Intellect has "being of itself"; it is True Being beyond generation or destruction that preserves the order and beauty provided in the universe by the Soul (IV.7.9.1–9).[111]

Within this framework, Plotinus in IV.3.5.5–8 maintains that Intellect as True Being never ceases to exist since the intelligibles exist in a complete unity. In the perfect intelligible world the intelligibles are indestructible since they are not corporeally divided (IV.3.5.6). Each intelligible remain simultaneously distinct in otherness and the same in being. For this reason, the intelligibles are without beginning or end in time and thus immortal and indestructible.

3.4.2 Indivisible and Self-identical

Building on the above foundation, Plotinus uses Parmenides fr. 8.5 and 8.25 in VI.4.4.25–27 to support the unity-in-plurality of Intellect:

> Ὁμοῦ γὰρ πᾶν τὸ ὄν, κἂν πολὺ οὕτως ᾖ· ἐὸν γὰρ ἐόντι πελάζει, καὶ πᾶν ὁμοῦ, καὶ νοῦς πολὺς ἑτερότητι, οὐ τόπῳ, ὁμοῦ δὲ πᾶς
> For Being is all together one, even if it is many things in this way; for "being is adjacent to being" and "all is together," and intellect is many by difference, not by place, and all together. [VI.4.4.25–27; trans. Armstrong modified]

This passage is a direct reference to Parmenides' indivisibility of Being. This can be shown first by the exact reference to Parmenides' fr. 8.25 "for Being is adjacent to Being"[112] in line 25, and second by the unusual use of Parmenides' ὁμοῦ πᾶν in lines 25 and 26. Both references are included in the *Index Fontium*, Roussos[113] and Armstrong,[114] but, despite its importance, VI.4.4.25–27 has not been noticed or discussed by any commentary or in any study about Parmenides. Parmenides' fr. 8.25 belongs to a whole argument on the indivisibility of Being (8.22–25) which was signposted in fr. 8.6.[115] Parmenides' argument is that Being is indivisible because the denial of non-Being rejects existential "gaps" in a succession of separate entities. Being is continuous, self-same in existence with no internal differences, one whole bound all together in unity.[116]

Although Plotinus in VI.4.4.25–27 seems to accept Parmenides' idea of Being's unity, all-togetherness and self-identity, he denies the indivisibility of Being by maintaining that Intellect is divisible by the Forms not in spatial terms but incorporeally. For this reason Plotinus reads Parmenides in the light of Plato's metaphysics of the Forms and supports the unity of Being along with the plurality of the Forms. This can be further supported by the quotation of Plato's *Timaeus* 35a2–3, on the divisibility of the bodies, in the next line of

VI.4.4 (28 ff.). Thus, in VI.4.4.25–27, Plotinus offers an interesting amalgamation of Parmenides and Plato in describing the unity-in-plurality of the intelligibles within Intellect. This plurality is complete, due to the all-togetherness of the intelligibles, and perfect in the eternal, changeless life of the intelligible reality.

3.4.3 Imperturbable and Changeless

The term ἀτρεμές[117] (imperturbable)[118] appears twice in the extant fragments of Parmenides' poem (frs 1.29 and 8.4). In fragment 1.29 Parmenides uses this epithet to denote the immutable and unshakable stillness of well-rounded truth (Ἀληθείης εὐκυκλέος)[119] contrasted with the unstable and unreliable opinion of mortals.[120] This fragment foreshadows the second occurrence of the word in fragment 8.4 where the epithet ἀτρεμές[121] appears as one of the predicates of Being connoting its immutable tranquillity; it characterizes the immutable and unvarying nature of Being in a steady unchanged state of inert calmness.[122] The imperturbable nature of Being reflects its immutability and timelessness (frs 8.26 and 8.28), remaining the same in the same ontological state in eternal perpetuity, completeness and self-identity (8.29–30). The term ἀτρεμές represents in Parmenides' poetic language a peaceful moment where the whole universe rests in stability and tranquillity, offering to the mind the ability to recognize the true nature of Being beyond the uncertainty of perceptible motion and change: *the unshaken heart of Truth*.[123]

According to Coxon, Parmenides' imperturbability of Being foreshadows Plato's account of the Form of Beauty in the *Symposium* 211b, and Aristotle's theory of the Unmoved Mover.[124] Moreover, before Plato and Aristotle, Parmenides' immutability of Being represents a strong criticism of the mobility of becoming in Ionic cosmology. Parmenides echoes Xenophanes earlier position on the unmoved God "remaining always in the same place" (fr. 26), as well as foreshadows Empedocles' theory of eternity in frs 17.11 and 26.10. It is this indirect connection of imperturbability and eternity between Parmenides and Empedocles that leads to Plotinus' attribution of ἀτρεμές to the eternal life of Intellect in the *Enneads*.

Plotinus uses the word ἀτρεμές, and the related ἀτρεμής, and ἀτρεμεῖν nine times in the *Enneads*, using the term to express the quiet solitude, calmness, and imperturbability of Intellect's eternal life.[125] The influence of Parmenides' immutability of Being on Plotinus' imperturbability of eternity has been noted by Henry and Schwyzer in the *Index Fontium* by pointing out two indirect references of Parmenides' fr. 8.4 to Plotinus' *Ennead* III.7.5.21, and III.7.11.3–4.[126] J. E. McGuire and J. E. Strange note the former reference but ignore the latter.[127] Roussos supplements these references with another allusion to ἀτρεμές in Plotinus' *Ennead* I.6.5.15,[128] while Kalligas in his commentary on *Ennead* I.1 recognizes another reference of the term at 9.23.[129] But all the other allusions to ἀτρεμές in the *Enneads* have not been recognized. Apart from the above citations, there is no further research in modern scholarship on the place of Parmenides' imperturbability of Being in Plotinus' thought and terminology, and the aforementioned Plotinian passages are also ignored by modern scholars and commentators and deserve our special attention.

Particularly in *Ennead* III.7.11.1–5 Plotinus uses the word ἀτρεμές twice to describe the *imperturbable life of eternity*.[130] Furthermore, in III.7.5.18–22 eternity is described as a God revealing and manifesting itself as [one who] *truly is*, and as a being which is imperturbable, self-identical, and firmly established in life:

> Eternity could well be said to be a God manifesting itself and revealing itself to be what it is, a being that is imperturbable, self-identical, and so has the property of being firmly stable in its life. [trans. McGuire-Strange modified]

For Plotinus this God is the true intelligible being; a Being that is imperturbable, the same and stable in its life. Since this Being is imperturbable then his life is also imperturbable.

Similarly, in the first lines of the eleventh chapter of the same treatise, where Plotinus' discussion of "time" begins, he defines eternity as a life which is imperturbable, all at once, limitless, altogether fixed without declination, a nature which rests in unity and is directed towards the One:

> We must return again to that condition which we said obtained in the case of eternity, to that imperturbable, all at once, actually limitless life, altogether fixed without declination, which rests in unity and is directed toward the One. [trans. McGuire-Strange modified]

In contrast to the nature of time and Soul, the nature of the eternal Being is "one in continuity" (III.7.11.53–4: ἐν συνεχείᾳ ἕν), a continuous unbounded whole held tight in unity. This passage echoes again passage *Ennead* VI.4.4.25–27 on the unity in plurality of the intelligibles. A comparison of the passages shows that Plotinus ascribes "imperturbability" both to the divine intelligible being and to intelligible life, for both refer to the intelligible condition of eternity where alteration and declination are denied.

Parmenides' influence in IV.3.5.5–8 and III.7.11.1–5 is therefore indisputable and especially the "continuity" of Intellect in III.7.11.53–4 clearly alludes to Parmenides' "continuity" (συνεχές) of Being in fr. 8.6. The linguistic similarities between the two philosophers lead to the conclusion that Plotinus' definition of eternity is inspired by Parmenides' terminology of Being. The difference between Parmenides' Being and Plotinus' eternity is that the former is "one all at once" and "limited," while the latter is "actually limitless in life" and becomes one "by self-returning towards the supreme One." But, more significantly, there is a difference in the metaphysical meaning that Plotinus applies to ἀτρεμές: for Plotinus' imperturbability of the eternal realm derives from the self-identity, unity and completeness of the intelligible life.

In further analysis, at the level of Intellect, the identity between Being and Intelligence, intelligible object and intelligible subject, manifests and reveals a constant life independent of anything external; a life which rests in tranquillity and partakes of the unity and perfection of the Forms. Intellect is imperturbable in itself without declination, partaking of a self-defined and self-sustained intelligible life. For this reason, Intellect is described in *Ennead* III.2.2.16 as imperturbable and quiet.[131] Intellect is the higher intelligible cause that formulates the universe in unperturbed quietness. The unperturbed quietness of Intellect is transmitted to the lower realities, but it cannot be sustained, and disintegrates under the multiple expansions of the perceptibles. Intellect exists in quietness since all the intelligibles remain eternally together in itself like the parts of the seed which remain always together in the same procreative state, before the seed extends and expands in spatial multiplicity and temporal mobility (III.2.2.18–33). Plotinus' immobility of Intellect reflects again Parmenides' immobility of Being.

Moreover, for Plotinus, the perceptible motion of the world derives from intelligible rest and the temporal perceptible life from the eternal intelligible life (III.2.4.15). The life of Intellect is a "life with no delight" (VI.9.11.50), which means that whereas in Intellect all the intelligibles persist in eternal life, in the perceptible world the souls continuously change by appearing in different bodily forms in different lifetimes (III.2.4). In the perceptible world, the quietness of eternal life is replaced and disturbed by the "clamor" (θόρυβος) of the bodies (I.1.9.23 ff.).[132] Here Plotinus, like Plato,[133] describes bodily life as full of changes and noise.[134] The intelligible quietness of the Soul disrupts into bodily life, blurred by the changes and clamor of external attachments and affections (I.1.9.25–27), but the Soul, focused on itself, can become imperturbable like Parmenides' Being, unaffected by the clamor of bodily changes.[135]

Indeed, when the Soul returns and rests in its true intelligible self, ignoring any bodily clamor and affection, it is able to experience the eternal tranquillity of intelligible life (I.1.9.23). When the Soul exercises its "inner sight" and contemplates the purity in itself, it becomes "true light" beyond measure, quantity, and dimensions (I.6.9) and ascends purified (I.6.7). The inner sight of Soul is contemplation in "silence" (σιωπή).[136] When the intellectual awareness of the Soul is silent and clear, the intelligible image is projected back pure and undisrupted, as happens with a mirror reflection when there is a smooth, bright, and untroubled surface (I.4.10.9–10). In this case, the "subject of intelligence" becomes united with "the object of intelligence," and the Soul attains the pure intelligible activity and identity prior to any kind of awareness (10.5–6).[137] Thus, the eternal imperturbability of intelligible life derives from the self-identity of intelligence and being at the level of Intellect, and the tranquillity of Being is the final state of ascent for the Soul.

The next step leads to the transcendent experience of the Soul and its final unity with the One, an experience of the Soul which is similar to that which true lovers of wisdom feel towards intelligible beauty (I.6.3–5). This beauty is not external, but internal: the inward beauty of the Soul beyond any color, shape, or size (I.6.5.9–10).[138] The "transparent soul" possessing true morality and all the purity of the virtues contemplates "its greatness, its righteous life, pure morality, courage with its noble look, dignity and modesty advancing in a fearless, calm and unperturbed disposition, and the godlike light shining upon all" (I.6.5.15). The unperturbed disposition of the Soul in I.6.5.15 echoes the eternal disposition in III.7.11.1–5. By returning within itself, the Soul contemplates Intellect, transcends the perceptible universe and finally ascends pure to the intelligible realm ready to be joined with the One (VI.9.5). With its ascent, the Soul discovers that its real self belongs to the eternal nature and becomes a fully actualized member of the intelligible world (IV.7.20.14–20; IV.8.1.1–10).[139] At the intelligible level, the Soul contemplates Intellect as a quiet and undisturbed motion and is able to contemplate the true intelligible being which has "all things in itself and is all things"; a multiple living reality of intelligibles (VI.9.5.14). The quiet and undisturbed motion of Intellect is the intelligible motion of Intellect returning towards the One. This constant focus of Intellect upon the One reveals the eternal undisrupted life of Being (IV.3.5.5–8).

For Plotinus, the return to the One[140] is the ultimate experience of the initiator within the process of the mysteries (VI.9.11).[141] The initiator transcends any multiplicity, even that of Intellect, and ascends to the highest Hypostasis of the One. The "contemplator" (ὁ ἰδών) becomes one with the "object of contemplation" (τὸ ἑωραμένον) within its own self (VI.9.11.1–9). This higher contemplation of the Soul is an experience both intellectual and visionary and, as J. R. Bussanich notes, the mystical awareness combines both cognitive and affective elements.[142] The ascent of the initiator is experienced as of one carried away by a divine power in a state of quiet solitude and calmness (VI.9.11.14). In this case, as in III.7.11.1–5 and I.6.5.15, the unperturbed disposition is the higher degree of experience before the unity with the One.

As Plotinus himself poetically describes it in *Ennead* V.5.8.3–7, it is this intelligible state of solitude where someone has to wait quietly until the One appears, "as the eye awaits the rising of the sun; and the sun rising over the horizon—from the Ocean the poets say—gives itself to the eyes to see." The man who is illuminated by the true light of the One ascends to the divine and apprehends eternity, purity, and immortality, and as Plotinus significantly recalls the poetic words of Empedocles' fr. 112, the man is able to say: "Greetings! I am for you an immortal god" (IV.7.10.38–40: χαίρετ', ἐγὼ δ' ὑμῖν θεὸς ἄμβροτος). Thus, the union with the One is the "end of the journey,"[143] the mystical state where the Soul flies "alone to the alone" (VI.9.11.45–51).[144]

To conclude: Plotinus' imperturbability of the eternal intelligible realm is inspired by Parmenides' theory of Being. Even if Plotinus does not refer directly to Parmenides' words at frs 1.29 or 8.4, the frequent use of ἀτρεμές in connection with the self-identity, completeness, unity, and immobility of Being makes Plotinus allusion to Parmenides practically certain. The use of ἀτρεμές in Plotinus justifies the reading of this word in Parmenides' fr. 1.29 over that of ἀτρεκές. The conclusion is reinforced by the fact that ἀτρεμές is rarely used by Plato and Aristotle, so in all probability the influence of Parmenides' ἀτρεμές on Plotinus is direct and original. Plotinus is using Parmenides' term as a crucial and almost technical term to express both the tranquillity of the intelligible life and the ultimate mystical experience of the contemplator before the unity with the One. Plotinus lead us to read Parmenides' philosophy of Being as the result of a mystical experience of tranquility, quietness and unperturbed disposition. In all cases, the "unperturbed disposition" applies to eternity and particularly to the life of intelligible world. The tranquil nature of eternity signifies a self-defined eternal life of Intellect contrasted with the clamor of temporal becoming. On this basis, let us see in the next section Plotinus' theory of time and eternity in relation to the Presocratic tradition.

Chapter 4

Eternity and Time

4.1 PLOTINUS' THEORY OF ETERNITY AND TIME

Plotinus' central discussion on eternity (αἰών) and time (χρόνος) appears in *Ennead* III.7, *On Eternity and Time*.[1] The treatise is divided into thirteen chapters: after a first introductory chapter in which Plotinus presents his method of research, in chapters 2–6, he speculates upon the nature of eternity, in chapters 7–10, he denies the older theories of time and especially that of Aristotle, and finally, in chapters 11–13, he presents Plato's theory of time and demonstrates his own Neoplatonic interpretation. According to Porphyry (*Life*, 5), Plotinus composed this treatise during the middle or second period of his writings (AD 263–268).[2] During this period, Plotinus seemed to be focusing on anti-Gnostic and anti-Aristotelian polemics. *Ennead* III.7 is related to the latter, on Aristotle's theory of time as "number [or measure] of motion" given in the fourth book of the *Physics* (217b–224a), which is criticized and refuted in chapter 9. Furthermore, Plotinus discusses and rejects some Pythagorean, Stoic, and Epicurean theories of time in chapters 8 and 10. All these theories are denied because they exhibit a constant connection of χρόνος with physical motion, bodily change, or properties of these. Plotinus' refutation is based upon two major arguments: (1) *since motion occurs in time, time cannot be identified with something occurring in it* (III.7.8.45–47); and (2) *motion can stop or be interrupted but time cannot* (III.7.8.6–8).[3] Plotinus interprets positively Plato's theory of time in *Timaeus* 37c–38d and, along with Parmenides' theory of the timelessness of Being in fragment 8, suggests a new philosophical direction for the subject.[4]

Armstrong places *Ennead* III.7 along with the Aristotelian discussion of time in the *Physics* as one of the two major surviving accounts of the subject in ancient Greek philosophy.[5] Surprisingly, he excludes Alexander Aphrodisias' short treatise, *On Time*, preserved in Latin and Arabic, Simplicius' corollary on Time *in Physica* (773.8–800.21), Proclus' influential work *De Aeternitate Mundi,* as well as Philoponus' response to the latter work in his *De Aeternitate Mundi contra Proclum*, a refutation which became a model for the controversy between Pagans and Christians concerning the eternity of the world and the existence of God.[6] Besides these works, ancient accounts of time survive as fragments throughout the Greek philosophical tradition.

With regard to the philosophical sources of Plotinus in *Ennead* III.7, Plato is the major thinker behind the text.[7] In particular, Plotinus relies upon the *Timaeus* in (1) the definition of χρόνος as the "moving image of eternity" modeled on the metaphysical analogy between "moving image" (εἰκών) and "eternal archetype" (παράδειγμα) of the *Timaeus* (37d3–7);[8] (2) the creation of the universe and the celestial bodies as markers and measures of time (38b6–39e2);[9] (3) the supreme status of the "ever-living being" (37d1), which "abides in eternal unity" (37d6);[10] (4) the "goodness" of the Divine Craftsman in the creation of cosmos (29e);[11] and (5) the distinction between "indivisible substance" and "divisible substance" (35a).[12] Finally, as well as the *Timaeus*, Plotinus uses in *Ennead* III.7 the Platonic terminology of the *Sophist* and the *Parmenides*.

Of these passages two are direct references to Plato himself (III.7.6.1–9 and 13.20–30); both passages are clearly directed to a Neoplatonic interpretation of Plato's words in the *Timaeus* as a nonliteral account. First, in the sixth chapter of the treatise, Plotinus traces back to Plato his discussion of the nature of eternity and the eternal life of being around the transcendent One (III.7.6.1–9). For Plotinus, eternity is the intelligible life of being in constant focus upon the One. Likewise, in Plato's work, eternity signifies the intelligible life of True Being, and this is how Plato's phrase "eternity remains in unity" at *Timaeus* 37d6 is to be interpreted. Second, Plato is for Plotinus the first philosopher to distinguish the eternal life of the Forms from the temporal life of becoming. But even if time is manifested through the perceptible phenomena, its real nature is neither as measure nor the object of measure. Hence, in the last chapter of *Ennead* III.7, Plotinus clarifies the account at *Timaeus* 39b–c, claiming that the real essence of time is beyond any kind of measure. Time is prior to the cosmos and space and not vice versa (III.7.13.20–30).

But Plotinus is aware that many of the philosophers, before and after Plato, worked widely on this concept and he shows the difficulties and absurdities of some of their definitions. Before establishing his own interpretation, Plotinus realizes that he must first acknowledge and then criticize the earlier theories, as he describes his method in III.7.7.10–17. The philosophical problem of time was an old issue in Greek philosophy, and, further, "the ancient and revered philosophers" (7.11–12), who worked on the concept of time, made "important contributions" to the subject (7.15–16). As Plotinus puts it, "some of the ancient and revered philosophers have found out the truth; but it is proper to investigate which of them has attained it most completely, and how we too could reach an understanding about these things" (1.13–16). Plotinus shows with the expression "the ancient and revered philosophers" a positive attitude to his predecessors, respectful but not uncritical. But his aim in *Ennead* III.7 is not to act as a historian of philosophy, but rather to refute the various preceding accounts of time (which primarily relate to time as the "measure of motion"), and then to suggest his own new thesis (10.12–17), a thesis which shows approval of Plato.

Within this framework, Plotinus offers an invaluable philosophical survey on time in a threefold division of the ancient theories (III.7.7.17–27). The key term for this division is the concept of "physical motion." For Plotinus, since time is a "moving/changing" nature and not a "stationary/unchanging" one, then the idea of "motion" (κίνησις) rather than that of "rest" (στάσις) is the correct description (7.20–22). In fact, Plotinus' method in III.7.7.20–22 goes back to Aristotle's discussion on time at *Physics* 218a30–b20 where Aristotle's program of investigation agrees that all the preceding accounts of time are related to "physical motion" or "bodily change."[13] Plotinus wants to distinguish "time" from "rest" and, probably, also answer the definition of time given by Aristotle's pupil Strato of Lampsacus that time is "the measure of all motion and rest."[14]

Agreeing with the Aristotelian classification in the *Physics*, Plotinus offers his own threefold division of the preceding theories of time (III.7.7.19–20):

> Case 1: Time identified with simple motion (κίνησις ἡ λεγομένη)
> Case 2: Time identified with the moving object (τὸ κινούμενον)
> Case 3: Time identified with something belonging to motion (κινήσεως τι).[15]

On the basis of this first classification, Plotinus proceeds in the following lines of the chapter (7.22–27) to a more detailed division of the ancient accounts. Of the philosophers who follow [Case 1], some say that χρόνος is "all motion" (πᾶσα κίνησις) [Case 1.1], and others that it is the "motion of the universe" (κίνησις τοῦ παντός) [Case 1.2]. Those who follow [Case 2], speak of the moving object as the "sphere of the universe" (τοῦ παντὸς σφαῖρα). Of those who follow [Case 3], some say that the "something" (τὸ τί), which belongs to motion, is either "the extension of motion" (διάστημα κινήσεως) [Case 3.1], or "the measure of motion" (μέτρον κινήσεως) [Case 3.2], or "the concomitant of motion" (παρακολούθημα κινήσεως) [Case 3.3]; and these philosophers refer either to "all motion" (πάσης κίνησις) [Case 3.4], or to "orderly motion" (τεταγμένης κίνησις) [Case 3.5].[16]

With the expression "the measure of motion" in [Case 3.2], Plotinus directs us straight to Aristotle's account of χρόνος at *Physics* 220b32 ff. For Aristotle, time is defined as "the number (or measure) of motion in respect of before and after" (*Physics* 219b1–2: ὁ χρόνος ἀριθμὸς κινήσεως κατὰ τὸ πρότερον καὶ ὕστερον),[17] using "motion" and "number" here without any precise distinctions. Plotinus is aware of this connection and testifies to it at *Ennead* III.7.9.1 ff. According to Strange, Aristotle perhaps called time a "number" because of the Platonic influence of the account of time in the *Timaeus*.[18] Similarly, Armstrong notes that Aristotle develops his idea of time as measure based upon an original Academic view.[19] Plotinus argues against Aristotle as follows: *since time is a continuous nature, it is unreasonable to identify it with number which is a discrete quantity.* It is noteworthy that this criticism was originally made by Strato of Lampsacus and, as Strange points out, Plotinus has in mind this criticism in the ninth chapter of the treatise.[20] Strato described χρόνος as a "quantity which exists in all actions" and, in contrast to Aristotle, removed the concept of "motion" from his definition (*apud* Sextus Empiricus *Adversus Mathematicos* X: 177). According to S. Sambursky, Strato succeeded in avoiding the confusion of "actions," including rest, with the uniform, constant flux of time by which these actions were supposed to be measured.[21]

Furthermore, in Cases 1.1, 1.2, 3.4 and 3.5 Plotinus refers to some Stoic accounts of time. The Stoics defined χρόνος as the "extension of motion" or as "the motion of the universe,"[22] and Plotinus also makes the distinction between "all motion" and "orderly motion." As Armstrong observes, it was only the Stoics who had previously made this distinction.[23] With the expression "extension of motion" in [Case 3.1], Plotinus refers to the Stoic Zeno and Chrysippus. For Zeno (*SVF* II: 510), time is the "extension of all motion" (πάσης κινήσεως διάστημα), while for Chrysippus (*SVF* II: 509–510) it is the "extension of motion" (κινήσεως διάστημα), or more exactly the "extension of the motion of the universe" (διάστημα τῆς τοῦ κόσμου κινήσεως). A. Graeser, in his study, *Plotinus and the Stoics*, comments on this passage and suggests that Plotinus offers an explanation that reverses the Stoic position: *time is not essentially a measure of movement, but only per accidens*.[24] Following Graeser's comment, we can conclude that Plotinus offered this new idea of the concept of time not only with an eye to the Stoics, but also to all the ancient accounts, including those of the Aristotelians, Epicureans, and Pythagoreans, who considered time as inherent to natural phenomena. Time is not the measured or *discrete* property of the periodic rotation of the universe, but an intelligible *continuous* entity prior to cosmic movement. On this basis, Plotinus, with "concomitant of motion" in [Case 3.3], alludes to the Epicurean theory of time,[25] and with "the sphere of the whole" in [Case 2] to the Pythagoreans.[26]

Epicurus' theory of time is discussed at length in the *Letter of Herodotus*. For Epicurus, χρόνος cannot be recognized by a particular concept, but it is rather a special kind of "accident" (σύμπτωμα).[27] As C. Bailey comments, "time differs from everything else in that we cannot have a general conception of it, i.e., a visual image resulting from a number of individual perceptions."[28] Epicurus' definition of time therefore depends primarily on empirical evidence. Time is an "accident" resulting from the associations or states of perceptibles and so time can be defined as an "accident of accidents concomitant of motion."[29] On this basis, Plotinus criticizes Epicurus not only for identifying time as "concomitant motion," but also for deducing its nature from perceptible experience.[30]

Within this framework and having in mind the earlier theories of time, Plotinus begins *Ennead* III.7 with the fundamental thesis that eternity and time are two different natures. The former belongs to being and the intelligible realm,[31] the latter pertains to becoming and the perceptible universe (III.7.1.1–3). Hence, eternity is connected to Intellect, the Second Hypostasis of Being, whereas time belongs to Soul, the Third Hypostasis of Being. Eternity is related to Intellect's stability, unity, indivisibility, sameness, and perfection, contrasted with Soul's restless motion, otherness, and divisibility.[32] On this basis, Plotinus defines eternity as the timeless life of Intellect (3.36–38) and time as the restless life of Soul (11.44–45). Eternity and time imply two different forms of intelligible life (ζωή): whereas αἰών is the life of Intellect around the One, χρόνος is the life of Soul around the Intellect. Eternity is an intelligible life existing in a timeless and durationless present; time is an intelligible life beyond the borders of physical motion related to the restless activity of Soul.

> For if eternity is life at rest, unchanging and identical and already unbounded, and Time must exist as an image of eternity, then we must say that there is, instead of an intelligible life, another life having, in a way of speaking, the same name as this power of the soul, and instead of an intelligible motion, the motion of a part of soul; and instead of sameness and self-identity and abiding, that which does not abide in the same but acts one after another, and instead of that which is one without distances, an image of unity that is one in continuity; and instead of an already complete unbounded whole, an always continuous unbounded succession, and instead of a whole all together a whole which is, and always will be, going to come into being part by part. [III.7.11.45–56 trans. Armstrong modified]

In the above passage, Plotinus stresses the distinction between eternity and time by using the expression "instead of" (ἀντί). This expression is crucial for the comparison; it denotes not an absolute distinction between the two notions but rather some interrelated analogies of their properties according to the realities in which they participate and are manifest.

Another passage that compares eternity and time appears in *Ennead* I.5, *On Whether Well-Being Increases With Time.* In the seventh chapter of the treatise, Plotinus claims a central position in the discussion for Well-Being in connection with eternity and time. Since the life of well-being is the good life and the best life is the eternal life of True Being then well-being must be related to the eternal life of True Being outside any temporal affections or influences (I.5.7.21–31). For Plotinus, eternity is again beyond temporal divisions, extension or duration. Eternity is an indivisible, unextended, and timeless nature, clearly related to the life of True Being and never to that of temporal becoming.

It is worth mentioning, as J. E. McGuire and J. E. Strange observe, that Plotinus' definitions both of the non-durational nature of eternity and of the idealistic theory of time are not completely new, but also belong to the Middle-Platonic and Neopythagorean traditions.[33] Indeed eternity as a durationless and timeless present appears in Plutarch's *De E apud Delphos* 393ab and time as the life of Soul both in Plutarch's *Platonicae quaestiones* 1007bc and Chalcidius' treatise, *In Timaeum* (ch. 101).[34] More striking is the definition of Philo of Alexandria (*De mutatione nominum*, 267) of αἰών as the "life of the intelligible world" (τοῦ νοητοῦ βίος κόσμου), and χρόνος as the "life of the perceptible world" (τοῦ αἰσθητοῦ βίος κόσμου). But, as R. Sorabji clarifies, Plotinus' theory is not the same as that of the Platonic or Middle Platonic tradition since in Plotinus we find not just two levels of reality but three.[35]

Furthermore, the association of eternity and time with the concept of life is an old issue in Greek philosophy.[36] For Heraclitus (fr. 30), the cosmos is a self-generating "ever-living fire" which kindles in measures and is quenched in measures. Empedocles speaks of an "eternal life" in frs 16, 17, 26, 110. For Plato in the *Timaeus* (29d–31a; 40a–b), both the intelligible world of Forms and the perceptible world are conceived of as living organisms; whereas the Forms are "intelligible living-beings," the celestial bodies are "divine living-beings," and the cosmos as a whole is an "ensouled animal." The Platonic intelligible world is everlasting due to the eternal being of the Forms, the physical universe due to everlasting temporal becoming. Whereas the world of Forms exists in an everlasting stable perfection, the world of the senses exists in an everlasting moving generation. Finally, for Aristotle (*Physics* 3.3, *De Anima* 3.2), the living Intellect is identical to its intelligibles. This living Intellect is God and God is ever-living because of its self-identity through self-thinking. Let us see these accounts in detail.

4.2 ETERNITY AND TIME IN THE PRESOCRATICS

The Presocratic term for "time" is χρόνος and for "eternity" the noun is αἰών and the adjective ἀίδιος. But whereas χρόνος[37] does not involve any difficulty in its meaning, αἰών and ἀίδιος are fluid terms, commonly associated in early Greek language with "life" and "everlastingness". While the word αἰών may be translated by "life," "lifetime," "age," "generation," "period of existence," and "long space of time,"[38] the word ἀΐδιος tends to mean "everlasting," "eternal," "without beginning or end."[39] Alongside αἰών and ἀΐδιος other terms such ἀέναον (ever-flowing) and ἀείζωον (ever-living) complement the Greek concept of "duration" determined by the subject to which it is applied, as, for example, "human life," "cosmos," and "god." More significantly, all terms, especially in their post-Homeric usage, have connotations of ἀεί (always), and are closely associated to being (ὄν). The etymological definition of αἰών as "always being" (ἀεὶ ὄν) was accepted by Aristotle and Plotinus, but was not clearly established before Plato's metaphysics.

It is noteworthy that there is no good evidences for any religious personification or cult of αἰών in the early Greek tradition;[40] it is probable that it was only after its philosophical importance was established that αἰών became a religious personification. The religious practice is suggested by the statue of Aion dedicated at Eleusis after the first century BC and from Epiphanius' testimony about a festival in Alexandria where an image was brought of the Koreion with the announcement that "Kore has brought forth Aion."[41] Suda also refers to a statue of Aion.[42] Finally, the identification between Χρόνος and Κρόνος appears only after Pherecydes' mythico-philosophical innovations.

In the Homeric poems the word αἰών is usually related to human soul (ψυχή).[43] Although αἰών is never itself a psychological element or factor, it is still associated with the "vitality," or the "life force" of the human soul;[44] αἰών signifies the "vital substance," or "the vital force of animated beings" that keeps the human soul alive and leaves the body at death.[45] For Homer the word seems to have both a temporal[46] and emotional context,[47] but not the sense of "lifetime" found in post-Homeric writers.[48] Following E. Benveniste, D. Claus observes that the root meaning of αἰών is to be found in the Homeric αἰόλος (nimble and changeful of hue) and αἰόλλειν (to shift to and fro), and that the original meaning of αἰών is more that of bodily "life-fluid," or "spinal marrow" than a term expressing "life-force" as an independent concept.[49] Indeed Hippocrates (*Epidem*, 7) and Pindar (fr. 111) defined αἰών as the life-fluid of spinal marrow. But Onians before Claus had observed the etymological controversy of the term and especially the problematic notional transition from the original meaning of life-fluid, or marrow to that of "soul-life," and finally "lifetime."[50] Onians reasonably concluded that "it is not difficult to see how a word designating the life fluid might come to mean the life which the fluid represents and so the life temporally considered the life dependent on it."[51]

From these etymological considerations, the post-Homeric usage of αἰών is clearly associated with "lifetime," denoting the period or length of life for both mortals and gods.[52] The temporal sense of the word seems to be increased by the association of αἰών with "always" (ἀεί), implying duration in this sense and then by extension "everlastingness," or, in the original meaning of the Heraclitean term, "ever-living." From this perspective, αἰών is related to the divine everlastingness of the cosmos and the Platonic ever-living Being. The association of αἰών with being leads both to the famous Aristotelian etymological definition as "always being"[53] (ἀεὶ ὄν), and to Plotinus' version in *Ennead* III.7.6.23–36 as an unconditionally timeless "truly being."

Particularly in Presocratic thought the concept of eternity has either (1) cosmological, or (2) ontological content. The cosmological includes (1.1) cosmogony and/or (1.2) the nature of material substance, while the ontological includes (2.1) mortal life (2.2), divine life (2.3), the nature of thinking and/or (2.4), the nature of being. The Presocratic words that usually denote these areas are αἰών and ἀίδιος. Second, other words such as ἀέναον, ἀείζωον, μακραίων, and δολιχαίων are seldom used, and denote only a particular aspect of eternality within the philosophical style of some particular Presocratic. The words ἀείζωον, μακραίων, and δολιχαίων are compound terms used poetically by Heraclitus (fr. 30), and Empedocles (frs 115, 21 and 23), and they are unique in early Greek philosophy. Finally, another crucial keyword in the understanding of the Presocratic concept of eternity is the temporal "always," ἀεί. This word is frequently used to denote temporal duration of the subject with reference to the three tenses of time: "past" (ἦν), "present" (ἔστιν), and "future" (ἔσται)—and so is crucial to the present argument. In tables 4.1 and 4.2, we can see in detail how these words are used along with their content and subject in the following extant Presocratic fragments.[54]

On the other hand, the Presocratic usage of χρόνος has exclusively a cosmological context. Table 4.3 presents the extant Presocratic fragments on time. These extant references of χρόνος can be supplemented by other important testimonies.[56] Keeping in mind these references on eternity and time in the Presocratics, we can now proceed to their philosophical analysis in the *Enneads*.

4.3 THE PRESOCRATIC THEORIES OF ETERNITY AND TIME IN THE *ENNEADS*

Plotinus' theory of eternity and time relates to Presocratic theories in the context of three topics: (1) the timelessness of being, (2) the eternal life of Intellect, and (3) the everlastingness of the cosmos. The first topic is primarily related to Parmenides' radical idea of the timelessness of Being in fr. 8.5, the second points to Heraclitus' eternal vitality of fire in fr. 30 and Empedocles' eternal life in frs 16, 17, 26, 110, and the third to the everlastingness of the cosmos found in particular in Pherecydes, the Milesians, the Pythagoreans, Heraclitus, and Anaxagoras.

Table 4.1.
Cosmological Fragments of Eternity

Presocratic (fr.)	*Extant Fragment*	*Subject*
Empedocles (16.2)	τούτων ἀμφοτέρων κενεώσεται ἄσπετος *αἰών*	The endlessness lifetime of Love and Strife in the construction of the Cosmos.
Empedocles (17.11)	γίγνονταί τε καὶ οὔ σφισιν ἔμπεδος *αἰών*	All mortal things have no abiding life.
Philolaus (21.14)	τὸ κινέον ἐξ *αἰῶνος* ἐς *αἰῶνα* περιπολεῖ	The active part of the Cosmos goes around from "eternity to eternity."
Philolaus (21.21)	κόσμον ἦμεν ἐνέργειαν *ἀί διον* θεῶ	Cosmos is the everlasting activity of God.
Philolaus (21.4–8)	(κόσμος) διαμένει τὸν ἄπειρον *αἰῶνα* ἐξ *αἰῶνος* καὶ εἰς *αἰῶνα* διαμενεῖ	Cosmos endures eternally, both indestructible and inexhaustible.
Philolaus (23)	τῶν κοσμικῶν *αἰωνίας* διαμονῆς κρατιστεύοισαν καὶ αὐτογενῆ συνοχήν.	Number is the controlling and self-generated bond of the "eternal" continuance of the Cosmos.
Philolaus (26.1–2)	περὶ δὲ φύσιος καὶ ἁρμονίαςτῶν πραγμάτων *ἀίδιος* ἔσσα.	The "eternal" things are self-determined by nature and harmony.
Heraclitus (30)	ἦν ἀεὶ καὶ ἔστιν καὶ ἔσται πῦρ *ἀείζωον*.	Cosmos is "everlasting" due to its inherent "everliving" fiery substance.

Fragments have DK numbering.

First, Plotinus accepts and develops Parmenides' radical conception of Being's timelessness in his definition of eternity in *Ennead* III.7.6.23–36. For Plotinus, Parmenides is a forerunner of Plato in his theory of Being, the one Presocratic who gave the correct description of Being through the ontological predicates (fr. 8). Parmenides' definition of the timeless Being (fr. 8.5–6) is the first Preplatonic statement of the stable and unified nature found in the eternal life of the Platonic Forms, and Plato uses Parmenides in developing his own radical concept of eternity in the *Timaeus*.[57] Plotinus makes use of both

Table 4.2.
Ontological Fragments of Eternity

Presocratic (fr.)	*Extant Fragment*	*Subject*
Empedocles (110.3)	μάλα πάντα δι᾽ *αἰῶνος* παρέσονται	Well-grounded thoughts have "lifelong" establishment in human mind.
Empedocles (129.6)	δέκ᾽ ἀνθρώπων καί τ᾽ εἴκοσιν *αἰώνεσσιν*	Human "generations" (indirect ref. to Pythagoras).
Empedocles (21.12; 23.8)	θεοὶ *δολιχαίωνες*.	The gods have "eternal life" highest in honor.
Empedocles (115.2)	θεῶν ψήφισμα παλαιόν, *ἀίδιον*.	The divine decree of necessity is "everlasting" and sealed by broad oaths.
Heraclitus (29)	κλέος *ἀέναον* θνητῶν	Human have to search for "everlasting" glory which is preferable than mortal things.
Heraclitus (52)	*αἰὼν* παῖς ἐστι παίζων, πεσσεύων·	Human "lifetime" is a child that plays.
Melissus (4)	ἀρχήν τε καὶ τέλος ἔχον οὐδὲν οὔτε *ἀίδιον* οὔτε ἄπειρόν ἐστιν	Things with beginning and end in Time are not "everlasting" nor infinite (like Being).
Melissus (7(i))	*ἀίδιόν* ἐστι καὶ ἄπειρον	Being is "everlasting," infinite, one and all homogenous.

The above fragments (DK) are supplemented by a series of later testimonies.[55]

sources throughout *Ennead* III.7. Parmenides' terminology along with Plato's is so evident that Steven Strange came to the conclusion that Plotinus' discussion of eternity is more a commentary on Parmenides than on Plato, though Plato himself is of course dependent on Parmenides fr. 8 at *Timaeus* 37e.[58]

Second, Plotinus refers to the Pythagorean theory of time as related to the heaven and the cosmic sphere in *Ennead* III.7.2.1–4. The Pythagoreans are clearly echoed some chapters later in 7.24–25.

Third, Plotinus refers directly to Heraclitus in *Ennead* II.1.2.10–12, and the everlasting flux of the heavenly bodies by alluding to the image of the Heraclitean sun in fr. 6. The latter passage can be clearly related to *Ennead* V.1.9.3–5, and particularly to the reference to Heraclitus' everlasting flux of

Table 4.3.
Cosmological Fragments of Time

Presocratic (fr.)	*Extant Fragment*	*Subject*
Pherecydes (1)	Ζὰς μὲν καὶ *Χρόνος* ἦσαν ἀεὶ καὶ Χθονίη	Time is an everlasting self-generative cosmic principle.
Anaximander (1)	κατὰ τὴν τοῦ *χρόνου* τάξιν	Time is the preserver and regulator of the Cosmos.
Pythagoreans (33)	τοῦ ὅλου κίνησιν εἶναί φασιν [τὸν χρόνον], οἱ δὲ τὴν σφαῖραν αὐτήν Πυθαγόρας τὸν *χρόνον* τὴν σφαῖραν τοῦ περιέχοντος εἶναι.	Time is the motion of the heavenly sphere.
Pythagoreans (34)	*χρόνος* = ἀριθμός	Time marks the time-periods of human life.
Pythagoreans (37)	ἄστρον δὲ τὴν γῆν ἔλεγον ὡς ὄργανον καὶ αὐτὴν *χρόνου*	Earth is an instrument of Time.
Xenophanes (18)	*χρόνωι* ζητοῦντες ἐφευρίσκουσιν ἄμεινον	The process in Time reveals the hidden knowledge of things.
Melissus (7)	ἐν τῶι παντὶ *χρόνωι*	Nothing is changing in the whole of Time.
Empedocles (7.29, 110.8)	περιπλομένοιο *χρόνοιο*	The Everlasting Recurrence of Time.
Empedocles (30.2)	τελειομένοιο *χρόνοιο*	The fulfilment of Time.
Empedocles (115.7)	διὰ *χρόνου* εἴδεα θνητῶν	Mortal forms are in continuous change through Time.

Fragments have DK numbering.

the bodies.[59] Keeping in mind these references, we can proceed to the comparative analysis of these three Presocratic theories in the *Enneads*.

4.4 THE TIMELESSNESS OF BEING

One of the most important contributions of Plotinus' account of eternity is a complete etymological analysis of αἰών at the sixth chapter of *Ennead* III.7.

With his etymological analysis, Plotinus for the first time in Greek thought removes any durational notion from the concept of eternity by clarifying the difference between the "always" (ἀεί) of eternity and the "always" (ἀεί) of time. According to Plotinus, the true nature of eternity has to be examined before temporal duration. His discussion is mentioned in advance at the end of the fourth chapter of the same treatise when Plotinus gives the etymology of the word (4.42–3). Plotinus reaches this conclusion after showing that the essence of the intelligible being is not only complete in terms of a *whole having all the intelligible beings present to it*, but also in *not having any deficiency and never having any nonbeing present to it* (4.37–43). This statement is an absolutely necessary theoretical presupposition of the intelligible being in order to be eternal: *being "always existing" and never having any deficiency or nonbeing added in it.*

For Plotinus, "always" refers to the eternal intelligible nature and clearly does not imply any duration. In the case of eternity, ἀεί refers to the self-sufficient unextended power of the intelligible world containing the whole simultaneously, without any durational connotation as in the case of time. For Plotinus, "being" (ὄν) and the "always being" (ἀεὶ ὄν) are one and the same, and the "always being" is identified with the Platonic True Being (ἀληθῶς ὄν). Here is the key passage:

> For "always" is perhaps not being used in its strict sense [in the case of eternity], but it is used to indicate the imperishable, and this could mislead the soul into imagining an increase of extension, and moreover one that was never going to give out. It would perhaps have been better to have used just the word "being." But even though "being" was sufficient to indicate substance, since people also thought that becoming was substance, it was necessary to add "always," so that what was being said could be understood. For "being" is not something different from "always being," just as a philosopher and a true philosopher are not different. But since there is also the pretence of philosophy, the word "true" was added. Thus, also "always" was added to "being," so that we say "always being." Hence this must be understood as meaning "truly being," and the "always" must be contracted into an unextended power that in no way requires anything beyond what it already possesses: it possesses the whole. [III.7.6.23–36; trans. McGuire and Strange]

Actually, Plotinus' etymological derivation of αἰών from ἀεὶ ὄν derives from Aristotle's *De Caelo* 279a125–28, where Aristotle points out not only that αἰών denotes "immortality" (ἀθάνατος), "divinity" (θεῖος), and the "everlastingness of being" (αἰεὶ εἶναι):[60]

> As a matter of fact, the name of eternity possessed a divine significance for the ancients. For the fulfilment which includes the time of life of any creature, outside of which no natural development can fall, has been called eternity (αἰών). On the same principle the fulfilment of the whole heaven, the fulfilment which includes all time and infinity, is eternity (αἰών)—a name based upon "always being," "immortal" and "divine." [*De Caelo* 279a25–28; trans. Stocks modified]

According to some modern scholars, Plotinus in the previous passage 4.37–43 and mainly at 6.23–36 seems to have in mind not only this Aristotelian passage, but also the whole of Aristotle's discussion.[61] But what has not been noted is that Aristotle says at the beginning of the passage that his etymology is the traditional one, and that the name of αἰών seems to have a divine significance for the ancients.

Who are the ancients who provide us with this etymology? Does Plotinus' etymology in III.7.4.37–43, and 6.23–36 refer only to Aristotle, or does he have in mind an older traditional etymological definition? Unfortunately, neither Aristotle nor Plotinus are more specific. The only assumption that can be made derives from the text that follows in *De Caelo* regarding Aristotle's discussion on the generation and destruction of the perceptible world (279a30–280a34). At 279b12–17, Aristotle maintains that there are two distinct theories on the generation of the cosmos: one speaks of an eternal generation and the other of a natural formation liable to destruction. According to Aristotle (279b16–17), the philosophers who support the "theory of destruction" are Empedocles and Heraclitus, and they also maintain that there is an alteration in the destructive process in an endless continuation. Some lines later, and in the same context, Aristotle refers to Plato's *Timaeus* (28a27–34). Criticizing Plato's account of the heaven, Aristotle sees him as the philosopher who accepts both that something which is not generated can be destroyed and that something which is generated persists unaffected. For Aristotle, Plato in the *Timaeus* supports the claim that the heaven, even if it *was* generated, will nevertheless exist in "everlasting time" (ἀεὶ χρόνον). Can we conclude from the above passages that Aristotle, in the definition of αἰὼν, had in mind Plato, Heraclitus, Empedocles and perhaps some other Presocratics? This hypothesis can be justified by returning to Plato' theory of eternity, Philolaus' eternal continuance, and Parmenides' timelessness of Being.

4.4.1 Philolaus' Eternal Continuance and Plato's Eternity of the Forms

Plato's theory of eternity is clearly outlined in *Timaeus* 37e–38b.[62] In this passage, Plato distinguishes eternity from time as referring to different ontological realms: eternity to the world of being, time to the world of becoming.

Plato's discussion focuses on the "forms of time" and how far they can be applied to eternal, changeless, and motionless being. Temporal forms such as past, present, and future tenses are perceptible motions, and as such they can be used only in the realm of perceptible becoming that unfolds in temporality. The realm of the Forms transcends perceptible motion and change; for "true being" only a timeless "is" (ἔστιν) can be applied to its nature. Hence, Plato excludes temporality from being by denying any perceptible change and motion to its essential nature. True Being is always changeless and motionless, with no spatial transitions and temporal divisions; only the Forms participate in an eternal nature.

With the *Timaeus*, Plato introduces a new philosophical meaning for αἰών. T. M. Robinson has discussed this novelty and he analyzed the use of the words ἀίδιος, αἰώνιος, and διαιώνιος in the dialogue.[63] He observes that whereas the term ἀίδιος is well known from Homer, the terms αἰώνιος (*Timaeus*, 37d3), and διαιώνιος (*Timaeus*, 38b8; 39e2) are originally Platonic and both are used to describe the eternal realm of the Forms and indeed the adjective αἰώνιος derives from the word αἰών. Based on this alteration, Plato seems to transform the original meaning of the term αἰών from "long space of time" to that of "eternity."

Significantly, the only Preplatonic extant occurrence of the term αἰώνιος appears in Philolaus' fragments 23, 21.7, and 21.14. Fragment 23[64] is quoted by Iamblichus *in Nicomachi arithmeticam introductionem* 10.22[65] in a series of ancient definitions of "number," including some dubious attributions to Thales, Pythagoras, Eudoxus, and Hippasus (*in Nicomach*, 10.8 ff.). For Iamblichus, Philolaus defines "number" as the controlling and self-generated bond of the "eternal continuance" (αἰωνίας διαμονῆς) of the things in the cosmos. According to C. A. Huffman, Philolaus' fragment 23 is spurious since all the vocabulary used has no parallel before Plato and Aristotle.[66] On the other hand, the vocabulary of fr. 23 fits almost perfectly with fr. 21.4–7 quoted by Stobaeus *Eclogae* I.20.2.[67] But, as in the case of fr. 23, Huffman regards fr. 21 as spurious for two reasons: first because of its anachronistic vocabulary, and second because of its irrelevant context; the emphasis on the eternity of the cosmos both in fr. 21 and fr. 23 is not genuine to the thought of Philolaus who mainly refers to generation.[68] For Huffman, therefore, the word αἰώνιος remains originally Platonic. In all probability, Iamblichus in fr. 23 and Stobaeus in fr. 21 used a technical vocabulary strongly influenced by the Platonic tradition.

But, *contra* Huffman, the linguistic similarity between the two fragments of Philolaus is so striking that it cannot be ignored. The possibility that the word αἰώνιος could exist before Plato in the vocabulary of Philolaus cannot be excluded. Philolaus' "eternal continuance" (αἰωνίας διαμονῆς) seems to be an expression of special significance since it appears verbatim twice in

Syrianus (*in Aristotelis metaphysica commentaria*, 123.6, and 142.24), and once in Proclus (*in Timaeus* I.239.2). Syrianus attributes the phrase to Philolaus as well as to other Pythagoreans. Proclus quotes "eternal continuance" in a work devoted to Plato's *Timaeus* and especially in a passage distinguishing temporal and eternal everlastingness. It is noteworthy, that Iamblichus, Proclus and Syrianus were frequently influenced by some pseudo-Pythagorean sources and, as Huffman himself notes, the term διαμονή is found in the pseudo-Pythagorean writings of Ocellus and the spurious report of Pythagorean doctrines by Alexander Polyhistor preserved by Diogenes Laertius.[69]

Thus, even if διαμονή has pseudo-Pythagorean origins rather than being original to Philolaus, this is not the case for αἰώνιος. Philolaus is aware of the concept of everlastingness as shown in fragment 6.[70] This fragment connects back to fr. 21.21 where the cosmos is presented as "the everlasting activity of God and generation." As Philolaus says,[71] God is the one leader and ruler of all things, an eternal being (θεός, εἷς, ἀεὶ ὤν) abiding immobile, selfsame, and different from all others.[72] This apocalyptic account prefigures not only Plato's conception of divinity, stability, and the immobility of the Forms, but also the Aristotelian etymology of eternity. From these considerations, it could be assumed that Philolaus or some other Pythagoreans may have influenced Plato's theory of eternity. In fact, Plato's contact with Pythagoreans, and especially Philolaus, Eurytus, and Archytas, is well known.[73] Thus, it can be supposed that Plato echoes with αἰώνιος an earlier Pythagorean notion of eternity and that Plato's contribution lies more in the expansion of αἰώνιος to διαιώνιος. The term αἰώνιος seems to be a Preplatonic term to express the everlastingness of the Cosmos which was later used in the metaphysical terminology of Plato to denote the eternity of the Forms in the *Timaeus*.

At the other end of the spectrum, Tarán rejects any technical terms in the *Timaeus*.[74] But, *contra* Tarán, even if Plato does not distinguish *explicitly* the eternity of Forms from the temporality of becoming, he still distinguishes the two realms *essentially*. I therefore intend to follow Robinson's threefold distinction of eternity in the *Timaeus* relating to: (i) the Forms, (ii) the Divine Craftsman, and (iii) the Receptacle.[75] The world of Forms and the world of becoming participate in the eternal nature in different ways. The realm of the Forms is timelessly eternal, while the realm of becoming is everlasting in endless temporal duration. However, there is considerable debate on whether Plato's conception of αἰών in *Timaeus* 37e–38b refers to a non-durational eternity of the Forms, or to an eternity in which the Forms endure everlastingly. Initially, the former position, which is regarded as the traditional one, was held by H. Cherniss,[76] the latter by F. M. Cornford[77] followed and supported by J. Whittaker.[78] In both approaches, the term under investigation is that of ἀεί.

Pace Cornford and Whittaker, the distinction between the ἀεί of becoming and the ἀεί of the Forms is also observable at *Timaeus* 28a. There it is said that, whereas True Being *always is*, ungenerated, that which belongs in the world of becoming *always comes-to-be* and *never* is a real being itself. The former is an unchanging intelligible nature which is grasped by reason and intelligence, the latter a changing sensible nature which is grasped by opinion and perception. Likewise, in the *Republic* (527b), the knowledge of the ἀεὶ ὄν is attainable only through the science of geometry. Geometry leads the human soul upwards to philosophical truth which describes what *always is* and not what *comes into being* and *passes away*. The true nature of the human soul is divine, immortal, and *always is* related to the nature of True Being and its stability (*Republic*, 611e–612a). Thus, any discipline such as geometry or mathematics which leads the soul upwards to the eternal knowledge of the Forms, refines and purifies it so that it may reach to its truest intelligible self and wisdom beyond temporality. Similarly in the *Phaedo* (79a), Plato distinguishes between beings that are *always* complete and beings that are *never* complete. In the light of the *Timaeus*, the former must be regarded as eternal, the latter as temporal. As Plato states in 38a3–4, the Forms are the intelligible beings which have the characteristic to remain *always* the same in themselves beyond change and motion. In this context, the word ἀεί, even if it implies duration in its primary sense, when it refers to the Forms must be regarded as beyond or in contrast to temporal becoming. For this reason, Plato argues in the *Phaedo*, 79d that the soul through self-investigation becomes connatural with that which *always exists* and passes into the reality of the Forms. That for Plato the state of True Being is the aim of philosophy is further illustrated from the *Symposium*. In Diotima's speech, the philosopher must be guided by the love of stable-real beauty which *always is*: as with the other Forms, intelligible beauty is ever the same, unchangeable, always one in form (*Symposium*, 211a–d).

From the above considerations, it may be the case that Plato fails to clarify whether the eternity of the Forms is durational or timeless not so much because of his unawareness of the problem but rather because of the lack of the appropriate metaphysical terminology. It is important to mention that Plato himself recognizes that his account is not completely accurate in the comment: "I don't suppose this is a good time right now to be too meticulous about these matters" (*Timaeus*, 38b3–4). Here Plato suggests a promise of a more exact analysis that is never fulfilled and seems to be aware that he is using an unsuitable "temporal" terminology to describe the eternity of the Forms. By using the word ἀεί of the realm of Forms, he undoubtedly applies a durational term to something which transcends temporal becoming. But in the *Timaeus* as well as in other dialogues, he seems to be more interested in distinguishing between the realm of becoming and that of the Forms and for him this discrimination between the two natures is more important than an accurate verbal description of them. Finally, it should not be forgotten that the whole dialogue in the *Timaeus* is a likely story and not an accurate account. For these reasons, Plato's theory of αἰών must be regarded as involving the idea of timelessness, but without a complete justification of it. However, this idea originates in Parmenides' timeless conception of Being.

4.4.2 Parmenides' Timelessness of Being

Despite the fact that Parmenides never uses αἰών or ἀίδιος, the concept of "timeless eternity" originates in his radical philosophical thought. As we have seen,[79] Parmenides envisages in his poem an indivisible and indestructible Being, existing changeless and immovable in a timeless present, all together in atemporal completeness, unity, and indivisibility (fr. 8.5–6):

> οὐδέ ποτ' ἦν οὐδ' ἔσται, ἐπεὶ νῦν ἔστιν ὁμοῦ πᾶν ἕν, συνεχές·
> It never was nor will be, since it is now all-together, one, continuous.

Prima facie these lines from the Way of Truth (fragment 8.1–49) exclude any temporality from Being: it *never* existed at any time in the "past" and *never* will exist at any time in the "future." *Being exists complete in a timeless present outside any temporal distinction.*

In fact, Parmenides' fragment 8.5–6 is usually regarded as a reply to Heraclitus' everlastingness of the cosmos in fragment 30 and in general to Ionian accounts of becoming. Parmenides' statement "it never was nor will be, since it is now all-together" (fr. 8.5–6) can be clearly contrasted with Heraclitus' thesis "it always was and is and will be" (fr. 30). Whereas Heraclitus' cosmos *always* "was," "is" and "will be" in the process of generation and destruction through the work of an *ever*-living fire, Parmenides' Being *never* "was" nor "will be," but is timeless, all together in a state of changeless unity where no generation and no destruction is taking place. Whereas Heraclitus' cosmos is self-generated (fr. 30), Parmenides' Being is not generated at all (fr. 8.6–21).

The key term that differentiates Parmenides' fr. 8.5–6 and Heraclitus' fr. 30 is that of ἀεί. While Heraclitus uses it twice to express the everlastingness of the cosmos as well as its ever-living fiery substance (*ἀεί*-ζωον), Parmenides omits ἀεί completely from his language in the extant fragments. Whereas Heraclitus' being subsists by an everlasting durational temporality, Parmenides' Being is sustained in a timeless non-durational atemporality. On the one hand, Heraclitus' Being refers to an A-series[80] *temporal present* (past → present → future), on the other, Parmenides' Being refers to a *timeless present*. Whereas for Heraclitus the universe is temporally divided into past, present, and future, for Parmenides Being is temporally undivided, having no past or future.[81]

Indeed, for Parmenides, the tenses of time are clearly denied and only a complete and timeless present of Being is accepted. This can be observed by his expression "it is now all-together" (νῦν ἔστιν ὁμοῦ πᾶν). Some modern scholars such as D. Gallop and J. Barnes erroneously translate νῦν and ὁμοῦ πᾶν separately by inserting a comma after νῦν ἔστιν, contrary to the editions of the ancient MSS, particularly in the four assurances in Simplicius' original.[82] On the other hand, Tarán, Coxon, Conche, and Roussos take the two terms as interconnected; the word "now" has to be glossed by "all together."[83] The one term complements the other by manifesting both the completeness and the timelessness of Being. For Parmenides it is exactly the completeness of Being as well as its oneness and spatial continuity that explains its timelessness. With non-Being rejected Parmenides argues: *since there is no beginning or end in time, therefore there is no sequence in time of one thing after another, and therefore no change in Time exists.*

In particular, Parmenides in fragment 8.5–6 denies the temporality of Being, and proves its timelessness through the long argument put forward by the goddess in lines 6 to 21. Throughout these lines, Being is justified as timeless outside any temporal transition, generation or destruction. But what is the subject of this denial? I do not intend to follow the suggestions of some scholars that the unspecified subject ('it') in line 5 can be glossed as "whatever can be spoken or thought of,"[84] or more generally "whatever we inquire into."[85] Parmenides clearly states that the subject is Being (fr. 8.3), that is, "whatever there is," characterized by its predicates as "ungenerated," "imperishable," "entire," "unique," "unmoved," and "perfect" (fr. 8.3–4). But what exactly is the timeless nature of Being? On this question, different scholars provide different and contradictory answers.[86] The following is a listing of the main interpretations.

First, according to H. Fränkel,[87] L. Tarán,[88] and D. Gallop,[89] the aim of Parmenides' fragment is just to stress the impossibility of generation and destruction and not timelessness These scholars maintain that Parmenides speaks of an everlasting Being including a temporal duration in its nature. This idea of everlasting duration seems to be followed also by M. Schofield[90] and D. O' Brien[91] in claiming that Parmenides' subject is not already over or still to come. Moreover, Gallop finds Parmenides' argument of timelessness problematic for two reasons: first, because of the use of the temporal terms "now" (νῦν) and "continuous" (συνεχές) in his verses and second, because of the fact that the premise "since it is now, all together" is insufficient to disprove past and future existence; an inference from "x exists now, all together" to "x never existed in the past," or "x never will exist in the future" is invalid.[92]

The second interpretation still keeps the concept of duration but in different terms. According to this interpretation, even if Parmenides denies an

A-series temporality of past and future, he does not exclude the idea of a static B-series temporality based on the concepts of "earlier" and "later."[93]

As a third view, Sorabji maintains his idea of a non-durational timeless Being.[94] Sorabji supports successfully the timelessness of Being via a thorough analysis of fr. 8.1–25 and especially Parmenides' argument of atemporality and indestructibility at lines 8.6–21. In the background of Sorabji's interpretation lies G. E. L. Owen's influential article "Plato and Parmenides on the timeless present." Sorabji goes a step further by omitting even the "present" from his interpretation.

Fourth, Owen argues that Parmenides postulates in his words the idea of a "timeless present." According to this view, the word νῦν ἔστιν (now is) in line 5 denotes an enduring present outside past or future,[95] but still Parmenides does not succeed in excluding present from Being. Owen supports his thesis by connecting fr. 8.5–6 with fr. 8.29–30: "remaining the same and in the same state, it [the Being] lies by itself and remains thus where it is perpetually"; the stability of Being in the present is a corollary of its timelessness.

A fifth view, that of Barnes, states that Parmenides' fragment speaks about a single instant in time *which is all the time there is*.[96] This is similar to a sixth view ascribed to Ammonius (*in Interpretatione* 133.15–27) which refers to a "sizeless present." According to his argument, *since the past is no longer and the future not yet then what remains is a "single eternal now."*[97]

J. Whittaker offers a seventh interpretation by cutting across the views of "timelessness" and "enduring present."[98] As Whittaker observes, since for the Greek mind before Plutarch "time is measured time" (a system of days, months, and years), then Parmenides' denial goes against a temporal system of measurement but not against an abstract concept of time.[99] Whittaker states, and Sorabji follows him here, that the denial of time cannot justify the concept of eternity,[100] for it cannot be proved that something outside temporality can be characterized as eternal. For J. Whittaker, and on this Sorabji disagrees, Parmenides' denial of time must be understood simply as a denial of measured time and not as a denial of duration of an abstract time. Yet it can be argued that in both cases timelessness is still included in Parmenides' thought, and his denial of past and future inevitably leads to the denial of an A-series flowing time. But it has to be admitted that justification of timelessness requires a special kind of metaphysics that was not available at the time of Parmenides. For this reason, Whittaker argues that Parmenides cannot possibly have propounded the doctrine of non-durational eternity.[101]

Finally, W. Kneale maintains a radical interpretation of fr. 8.5–6.[102] Kneale's justification is fr. 8.41–44 where Parmenides compares Being to the bulk of a spherical ball which is equally poised in every direction from its center. He adopts the hypothesis that this view originated with the Pythagoreans since a sphere has no beginning or end in time and every single point of its finite volume can be equally characterized as past, present, and future within a continuous enduring present. Consequently, the tenses of time can be easily telescoped within a single point and so eliminated by the cyclical nature of Being.

The above interpretations could be further reduced to three different categories: Parmenides' Being is (1) everlasting, or (2) timeless, or (3) at a state of enduring present. The first implies everlasting duration, while the second denies it completely. The third view allows a special kind of enduring temporality encompassed in a single present or instant. Of these interpretations, the "timeless" option, should be accepted for the following reasons.

The terms νῦν and συνεχές show Parmenides' linguistic limitations in expressing timelessness rather than unawareness of the subject, and they are the best possible expressions to denote timelessness and indivisibility. If these terms are taken together with the unity and completeness given in the summary at fragment 8.5–6, the result is a stable, timeless, complete, and unified Being. The "now" of Being is not the temporal now but a timeless "now" that involves the Being's oneness, completeness, and indestructibility. Paraphrasing Parmenides' words, we can reconstruct his thought as follows: since temporality implies incompleteness, multiplicity, and divisibility and Being *has to be* one and indivisible; Being must inevitably be conceived of as timeless, outside any tenses of past (was) or future (will be). Being's timelessness is encapsulated within an undivided present; a timeless *now* which denotes neither a single instant, nor the *now* in temporality but the *now* of simultaneity.

Parmenides' timelessness of Being could be further supported through the complementary reasoning of fr. 8.6–21. The kernel of Parmenides' argument in 8.6–21 is the following: *since non-being is impossible then generation and destruction are also impossible. Therefore, since generation and destruction are impossible no beginning or end in time is possible for what there is.* Parmenides' argument starts from generation and offers a dilemma: if there is generation for Being, then either Being arose from *what-is-not* [Case 1], or it arose from *what-is* [Case 2].[103]

Case 1 is impossible for two reasons: first, since it is inconceivable that anything is-not, then it is impossible for Being to originate from what-is-not (fr. 8.7–9); non-Being cannot be the source of Being (cf. fr. 8.12); second, if Being arose from what-is-not what compulsion was there for it to arise later rather than earlier? (fr. 8.9–10).[104] Parmenides maintains that a generated Being "needs" (8.9: χρέος) necessarily to contain within it some principle of development sufficient to explain its generation.[105] But what principle can derive from what-is-not? Consequently, from the above Parmenides concludes that Being "must either be all at once or not at all" (8.11). But since what-is-not is rejected then the only possible way is that what-is is "all at once."

Case 2 is rejected because of the perfection and completeness of Being. Since there is nothing else besides what there is, it cannot be generated from anything else besides itself (fr. 8.36–38). "Justice" (δίκη) is the principle that holds Being fast around its fetters and never allows generation or destruction (fr. 8.13–15). Being is "immobile" within the limits of "strong necessity," "without beginning," and "without end," changeless "in the bonds of great chains" (fr. 8.26–32). Because of Necessity, Being remains "the same and in the same state" lying firmly by itself, "remaining perpetually in sameness" (8.29–30). For Parmenides, the immobility and stability of Being ensures its completeness and perfection (8.31–32). Therefore, since Being is perfect and complete then there can be nothing else besides itself to come-to-be or pass away, start or finish.

Based on the above, the whole issue for Parmenides is between two possible ways: *it is or is not* (8.16). But since the way of non-Being has been denied then only the way of Being is permitted. From this Parmenides argues for timelessness: *since generation implies a temporal start in the past and destruction a temporal end in the future and since "past" refers to "what is not" and "future" to "what is not yet" then both temporal tenses describe non-Being and never Being*. Any temporal tenses are contradictory for Being and so only a timeless present can refer to it.

Significantly, the timelessness of Being can be also justified by Parmenides' words in 8.36–38:

> οὐδὲ χρόνος ἐστὶν ἢ ἔσται ἄλλο πάρεξ τοῦ ἐόντος, ἐπεὶ τό γε Μοῖρ᾽ ἐπέδησεν οὖλον ἀκίνητόν τ᾽ ἔμεναι·
> And time is not nor will be another thing alongside Being, since this was bound fast by fate to be entire and changeless.[106] [trans. Coxon]

With regard to the text, according to A. H. Coxon, the two variants that Simplicius provides are not variants at all; Coxon reconstructs, and Conche follows, Parmenides 8.36 as οὐδὲ χρόνος ἐστὶν ἢ ἔσται and justifies the timelessness of Being provided in fragment 8.5–6.[107] On the other hand, other scholars such as Diels-Kranz, Taràn, and Gallop change the text in οὐδὲν γὰρ <ἢ> ἔστιν ἢ ἔσται by keeping vague the idea of timelessness.[108] H. Diels-Kranz admits that Simplicius' reading οὐδ᾽ εἰ χρόνος is both metrically correct and fits the general context of timelessness based on the perfection of Being, but not the context of the particular verses.[109] Taràn and Gallop deny completely the idea of timelessness in the text. But, in my view, the latter readings are based more on a misinterpretation of Parmenides' thought than on an accurate reconstruction of Simplicius' original transcription.[110] As M. Conche asks, "Pourquoi en ce cas, préférée le οὐδ᾽ εἰ χρόνος de *Physics* 146, quitte à le corriger?"[111] Indeed, since verse 8.36 is both metrically correct and philosophically consistent with the Parmenidean concept of timelessness in 8.5–6 why would Simplicius' reading be wrong? As Coxon puts it, "it seems certain that what Simplicius had in his manuscript of Parmenides is what he copied in his careful transcription of the whole text of fr. 8.1–52."[112] Coxon simply corrects οὐδ' εἰ χρόνος to οὐδὲ χρόνος in order to remove any ambiguity from the text. The same form of expression can be found also in Aristotle's *De Caelo* 279a12 (οὐδὲ χρόνος ἐστὶν ἔξω τοῦ οὐρανοῦ), as well as in Plotinus' *Ennead* IV.3.25.14–15 (οὐδὲ χρόνος, ἀλλ' αἰὼν περὶ τὸ ὄν). The latter reference echoes Parmenides' timelessness of Being and provides us with an interesting reading which will be evaluated in the next chapter. Finally, Simplicius' quotation of the negative οὐδέ in this fragment can be also justified by the repetitive usage of the same word in fragment 8.5–6.

Thus, Parmenides' elimination of time in fragments 8.5–6, 6–21, and 8.36–37 results in the timelessness of Being; Being is beyond any divisions of time since it is essentially indivisible and changeless. Duration must be excluded since duration presupposes some kind of process or transition which would reduce the perfection and completeness of Being. On this basis, temporal duration is also impossible since any transition from "prior" to "posterior," "earlier" to "later" are eliminated by the immovability of Being. Consequently, the only possible way for Parmenides' Being is that of a timeless eternity. Timelessness, along with indivisibility, indestructibility, and immovability, signifies the completeness, unity, and perfection of Being.

Parmenides' timelessness of Being was not, however, continued in the Presocratic tradition. Melissus of Samos, the third important figure of the Eleatic movement, agrees with Parmenides' main arguments on the indestructibility, immobility, indivisibility, oneness, completeness, changelessness, and perfection of Being, but he adopts a different viewpoint on atemporality and finitude of Being. While Parmenides' Being is timeless and complete, Melissus' Being is everlasting and without limits. Melissus' modification of Parmenides' thought is prima facie observable in his philosophical language. In contrast to Parmenides, Melissus frequently uses ἀεί[113] and ἀίδιος[114] to denote the everlastingness of Being. Whereas Parmenides' Being "never was" in the past, "never will be" in the future, but "is now" in a timeless present, Melissus' Being "is" and "always was," and "always shall be" in an everlasting duration (fr. 2.2). For Melissus, the denial of ex nihilo creation results in a Being which is eternal not in terms of Parmenides' timelessness but in terms of an enduring presence in continuous everlastingness beyond generation or destruction (fr. 1.7–8). Since Being is ungenerated, it has no temporal beginning, and, since it is indestructible, it has no end (fr. 2.4). Therefore, since Being neither began nor ended, it *always was* and *always shall be* everlastingly. Due to its everlastingness, Being is entire (fr. 8.38), since what is not entire cannot always be (fr. 2.6). On the basis of the everlastingness of Being, Melissus deduces its lack of spatial limit. Since Being is everlastingly eternal with no beginning nor end in temporality, it has *necessarily* to be without spatial limits (fr. 3).[115] Melissus' limitlessness of Being is the second crucial point where he differs from Parmenides' fr. 4.[116]

Despite the evident difference between the two forms of eternity in the Eleatic tradition, some modern scholars attribute the concept of everlastingness to Parmenides back from Melissus' account.[117] But Melissus and Parmenides infer almost the same attributes of Being from the denial of non-Being, yet Melissus' argument on the infiniteness of Being is in strong contrast to Parmenides' concept of the finitude of Being. While Parmenides' Being is finite *like* the bulk of a well-rounded sphere equally balanced about the center in every direction (fr. 8.42–49), Melissus' Being is with no shape and limits. Being is *like* a sphere, but, being careful in his language, Parmenides does not say that it is actually *spherical* or *finite* in the sense of having a spatial limit. Parmenides' Being as *complete* and *balanced* does not logically entail a spatial boundary. Melissus goes further on this and in denying *is-not* spatially to Being argued that there has therefore to be no limit spatially. Thus, whereas for Parmenides there is no *is-not* temporally to limit *is*, Melissus claims that no *is-not* spatially limits *is*.

Keeping in mind these considerations we can return to Plotinus' theory of time and the timelessness of the Plotinian Being.

4.4.3 Plotinus' Timelessness of Eternity

In *Ennead* III.7.6.21–6, Plotinus, as has been mentioned, points out that the usage of ἀεί in the case of αἰών is not in the strict sense, but should be taken as the only term which can denote the incorruptibility of the intelligible being. In this case, Plotinus recognizes the metaphysical limitations of language. When a "temporal" term such as ἀεί is used to describe a timeless nature, it misleads the human mind into imagining a continuous expansion of something which is essentially incorruptible and non-expansible. For this reason, Plotinus suggests that only an unconditional being can be better used to describe intelligible nature. But, again, since being can also mislead us into adopting "the being" of becoming, then "always" was necessarily added to 'being' in order to discriminate the 'being of becoming' from the 'being of eternity' (6.23–36). Arguing from this passage, Sorabji correctly points out that Plotinus' explanation of the eternal realm as having no duration is a successful way of resolving the ambiguity left by Plato at *Timaeus* 38a concerning the question whether eternity is timeless or has an everlasting duration.[118]

But, as well as this clarification, Plotinus also aims to highlight the limitations of language in defining subtle metaphysical terms. The word ἀεί, even when it has a particular meaning, can still be used conventionally to describe different metaphysical and ontological qualifications. While ἀεί in χρόνος implies *temporal duration*, ἀεί in αἰών implies *timeless being*. Within the same framework we can place the word νῦν, "now." While the temporal "now" indicates the present in contrast with other temporal tenses, the eternal "now" signifies a timeless present.[119] In other words, whereas the now of eternity refers to the simultaneous timeless presence of the intelligible being, the now of time indicates temporal present as a joining link between the tenses of past and future.

Within this framework, Parmenides' timelessness of Being corresponds to Plotinus' timelessness of Intellect. For Plotinus every act of intelligence is timeless (IV.4.1.12: ἄχρονος πᾶσα νόησις). The "real being" involves eternity and not time (II.5.3.8), therefore the intelligible nature is characterized by the lack of any temporal tenses. Eternity possesses all things at once, in a partless completion, as if all things were centralized in a single point and never outflowing from this point, but remaining in the same state of a timeless and changeless existence, always being in the present (III.7.3.18–22). But again the "present" (παρόν) of eternity is not the same as the present of time, and the tenses of time cannot be applied to the nature of eternity. No past nor future, no was nor will-be, no previous nor afterwards are attributes that can describe the eternal nature (III.7.3.25). Every notion of change, becoming or passing-away is absolutely incompatible with the eternal nature. For Plotinus, the eternal being exists in a state of timeless present, in unity and stability, outside any succession of the tenses of time (3.34–35: μήτε ἦν, μήτε ἔσται, ἀλλ᾽ ἔστι μόνον). The latter phrase is clearly an expression of Parmenides' fr. 8.5–6.

On this, as for Parmenides' Being, the timelessness of Plotinus' eternity stems from the completeness of Being (III.7.5.1–7). This higher Being is not just "always being" (ἀεὶ ὄν) but "always complete being" (ἀεὶ ὅλον ὄν) (III.7.5.12–18). In respect of a nature which is always the same, eternity does not involve any sort of succession from "one thing to another," and, since succession is impossible, eternity cannot be extended, unrolled, prolonged, or stretched-out (6.15–17). Consequently, "before" and "after" are also impossible and therefore temporality must be excluded from eternity (6.17–18). For Plotinus, eternal being only *is* and this unconditional *is* describes the essence of the intelligible life: αἰών. Eternity is a nature that is not going to be but already *is* in a perfect condition, without beginning and end, unaffected, altogether in a timeless present; a nature which self-includes everything in perfection because there is nothing other than itself (3.30–35).

4.5 THE ETERNAL LIFE OF INTELLECT

In the third chapter of *Ennead* III.7, Plotinus defines eternity as "the life which exists around being, all together and full, completely without extension" (3.36–38).[120] For Plotinus, αἰών and the intelligible nature are both majestic and self-inclusive (III.7.2.5–10). But even if eternity is something majestic and Intellect is conceived of as the highest degree of majesty and beauty, we should not confuse both notions and conclude that eternity and Intellect are identical (2.15–17). Equally, concerning inclusiveness, since the intelligible nature includes its whole "in parts" and eternity includes the intelligible "whole all at once and not as a part of eternity," then there is here a different kind of inclusiveness. While eternity includes the intelligible substance simultaneously, every intelligible being is eternal in virtue of eternity. This logical consequence leads Plotinus inevitably to search for the identity of eternity in the Platonic doctrine of the five Platonic Genera described in the *Sophist* 254d–e.[121] Plotinus suggests that as long as time exists in virtue of motion then probably eternity will exist in virtue of rest. But if eternity is identified with "rest," we must then clarify whether the identification refers "simply to rest,"[122] or "to rest which resides in substance."[123] Plotinus argues that none of the above identifications are valid.

Eternity does not derive accidentally from something external but belongs to and originates from the intelligible nature and manifests the very substance of the intelligible realm (III.7.4.1–6). Eternity pertains to an intelligible nature where all the primary and blessed beings constantly exist. It has a primary existence, and, as a primary being, must necessarily exist among the primaries in the higher ontological level of them. Eternity, Beauty, and Truth belong to and derive from the primaries,[124] being self-defined and self-identical in accordance solely to their nature.[125] The intelligible world as a whole, where αἰών is inherent, is a true whole, deficient in nothing, lacking in nothing, and unaffected in any way (4.12–37). Since nothing can happen contrary to the intelligible nature, then the eternal, primal, and blessed intelligible beings have no aspiration for the future, are already the whole of what they are, have a full life of their own, and seek nothing, since there is nothing that is going to be for them, nor that in which what is going to be can develop.

Thus, αἰών manifests the perfection of the intelligible world and this perfection derives from self-completeness, self-knowledge, self-inclusion and self-intellection of Intellect; Intellect encompasses all intelligibles in true and divine eternity (V.1.4.10–19). Hence, Plotinus identifies eternity in *Ennead* III.7.5.19–22 with a "God manifesting and revealing itself as it is."[126] This God is the true intelligible eternal being; a being that is imperturbable, the same and stable in its life. Since this being is imperturbable then his life is also imperturbable, "which is all at once, altogether fixed and without limitation or declination, resting in and towards the One" (III.7.11.1–5). Eternity is not just the substrate but as it were shines from the intelligible substrate (III.7.3.24–25), embracing the unity, stability, and order of the intelligible realm (VI.6.18.35–36; III.7.6.4–10).

Within this context, eternity signifies the life of "true being" (IV.3.25.15); eternity is a single life in simultaneous unity, selfsame and always without extension (IV.3.3.12–13). It is the form of intelligible life which manifests the inexhaustible activity of the intelligible realm; a self-thinking nature outside any otherness or difference. Eternity is a life all-together, always in a present state of being, unchanging, a nature which abides always in the same condition. Hence, eternity is a complete life and unlimited; unlimited in virtue of expending nothing of itself; a life which never gives out in becoming or change (IV.3.5.23–30). Thus, eternity is a life belonging in the essence of being, all at once, full and unextended.

Plotinus stresses the need not to confuse eternity with the everlastingness of time, or something unextended with something extended (I.5.7.16–31). Eternity is unextended, undivided, and timeless, it is the "life of eternity which is not made up of many times but is altogether from the whole of time." While "true being" lives in a single, timeless, and unextended present, time fragments the eternal presence of being in temporal tenses. That is the reason why time is called "the image of eternity"; since time intends to bring about the disappearance of what is permanent in eternity, by taking this permanence and destroying it through its own temporal dispersion. That is why well-being has to be searched for not in temporal life but in the eternal life of real being which remains in unity and stability.[127]

Now since the metaphysical association of Plotinus' eternity with the life of Intellect has been demonstrated, it is appropriate to turn to the Presocratic association of eternity with the concept of life. This association echoes Presocratic hylozoism and is found most significantly in Heraclitus and Empedocles.

4.5.1 Eternity in Heraclitus

Heraclitus' view of eternity is found in fragments 52 and 30. Fragment 52 is one of the most important surviving passages about the Presocratic αἰών, and it is preserved by Hippolytus in *Refutatio* IX.9 along with fragments 50 to 58.[128] According to this fragment, αἰών is personified as a child playing the ancient board game of πεσσεία. The language of the fragment is clearly poetic, and includes the common Heraclitean *motif* of rhythmical repetition: παῖς, παίζων, πεσσεύων. The context of the fragment is primarily cosmological, with an indirect criticism of Ephesian politics[129] and a reference to Heraclitus' misanthropy towards ordinary people who do not understand the real nature of things.[130] Not unexpectedly, the nature of the fragment is enigmatic—a riddle in typically obscure Heraclitean language. Due to this obscurity, there are many interpretations and various readings in both ancient authors and modern scholars, but the riddle remains unsolved. All the attempts to answer the riddle focus on three main questions related to the context of the fragment: Who is αἰών? What is the nature of the ancient board game? What is the kingship of the child?

With regard to the nature of αἰών, there are two suggested and probably interrelated interpretations. The αἰών is either (i) the symbolic personification of a divine deity or god, or (ii) an allegorical representation of human age, lifetime, or destiny. The former theological interpretation seems to be a common view in some ancient authors such as Hippolytus (the primary source for fr. 52), Lucian (*Vitarum Auctio*, 14),[131] Clement (*Paedagogus* I.21.4), *Plutarch* (*De E apud Delphos*, 393), Proclus (*in Timaeus* I.334.1), and Philo (*De Aeternitate Mundi*, 42).[132] For M. Marcovich, all these references are misinterpretations of fr. 52. Hippolytus draws an analogy between God, the Father of the world, and the Creator God-Son, and erroneously infers identification between αἰών and the God-Son. Likewise, Clement relates αἰών to Zeus, while Plutarch, Philo, and Proclus to the divine Craftsman or the Demiurge of the cosmos. Marcovich maintains that these testimonies contain either a Stoic identification of αἰών with Zeus, or an anachronistic projection in Heraclitus' thought forward to the Platonic Demiurge, or a misinterpretation of the Homeric child-image.[133] But the idea of a divine Creator who fashions the world is completely irrelevant to Heraclitus' philosophy, since in fragment 30 the cosmos is explicitly said not to be the external product of any human or divine activity.

On the other hand, the relationship between αἰών and Zeus should not be regarded as completely irrelevant to Heraclitus' thought. If we suppose that the αἰών of fragment 52 is related to the ever-living fire of fr. 30, and πῦρ is further related to "bright Zeus" (fr. 120), the thunder-ruler of everything (fr. 32), and the "one wise god" with the name of Zeus (fr. 64), then the connection between αἰών and Zeus is not absurd. Furthermore, the connection of Zeus to πῦρ can be found in Empedocles' identification of πῦρ with "bright Zeus" (fr. 6), and his reference to Zeus as King (fr. 128). If we were to risk correlating Heraclitus' αἰών child of fr. 52 with Empedocles' young girl playing with the time-instrument of the clepsydra in fr. 100, then the connection of αἰών with "time" personified in the figure of a god-child becomes even more important. The resemblance between Heraclitus and Empedocles leads to the possible conclusion that Heraclitus probably had in mind a correlative analogy between αἰών, πῦρ, and Ζεύς.[134] This means that Heraclitus' αἰών is not an abstract concept; it refers to a symbolic representation of a divine entity, a cosmic player, who controls with his game the destiny of the world. The cosmic player is represented by the double image of αἰών in the form of both an immature child and a mature and wise old man in order to show the cycles of human generations. This idea probably influenced Hellenistic and later images of αἰών.[135]

From this point of view, Heraclitus' αἰών is related to the traditional meaning of "lifetime," "human age," "generations," and "destiny." The lifetime translation and interpretation of αἰών is commonly followed by most modern scholars. Marcovich, for example, links αἰών to human age, but keeps the lifetime meaning, which is also followed by C. H. Kahn, M. R. Wright, and E. N. Roussos.[136] This is indeed Euripides' image of Μοῖρα as child (παῖς) of Χρόνος and Αἰών in *Heraclidae* 900. Euripides is probably influenced here by Heraclitus. Philo in *De vita Mosis* I.31 also echoes Heraclitus in saying that "chance" (τύχη) plays with human lives and Gregory Nazianzenus in *Carmina de se ipso* I.334.3 compares χρόνος to the game of πεσσεία.[137] But chance cannot be easily found in Heraclitus' thought since *logos* as the cosmic rhythm which underlies the world with measure and order, and eliminates chance or randomness. The image of the game in fragment 52 is more important for its structure and rules, which represent the Heraclitean order of the ἀεὶ *logos* (fr. 1), and for the skills of the player rather than for the chance of dice. This gives a backhanded political meaning to fr. 52, for whether or not ruling a city presupposes a man with skills and maturity, the King of the city behaves like an immature child who does not know how to play according to the correct rules of the game. For this reason fr. 52 would then link with the criticism of the leadership of Ephesus in fr. 121.

On the other hand, within a cosmological framework, in the background of Heraclitus' game lies the opposition between the everlastingness of the cosmos and the temporality of human lifetime. Whether αἰών is either a young child or an old king there remain two different but unified views of the same cosmic principle: πῦρ. The circular transformations of fire (fr. 31) mark a unity and everlasting circular continuity between life and death, awake and sleep, young and old (fr. 88). C. Kahn suggests that Heraclitus' πεσσεύων in fr. 52 has to be understood in the light of μεταπεσόντα, the "things transposed" in fr. 88. According to Kahn's suggestion, Heraclitus' image of the cosmos could be that of a playing field where a cosmic divine player moves pieces back and forth on a board where the pieces represent humans becoming old and young, living and dying, waking and sleeping. The view of human destiny as the subject of a game can also be found in Plato's *Laws* 903d where the πεσσευτής promotes a soul with a promising character to a better condition in order to meet the fate which it deserves. But, more importantly, it links fr.52 with Heraclitus' fragment 53 (the next one quoted by Hippolytus) where "war" (πόλεμος) is the father and king of all. The player in fr. 53 is now πόλεμος, playing with opposite forces and shows some as gods and others as men, some as slaves and others as free. In this fragment, the playing field becomes a battlefield of opposites where there is a general exchange, and some become winners and others losers (frs 90 and 36).

Finally, the game of αἰών represents the circular kindling and quenching self-generative process of ever-living fire (fr. 30). This cosmic process is endless like the continuous play of a child in fr. 52 who starts his game over and over again.[138] As Kahn puts it, the cosmological meaning of αἰών represents the "everlasting child," who remains forever youthful through his lifetime, playing the game of eternal kingship in a series of births and deaths across the generations.[139] It is the everlasting life of αἰών, personified in the unfailing vitality of the child, which keeps the universe in an eternal state of enduring becoming. The cosmos remains ever-new by the ever-living rekindling of its own fiery source. Heraclitus' game of αἰών is not the game of many players but the game of an individual player who plays with itself like the self-generative process of the ever-living fire, producing the whole cosmos by its own inner revolving harmony. Thus, αἰών in Heraclitus is connected to the Presocratic concept of life elaborated explicitly in Empedocles' philosophy.

4.5.2 Eternal Life in Empedocles

Empedocles' work is an invaluable source for our understanding of αἰών and χρόνος in early Greek philosophy. He is the only Presocratic who systematically uses within his poetic-philosophical context the words αἰών,[140] ἀίδιος,[141] and χρόνος,[142] as well as the ἀεί.[143] He also introduces the composite poetic words δολιχαίων[144] and μακραίων[145] to express the life (βίος) of *daimōns* and gods. It is noteworthy that δολιχαίων is unique in extant ancient Greek literature, while μακραίων can be found in Greek tragedy and later Greek philosophy.

Empedocles is the first Presocratic to relate eternity and time to life in a philosophical sense. He applies αἰών and χρόνος to three different ontological levels of life arranged in a hierarchical order: (1) the everlasting life of the divine and imperishable principles at the immortal level, (2) the long-lasting life of *daimōns* and gods at the level of soul, and (3) the temporal short-life of mortals at the level of temporal becoming.

According to these references, Empedocles' four roots are the *eternal* material elements with no beginning or end in time, or spatial variation, or addition, or abstraction from the totality of the cosmos.[146] Love and Strife are the *eternal* motive forces which combine and separate the elements within the cosmic cycle. Both the motive principles contain an "everlasting life" (ἄσπετος αἰών) which always was, will be, and never is going to be extinguished or exhausted in the future (fr. 16).[147]

The inexhaustible everlasting life highlights the ontological difference between mortal and immortal beings. For Empedocles, the continual temporal exchange of mortal life during the mixing phase of Love and the separating phase of Strife makes it incompatible and inferior to the "everlasting abiding" (ἔμπεδος αἰών) of immortal life (fr. 26.10). While the θνητά are subject to the temporality of becoming, the "immortals" participate in everlasting stability outside the alteration of coming-to-be and passing-away (fr. 17.9–13). On the one hand, immortals have an everlasting life remaining *always* unaltered and unmixed in the cyclical structure of the cosmos,[148] on the other, mortals

Table 4.4.
Hierarchy of Lives in Empedocles in Connection with αἰών and χρόνος

immortal level everlasting life	*ἀθάνατα* The Four Roots, Love, Strife	frs 17.11 et 26.10: ἔμπεδος αἰών fr. 16.2: ἄσπετος αἰών fr. 110.3: ταῦτά (v. immortals) μάλα πάντα δι' αἰῶνος παρέσονται
soul level long-lasting lifetime	*δαίμονες and θεοὶ* Daimōns and gods and some wise men	fr. 115.1–2: θεῶν ψήφισμα . . . ἀίδιον fr. 21.12; 23.8: θεοὶ δολιχαίωνες fr. 115.5: δαίμονες οἵτε μακραίωνος λελάχασι βίοιο fr. 129.6: (the wise ἀνὴρ) δέκ' ἀνθρώπων καί τ' εἴκοσιν αἰώνεσσιν
mortal level short lifetime	*θνητά* Humans, animals and plants	fr. 115.7: . . . διὰ χρόνου εἴδεα θνητῶν frs 17.29 et 110.8: περιπλομένοιο χρόνοιο fr. 30.2: τελειομένοιο χρόνοιο

Fragments have DK numbering.

are born and die in continual temporal exchange as the circle moves round in a recurring time within the cosmos (fr. 26.1).[149]

Empedocles' God is also immortal and everlasting, described as a rounded sphere rejoicing in encircling stillness (fr. 27.3 and 28.4), equal to itself in every direction, without any beginning or end (29.3).[150] Empedocles' σφαῖρος is an echo of Parmenides' Being described as *like* a well-rounded sphere. But, in contrast to the completeness of Parmenides' Being, Empedocles' God is infinite in every direction. Empedocles' σφαῖρος contains holy-mind which embraces all the immortal principles of the cosmos, a God who has little in common with the traditional anthropomorphic gods (fr. 134). In this, Empedocles' God echoes Xenophanes' divine mind (frs 23–26) as Mind alone, holy and inexpressible darting through the whole cosmos with swift thought.[151] Love, Strife, and the four Roots are the immortal and intelligible contents of God and as such they can be grasped not by the senses but only with human mind.[152] The senses are not reliable sources of knowledge and humans have to use their thinking in order to grasp a reality which is primarily intelligible and exists beyond the perceptible phenomena (fr. 3). As a whole, the divine nature is conceivable only through mind (frs 132–134). The senses can tell us, in the visible sun, air, earth, and sea, about the roots, and inner feelings of love and hate are expressions of the cosmic motive forces. Only thinking reveals the real nature of each thing and leads to true knowledge (fr. 3.8), and contemplation of immortal truths is the only process for the understanding of the divine principles and the recognition of their nature through human life (fr. 17.3). Humans with correct thinking become δολιχόφρονες (fr. 11.5) and ascend to the level of the δολιχαίωνες δαίμονες (frs 21.2; 23.8).[153]

Yet Empedocles' δαίμονες are not immortal or everlasting (fr. 115).[154] They are subject to the alterations of the four elements under the act of Love and Strife, ratified by the "eternal oath" (ψήφισμα ἀίδιον), which rules the formation and separation of all mortal things (fr. 115.1–2). Empedocles' δαίμονες are not outside this "decree of necessity" and so their αἰών is not perfect and immortal (fr. 115.1–8). The αἰών of the δαίμονες is μακραίων, a "long-lasting lifetime" between the temporal life of the mortals and the everlasting life of the immortals (fr. 115.5).[155] As Wright observes, the excellence of the *daimōns* is in the harmony of their constitutive elements.[156] This "excellence in harmony" marks the superiority of their αἰών in contrast to the lifetime of humans. Whereas, the δαίμονες have a long-lifetime within the eternity of the σφαῖρος, humans have only a short lifetime with limited knowledge and capabilities (fr. 2). Within their life (βίος) humans can observe and participate in only a small part of the whole eternal life (ζωή). In different degrees of excellence, the life of mortals (βίος) is related to the level of impermanent becoming, the life of the δαίμονες to the middle level of divine soul, while there is "unlimited" life (ζωή) for the immortal nature.

To summarize: from the extant evidence Empedocles is the first Presocratic philosopher to treat systematically the idea of eternity related to the notion of life. On the one hand, he keeps the traditional meaning of "long-extending life" and attributes it to the level of the soul of the δαίμονες, while, on the other, he recognizes a higher level of "everlasting life" enjoyed by the divine nature of the holy mind. Influenced by Parmenides, Empedocles relates this divine life to the immobility, stability, completeness, and immutability of Being, but he does not follow Parmenides' idea of timelessness. Empedocles' divine αἰών is everlasting but not timeless. For this reason he remains loyal to the Ionic tradition and especially to Heraclitus' concept of an everlasting cosmos sustained by the ever-living fire. Empedocles describes a universe full of life, the origins of which are immortal and intelligible; everything mortal originates from the immortal, everything temporal from the eternal. Thus, Empedocles, like Plato, distinguishes between the temporality of the mortal world and the everlastingness of the divine, and Empedocles' concept of αἰών as endless life echoes in Plotinus' association of eternity with the life of the Forms.

4.6 THE EVERLASTINGNESS OF TIME

In the eleventh chapter of *Ennead* III.7, Plotinus defines time as "the life of Soul in a transitory motion from one stage of life to another" (11.44–45). With this definition, Plotinus aims to stress the fact that the life of the Soul is not a form of *animal life* (ζωή), but a mode of *intelligible life* (βίος),[157] transiting discursively in otherness.[158] Whereas the Intellect contemplates the whole intelligible realm *simultaneously* in a single timeless vision, the Soul thinks Intellect *discursively* in a multiple transition by moving from one intelligible to another (III.7.11.35–43). The real nature of time is intelligible and hence it has to be essentially distinguished from physical motion and the alterations of natural phenomena. Time is the "moving image of eternity" in Plato's words because the Soul follows, imitates, and manifests in restless discursive thinking the eternal non-discursive unity of Intellect.

Soul's temporal succession of psychic events, as Strange puts it, derives from the psychological succession of its own thoughts.[159] When Soul turn towards and looks to the past it produces memory, and memory causes the division of time in tenses (IV.4.15.5 ff.). Looking to the past is an intelligible motion in otherness, a motion which causes the fragmentation of eternal life in the everlasting temporality of a continuous transition of past, present, and future.

Thus, while the nature of Soul is originally eternal its by-products are temporal. Since Soul's life generates time (III.7.12.21–22), time belongs to the Soul and so all the universe is the by-product of its vital activity; *the whole universe moves within the time of the Soul* (III.7.12.22–25). Time transcends physical phenomena and the instability of becoming. It has its origins in the higher levels of being; it is an intelligible and incorporeal nature, not present in any perceptible particular, but all the perceptible particulars seem to be present in it. Time is the cause of physical motion and not vice versa.

Time, as the life of Soul, is posterior to Soul, and by extension that which exists in temporality is less than time itself (IV.4.15.15). Whereas beings which exist temporally in becoming presuppose necessarily the condition of future; their being is necessarily dependent on the being of time (III.7.4.19–28). But *being in time* is not a fundamental form of being. The beings of becoming base their existence in the future and their life span seems to be diminished when this temporal form of being progressively lessens in the everlastingness of time. Whereas the intelligible world has a life abiding in a *timeless present* (ἀεὶ παρόν: III.7.3.16–17), the perceptible world has a life unfolding in *temporal everlastingness* by means of what is going to be (ἀεὶ μέλλον: III.7.4.34). The everlasting existence of the cosmos is not an existence based on the sameness of the "present" but on an otherness of the "future," which produces a transient imperfect motion (III.7.11.35–43).

So the everlastingness of time is different ontologically from the timelessness of eternity, and this distinction is the cause of the continuous circular motion of the universe towards future aspiration.[160] The existence of temporal entities does not belong to the temporal beings themselves but to the intelligible and eternal substance which outflows their existence to the entities existing in temporality, and the universe manifests in temporal everlastingness the eternal life of the Intellect through Soul. Thus, the universe exists in a state of temporal imperfection as it continuously hastens towards the future, aspiring to the perfection of the intelligible substance (III.7.4.28–33). For Plotinus, the circular motion of the universe imitates in everlastingness eternal timelessness and follows the intelligible movement of the Soul around the Intellect (V.1.4.17–19). Being in time the universe needs to put forth its own being in everlastingness, since the temporal being of the universe stands outside the self-sustained eternal being of Intellect.

Here it is noteworthy that Plotinus' distinction between eternal being and temporal becoming echoes Plato's initial distinction of being and becoming at the *Timaeus* (27d6–28a1). For Plato, as for Plotinus, the lesser temporal becoming derives from the higher eternal being of the Forms. For Plotinus, the cosmos is "in time" and the movements of the stars are accidentally relative indicators of time and not time itself (III.7.8.10 ff.).[161] Thus, when Plato relates time to the motion of the heavenly spheres, calling the courses of stars "times," he does not mean that time is the physical motion of the heavenly sphere, but the intelligible cause of this motion, the intelligible motion of the Soul's life before the universe (III.7.13.20 ff.).

If we as humans, says Plotinus, count time by measuring the physical motion of the celestial bodies, it is because our Soul is not able to delimit time in itself. That is why Plato speaks of the "divisions of time" and comes to the concept of number in the *Timaeus*. Since we cannot count an incorporeal nature, we count its manifestations, measuring the intervals between one sunrise and the next, since this kind of motion is the only order and perfect (III.7.12.28–37). Then, as Plotinus concludes, we use these intervals as a measure, but this measure is not time, because time is outside physical space, belonging with a higher nature which cannot be measured or counted at all (III.7.12.58–61).

4.6.1 The Myth of Time

But what is the cause of Soul's departure from eternity to time? Plotinus gives a common metaphorical answer throughout the *Enneads*: the Soul includes an "officious nature" (III.7.11.15: φύσις πολυπράγμονος), an "unquiet power" (11.20: δύναμις οὐχ ἥσυχος), which continually wishes to produce something more than it possesses.[162] Soul is like a λόγος unfolding itself from a quiet seed (III.7.11.25–26), and, as it advances in plurality and largeness, it diminishes its internal unity and grows weaker as it extends and multiplies. Soul becomes a "slave of time" (δουλεύειν χρόνῳ) by making the whole of itself and its processes to be within temporal limitations (11.31–34).

Based on this idea and having in mind the nature of the narrative of the *Timaeus*, Plotinus denies any literal reading of the text, which was common to some Aristotelian and Middle-Platonic commentators, but follows the mythological-allegorical one:

> We must return again to that condition which we said obtained in the case of eternity, to that imperturbable life, which is all at once, and is altogether fixed and actually unlimited, which is without any sort of turning away, and rests in and is directed towards the One. There was not yet time, at least for the things of that realm, but we shall generate time by the account and nature of what is posterior to it. Since these beings were at rest in themselves, one could hardly call upon the Muses, who did not yet exist, to tell us this, "how time first issued forth." But perhaps—even if the Muses did exist then after all—one might ask time itself, when it had come into being, how it is that it was revealed and had come into being. It might say something like this about itself: that before, when it had not generated this "before" or felt the need of the "after," time rested along with eternity in being, but was not yet time, but it too was at rest in eternity. But since there was an officious nature that wished to rule itself and belong to itself and that chose to seek for more than it presently had, this nature moved, and time moved with it, and in always moving on to what comes next, to what comes after and is not the same, and having made progress in this journey, we produced time as the image of eternity. [III.7.11.1–20; trans. McGuire and Strange modified]

Plotinus' mythical personification of time has attracted the interest of modern scholars.[163] His reference to the Muses in lines 8–9 is an allusion to Homer' *Iliad* 16.112–113 and Plato's *Republic* 545d.[164]

This odd Plotinian myth, a "parody" of the Platonic myths as Strange puts it, indicates that time does not literally have a temporal beginning.[165] Plotinus is here taking up a position on an endemic problem of Platonism: on the one hand, Plato in the *Timaeus* states that the cosmos had a temporal beginning (28b–c) and, on the other, that it is ever-existing because of the unending power of the Divine Craftsman (41b). Some Platonists such as Plutarch adopted the former position, while others such as Atticus accepted both.[166] For Plotinus, Plato's account in the *Timaeus* is not a literal description of the creation of the cosmos and Soul by a Divine Craftsman, but an allegorical account of a Divine Creation which cannot be communicated except within strict and limited philosophical argument (II.1.1).[167] Plotinus' myth of time implies its self-generation and everlastingness. Both implications take us back not only to Plato's mythical account of the *Timaeus* but also to the Presocratic concept of Time as self-generated and everlasting.

4.6.2 The Everlastingness of the Cosmos

Originally the concept of the everlastingness of the cosmos derives from early Presocratic thought. In Pherecydes and the Ionian thinkers everlastingness seems to be an inseparable attribute of the cosmos. Pherecydes is the first ancient author to introduce the concept of everlastingness. In his cosmogony, time appears as an everlasting procreative cosmogonical principle,[168] Χρόνος is personified as one of the three primal everlasting principles[169] that initially began the generation of the cosmos.[170] The word ἀεί in Pherecydes' fr. 1 highlights the everlasting nature of the three deities which "always existed" (ἦσαν ἀεί).[171] With Pherecydes Time takes on another meaning, which may have been responsible for the later connotations of time as everlasting. Pherecydes' Χρόνος exists before the beginning of the cosmos and is responsible for the whole cosmic generation. This is testified by Damascius' description of Pherecydes' Χρόνος as a self-creative principle which initially produces from its own seeds the three primal elements: fire, breath, and water.[172] Pherecydes' Χρόνος is the eternal and ultimate power which steps out of eternity to create a temporal world.[173] The self-creative nature of time keeps Pherecydes loyal to the philosophical tradition of eliminating ex nihilo creation. The cosmos cannot result from non-being, but only from some basic procreative and self-creative everlasting principle. Pherecydes' view comes to be extremely influential on Presocratic thought and especially on Anaximander's everlastingness of the ἄπειρον.[174] Anaximander's ἄπειρον signifies a derivative source *with no defined limits temporally or spatially*. It is noteworthy that Anaximander's conception of spatial and temporal limitlessness can be found later in Anaxagoras' theory of Mind. Anaxagoras' Νοῦς is always existing (fr. 14.1: ἀεί ἐστι) without beginning or end in time (fr. 13).

For Anaximander all things in the cosmos originate from the ἄπειρον and return to the same everlasting source. This continually recurring process of generation and destruction is an important innovation in Greek thought. Anything existing would have to be *either* mortal, with beginning and end, *or* immortal, without beginning or end, so that the traditional notion of gods with birth but no death would be seen as illogical. Whereas the gods of Greek tradition are born but then have an endless life, Anaximander's primal substance is everlasting, with no beginning or end, temporally or spatially; it is a substance beyond mortality from which all things in the cosmos originate and eventually return.

As Hippolytus testifies,[175] the ἄπειρον is everlasting and ageless, a nature which *always* includes all the possible worlds within.[176] Hippolytus' testimony supplements Simplicius' comment (=DK 12A9) on an important point: he attributes everlastingness (ἀίδιον) to the ἄπειρον. Hippolytus offers an interesting comparison between the "unlimited" everlasting nature of the ἄπειρον and the "limited" nature of temporal becoming. Pseudo-Plutarch describes how, for Anaximander, coming-to-be and passing away recur in cyclical processes from a limitless αἰών.[177]

Anaximander's everlasting ἄπειρον is further characterized by an "eternal motion" (ἀίδιος κίνησις). On the importance of the eternal motion in Anaximander, there is agreement between both Simplicius (=DK 12A9) and Hippolytus (12A11) as well as Hermias (12A12).[178] The source of all these references is Theophrastus, who also ascribes eternal motion to Anaximenes[179] as the cause of the qualitative change of the air (ἀήρ),[180] and to Leucippus' random movement of the atoms in all directions.[181] Furthermore, Plutarch attributes eternal motion to Anaximenes and explains it as motion originating from eternity.[182] Generation out of and destruction into the ἄπειρον follow the cycles of mortal life and death, but Anaximander's everlasting motion does not imply any circularity either to the ἄπειρον or to κίνησις as some scholars suppose, but, as Kahn points out, it means nothing more than an everlasting motion which always was, is, and shall be enduringly in time, manifested by the endless series of astronomical occurrences.[183]

However, the only evidence for Anaximander distinguishing between eternity and time is to be found in the "ordering" or "assessment of time" (χρόνου τάξις) of fr. 1. Anaximander with a poetic and political metaphor describes temporal generation as an unjust action for which compensation has to be paid under the ordering of Time.[184] Temporal beings become limited as they emerge from their primary infinite and everlasting origin. Whereas τάξις signifies the temporal limits of generation and destruction, the ἄπειρον signifies everlastingness and lack of limitation. The "assessment of time" therefore denotes the cosmic process of balanced opposition and equilibrium between opposite forces acting and reacting on each other with mutual gains and losses.[185]

Here it has to be mentioned that Anaximander's view of time distinguishes his philosophy from Pherecydes' earlier mythical conception of time. Whereas for Anaximander time is the preserver and regulator of the cosmos, the ordering principle of temporal becoming, for Pherecydes' Χρόνος is the initial generator of the cosmos before any temporal creation.[186] While for Anaximander χρόνος is a cosmological principle related to order, in Pherecydes, it is a cosmogonical one before there is an order. The common element between the two philosophers is that the source of the universe is an everlasting principle, but whereas for Anaximander this principle is an unconditional and indefinite ἄπειρον, for Pherecydes it is a particular personified "time-god."[187] For this reason, Anaximander's cosmology is more clearly a step towards discrimination between an eternal and temporal condition of the cosmos. In Anaximander, an everlasting source becomes the origin of temporal becoming which preserves in its turn the everlastingness of its originative source in different recurring temporal conditions.

Nevertheless, for Plotinus, the Presocratic who clearly asserts the everlastingness of the cosmos is Heraclitus.[188] In *Ennead* II.1 *On Heaven*,[189] Plotinus alludes constantly Heraclitus' flux of becoming,[190] and the Heraclitean term for "flux," ῥεῖν (flow), can be found not only in this treatise,[191] but throughout the *Enneads*.[192] Of course, these references are not all direct allusions to the Heraclitean theory of flux since the verb ῥεῖν was already a common expression for both Platonists and Stoics to express cosmic flux.[193] Heraclitus' influence is mainly apparent in the second chapter of *Ennead* II.1 where Plotinus recalls by name the Presocratic (10–12: τῷ Ἡρακλείτῳ), and the other natural philosophers (6–7: οἱ περὶ φύσεως εἰρηκόσι). These early philosophers are in agreement with Plato's theory of the continual flux of the heavenly bodies:

> If, then, we accept this view and maintain that the heaven and everything in it last forever as individuals, but the things below the sphere of the moon are only everlasting in form, we must show how heaven, which has a body, can have proper individual identity, in the sense that each particular detail remains unchanged, when the nature of body is in continual flux. This is the view held by Plato himself, as well as by all the other natural philosophers, not only about other bodies but about the heavenly bodies themselves. For "how," he says, "when they have bodies and are visible can they be unchangeable and always the same"—agreeing, obviously, in this, too, with Heraclitus, who said that the sun becomes everlastingly. [II.1.2.1–13; trans. Armstrong modified]

Plotinus' aim in this passage, as in the whole of *Ennead* II.1, is to defend his theory of the incorruptibility, inalterability, and everlastingness of the heavenly bodies as individual entities. He knows that his theory, which was followed by most pagan Neoplatonists, is in contrast not only to Plato's (*Republic* 530b2–3), but also to the Presocratic philosophers who maintained the continual flux of material bodies.[194] As P. Kalligas notes, this is one of the rare cases in the *Enneads* where Plotinus may be openly contrasted with Plato.[195] But Plotinus' arguments are directed more against the Stoics and Stoicising Platonists. These are the philosophers, according to Armstrong, who erroneously interpreted the *Timaeus* as meaning that the heavens are "subject to change in a regular ever-ending cycle, and that there was a real community of substance and interaction between the regions below and the regions above the moon."[196]

For Plotinus, the cosmos is everlasting because it has no temporal beginning (II.1.4.25). The universe is everlasting because it is governed and ruled by a better eternal Soul which is primarily intelligible and belongs to a higher eternal nature.[197] As he puts it in II.9.7.1–2: "the cosmos did not begin and will not come to an end but exists always as long as the intelligible realities exist." Whereas the perceptibles are everlasting, like the nature of the perceptible world (II.4.5.27), the intelligibles are eternal, like the nature of the intelligible world (5.28). Hence, for Plotinus, the true meaning of the *Timaeus* is that the heavenly bodies do not contain any admixture of the material elements of the sublunary world (II.2.6–8). The heavenly bodies exist in an everlasting flux for they are under the direction of an eternal Soul, which is too weak to keep the eternity of Intellect in absolute stability, but imitates eternity in the form of an everlasting and unchanging temporality (8.20–27).

For Plotinus, Heraclitus' conception of the everlastingness of the cosmos is encapsulated in the image of the ἥλιος, which is *always* new everyday (II.1.2.10–12: Συγχωρῶν καὶ ἐπὶ τούτων δηλονότι τῷ Ἡρακλείτῳ, ὃς ἔφη ἀεὶ καὶ τὸν ἥλιον γίνεσθαι). Plotinus here paraphrases Heraclitus' fragment 6: ὁ νέος ἐφ' ἡμέρῃ ἐστίν. The main source of the fragment is Aristotle's *Meteorologica*, 354b33. Aristotle interprets the phrase as denoting not only the everyday renewal of the sun but also its everlasting renewal.[198] The latter seems to have a parallel in fr. 106 where the nature of every day is *always* the same in essence. Moreover, fragment 6 is related to Theophrastus' account where the sun is described as a celestial bowl in which the hot and moist exhalation is ignited every morning and extinguished every night.[199]

Plotinus' reference to Heraclitus' fr. 6, however, has not been mentioned by modern scholarship on Heraclitus, but it has been recognized as an allusion to Heraclitus by Roussos, Armstrong, Kalligas, and the *Index Fontium* of Henry and Schwyzer.[200] Armstrong and Roussos assume that Plotinus' source of II.1.2.10–12 is Aristotle's *Meteorologica* 354b33, and Roussos particularly denies Lassale's suggestion that Plotinus in II.1.2.10–12 had in mind another point of Heraclitus' teaching.[201] But none of the above positions seems to be a correct interpretation of the text in the *Ennead*.

Whereas Plotinus' reference to the ἥλιος leads us undoubtedly to Heraclitus' fragment 6, this does not necessarily mean that his source was Aristotle. As is evident from the text, Plotinus' aim is to relate Heraclitus' everlasting flux of becoming to Plato rather than Aristotle. Aristotle is discussed in connection with the theory of the fifth body (*De Caelo* 270b) in the next lines where the context is different (2.14 ff.). Plotinus focuses more on the concept of everlastingness, and this is the emphasis of the parallel passage in *Ennead* V.1.9.5 where Plotinus speaks of the Heraclitean flux of the bodies. Thus, in II.1.2.10–12 Plotinus discovers in Heraclitus' thought a connection between the "sun" (ἥλιος), representing "fire" (πῦρ), "flux" (ῥεῖν), "becoming" (γίγνε-ται), and "everlastingness" (ἀεί): *becoming exists in a state of everlasting flux underlined by the ever-living force of fire*. It is significant that in *Ennead* VI.4 Plotinus uses again the image of ἥλιος to justify the necessary flux of becoming:

> Yet if the sun were to stay fixed in any particular place, it would give the same light to the same regions; but if everybody were to say, not the same light, he would confirm by this that the body of the sun was flowing away. [VI.4.10.26–28; trans. Armstrong]

The concluding phrase of the above passage (τὸ σῶμα ῥεῖν τοῦ ἡλίου) leads us inevitably again to II.1.2.10–12, and V.1.9.5, and, by extension, to Heraclitus' terminology. This reference has not as yet been picked up by scholars of Plotinus.

Here it has to be noted that in VI.4.10.26–28, Plotinus' rationale follows the metaphysical "path" of Plato and not the cosmological one of the Ephesian. On the other hand, it is significant that Heraclitus' terminology survives the transfer to Plotinus' metaphysical thought. Initially, the transfer is shown in Plotinus' conscious connection between Heraclitus and Plato in II.1.2.10–12. We have already seen in V.9.5.26–32 a similar case where Plato and Heraclitus appear in the same passage. Likewise in II.1.2.10–12, Plotinus establishes the philosophical link between the two thinkers with the affirmative συγχωρῶν in line 10. More importantly, the emphatic καὶ ἐπὶ τούτων can lead to the assumption that for him the two philosophers seem to agree on more issues than this particular subject. Plotinus is not wrong to find a parallel between the two philosophers since Heraclitus' thought is evident in Plato's cosmology of the *Timaeus*, the *Republic*, the *Cratylus*, the *Statesman*, and the *Laws*.[202] However, a reconciliation between the two philosophers is unlikely if we remember Plato's polemic against Heraclitus especially on his theory of "continual flux" in the *Theaetetus* (181a1 ff.), where Plato argues against the Heracliteans, and in the *Sophist* (242c8 ff.), where Plato speaks ironically of Heraclitus and Empedocles as the "Ionian and Sicilian Muses." Therefore, Plotinus' source of II.1.2.10–12, if he does not recall Heraclitus' original, could easily be Plato and more precisely the *Cratylus* (402A), where the theory of cosmic flux is recalled.

Plotinus seems to accept Heraclitus' position that the everlastingness of becoming is expressed in the form of an endless cosmic flux. The everlasting flux of becoming is maintained by an ever-living πῦρ and its unending vital force (fr. 30). Despite its transformations the Heraclitean πῦρ remains always an everlasting material source (fr. 31). Plotinus recalls Heraclitus' everlastingness of πῦρ in II.1.3.25–30:

> . . . but if there is no loss by flux in heaven there is no need for nourishment. If anything was lost there through fire being extinguished, other fire would have to be kindled; and if it had this other fire from something else and that something else lost it by flux, that again would have to be replaced by other fire. But as a result of this the universal living creature would not remain the same thing, even if it remained the same sort of thing. [trans. Armstrong]

In this passage, Plotinus with the expressions ἐξάπτεσθαι and ἀποσβεννύμενον in line 27 recalls Heraclitus' ἁπτόμενον and ἀποσβεννύμενον in fr. 30. These measures manifest the limitations of fire which fix the limitations of the sun so that it does not overstep its measures (fr. 94). The limitations of fire are also mentioned by Plotinus in II.9.3.6: "fire is limited by ratio." In VI.7.11.6, Plotinus again recognizes the vital power of fire. Heraclitus seems to be behind Plotinus' question "How does fire live?" (πῶς πῦρ ζῇ). Plotinus offers some lines later a Platonic answer (43–48):

> Soul is a life and a forming principle, both one and the same. This is why Plato says that there is a soul in each of the elements, in no other way than this perceptible fire. So then what makes the fire here below is also a fiery life, a truer fire. The transcendent fire, then, since it is more fire, would be more in life; so then absolute fire also lives. [trans. Armstrong modified]

It is significant that Plotinus' conclusion is justified within the rationale of a living soul (43–44). Prima facie Heraclitus would not disagree with this position;[203] for him the fiery souls "always flow" (fr. 12: ἀεὶ γίνονται) as the sun is "always new" (fr. 6: ἀεὶ νέος συνεχῶς). Finally, in III.7.8.40–41, Plotinus uses the image of the flow of water to denote the everlastingness of time:

> . . . time will not appear or come into one's mind but motion which keeps on coming again and again, just like water flowing which keeps on coming again and again . . . [trans. Armstrong modified]

Can we suppose that behind the last phrase there is an echo of Heraclitus? This is not explicitly in the text, but the image of "ever-flowing water" is a reminder of Heraclitus' "ever-flowing river" in frs 12, 91, and 49a.[204]

4.6.3 The Movement of the Spheres, Eternal Recurrence, and Spiral Time

In *Ennead* III.7, Plotinus refers twice to the Pythagorean doctrines of time: in the first passage (2.1–4), time is identified with the whole heaven and the cosmos, while in the second (7.24–25) it is related to the sphere of the universe.

> Τίνα οὖν ποτε χρὴ φάναι τὸν αἰῶνα εἶναι; Ἀρά γε τὴν νοητὴν αὐτὴν οὐσίαν, *ὥσπερ ἂν εἴ τις λέγοι τὸν χρόνον τὸν σύμπαντα οὐρανὸν καὶ κόσμον εἶ ναι; Καὶ γὰρ αὖ καὶ ταύτην τὴν δό ξαν ἔσχον τινές, φασι, περὶ τοῦχρό νου.*
> So, what would you say that eternity is? Is it intelligible Substance itself, as someone might say that time is the whole of the heaven and the cosmos? For they say that there are some who have held this opinion about time. [III.7.2.1–4trans. McGuire and Strange]

> . . . οἱ δὲ τὸ κινούμενον λέγοντες τὴν ***τοῦ παντὸς ἂν σφαῖραν** λέγοιεν*
> . . . those who say that time is what is moved would say that it is the sphere of the universe. [III.7.7.24–25; trans. McGuire and Strange modified]

The above passages are indirect references to the Pythagoreans. Plotinus' allusion lies behind the phrases "there are some who have held this opinion about time" (III.7.2.4: ταύτην τὴν δόξαν ἔσχον τινές, φασι, περὶ τοῦ χρόνου), and "those who say that time is . . ." (III.7.7.24: οἱ λέγοντες). In the former case, Plotinus echoes Aristotle's *Physics* 218b1,[205] and Simplicius (*in Physica* 700.19–20),[206] who testifies the Pythagorean doctrine of time identified with the cosmic sphere.[207] Thus, Plotinus' III.7.2.1–4 and III.7.7.24–25 have to be accepted as Pythagorean allusions from a Peripatetic testimony.

Plotinus' references to Pythagorean Time in III.7.2.1–4 and III.7.7.24–25 have been recognized by Armstrong,[208] McGuire, and Strange,[209] and the *Index Fontium* of Henry and Schwyzer. There is no doubt that some Pythagorean and Orphic doctrines of χρόνος seem to be influential in the Neoplatonic tradition. More precisely, the mythical image of χρόνος is presented in the late Neoplatonic accounts of Orphic cosmogonies.[210] For example, for Damascius, in the Orphic Rhapsodies, χρόνος is the "one un-ageing origin of all,"[211] and for Athenagoras it is personified as a living creature in the form of a snake with a lion's head (fr. 13).[212] Moreover, for the Orphics, Χρόνος wound around Necessity, and this probably influenced the Pythagorean definition of time as the "sphere of the encompassing,"[213] as well as the concept of the Pythagorean Necessity that "lies around the universe."[214] It is also worth quoting Plato's conception of the axis of the universe girt around by a bond of light.[215]

Pythagorean χρόνος was also expressible in numbers. This is testified by Eudemus quoted by Simplicius *in Physica*.[216] Alexander declares that "seven" was the number for καιρός, the crucial stages of human life and the sun, the seventh of the heavenly bodies counting towards the center, the celestial body which marks the crucial periods of human life.[217] Aristotle testifies that for the Pythagoreans the Earth was also an instrument of time.[218] Based on the recurring cyclical movement of the celestial bodies, the Pythagoreans held that events recur endlessly in certain time cycles.[219] Since for the Pythagoreans χρόνος was measured by the movements of the planets, and the positions of the planets recur again within the cycle of the Great Year, historical events in human life recur in certain time cycles and so whatever happens in each cycle will be endlessly repeated in time.[220] The Pythagorean doctrine of "endless recurrence" echoes in Eudemus' joke of the lecture "endlessly repeated" (fr. 51) quoted by Simplicius *in Physica* 732.26.

The Pythagorean idea of the endless recurrence of events is also found in Plotinus' pupil Porphyry (*Life of Pythagoras*, 19) in connection with the Soul's reincarnation. According to Porphyry, Pythagoras was the first to introduce the immortality and reincarnation of the Soul as well as the belief that events recur in repeating cycles.[221] According to Plutarch, when Pythagoras was asked what χρόνος was, he answered that it was "the soul of the universe" (*Quaest. Plat.* VIII.4). Soul has a number following its cycle of reincarnations (Aristotle *Metaphysics* 985b30). In death the Soul departs this world, as a shadow, to the underworld; in birth, it comes back from the underworld to this world. Within this context, Alcmaeon of Croton tells us that the Soul is immortal, because it has always a circular motion like the heavenly bodies (= DK 24A12), yet we die because we cannot join the beginning with the end (fr. 2).

Furthermore, the Pythagorean doctrine of endless recurrence echoes in Empedocles' theory of the recurring cosmic cycles (fr. 17) in which the four immortal elements periodically mingle into compounds and separate, generating various mortal forms within temporal becoming. Likewise, the Pythagorean doctrine appears later in the Stoic idea of the periodic universal conflagration and eternal recurrence in continuous time.[222] According to M. R. Wright, "the Stoics linked periodic thermal destruction and regeneration with cycles of eternal recurrence for the cosmos and individual."[223] In fact, the evidence goes back from Nemesius to the Stoic Chrysippus.[224] Chrysippus' conception of eternal recurrence echoes clearly the Pythagorean doctrine of endless recurrence. The Stoic theory lies fundamentally in the position that "many times recur again without end into infinity." The inclusion of "infinity" in the whole rationale, which probably derives from Empedocles' eternal cyclical motion,[225] leads us from Pythagorean endless recurrence to the Stoic eternal recurrence.[226]

For the Pythagoreans, then, the definite duration of time entails a cyclical cosmos with no temporal beginning or end, where events reoccur eternally. Pythagorean time as a definite number has to be regarded as independent from perceptible change and alteration: *a definite mathematical principle which underlies the numerical cyclical sequence of events ad infinitum.* This conclusion is supported by Hippasus,[227] who said that the periodic cycle of events and changes in the universe are underlined by a definite Time which is the cause of an ever-moving universe.[228]

For Plotinus, likewise, the movement of the heaven is circular, imitating the aspiration of the Soul around Intellect. This theory is clearly demonstrated in *Ennead* II.2 *On the Movement of Heaven.*[229] Nature is just what has been ordained by the Soul (II.2.1.6–50). The heaven has an everlasting circular motion because it follows the self-concentrated awareness and intellection of the Soul around Intellect.[230] The movement of Soul is not spatial, bodily and external, but temporal, intellectual, and internal. Since the life of the body is movement, and this life belongs to the Soul's intelligible and ordained movement, the animated universe does not stay still but encompasses in unity the circularity of Soul's movement. If Soul stayed still, the heaven would stand still too, but it draws the universe everlastingly to itself not in a straight line but in a circle. By moving in a circle of its own accord (II.2.1.26–27), the universe encompasses in its circularity both movement and rest (II.2.3.21–22).

> The universe seeks to go on in a straight line, but has no longer any place to go to, so it slips round, we may say, and curves back in the regions where it can; for it has no place beyond itself; this is the last. So it runs in the space it occupies and is its own place; it came to be there not in order to sit still but to move. The center of a circle naturally stays still, but if the outside circumference stayed still, it would be a big centre. So it can rather be expected, in the case of a living body in its natural state, to go round the centre. In this way, then, it will direct itself towards the centre, not by coinciding with it—that would abolish circles—but, since it cannot do that, by rotating around the centre; for in this way alone can it satisfy its impulse. [II.2.1.27–37; trans. Armstrong modified]

As a result, the movement of the universal body is not a simple circular movement but a spiral movement that "slips round" (περιολισθάνον) or "rotates around" (περιδινήσει) an intelligible center. In *Ennead* VI.3.13.26, Plotinus distinguishes between three different kinds of line: straight, circular, and spiral. Similarly, Proclus *in Euclid* 112.21 offers us the same division.[231] The ἕλιξ is a combination of linear and circular line. This is also described by Damascius *in Parmenidem* 122.22–23,[232] as well as Proclus *in Platonis Timaeum* III.21.4.[233]

From the above it can be assumed that the movement of Plotinus' universe can be described as a ἕλιξ that combines both linear and circular movement in one single motion. So we can draw the follow hypothesis about Plotinus' theory of time: *since time is the movement of the life of the Soul around Intellect and the movement of the Soul produces the spiral movement of the heavenly sphere then time is manifested in spiral motion.*

Plotinus' concept is not unique. Plato in the *Timaeus* 38e–39a relates time and the movement of the heavenly bodies to ἕλιξ. The heavenly bodies revolve according to the cycles of the Different and the Same in a "spiral twist" by moving in two contrary directions at once (39a6).[234] Additionally, Plato speaks about a vortex movement (δίνη) in the *Cratylus* (439c5) criticizing ever-flowing becoming, in the *Phaedo* (99b6) related to the heavens, and in the *Republic* (620e3) connected to the revolving spindle of Clotho in the Myth of Er. Proclus (*in Platonis Timaeum* III.40.41) testifies that for Plato and the theurgists χρόνος is named and worshiped as ἑλικοειδής, since it self-includes linear and circular movement.

But originally the spiral-vortex images of ἕλιξ and δίνη appear in the cosmology of the Presocratics and especially in Anaximander, Empedocles, Anaxagoras, and the Atomists. For Anaximander and Anaximenes, according to the testimony of Aëtius II.2.4 (= DK 13A12), vortex is related to the movement of the cosmos. In Anaximander's cosmogony, there are evidences of a vortex-action during the first separation of the elements from the ἄπειρον.[235] Aristotle seems to have in mind Anaximander and some other early Presocratic cosmogonies when he describes the nature of vortex-motion in *De Caelo* 295a–b. In all probability, the whole Anaximandrean ἄπειρον is in vortex-motion to explain the tendency of heavy bodies to stay in the center (*De Caelo* 295b10).[236]

Moreover, in Empedocles' fr. 35 the movement of "spiral vortex" is clearly related to the rotation and generation of the cosmos. As Wright observes, δίνη (35.3) and στροφάλιγξ (35.4) refer "to the cosmic rotation started at the separation of the four masses."[237] According to Simplicius (*in De Caelo* 529.17–18), δίνη and στροφάλιγξ are identified in fr. 35. While Strife has reached the lowest depths of the vortex, Love arises at in the center of the eddy and gradually brings the cosmos into unity from plurality.[238]

In addition, for Anaxagoras, according to the testimony of Diogenes Laertius (II: 6–15), vortex-motion is related to the heaven.[239] In fr. 12.14–17, Anaxagoras describes how Mind initiated the rotation in the primary mixture: Mind imparted the first vortex-motion at a high speed, and the revolution caused the progressive separation of the ingredients.

Finally, in the cosmogony of the Atomists vortex-motion played an essential role in the formation of the cosmos. For Leucippus, according to the testimony of Diogenes Laertius IX.31, the world comes into being when atoms of all sorts and shapes come together and produce a single whirl or vortex, and after colliding they revolve and begin to separate apart. Similarly for Democritus, as Diogenes Laertius IX.45 again testifies, vortex is the generative cause of all things and is further identified with necessity.[240] According to Aristotle (*Physics* 196a24), vortex and movements arose accidentally by separation, and brought the universe into its ordered condition. Simplicius follows the latter testimony and provides the further information that vortex separated off from the whole by accident or chance.[241]

With regard to the concept of vortex therefore Plotinus remains loyal not only to the Platonic tradition of the generation of the cosmos by a divine intelligence, but also echoes the original image of vortex-spiral in connection with the production of the cosmos and, by extension, the description of time in terms of spiral image. Plotinus differs from the Presocratics in that he adapts the image of the spiral to a metaphysical context, but the subject matter is always the same: the formation of the cosmos. Whereas for Plotinus and the Platonists the cosmos originates from the intellectual movement of a higher Soul, for the Presocratics the cosmos has a material cause ordained by the physical forces of nature.

Chapter 5

Matter and Soul

5.1 MATTER AND ENSOULED BODY IN PLOTINUS

Plotinus' theory of Matter (ὕλη)[1] is a philosophical synthesis of Plato's Receptacle of becoming (ὑποδοχή) in the *Timaeus* (48e–52d), and Aristotle's theory of matter as Substrate (ὑποκείμενον) in *Physics* 192a3 (II.4.1; III.6.13–14).[2] For Plotinus, matter is sterile and undesignated nonbeing, the formless and insubstantial receptacle of the Platonic Forms; the unqualified underlying substratum that inactively reflects the intelligible beings.[3] On this basis, the insubstantiality of Plotinus' ὕλη is closer to the Aristotelian ὑποκείμενον than the Platonic ὑποδοχή,[4] and, like many earlier Platonists, he identifies the ὑποδοχή with the ὑποκείμενον with the aim of rejecting the natural interpretation of the identification of matter with "space" (χώρα) in the *Timaeus* (51a–52a). Plotinus position is that since matter is indefinite, it cannot have the definite quality of spatial extension, but is an inert and formless neutral entity that causes evil in its sterility and privation.[5] Yet ὕλη is neither absolute nonexistence nor an independently existing principle (I.8.3; II.4.16). It is, as R. T. Wallis puts it, "the point at which the outflow of reality from the One fades away into utter darkness."[6]

Plotinus defines ὕλη as "pure privation" (στέρησις: II.4.16.3), "utter sterility," "essential negation," "absolute poverty," "underlying substrate" (II.4.1.2, 6.3, 12.23; II.6.7.1; VI.3.4.24–8: ὑποκείμενον); "potentiality that can never been actualized" (I.8.3.16; II.5.4–6; III.6.14.5–15).[7] As he puts it in II.5.5.6–7: "its potential existence is not being something, but being potentially everything; and since it is nothing in itself—except what it is, matter—it does not exist actually at all." Hence, ὕλη is frequently described in negative terms as "incorporeal" (ἀσώματος),[8] "impassive" (ἀπαθής),[9] "indeterminate" (ἀόριστος),[10] "formless" (ἄμορφος),[11] "invisible" (ἀόρατος),[12] "indestructible" (ἀνώλεθρος),[13] "indefinite" (ἄπειρος),[14] "without quality" (ἄποιος),[15] "without magnitude" (III.6.16.25), and "without alterations" (III.6.10.20–21).[16] It is a "weak" and "dim" phantasm unable to receive a shape of its own (II.5.5.21–22).[17] It is "true falsity" (II.5.5.23),[18] an entity which is "nothing in itself" (5.6), "truly nonbeing" (III.6.7.12–13): that which is "really unreal" (II 5.5.24).[19] Matter is, in L. P. Gerson's words, "the unintelligible element in nature."[20] It is an insubstantial nature which cannot posses any actual reality but is left in sterile potentiality to reflect the images of the unrestricted intelligibles (II.5.2.27–8).

For Plotinus, the apparent actuality of the perceptibles is a reflection of intelligibles upon matter (V.1.9.20–34). It is metaphorically portrayed as the Mirror of Dionysus (IV.3.12.1 ff.; III.6.7–13), the unaffected mirror which reflects the images of the intelligibles as *pseudo*-existences through the medium of the Soul. The projection of the intelligibles upon matter is an illumination which does not separate them substantially from their intelligible origins nor cause a division in their incorporeal unity in space or time (III.6.13.49). For this reason, and following Aristotelian *hylomorphism*, Plotinus conceives of the perceptible bodies as composite entities of matter and form (II 4.2.15), but still mere representations: "they are images drawn on the shadow" (VI 3.8.35–36). As Plotinus vividly puts it, the image of the "form" slips away on the alien mirror of "matter" like an "echo from smooth flat surfaces" (III 6.14.25). The intelligible form manifests in the bodies, like a statue reflected in the mirror. If we remove the image from the mirror, the statue itself is not affected. In the same way, if the image of the statue is removed from the mirror, the mirror is also not affected; in fact, the mirror remains formless.[21] Matter remains unaffected on receiving the Forms, and the Forms remain unaffected because their intelligible nature is undivided. Whereas matter and form are substantially unaffected, affection belongs to the divisible bodies (III 6.19.7). Thus, the perceptible world is nothing but an image of the intelligible world. What our senses perceive are only the shadows of the images existing as archetypes in the transient world of the Platonic Forms. The perceptible world is somehow an illusion in terms of being a reflection of the intelligible realm and so substantially unreal.

On the other hand, ὕλη is fundamentally important in the formation of living bodies (II.4.12). Without the contribution of matter bodies would be "without size" (ἀμεγέθη) and "without substance" (ἀνυπόστατα) (II 4.12.4), and no bodies would exist without the preexistence of material substratum to receive the Forms. If matter was completely without existence it would be impossible to receive even this dim existence of the Forms, so Plotinus' ὕλη should not be thought of in completely negative terms as the Gnostic "darkness" (II.9.2.12.39 ff.).[22] Matter *is there when nothing is there*, when the divine outflowing process ultimately runs out.

This positive view of matter is presented in *Ennead* IV.8 *On the Descent of the Soul into the Bodies*. In the eighth chapter of the treatise, ὕλη appears to be not only existing, but also related to the supreme divine splendor and goodness (IV.8.6.16–23). Plotinus makes it clear that, since matter is not an intelligible self-existing entity, it has to receive existence from something prior to and beyond it: the intelligibles. Likewise the perceptible bodies that project on matter are conditioned and dependent on the intelligibles, receiving their life through their participation in Intellect. The supplier of this life is Soul; Soul acts as the intelligible agent that illuminates the nature of Intellect on matter and finally formulates matter into a bodily appearance within the flow of becoming.

Plotinus' theory of Soul pervades the nine treatises of *Enneads* IV. The Soul, as the Third Hypostasis of Being, is an expression of Intellect, just as Intellect is of the One, and, as Intellect illuminates Soul by contemplating the One, the Soul illuminates the cosmos by contemplating Intellect. As it contemplates the Intellect in itself, the Soul pours forth its intelligible living light, beauty, and perfection on matter and formulates the cosmos (III.8.4). Hence, the cosmos is an organic unity originally driven by the intelligible vitality of Soul, the expressed image of an intelligible archetype in perceptible multiplicity. As such, the perceptible world is a work of beauty, light, and splendor, generated from an act of contemplation—the self-contemplation of the Soul towards the excellence of Intellect. Hence, human mind is able through the perceptible realm to know the intelligible realm. When human mind contemplates the perceptible images, it remembers their intelligible archetypes, and through this process it is able to recognize the truth of the intelligibles by the resemblance of the perceptibles to them. Through contemplation, the mind ascends from the cosmos to Soul, from Soul to Intellect and from Intellect to the One (III.8.8.1–2).

Furthermore, the Plotinian Soul can be theoretically divided into World Soul and Individual Soul. Contrasted with the World Soul, the Individual Soul has acted from an embryonic revolt against its perfect intelligible priors and an urge of unmanageable selfishness, whereas the World Soul governs, cares, and directs the universe with its comprehensive power, transcendent in the divine superior part (IV.8.2.26–38). Soul has an "amphibious" nature (IV.8.4.32), living and participating in both the intelligible and the perceptible worlds (IV.8.8.11–13). Soul has a "double life" (IV.8.4.19), and thus a "double nature," partly intelligible and partly perceptible (IV.8.7.1). For this reason, Soul has a share in both realms, occupying a "middle rank" (μέση τάξις) at the boundary between the perceptible and the intelligible nature (IV.8.7.5).

Soul, as an intelligible entity, includes within itself the intelligible seed in the form of λόγος; the formative principle. This formative principle is the expression and the activity of the Intellect in the Soul (V.1.6.45). But since the nature of λόγος in the Soul has not the perfection of Intellect, it is an image of Intellect. Thus, the formative activity of Soul succeeds by reason of its innermost formative principle that originates from the transient Intellect (II.4.3.5–11), and λόγος is exactly this intellectual spermatic generator of the perceptible world in the Soul (III.6.19.26–29). As Kalligas observes, λόγος "is a formative principle, organizing passive, chaotic matter into a well-articulated cosmos, and governing it as Nature. It acts like a seminal power embedded in each particular perceptible object, regulating its individual character and development. It is both unified and unifying, while possessing the "seeds of variety and multiplicity which are brought forth by its action."[23] The Soul animates the material bodies through λόγος (IV.3.10.35–42) and so the perceptible bodies are the intelligible projections or illuminations of Soul onto matter.[24] Thus, for Plotinus, Soul should not be conceived as present in the body but the body as present in the Soul; *the material universe is not an embodied soul but an ensouled body* (IV.3.22–23).

In the development of Plotinus' theory of matter and the nature of the ensouled body, important Presocratic theories are present in the discussion, especially in *Ennead* II.4 on the nature of matter and in *Ennead* IV.8 on the ensouled bodies. These two treatises therefore are the focus of the next two sections of this chapter.

5.2 PLOTINUS' CRITICISM OF PRESOCRATIC MATTER

In the seventh chapter of *Ennead* II.4, Plotinus puts forward an important criticism of Presocratic theories of matter with special reference to Anaximander, Empedocles, Anaxagoras, and the early Atomists, Leucippus, and Democritus. His argument against the Presocratics is that they do not recognize the insubstantiality and sterility of matter. As Kalligas notes, Plotinus criticizes the Presocratics in II.4.7, because of their inability to recognize the *tertium quid* which is subject to the interchangeability of the opposites.[25] Here Plotinus does not keep to a chronological line of criticism, but his treatment of Anaximander follows Empedocles and Anaxagoras, and precedes the Atomists. This flow of criticism reflects, as in many other cases throughout the *Enneads*, his spontaneous style of philosophizing. Nevertheless, II.4.7 involves the four most influential early philosophical theories of matter corresponding to three different schools of Presocratic thought: (1) Anaximander and the early Ionic thinkers of Miletus; (2) Empedocles and the Presocratic-Pythagorean movement of South Italy; (3) Anaxagoras and the Atomists' pluralistic natural philosophy of the late Ionic tradition.

Within this framework, Plotinus aims to set out a theoretical line of investigation. This interpretative line moves from the definite principle of Empedocles' theory of the "four elements" (lines 1–2), to the indefinite originative substance of the Anaximandrean "unlimited" (lines 2–13), then to the indefinite multiple units of the Anaxagorean "stuffs" (lines 13–20), and finally to the indivisible absolute principles, the "atoms," of Leucippus and Democritus (lines 20–28). Here it is noteworthy that while in lines 1–2 and 2–13 Plotinus refers directly by name to Empedocles and Anaxagoras, in lines 13–20 he refers indirectly to Anaximander and in lines 20–28 to the Atomists (line 20).

These allusions to Anaximander, Empedocles, and Anaxagoras have been indicated only by the *Index Fontium* of Henry and Schwyzer, Roussos,[26] and Kalligas.[27] Despite the documented significance of the source in Plotinus, H. Diels did not take *Ennead* II.4.7 into account as Presocratic testimony and modern scholarship lacks any detailed study of Plotinus' criticism of the Presocratic theories of matter. Armstrong notes on II.4.7 that Plotinus' criticism does not indicate any independent study of the Presocratics but is based on Aristotle's theory of matter[28] and is entirely Peripatetic in spirit.[29] Likewise Kalligas,[30] following É. Bréhier, suggests that Plotinus in II.4.7 probably has in mind Aristotle's *Metaphysics* 1069b20–3, or a Peripatetic commentary of the Aristotelian work; this consideration is based on Aristotle's reference to the same Presocratics as Plotinus in II.4.7.[31]

But the whole tenor of the criticism in II.4.7 reflects Plotinus' own thought rather than that of Aristotle or any other Peripatetic source. The similarities belong with Plotinus' own theory of matter and not the Aristotelian, and it is from this perspective that II.4.7 is of central philosophical importance. In support of this claim, the next four sections analyze the four Presocratic theories of matter as they appear in II.4.7 and discuss them in comparison with Plotinus' own theory of matter, in the chronological order of (1) Anaximander's theory of the *apeiron*, (2) Empedocles' theory of the four elements, (3) Anaxagoras' theory of the primeval mixture, and (4) Leucippus and Democritus' theory of atoms.

5.2.1 Anaximander's apeiron

Plotinus gives the following critique of Anaximander's theory of ἄπειρον at II.4.7.13–20:[32]

> Ὁ δὲ τὸ ἄπειρον ὑποθεὶς τί ποτε τοῦτο λεγέτω. Καὶ εἰ οὕτως ἄπειρον, ὡς ἀδιεξίτητον, ὡς οὐκ ἔστι τοιοῦτόν τι ἐν τοῖς οὖσιν οὔτε αὐτοάπειρον οὔτε ἐπ' ἄλλῃ φύσει ὡς συμβεβηκὸς σώματί τινι, τὸ μὲν αὐτοάπειρον, ὅτι καὶ τὸ μέρος αὐτοῦ ἐξ ἀνάγκης ἄπειρον, τὸ δὲ ὡς συμβεβηκός, ὅτι τὸ ᾧ συμβέβηκεν ἐκεῖνο οὐκ ἂν καθ' ἑαυτὸ ἄπειρον εἴη οὐδὲ ἁπλοῦν οὐδὲ ὕλη ἔτι, δῆλον.
> As for the man who maintains that matter is the *apeiron*, let him explain what it is. If the *apeiron* means endless extension, it is obvious that there is no such thing among beings; neither can it be unlimited in itself, nor an unlimited that exists in another nature, as an accident of some body; there is no unlimited in itself, since its parts too would be necessarily unlimited, and no accidental unlimited, since that of which it was an accident could not be unlimited in itself; it would not be simple nor even matter any longer. [trans. Armstrong modified]

In this passage, Plotinus refers indirectly to Anaximander in lines 13–14 with the masculine article ὁ; the reference would be recognizable since Anaximander's ἄπειρον was well-known.

Originally Anaximander's ἄπειρον signified the derivative source of all things without limits in space and time, and without any particular quantity or quality.[33] According to Simplicius (*in Physica* 24.13 ff.), who preserves the only extant fragment of the Presocratic, Anaximander is the first philosopher to say that the principle and element of all that there is is the "unlimited" (τὸ ἄπειρον). According to Aristotle, for Anaximander's ἄπειρον there was no beginning, but it is itself the beginning of all things (*Physics* 203b7). From this unlimited nature all things have their origin and end (fr. 1): "for they suffer punishment and make reparation to one another for their injustice, according to the assessment of time."

Anaximander's ἄπειρον marks a different position from the other Milesians on the material principle of the cosmos. Whereas Thales and Anaximenes define the originative substance as water and air respectively and thus associate it with a particular material element, Anaximander speaks of an unlimited substance, which lacks any materiality and mortality; in this, the ἄπειρον echoes the ontological neutrality of the Hesiodic Chaos. As Kahn puts it, Anaximander's ἄπειρον is a "huge inexhaustible mass, stretching away endlessly in every direction."[34] So Anaximander's primal principle is to be thought of as that unqualified immaterial and immortal substance that is the source of qualified, material, and mortal things in the cosmos; it is the unlimited source of being beyond any spatial, temporal, quantitive, or qualitive predication. As M. Schofield summarizes, the ἄπειρον is the *beyond*: "what necessarily lies outside our experience of space and time, pictured as stretching away boundlessly outside the limits of the cosmos which it encloses."[35]

Unfortunately, most of our information on Anaximander's ἄπειρον derives from later sources, such as Aristotle and Theophrastus, and then from the Neoplatonic Simplicius *in Physica* 24.13, Hippolytus *Refutatio* I.6.1–2, and pseudo-Plutarch *Stromateis*.[36] Plotinus' testimony of Anaximander's ἄπειρον in II.4.7.13–20 is therefore of great philosophical and doxographical importance. Armstrong states that Plotinus' criticism of Anaximander shows how closely he is following the Peripatetic tradition,[37] but this position lacks support in the text. If Plotinus had followed the Peripatetic tradition, he would have just repeated Aristotle's criticism and not given his own, but the identification of the ἄπειρον with ὕλη as the indefinite substratum of beings (II.4.15; III.6.7) shows that Plotinus did not have in mind Aristotle's interpretation of Anaximander's ἄπειρον at *Physics* 204a–b.[38] Plotinus sets out his own interpretation of Anaximander's principle and to some extent appears to agree with it.

Plotinus' opening words in II.4.7.2–13 testify that the exact nature of Anaximander's ἄπειρον was still in his time a disputable issue. He therefore proceeds to interpret the notion of the ἄπειρον in his own terms. If Anaximander's ἄπειρον means "endless extension" (ἀδιεξίτητον), it would be related to the concept of unlimitedness and not the indefiniteness that is preferable for matter (VI.6.17.14).[39] For Plotinus, such an interpretation of ἄπειρον (as the unlimited) cannot be accepted for the following reason (II.4.7.15–20): ἄπειρον has to be either "unlimited in itself" (αὐτοάπειρον), or "accidentally unlimited" (συμβεβηκός). The former case is denied since it is absurd for every part of the unlimited to be unlimited too (17–18). The second case is denied since every particular in which the accidental unlimited participates cannot be unlimited apart from that accident, so it cannot be a simple principle, and therefore not to be identified as matter (18–20).

As Plotinus concludes only if Anaximander's ἄπειρον has the meaning of the *unqualified and indefinite substratum that underlies the physical bodies* is accepted as an appropriate definition of matter. This position is explained at II.4.15.

> But matter is set in order, as are all things which are not matter in so far as they participate in it or are reckoned as matter; so matter must be the indefinite, but not indefinite in the sense that it is so incidentally and that the indefinite is an incidental attribute of it. . . . So the indefinite is not an incidental attribute of matter; the indefinite is matter itself. [II.4.15.8–17; trans. Armstrong modified]

According to this passage, Plotinus defines ὕλη as the "indefinite" only if the term ἄπειρον is not used as an incidental attribute or as *logos*. Since matter cannot be definite or something defined, it has to be identified with the indefinite itself and not its possible predicates.

In the following lines of the same chapter, Plotinus therefore explains the ontological difference between "intelligible matter" and "perceptible matter": "they differ as the archetype differs from the image" (II.4.1522). But in this case the Platonic model is reversed.[40] Whereas the vitality of the perceptible world is a lesser copy of the intelligible realm, the indefiniteness of perceptible matter is contrasted with the archetype of the intelligible indefiniteness:

> For indefiniteness is present in a higher degree in that which is less defined; and less in the good is more in the bad. That which is in the intelligible world, which has a greater degree of existence, is indefinite only as an image. In contrast, that which is in the perceptible world has a less degree of existence, and in proportion, since it has escaped from being and truth. And sunk down into the nature of the image, it is more truly indefinite. [II.4.15.24–28; trans. Armstrong modified]

Thus, the indefiniteness (ἀπειρία) of perceptible matter is the original version of indefiniteness and not vice versa. Due to the sterile and negative nature of matter contrasted with the perfection of Intellect, matter is characterized as the archetypal indefinite by opposition to the excellence of the formative principle (II.4.15.29–37).[41]

This is why the Plotinian ὕλη is truly nonbeing, always indeterminate, insatiate, and in complete poverty, an insubstantial existence nowhere stable in being, an invisible phantom which remains unseen, a lie in the imagination of fleeting frivolity, a mirror reflected in another mirror, an imitation filled with nothingness, a formless ghost beyond definition and intelligence.[42] As such ὕλη can be identified only with evil itself: a kind of "unmeasuredness contrasted with measure" (ἀμετρίαν πρὸς μέτρον), "formlessness contrasted with form" (ἀνείδεον πρὸς εἰδοποιητικὸν), "insufficiency contrasted with self-sufficiency" (ἀεὶ ἐνδεὲς πρὸς αὔταρκες), "indefiniteness contrasted with limit" (ἄπειρον πρὸς πέρας) (I.8.3.12–15).

The latter rejection clearly removes the original notion of "unlimited" from Anaximander's ἄπειρον and elucidates Plotinus' interpretation of ἄπειρον as "indefinite." Since indefiniteness signifies imperfection and this imperfection exists only in matter, true indefiniteness subsists originally at the level of matter and not at the level of Intellect (II.4.5.28). Consequently ὕλη, because of its ἀπειρία, must be called ἄπειρον in a sense that signifies its indefinite, insubstantial, unqualified, and unintelligent nature. Only with this precondition can Anaximander's ἄπειρον be accepted as an appropriate definition of Plotinus' ὕλη—as the *indefinite substratum of beings.*

But whereas Plotinus adopts a more or less affirmative position towards Anaximander's conception of ἄπειρον, he is totally critical of the theories of Empedocles, Anaxagoras, and the Atomists.

5.2.2 Empedocles' Theory of the Four Elements

Plotinus' criticism of Presocratic concepts of Matter begins with a direct reference to Empedocles (II.4.7.1–2), who is castigated for classifying the four elements (fire, air, water, and earth) as ὕλη. For Plotinus, the destructibility of the elements tells against Empedocles' position:

> Ἐμπεδοκλῆς δὲ τὰ στοιχεῖα ἐν ὕλῃ θέμενος ἀντιμαρτυροῦσαν ἔχει τὴν φθορὰν αὐτῶν.
> Empedocles, who identifies the elements with matter, has their destruction as evidence against him. [II.4.7.1–2; trans. Armstrong modified]

This passage can obviously be compared with the parallel of *Ennead* V.1.9.5–7. As in V.1.9.5–7, in II.4.7.1–2, Plotinus refers again to Empedocles' theory of the four material elements, but whereas in V.1.9.5–7 Plotinus simply refers to Empedocles' theory, in II.4.7.1–2, he further explains and criticizes it.

For Empedocles, the four "roots" (ῥιζώματα) are the distinct and equally balanced material elements of the cosmos.[43] Within his poetic language, he uses different names, initially of divine figures, to describe their distinct nature (fr. 6): "Hear first the four roots of all things: bright Zeus and life-bringing Hera and Aidoneus and Nestis, whose tears are the source of mortal streams."[44] According to Wright, the botanical terms "roots" indicate the vitality of the substructure, their unseen depths and the potentiality for growth, while the divine names indicate their potency and sempiternity.[45]

Empedocles defines the four elements as the immortal material principles that make up and give form to the countless types of mortal beings, while they themselves remain fundamentally immobile, unchanged and imperishable (fr. 35; fr. 12). They are "the only real things" (fr. 21.13), "equal," and "alike in age" (fr. 17.27), while each has its particular prerogatives and properties (fr. 17.28). Like Parmenides' Being, the Empedoclean elements are 'unborn' (fr. 7), 'indestructible' (fr. 17.31), and 'always the same' (fr. 17.35). Due to the completeness of the four elements, being is continuous, without spatial gaps: "there is no part of the whole that is empty" (fr. 13).[46] Empedocles accepts Parmenides' thesis that nothing comes-to-be or passes-away. Generation and destruction have to be denied; so-called generation is merely the mixing (μίξις) of the elements in various proportions, while destruction is the separation (διάλλαξις) of the various compounds into their original elements (fr. 8.6; fr. 21).[47]

Consequently, Empedocles' cosmos is a multidivergent synthesis of the elements expressed in various kinds of things. He describes this diversity by the simile of the painter who produces all his figures and objects in his artifact through the combination of four basic colors:

> As painters, men well taught by wisdom in the practice of their art, decorate temple offerings—they take in their hands pigments of various colours, and after fitting them in close combination, more of some and less of others, they produce from them shapes resembling all things, creating trees and men and women, animals and birds and water-nourished fish, and long-lived gods too, highest in honour; so let not error convince you in your mind that there is any other source for the countless perishables that are seen, but know this clearly, since the discourse you have heard is from a god. [fr. 23; trans. Wright]

In this context, the testimony of Aëtius IV.14.1,[48] in which the parts of the four roots that are in the composition of the mirror set the emanations from the reflected object becomes relevant.[49] Empedocles' conception of the mirror reflections in connection with the material elements is a striking precursor of Plotinus' metaphor of matter identified with the mirror of Dionysus on which the Forms are reflected (IV.3.12.1; III.6.7–13).

However, unlike Plotinus II.4.7.1–2, the terms "matter" (ὕλη) and "element" (στοιχεῖον) do not appear in Empedocles' extant fragments. The term στοιχεῖον as "the material primary component immanent in things" seems to be Aristotelian (*Metaphysics* 1014a25–35) and not originally Presocratic. Hence, the source of II.4.7.1–2 is usually thought to be Aristotle (*Metaphysics* 985a31–33).[50]

But in quoting Empedocles in *Ennead* II.4.7.1–2, Plotinus does not necessarily have in mind Aristotle or any another Peripatetic source, and indeed there are no strong textual or philosophical similarities between the Aristotelian and the Plotinian texts. As in *Metaphysics*, Aristotle links matter and the elements in his work *On Generation and Corruption* 322b1–10 but without further clarifying this position. Plotinus is surely relying on his own evidences as the term ἀντιμαρτυρεῖ in line 1 presents. Moreover, whereas Aristotle diminishes the fundamentality of the Empedoclean elements by referring to them as the so-called elements (*Gen. Cor.* 322b1–5) and "simple bodies" (for instance in *De Caelo* 298a27 ff.), Plotinus criticizes Empedocles on a different philosophical ground: *the destructibility of the elements*. Consequently, even if Plotinus' theory of matter is influenced by the Aristotelian theory and the conception of ὕλη in connection to Empedocles seems to be originally attributed by Aristotle, the critique in II.4.7.1–2 is clearly Plotinian in spirit.

Moreover, II.4.7.1–2 is a continuation of Plotinus' discussion on the nature of elements in chapter 6. For Plotinus, the interchangeability of the elements leads inevitably to the conclusion that ὕλη has to be different from bodies, and related to the indestructible substratum that underlies bodies (II.4.6.1–14). The elements in turn have to be understood as *hylomorphic* composites (II.4.1.8–11). Plotinus' argument in II.4.6.14–20 goes as follows:

1. The elements could be Form, Matter, or composite of Matter and Form;
2. They are not Form because they have dimension and magnitude;
3. They are not Matter because they are destructible;
4. Therefore, the elements are composites of Form (in quality and shape) and Matter (in indefinite and formless substrate).

As Plotinus further explains in *Ennead* I.8.6.49–54, the elements have to be established on a common material substrate which is constitutive of their being. Since the elements are bound by a common substrate, they are not independent existences and so they are not contraries.[51]

Despite the fact that the elements are constituted from contrary qualities—fire from hot and dry, water from cold and wet—they cannot be contraries themselves, but the contrary qualities occur as accidents (I.8.6.49.54). Each of the elements corresponds to different degrees of bodily purity, ontological complexity, and organizational unity (III.6.6.40 ff.; V.9.3.15–20). Whereas fire has less of body and more purity and so it is closer to the unity of the intelligible realm, Earth has more of body and less purity and so is closer to the perceptible realm (III.6.6.49–58).

For the above reasons it is clear why Plotinus criticizes Empedocles' theory of the four elements as ὕλη. This criticism leads on to the next Presocratic theory of matter, that maintained by Anaxagoras.

5.2.3 Anaxagoras' Theory of Matter

After the criticism of Empedocles in II.4.7.1–2, Plotinus tackles Anaxagoras' theory of matter next in II.4.7.2–13, in particular Anaxagoras' theory of primeval mixture and its nonteleological relationship to Nous. This passage can be read as direct parallel to *Ennead* V.1.9.1–3 on Anaxagoras' Mind. But in II.4.7.2–13, Plotinus shows a deeper understanding of Anaxagoras' thought:

> Ἀναξαγόρας δὲ τὸ μίγμα ὕλην[52] ποιῶν, οὐκ ἐπιτηδειότητα πρὸς πάντα, ἀλλὰ πάντα ἐνεργείᾳ ἔχειν λέγων ὅν εἰσάγει νοῦν ἀναιρεῖ οὐκ αὐτὸν τὴν μορφὴν καὶ τὸ εἶδος διδόντα ποιῶν οὐδὲ πρότερον τῆς ὕλης ἀλλ' ἅμα. Ἀδύνατον δὲ τὸ ἅμα. Εἰ γὰρ μετέχει τὸ μίγμα τοῦ εἶναι, πρότερον τὸ ὄν· εἰ δὲ καὶ τοῦτο ὂν τὸ μίγμα, κἀκεῖνο, ἄλλου ἐπ' αὐτοῖς δεήσει τρίτου. Εἰ οὖν πρότερον ἀνάγκη τὸν δημιουργὸν εἶναι, τί ἔδει τὰ εἴδη κατὰ σμικρὰ ἐν τῇ ὕλῃ εἶναι, εἶτα τὸν νοῦν διὰ πραγμάτων ἀνηνύτων διακρίνειν ἐξὸν ἀποίῳ οὔσῃ τὴν ποιότητα καὶ τὴν μορφὴν ἐπὶ πᾶσαν ἐκτεῖναι; Τό τε *πᾶν ἐν παντὶ* εἶναι πῶς οὐκ ἀδύνατον;
> Anaxagoras, when he makes his mixture matter, and says that it is not a capacity for everything but contains everything in actuality, does away with Mind which he introduces by not making it the giver of shape and form, and not prior to matter but simultaneous with it. But this simultaneity is impossible. For if the mixture participates in being the existent is prior; and if both this mixture and being are existent, there will be need of a third over them, different from them. If then it is necessary for the maker to be prior, why did the forms have to be in small pieces in the matter, and why did mind have to separate them out with endless trouble, when it could, as matter is without quality, extend quality and shape over the whole of it? And how is it not impossible that everything should be in everything? [II.4.7.2–13; trans. Armstrong modified]

Despite its undoubted significant as an ancient source, this passage is missing from modern studies and commentaries of Anaxagoras as well as the source of II.4.7.2–13, like most of the Presocratic allusions in the *Enneads*, appears to be a controversial issue.

More precisely, Plotinus' identification of "mixture" (μῖγμα) with "matter" (ὕλη) in II.4.7.2–13 has no parallel in Anaxagoras' extant fragments and testimonies. So, according to Kalligas, Plotinus' criticism of Anaxagoras' μῖ γμα is based on Aristotle's *Physics* 187a23 and *Metaphysics* 1012a28 as well as the description of μῖγμα as "containing everything in actuality" found in Aristotle's *Metaphysics* 1069b1.[53] Moreover, the term μῖγμα appears three times in Simplicius' testimonies: (1) before the quotation of Anaxagoras' fr. 1 *in Physica* 155.23; (2) in the concluding comment after the quotation of fr. 5 *in Physica* 156.9; and (3) *in Physica* 154.29. These references can be supplemented with Aristotle's *Physics* 203a19. In the light of the above sources, the term μῖγμα seems to be an original Anaxagorean term.[54]

Yet, as Armstrong admits, II.4.7.2–13 is less Peripatetic than the rest of II.4.7; it implies Plotinus' own views on Intellect and Being,[55] and the *Index Fontium* of Henry and Schwyzer and Roussos[56] consider II.4.7.2–13 as an allusion to Anaxagoras' fr. 12.[57] However, Armstrong condemns Plotinus' criticism in II.4.7.2–13 as obscure,[58] but *contra* Armstrong there are no obscurities nor uncertainties in the passage if it is understood that Plotinus' criticism of Anaxagoras' theory of matter is an anachronistic interpretation of the Presocratic physical theory based on Plotinus' own metaphysical accounts of matter and Intellect. Moreover, it will be shown that II.4.7.2–13 leads to more fragments of Anaxagoras than just fragment 12.

Originally in Anaxagoras' natural philosophy, in the beginning of the cosmos everything was mixed together in a primeval mixture, and in the mixture nothing was distinguishable from anything else (fr. 1). The revolutionary formation of the cosmos started when this primeval mixture began to be separated out by the motive power of Nous (frs 11–13). Nous initiated the rotation of the mixture, resulting in the predominantly heavy parts coming to the center of the vortex and the finer parts moving away from it (fr. 12).[59] Matter under the control of Nous expands continually and indefinitely outwards from the original microdot which contained everything in the whole universe (fr. 13). The compact ingredients (χρήματα) of the primeval mixture were the opposite qualities of the wet and the dry, the hot and the cold, the bright and the dark that correspond in some way to Anaximander's opposites (4.14–17); the four Empedoclean elements earth (fr. 4.17), water (fr. 16), air, and fire (fr. 1.4 and 2), and an unlimited number of seeds (fr. 4.17–18).

Anaxagoras' theory of matter,[60] and especially the nature of "the seeds" (σπέρματα), has attracted a great deal of interest.[61] According to G. B. Kerferd, the ancient tradition, and more precisely Aristotle and Simplicius, attribute five principles to Anaxagoras' theory of Matter: (1) the canon of non-becoming, (2) indefinite divisibility, (3) universal mixture, (4) predominance, and (5) homeomereity.[62] In modern times, Anaxagoras' physical view about the material world is an extremely controversial issue, especially with reference to the primal elements of his natural philosophy. Some modern commentators maintain that the real elements in Anaxagoras' thought are the opposites and that the seeds are just quality substances.[63] C. Strang interprets the seeds as natural substances and not as biological particles.[64] On the other hand, C. C. W. Taylor defines the σπέρματα as "the genetic constituents of organisms,"[65] and this biological interpretation of Anaxagoras' seeds is followed by G. Vlastos who understands the seeds as the compounds of all the essential constituents of the living organisms and, for this reason, generalizes the "principle of germination from biology to cosmology, extending it to any process of generation."[66] Schofield accepts the biological context of the Anaxagorean seeds, but he denies agglomeration in favor of a zoological and agricultural interpretation.[67]

Whatever the details and as it is exposed in Anaxagoras' extant fragments, all material things in the cosmos originate from the primordial mixture of the basic σπέρματα (frs 1–6). But none of the σπέρματα is generated or destroyed; they are the ultimate combined, indivisible, and imperishable elements, unlimited in number, and different in shape, color, and taste, with each seed containing everything (frs 3–5). According to Aristotle,[68] the elements in Anaxagoras are not elemental principles, as in Empedocles, but aggregations of the *homoiomere*.[69] *Homoiomeria* means that for any given substance, its greater ratio is comprised of an infinite number of smaller particles having the same nature as the whole (and thus of all particles in existence), included in all physical mixtures.[70] On this basis, some modern scholars maintain that Anaxagoras' theory of the seeds as nonelemental particles is a reply to Empedocles' theory of elements.[71] But, as S. Teodorsson counters, this interpretation is in conflict with Anaxagoras' own words.[72] By following Aristotle's terminology, later ancient authors such as Diogenes Laertius II.6–15, Plutarch *Pericles* 4, Simplicius *in Physica* 27.2, and Galen *De Naturalibus Facultatibus* II.8 refer to the Anaxagorean σπέρματα as *homoiomere* meaning the elemental particles of like kind from which the whole universe is constructed. Likewise, Plotinus throughout the *Enneads* uses the term ὁμοιομερῆ in the Aristotelian and not in the Anaxagorean sense.[73]

Plotinus' discussion in *Ennead* II.4.7.2–13 refers precisely to this primordial mixture of Anaxagoras and the formation of the cosmos under the control and activity of Nous. Plotinus refers also indirectly to the Anaxagorean mixture when he denies the corporeality of the heavenly bodies at II.1.6.17–24. Plotinus criticizes Anaxagoras indirectly for putting "a great portion of earth" in the original mixture rather than of fire which is the most intangible of the elements. However, Plotinus' criticism of Anaxagoras in II.4.7.2–13 is prima facie an odd but unique ancient reading, strongly influenced by his Platonic background. Plotinus' criticism is threefold: directed (1) at the nature of the seeds as particular qualities; (2) at the nonteleological priority of Nous over matter; and (3) at the dictum "everything is in everything" as a principle working at the level of matter.

In a further analysis, with the phrase "the forms have to be in small pieces in the matter" (line 10), Plotinus alludes to the "smallness" of the σπέρματα in fragments 1.1–3, 3, 6.3, and 12.14, the term "forms" (εἴδη), denoting the Platonic exegesis of Plotinus. For Plotinus therefore, Anaxagoras' σπέρματα are conceived as Platonic Forms encapsulated in material beings, namely, the formative principle of Soul (VI.4.11). For Plotinus there is an organic analogy of the seed and its parts: "the seed is a whole and the parts into which it naturally divides derive from it, and each part is a whole and the whole remains an undiminished whole and all parts are one."[74] Hence, Plotinus' image of the seed echoes clearly Anaxagoras' principle of ὁμοῦ πάντα to express the self-inclusive unity of the seed (II.6.1.10; III.2.2.18–19). Plotinus' concept of the seed includes in one concept the two fundamental Presocratic principles of ἕν πάντα and ὁμοῦ πάντα and so strengthens the claim of Presocratic influence in Plotinus, especially that of Heraclitus and Anaxagoras. Of course, for Plotinus, perfect self-inclusiveness is evident only at the level of Intellect where the real beings, the intelligibles, are truly self-existent and all together in one unified whole.[75] As Plotinus clearly puts it at III.3.7.8–9: "the unity of all things into one is the principle in which all are together and all make a whole." Both the above references echo Anaxagoras' thought at a metaphysical level.

Despite the Platonic origins of Plotinus' interpretation, the εἴδη at II.4.7.2–13 could have an original allusion to the ἰδέας of Anaxagoras fr. 4.3. But from the evidence of the Enneadic text this can be no more than a hypothesis. What can be said for sure is that Plotinus conceives the Anaxagorean σπέρματα not at the level of matter but at the level of Soul, and on this basis he criticizes Anaxagoras' theory. Plotinus criticizes Anaxagoras' Nous in frs 11–14 as the separating motive principle that initiates, controls, and arranges all things in the universe on the grounds of its nonteleological nature and its ontological simultaneity with matter. On this basis, at the beginning of II.4.7.2–13, Plotinus sets out the following argument (2–6): since (1) the primordial mixture contains everything in actuality, and so (2) it is not the capacity of everything, therefore (3) Nous is not prior to matter but simultaneous with it. Both the intermediate conclusion of premise 2 and the final conclusion of premise 3 are original to Plotinus. Whereas premise 2 is based on Plotinus' view of matter as an unqualified capacity of everything, premise 3 is based on Plotinus' view of Intellect as the supplier of shape and form. Thus, since Nous is the transcendent intelligible provider of Being and Form prior to any existence, matter cannot be self-existence and simultaneous to Nous but posterior to it. When Anaxagoras introduces being to matter, he denies at the same time the priority of Nous.

As a result, Plotinus concludes that the simultaneity of matter and Nous is impossible. He denies this simultaneity by following an ontological-teleological analysis (6–9): (1) if the mixture participates in being, then being has to be prior to mixture; (2) if mixture and being are both existent in different terms there must be a third principle prior to them that will provide them with their necessary existence; (3) consequently, in all cases, the simultaneity of matter and being is impossible. Based on this rationale, Plotinus ends his criticism by following a Neoplatonic interpretation regarding Nous as the Platonic Demiurge (9–13): since Nous is necessarily prior to its products and matter is totally unqualified and formless, it is absurd for matter to include the Forms in small pieces—as seeds in the original mixture and for Nous to separate the small pieces from the primordial mixture. Here Plotinus' criticism echoes Socrates' criticism of Anaxagoras' mechanistic nature of Nous at *Phaedo* 97b–99c.

Finally therefore it is impossible for Plotinus to accept Anaxagoras' statement that "everything is in everything." Plotinus' doubt echoes the well-known Anaxagorean dictum found in frs 6.3–4, 11, and 12.5–6. But what is the correct meaning of Anaxagoras' original statement? According to some scholars the correct interpretation of Anaxagoras' dictum is that "everything has a share in everything," meaning that in every substance there is share of every other substance since it includes somehow a portion of the initial mixture.[76] *Contra* this interpretation, Taylor follows a literal reading of the dictum, suggesting that "everything is in everything" means that, since every stuff is a component of every stuff, no stuffs are elementals relative to other stuffs, only compared to the constructed bodily entities.[77]

On the other hand, whereas Plotinus seems to understand the original meaning of Anaxagoras' dictum, he again criticizes it from his Neoplatonic perspective. The rhetorical question *how is it not impossible that everything should be in everything* finds an answer within his own philosophical system. For Plotinus, the self-inclusive interoperability that the Anaxagorean "everything is in everything" denotes should be applied at the level of Intellect and not at the level of matter. Although, despite II.4.7.2–13, the Anaxagorean dictum does not literally appear in the *Enneads*, in a passage of V.8, Plotinus explains how at the level of Intellect *everything is in everything* due to the incorporeal and spiritual transparency of the intelligibles:

> For all things in the intelligible world are transparent, and there is nothing dark or opaque; everything and all things are clear to the inmost part to everything; for light is transparent to light. Each intelligible there has everything in itself and sees all things in every other, so that all are

> everywhere and each and every one is all and the glory is unlimited; for each of them is splendid, because even the small is splendid; the sun there is all the stars, and each star is the sun and all the others. [V.8.4.5–11; trans. Armstrong modified]

According to this vivid description of the intelligible world, the Anaxagorean dictum is relevant for Plotinus *only* at the level of Intellect.[78] Paraphrasing Anaxagoras' words of fr. 11, Plotinus could say that "in everything there is a share of everything, but only in Nous."

To summarize: Plotinus' criticism of II.4.7.2–13 should not be limited only to Anaxagoras' fr. 12; his interpretation of Anaxagoras has to be regarded more as a Neoplatonic misinterpretation of the Presocratic. Plotinus' anachronistic reading belongs in the metaphysical framework in which he reads Anaxagoras' natural philosophy. As a result, Plotinus' criticism is not directed against Anaxagoras' theory of matter as such, but rather against its alleged ontological simultaneity with Nous. In spite of this, the presence of Anaxagoras in II.4.7 shows the significant role that the Presocratic played in the theories of matter of later philosophical antiquity.

5.2.4 The Atomic Theory of Matter

Plotinus ends his criticism of the Presocratic theories of matter with the early Atomists (II.4.7.20–28). He appears to be completely negative with regard to this Presocratic theory:

> Ἀλλ' οὐδὲ αἱ ἄτομοι τάξιν ὕλης ἕξουσιν αἱ τὸ παράπαν οὐκ οὖσαι· τμητὸν γὰρ πᾶν σῶμα κατὰ πᾶν· καὶ τὸ συνεχὲς δὲ τῶν σωμάτων καὶ τὸ ὑγρὸν καὶ τὸ μὴ οἷόν τε ἄνευ νοῦ ἕκαστα καὶ ψυχῆς, ἣν ἀδύνατον ἐξ ἀτόμων εἶναι, ἄλλην τε φύσιν παρὰ τὰς ἀτόμους ἐκ τῶν ἀτόμων δημιουργεῖν οὐχ οἷόν τε, ἐπεὶ καὶ οὐδεὶς δημιουργὸς ποιήσει τι ἐξ οὐχ ὕλης συνεχοῦς, καὶ μυρία ἂν λέγοιτο πρὸς ταύτην τὴν ὑπόθεσιν καὶ εἴρηται· διὸ ἐνδιατρίβειν περιττὸν ἐν τούτοις.
> Atoms again cannot hold the position of matter; for there are no atoms at all; all body is divisible endlessly; again the continuity of bodies and their flexibility, and everything that exists, is not explicable apart from mind, or apart from the soul which cannot be made up of atoms—out of atoms generation could produce nothing but atoms, since no maker could produce anything from a discontinuous material—and innumerable reasons might be brought, and have been brought, against this hypothesis and it need detain us no longer. [trans. Stephen Mackenna and B. S. Page modified]

In this passage, Plotinus not only considers the whole concept of atoms erroneous, but he also completely refutes their existence as such. Plotinus brings three interrelated arguments against the Atomic theory: (1) the endless divisibility of bodies, (2) bodily continuity and flexibility, and (3) the impossibility of generation of physical continuity from a discontinuous material. As it is obvious, Plotinus' criticism is clearly Platonic in spirit. Since physical bodies are wholly divisible, continuous, and flexible, it is impossible to regard as their cause the atoms that are fundamentally indivisible, discontinuous, and inflexible. Thus, the primal cause of physical bodies has to be a transcendent intelligible cause and not a corporeal one. Moreover, at the end of II.4.7.20–28, Plotinus admits that his arguments are not the only ones that had been brought against the Atomic theory, and he quickly closes the discussion with no further analysis. With the last lines of the passage, he probably refers to his own criticism of the Atomic theory in *Enneads* IV.7, *On the Immortality of the Soul*, and III.1, *On Destiny*; both treatises could be read in parallel not only with II.4.7.20–28, but also with the whole of II.4.7.

In *Ennead* IV.7, Plotinus states that the formative principle of all physical bodies exists in the Soul and not in matter. He therefore rejects the materialistic theories of Presocratic hylozoism (ch. 2), the Atomic theory (ch. 3), Stoic corporealism (chs. 4–8[3]), the Pythagorean soul-harmony theory (ch. 8[4]), and Aristotle's entelechy (ch. 8[5]). All these are denied in the light of Plato's authority and Plotinus' own hylomorphism (chs. 9–14).[79] For Plotinus, since bodies are composites of matter and Form, and life (as form and intelligence) is present fundamentally in the Soul then the formative vital cause of bodies exists only in the Soul and not in matter (IV.2.2–26). Since the four elements—fire, air, water, and earth—are lifeless of themselves, they cannot be regarded as a formative principle of bodies. It is impossible for a lifeless element to produce life, or for a mindless or disordered thing to generate mind and order (V.9.3.15 ff.). This criticism is directed against the Presocratic hylozoism not only of Empedocles' four-element theory, but also the Milesians, Heraclitus, Xenophanes, and in general of the Presocratic thinkers who maintain the materialistic causality and vitality of bodies.

As a Platonist, Plotinus maintains that the real cause of every composite corporeal nature should be found in the transcendent realm of the Forms and not internally in its matter substratum. It is this eternal vitality of the intelligible world expressed and manifested in *logos*—the inherent principle of Soul that formulates the bodies (IV.2.2.23–25)—that is the real cause of all corporeal entities. Likewise the unity of bodies cannot derive from partless units or particles as is supposed in the case of the Atomic theory (3.5–6):

> But if someone says that it is not so, but that atoms or other partless units can produce the soul by coming together in unity and identity of

> experience, he could be refuted by their juxtaposition, and that not a complete one, since nothing which is one and united with itself in identity of experience can come from bodies which are incapable of unification and sensation, but soul is united in itself in identity of experience. [IV.3.1–6; trans. Armstrong modified]

This obscure passage can obviously be compared with the criticism of the Atomic theory at II.4.7.20–28. Here again Plotinus attacks the Atomic theory on the basis that bodily unity and the identity of experience (ὁμοπάθεια)[80] are due to Soul's self-unity and self-sensitivity and not to the mere juxtaposition of atoms.

For the same reason Plotinus criticizes the Atomic theory at *Ennead* III.1.2–3. In this treatise he refutes the non-Platonic deterministic explanations of the material world (III.1.2–7) in favor of the Platonic teleological position (III.1.8–10).[81] He focuses on the Atomists and rejects their materialistic theories of being and the cosmos initially at chapter 2 and more extensively at chapter 3. For Plotinus, physical and psychological phenomena cannot be derived from corporeal principles such as atoms. Atomic motion, collision, combination, and agglomeration cannot determine our impulses and states, nor atomic necessity our various states of being (III.1.2.10–15). It is absurd to regard universal order, reason, and *logos* as being produced by the disorderly motion of atoms, and impossible to account for the production of atoms per se (III.1.3.3). Plotinus supports his position with the following argument:

> Suppose that atoms exist: these atoms are to move, one downwards—admitting that there is downward movement—another slant-wise, all haphazardly, in a confused conflict. Nothing here is orderly; order has not come into being, though the outcome, this universe, when it achieves existence, is all order; and thus prediction and divination are utterly impossible, whether by the laws of the science—what science can operate where there is no order?—or by divine possession and inspiration, which no less require that the future be something regulated. Material entities exposed to all this onslaught may very well be under compulsion to yield to whatever the atoms may bring: but would anyone pretend that the acts and states of a soul or mind could be explained by any atomic movements? [III.1.3.9–20; trans. Mackenna and Page modified]

This argument could be again compared with II.4.7.20–28, where again Plotinus refutes generation from disorderly atomic motion. As in II.4.7.20–28 Plotinus repeats in III.1.3.5–6, without clarifying again his source, that many sound arguments have been brought against the theory of atoms. This similarity between the two texts suggests that Plotinus had in mind the same argumentation and probably the same source *contra* the Atomic theory.[82]

However, passage IV.7.3.1–6, and the discussion in III.1.2–3 are usually regarded as a refutation of the late Epicurean theory of atoms and not that of the early Atomists Leucippus and Democritus. *Contra* this interpretation, the *Index Fontium* of Henry and Schwyzer reinstates the Presocratic origin of IV.7.3.3 as an allusion to Democritus' testimony found in Aristotle *De Anima* 403b–404a, Alexander of Aphrodisias *De Mixtione* 2, and Philoponus *De Anima* 35.12. Alexander's testimony is also alluded to at *Ennead* II.7.1.4–8 where Plotinus refutes the material transfusion of bodies due to the mechanical juxtaposition of elemental particles.[83] Moreover, as Armstrong observes, this passage is also an echo of Anaxagoras' testimony found in Aëtius I.17.2.[84]

Indeed, a careful look at IV.7.3.1–6, and III.1.2–3 reveals the terminology of the early Atomists. In the light of the extant fragments and testimonies of Leucippus and Democritus, we can make the following observation. By denoting the atoms as partless things in IV.7.3.1, Plotinus echoes Simplicius' testimony *in Physica* 925.10, and Aëtius I.16.2. It is noteworthy, that Simplicius reports that Epicurus denied the partlessness of atoms in favor of their indestructibility. This evidence leads again to the conclusion that Plotinus at IV.7.3.1–6 had in mind the early Atomists and not the later Epicurean atomic theory.

More clearly, the early Atomic theory is evident in III.1.3.2–3 where Plotinus describes the nature of atomic motion. With "disorderly motion" Plotinus alludes to Aristotle's *De Caelo* 275b29, and Aëtius I.26.2.[85] The term πληγή in the latter source as well as in Simplicius *in Physica* 42.10 goes back to the reference of the atomic πληγαῖς in III.1.2.11, and III.1.3.20. Again, with the phrase συμπλοκαῖς πρὸς ἄλληλα in III.1.3.2–3, Plotinus echoes Theophrastus' important testimony in *De Sensu* 66.8. Likewise, the multidivergent downward, upward, and sideward movement of the atoms in space expressed in III.1.3.9–11 leads to the positioning of atoms reported by Aristotle in *Physics* 188a22, and Galen's vivid description in *De Elementis* I.2, and Theophrastus' *De Sensu* 66.8. In addition, the identification of atoms with elements in III.1.3.1–2 echoes Simplicius *in Physica* 28.15, Hippolytus *Refutatio* I.13, Aristotle' *Physics* 265b24, Aëtius I.15.8.

Finally, but no less importantly, with the term Necessity (ἀνάγκη) in III.1.2.14, 3.8, 3.19, Plotinus refers indirectly to the Atomists' concept of necessity mentioned in Leucippus' fr. 2 "nothing happens in vain, but everything from reason and by necessity," and Democritus' frs 118 and 181.[86] Strikingly, the source of Leucippus' fr. 2 is Aëtius I.25.4 where the context of the passage is on Destiny (εἱμαρμένη) as the subject-matter of Plotinus' *Ennead* III.1. In this *Ennead*, an indirect allusion appears between Heraclitus' testimony DK 22A8 (=Aëtius I.7.22), and Plotinus' III.1.2.35 with regard to destiny and justice. It may well be that Plotinus and Aëtius had in mind the same passage or the same source, but unfortunately both authorities are silent on the issue.

Originally for the Atomists, on Aristotle's authority (*Physics* 196a24), necessity is connected to accidence (τὸ αὐτόματον). Plotinus seems to be aware of this detail of atomic theory. In particular, in *Ennead* III.2, *On Providence I*, Plotinus criticizes the atomic conceptions of "accidence" (αὐτόματον) and "chance" (τύχη): "to attribute the being and structure of this universal whole to accident and chance is unreasonable and belongs to a man without intelligence or perception" (III.2.1.1–2). This criticism is usually thought to be directed only to the Epicureans.[87] But from the above evidence, it is obvious that the idea of τύχη derives from the early Atomists, to whom in all probability Plotinus is replying directly. A similar criticism appears in *Ennead* IV.7.8[4].23–28:

> And in general these people also make ensouled things out of soulless, and things casually arranged out of things in disorder, and do not make order arise from the soul, but say that soul has received its existence from a chance arrangement. [trans. Armstrong]

With this passage, Plotinus again counters the Atomic theory of chance.[88] Similar responses to spontaneity and accidence can be found at VI.7.11.37; VI.8.8.26, 14.40, 18.30; VI.9.5.1–5. Yet none of these passages have been recognized as critical allusion to the early Atomists.

In a further analysis, the early theory of atoms[89] is based on the following fundamental tenets: (1) matter consists of separate, partless, solid, eternal, immutable, invisible, and intangible unit-particles which are physically and theoretically indivisible, and named, in the original Presocratic language, the "uncuttable" (ἄτομα);[90] (2) the atoms differ in shape (A from B), position (Z from N), and order (AN from NA) but not in quality; (3) empty space or void is necessary for the movement of atoms; (4) perceptible change and plurality are the result of the transfer of momentum by the moving atoms and such transfer occurs only by contact and not by distinct action. Actually, the theory of indivisible atoms should be regarded as a direct reply to Eleatic monism and in particular to Zeno's argument of infinite divisibility.[91] By taking a different position from the Eleatic absolute denial of nonbeing, the Atomists state that nonbeing exists as emptiness: *what-is* is the plenum of atoms, while *what-is-not* is the emptiness of void (fr. 156).[92] Emptiness can explain natural phenomena and physical plurality; *what-is-not* is in existence spatially as the fundamental prerequisite of physical motion. This mechanical motion is the result of reason and necessity and not of divine justice or moral law. Generation is an arbitrary motion from one state of atomic conglomeration to another through void. A structure of infinite uncuttable and invisible atoms lies behind the world of everyday experience (frs 6, 7, 11 and 117), and consequently perceptible qualities are merely "by convention": in reality there are only atoms and void (fr. 9 and fr. 125: νόμῳ χροιή, νόμῳ γλυκύ, νόμῳ πικρόν, ἐτεῇ δ' ἄτομα καὶ κενόν).

Plotinus is aware of the latter position in *Enneads* III.6.12.22–24, and IV.4.29.32–34.[93] In both passages, he seems to agree (III.6.12.24) with Democritus' theory that bodily qualities exist only by convention. In III.6.12.22–24, Plotinus states that since matter cannot be affected by form either in shape or size, then bodily alteration happens only by convention:

> If, then, anyone at this point should quote "colour by convention and other things by convention," because the underlying nature has nothing in the way which it is conventionally supposed to, his quotation would not be out of place. [trans. Armstrong]

Similarly, in IV.4.29.32–34, Plotinus follows the same argument:

> So, then the light of bodies which have perished would remain, but the repercussion, which is the result of all the visible qualities, would not remain. One might of course say that one sees by convention, and that the so-called qualities are not in their substrates. [trans. Armstrong]

From the above passages, it is obvious that Plotinus refers indirectly to Democritus. This is obvious in the use of the phrases τὸ νόμῳ χροιὴ καὶ τὰ ἄλλα νόμῳ at III.6.12.22–24, and νόμῳ ὁρᾶν at IV.4.29.32–34 that both to allude the original term νόμῳ of frs 9 and 125. But neither Plotinian passage is included as testimony in Diels, or in any other commentary or study of Democritus. The same rationale is followed in VI.3.25 where Plotinus refutes qualitative "alteration" (ἀλλοίωσις) in terms of corporeal "composition" (σύγκρισις), and "dissolution" (διάκρισις). This refutation leads clearly to Simplicius *De Caelo* 294.33, Aristotle *Metaphysics* 985b4, and Aëtius IV.4.6. But the *Index Fontium* of Henry and Schwyzer relates VI.3.25.1–5 only to Aëtius, and VI.3.25.34 to Aristotle; it omits Simplicius' source.

Finally, Plotinus accepts Democritus' principle "like is known by like" reported by Sextus (*Adversus Mathematicos* VII.116: τὰ ὅμοια τῶν ὁμοίων εἶναι γνωριστικά) in *Enneads* II.4.10.1–5, and VI.9.11.30–32. In the former treatise it is said that τῷ ὁμοίῳ τὸ ὅμοιον is the only possible and appropriate metaphysical way to conceive the indefiniteness of matter: "for if like is known by like, the indefinite is known by indefinite." Moreover the same principle can be applied by the initiator to succeed in the final mystical union with the supreme principle: the One (VI.9.11.30–32): "he sees principle by principle and that like is united with like" (31–32).

5.3 PLOTINUS' THEORY OF THE ENSOULED BODY

Plotinus' *Ennead* IV.8, *On the Descent of the Soul into the Bodies*, concerns the nature of matter and the ensouled bodies. Plotinus' intention in this early treatise, as later in *Ennead* II.9, is to attack the Gnostic pessimistic interpretations of Greek philosophy, especially concerning the living bodies and the purpose of the material world. In support of the Greek philosophical tradition, Plotinus recalls Heraclitus, Empedocles, the Pythagoreans, and Plato. It is noteworthy that Plotinus in II.9.18 comments on the misinterpreting accounts of the Gnostics with a borrowing of Heraclitus' expression of the Sibyl's "raving words" in fr. 92 (20: ἀπαξιοῦσιν ἀδελφοὺς λέγειν οὐδὲ τὴν κόσμου ψυχὴν *στόματι μαινομένῳ*.).[94]

Plotinus begins *Ennead* IV.8 by exposing the traditional dualistic views of the Presocratic and the Platonic theories related to the problem of the ensouled bodies (chs 1–4). Then Plotinus reconciles the alleged contradictions between the ancient theories with regard to the Soul's "sin," or "fall" into the body (ch. 5), and afterwards states his own positive perspective of the material world as the necessary effect of the divine splendor (chs 6–7). He concludes with his own innovative theory according to which every individual soul is not descended as a whole, but its intelligible part always remains at a higher level (ch. 8).

Plotinus' central question of *Ennead* IV.8 seems to be the following: *since Soul belongs to the higher intelligible realm how has it descended into a lesser corporeal body?* Initially, Plotinus searches for an answer in the Presocratic theories of Soul found in Heraclitus, Empedocles, and the Pythagoreans (1.11–27). But since the Presocratics neglected to clarify their accounts exactly, he turns his thought to Plato; his main philosophical authority (1.23–50). But Plato's accounts are unfortunately contradicted. Plotinus correctly sets out, on the one hand (1.27–40), Plato's pessimistic view of the material world found in the *Phaedo* (62b2–5, 65d1, 67d1), in the *Cratylus* 400c2, the cave of the *Republic* (514a–515c, 517b4–5, 532e3, 619d7), and the myth of the *Phaedrus* (246c–d, 247d5, 249b2), and, on the other (1.40–50), Plato's optimistic view found in the *Timaeus* (34b8, 30b8, 92c8, 29a3, 30b3, 39e7–9). Whereas in the former case, Plato disapproves the material world as a "cave" (the "den" in Empedocles' terminology) into which the Soul is fettered and buried, in the latter, he praises the material world as the most beautiful product of divine splendor and providence.[95]

But the problem of the ensouled body then remains inexplicable. Since the traditional Presocratic and Platonic accounts are contradicted, Plotinus searches for his own answer to the problem. Plotinus exposes a positive view of matter described as a necessary reality that reflects the higher splendor of the intelligible realm.[96] Plotinus states that there two kinds of bodily care: (1) the universal supervision, and (2) the particular direction (2.26–30). Whereas the first case involves the World Soul's untroubled government and order of the universal body, the second case involves the Individual Soul's active direction of the individual body.

On the one hand, the World Soul governs effortless the body of the universe. The World Soul, as the purest form of Soul, focuses constantly on the perfect and blessed intelligible realities and orders the universal body with its unlimited power. At this pure ontological level: "the World Soul does not belong to the body, but the body belongs to the World Soul" (2.49–53). Since the universal body is perfect, self-sufficient and always self-identical (2.14–21), the World Soul remains free from desires, unaffected, and free from compulsion and wants. The World Soul never leaves its eternal nature but belongs constantly to the divine intelligible realm (2.34–38).

On the other hand, the individual soul governs its lesser body with great difficulty. For Plotinus, there are two interrelated reasons why the ensouled body becomes displeased (2.47–53): (1) the body hinders the intellective act of the Soul, and (2) the body fills the Soul with pleasures, desires, and pain. Indeed, by directing all of its powers to its bodily part, the Soul becomes less actualized, absorbed in the particular rather than the universal (4.17–21). By looking to its part, the Soul separates from the whole and concentrates on one single thing, the individual body. Hence, the life of the individual soul becomes constrained, full of desires and difficulties. But for Plotinus neither of these problems really affects the real nature of Soul (2.46–53). Fundamentally, the Soul originates from the higher realm of the divine Intellect and its highest part is always directed to the eternal reality of the intelligibles. Bodily care is just a temporal misdirection from the eternal perfection of the intelligible world.

The descent of the Soul into the body is not immediate but follows a series of phases: (1) *the intelligible origins*: the Soul was originally a complete, perfect, and pure intelligible being among the intelligibles (4.5–7); (2) *the decision of separation*: due to an inner unquiet power the Individual Soul decided to abandon the entirety of the intelligibles and descend into the perceptible realm (4.7–10); (3) *the partition*: the decision of the Individual Soul changed its state, from whole to part, from completeness to incompleteness, from perfection to imperfection. It became isolated, self-centred, belonging to itself by departing to its own individual life, away from the intelligible entirety (4.10–12); (4) *the self-isolation*: when the Soul lives continually in this departing state, without contemplating the intelligibles, it becomes a distinct separate part and deepens its isolation (4.12–17); *the care of the body*: by self-isolating, the soul becomes weak, focusing only on its bodily part.

Hence, for Plotinus, the main reason for the problem of the Soul's descent lies in its struggle to govern a lesser body. When the ensouled body suffers in the bodily condition, the problem lies in its bodily part and not its intelligible part (IV 8.7.17–26). That is because the Soul does not descend entirely into the body but there is always something of it in the intelligible. For this reason, the spiritual outflowing is actually a kind of illumination of Soul directed from the intelligible realm to the lower reality of matter and not a complete separation from the intelligible world.

5.3.1 The Presocratic Theories of the Ensouled Body in the Enneads

The Presocratics are present throughout *Ennead* IV.8. It is the only occasion where Plotinus refers by name—just in a single treatise—twice to Heraclitus (1.11; 5.6) three times to Empedocles (1.17; 1.33; 5.5), and once to Pythagoras and his followers (1.21). Throughout these passages, Plotinus refers to Heraclitus' fragments 60, 84a, 84b, 90 and 101; Empedocles' fragments 115 and 120 and the Pythagorean doctrine of soul without any particular reference to an extant fragment. These Presocratic references and allusions have been recognized by most modern scholars but doubts have been cast on their importance in IV.8 as a whole. For Armstrong, commenting on IV.8.1.11–23, Plotinus "spends little time in considering the Presocratics and does not seem to find them very helpful."[97] Other scholars such as M. Marcovich (1967), and C. H. Kahn (1979) distrust the reliability of Plotinus' sources. However, Plotinus' references are extremely important not only for his philosophical discussion, but also for the authentic reestablishment of the Presocratic terminology and concepts. Hence, the following two sections discuss Heraclitus and Empedocles in the context of Plotinus' theory of the ensouled body.

5.3.2 Heraclitus' Theory of Soul and Physical Alteration

At IV.8.1.11–17 Plotinus' refers directly to Heraclitus' theory of soul.

> Ὁ μὲν γὰρ *Ἡράκλειτος*, ὃς ἡμῖν παρακελεύεται ζητεῖν τοῦτο, ἀμοιβάς τε ἀναγκαίας τιθέμενος ἐκ τῶν ἐναντίων, ὁδόν τε ἄνω κάτω εἰπὼν καὶ μεταβάλλον ἀναπαύεται καὶ κάματός ἐστι τοῖς αὐτοῖς μοχθεῖν καὶ ἄρχεσθαι εἰκάζειν ἔδωκεν ἀμελήσας σαφῆ ἡμῖν ποιῆσαι τὸν λόγον, ὡς δέον ἴσως παρ' αὐτῶν[98] ζητεῖν, ὥσπερ καὶ αὐτὸς ζητήσας εὗρεν.
>
> Heraclitus, who urges us to examine this, positing "necessary changes" from "opposite to opposite," and saying "way up and down" and "changing it is at rest," and "weariness to toil for and be ruled by the same," left us guessing, since he has neglected to make clear to us what

> he is saying, perhaps because we ought to seek by ourselves, as Heraclitus "himself sought and found." [trans. Armstrong modified]

In this passage, Plotinus offers an amalgamation of Heraclitus' accounts of physical alterations, the cosmic cycles of fire and the unity of opposites. First, with the phrase "necessary changes from opposite to opposite," Plotinus alludes to Heraclitus' concept of cosmic necessity and his theory of opposites.[99] Second, with "way up and down," Plotinus refers directly to Heraclitus' fr. 60. Third, with the phrases "changing it is at rest," and "it is weariness to toil for and be ruled by the same," he quotes directly Heraclitus' frs 84a and 84b on the changes of soul. In fact, the same reference to fr. 84a can be found in the phrase "rest in flight" (ἀνάπαυλα ἐν τῇ φυγῇ) at IV.8.5.6–7. Finally, with the statement "as himself sought and found," Plotinus refers indirectly to Heraclitus' fr. 101. The latter fragment is clearly alluded to again at V.9.5.31 as well as the relevant discussion about the nature of self-knowledge.[100]

Except for the latter allusion to fr. 101 in IV.8.1.17, all the other Heraclitean fragments quoted in IV.8.1.11–17 have been recognized by the *Index Fontium* of Henry and Schwyzer. In addition, for modern scholarship, IV.8.1.11–17 is the most important evidence of fragments 84a and 84b. It is significant that in Diels' study Plotinus' *Ennead* IV.8 is the sole source of frs 84a and 84b. Hence, G. S. Kirk,[101] Marcovich,[102] Roussos,[103] and Kahn[104] refer extensively to the context and the genuineness of the fragment as well as its importance in Plotinus. Similar ancient allusions to fragments 84a–b can be also found in Iamblichus' *De Anima* (*apud.* Stobaeus *Anthologium* I.49.39.40–44), and Aeneas Gazeus' *Theophrastus* 9.[105]

Iamblichus' citation echoes interestingly Plotinus' quotation of Heraclitus at IV.8.1.1–17.[106] Iamblichus obviously cites Heraclitus' fragments in the same way as in Plotinus' IV.8. The context of Iamblichus' passage is again the descent of the Soul. Thus, in all probability, Iamblichus' reference in *De Anima* is Plotinus' *Ennead* IV.8 which, as Kirk,[107] and Roussos[108] note, is the earliest and the most exact. Kirk, on the authority of Diogenes Laertius IX.8, maintains that the Heraclitean fragments quoted by Plotinus are "clearly dependent upon Theophrastus,"[109] but this position lacks support in Plotinus' text. As Roussos correctly replies, Plotinus seems to be aware of the original text of Heraclitus and not through an intermediate source such as Theophrastus or Diogenes Laertius.[110] This position can be further justified with the other Heraclitean allusions throughout the *Enneads* as well as the fact that Heraclitus' book was undoubtedly known during the third century AD.[111]

But despite its importance in later ancient authors, the reliability of Plotinus' citation in IV.8.1.1–17 has been doubted. For instance, Marcovich regards Plotinus' source as untrustworthy, highly enigmatic, and very hypothetical.[112] The same scholar notes that Plotinus gives no clue to the understanding of the Heraclitean fragments and the reason for him quoting Heraclitus' words is to imply the necessity of change in order to explain the nature of the living bodies.[113] Likewise, Kahn states that Plotinus' brief citations do not provide us with a "firm grip" of the Heraclitean text: "Plotinus quotes from memory, and we have no way of telling how far his memory reflects his own reading of Heraclitus or some more traditional account."[114] But even if Plotinus cannot be used as a literal source for Heraclitus—since he does not regard himself either as a historian of philosophy or a philologist—the philosophical importance of IV.8.1.1–17, as it will be shown in this chapter, cannot be doubted.

Concerning the content and context of the fragments in Heraclitus' book, modern scholars again deviate. Whereas, Bywater,[115] Gilbert,[116] Gigon,[117] and W. K. C. Guthrie[118] regard frs 84a and 84b as two separate and independent fragments, H. Diels, G. S. Kirk,[119] J. Burnet,[120] M. Marcovich,[121] E. N. Roussos,[122] and C. H. Kahn[123] regard frs 84a–b as one single fragment and link the meaning of both quotations together. Plotinus certainly quotes Heraclitus within the framework of his theory of Soul and reflects the Heraclitean opposites. With regard to the context of frs 84a–b, Diels and Marcovich agree that "fire" (πῦρ) is the subject of both fragments.[124] This conclusion is obviously erroneous since the context of Plotinus' passage is psychological and not cosmological, and the same context appears in the aforementioned passages both of Iamblichus and Aeneas Gazeus.

For Plotinus, and originally for Heraclitus, the subject of 84a–b is the soul (ψυχή). This is argued for by Roussos in his relevant study on Heraclitus and Plotinus.[125] Both fire and soul are interrelated for Heraclitus, since fire is the material substance of soul and soul follows the cosmic transformations of fire, the principal element of cosmic vitality.[126] Like the cosmos which is sustained by the "transformations of fire" (fr. 31), so for the soul "it is death to become water, for water it is death to become earth; out of earth water becomes and out of water, soul" (fr. 36). By means of this circular pattern of cosmic alterations, fire is transformed from one physical state to another: "cold things warm, warm cools, wet dried, parched is moistened" (fr. 126). Likewise, the soul alters from water to earth and from earth to water and then returns back to the original fiery condition.[127] The entrance of water into the fiery soul decreases its power and means the beginning of soul's death. Hence, the "wet" soul is powerless and weak like that of the drunkard who is unable to control his body and language (fr. 117). When the soul fails to control its *thumos* (fr. 85) and indulges its desires and anger, it loses its fiery substance and becomes "wet."[128] On the other hand, the dry soul is wisest and best (fr. 118); the soul closer to its fiery substance.

Heraclitus further relates fire and soul to *logos*. *Logos* governs fire and, by extension, both soul and the cosmos. Hence, the power of *logos* is represented in the image of thunder which rules and articulates everything (fr. 64).

The *logos* of soul has an immense depth, deep in the inner structure and causality of life (fr. 45): "you could not find the limits of soul though you traveled the whole way—so deep is its *logos*." If we seek for the ends of the soul we will be like the gold diggers who search through much earth and find little gold (fr. 22). The ultimate discovery will be the understanding of *logos* in fire, the primal material substrate of soul. Similarly, for Plotinus, the nature of matter hides deep into indefinites. As he explains, using the same words as Heraclitus, if someone, by a deep investigation, is able to distinguish the indefinite nature of matter from the other existing beings the result will be to understand that matter is originally an insubstantial nature (III.6.15.14–15: ἀλλ' εἴ ποτε ἐξεύροι αὐτὴν λόγος βαθύς τις ἐξ ἄλλων ὄντων).[129]

Furthermore, the Heraclitean soul extends and increases according to its innermost principle of *logos* (fr. 115: ψυχῆς ἐστι λόγος ἑαυτὸν αὔξων),[130] and in the same way, at VI.5.9.12–15, Plotinus recalls Heraclitus' fragment 115 to describe the limitless nature of the Soul (οἱ δὲ λόγον αὐτὸν αὔξοντα τὴν φύσιν αὐτῆς).[131] Since the Plotinian Soul is unbounded, the body of the universe, as an ever-expanding organic unity, follows the intelligible expansion of the Soul (IV.3.9.36). For this reason, the Soul totally enfolds and surrounds with its intelligible power the universal body and so the universe extends as far as the Soul extends (9.36–51). But the "expansion" should not be regarded literally in spatial terms (VI 5.9.18–23). The Soul does not expand either spatially or temporally. It is actually the first "intelligible expansion" after Intellect, an unlimited vital extension of an unbounded intelligible perfection and unity (IV.4.16.21–31; IV.3.17).

Consequently, the Plotinian Cosmos is an organic whole causally ordered and driven by *logos*: the formulating power of Soul. *Logos* for Plotinus is the intelligible container of the Forms within Soul; the intelligible principle implanted into the Soul's infinite ends (I.8.11–17; III.8.8.46). It is the intelligible seed; the interconnecting principle throughout the being of the perceptible world. While Intellect is a double capacity of intelligence and being, *logos* is the double divine root, the intelligible potentiality of thought and life in Soul. When *logos* unfolds, intellection and life are both manifested. *Logos* underlies the organic coherence of the cosmos and manifests the absolute unity of Intellect into a unified multiplicity. Hence, the cosmos is the extended image of the intelligible plurality into perceptible multiplicity. Thus, since Soul extends as far as the universal body, the seeds of *logos* exist *potentially* everywhere in the perceptible world, ready to be *actualized* by the Soul (IV.3.10.38–41; IV.7.2.20–25).

Likewise in Heraclitus' thought, the unlimited nature of *logos* stands in opposition to the limited and measurable nature of fire (fr. 31). The Heraclitean cosmos is a limited view of an unlimited nature. Following the structure of *logos* nature becomes observable because of its limited measures. If the sun oversteps its measures the sun will be punished by the dark guardian powers of Justice: the Ἐρινύες (fr. 94). The punishment of the sun involves loss of its kingdom and absolute darkness. Hence, the Ἐρινύες represent the unbounded darkness beyond the kingdom of the sun. Thus, the Heraclitean world is the ordered outcome of the hidden *logos*. The regular orbits of the sun, the circular transformations of fire, the divine unity within plurality are representations of the same *logos,* the necessary condition for a limited world of appearances in time under the government of an infinite and indefinite harmony. For Heraclitus, the real constitution of nature hides behind the natural phenomena (fr. 123). The Heraclitean *logos* is constantly associated with and inherent to every single being (fr. 1) because it is "common" (fr. 2) and "wise" (fr. 50), shared by all (fr. 114). This *logos* is the causal principle of nature, the element of unity within multiplicity (fr. 41), the universal law (fr. 33) that governs all things. For this reason, the unseen harmony of *logos* is stronger and better than the apparent one (fr. 54). Cosmic harmony occurs in accordance with the hidden *logos* and the apparent interrelationship of the opposites (fr. 51); from opposition comes conjunction, and from tones at variance the perfect harmony (fr. 8). Everything is at variance with itself and returns back on itself (fr. 48). The soul, which recognizes the hidden underlying *logos*, becomes truly wise (fr. 93, 107).

Like the hidden and unseen harmony of Heraclitus', becoming is underlined by the unity of *logos* (fr. 113: *ξυνόν ἐστι πᾶσι τό φρονέειν*), Plotinus' becoming is the living offspring of a concealed and common *logos* that underlies the unity of the natural world (VI.5.10.12: καὶ γὰρ καὶ τὸ φρονεῖν πᾶσιν ὅλον· διὸ καὶ *ξυνὸν τὸ φρονεῖν*). It is Soul's self-contemplation in silence, the inner contemplation of the unseen *logos* (III.8.6–8). Likewise, for Heraclitus, life is a manifestation of fire spread out in the cosmos as the vital extension of the hidden harmony of *logos* (frs 8, 51, 54). The revealed ἁρμονία is actually the harmony of opposites (fr. 8) where simultaneously everything that "conflicts with itself agrees with itself" (fr. 51). The Heraclitean image is that of the bow and the lyre which require tension between the parts to function, and whereas for the bow the name is life, its work is death (fr. 48). Thus, the same thing exists in us as "living and dead," "waking and sleeping," "young and old" (fr. 88). Within the cosmic circle of birth, death, and rebirth the descent of fire to water and from water to earth is endlessly repeated in the reverse ascending order from earth to water and from water to fire.[132]

Thus, the law of opposition arises from the conjunction of the opposites through *logos*. For Heraclitus the conflict of oppositions is represented by the image of "war" (πόλεμος) that makes gods and mortals, free and slave (fr. 53) and keeps the cosmos in material equilibrium and harmony (fr. 8). In the Heraclitean cosmos of opposition, the soul feels the conflict of the different tensions in experiencing a series of contradictory feelings: it is the experience of disease that makes health important, the experience of hunger that makes satiety sweet, the experience of weariness that makes rest good (fr. 111). By extension it is the experience of the bad that makes the good understandable: there would be no right without wrong (fr. 23), no life without death, or death without life. In Heraclitus' mind, cosmic conflict, expressed in the image of war (frs 80 and 53), is the common rule, the *logos,* between the different species in nature; hence, all things happen by strife and necessity (fr. 80).

Similarly, Plotinus states that πόλεμος represents the necessary and continuous conflict of life for both animals and humans (III.2.15.5). As he further explains in III.2.16, a chapter which reflects Heraclitus' language and thought, life is the battlefield of beings. Since all individual entities are never isolated but interwoven by the principle of *logos*, war and battle in life derive from *logos*, setting in conflict the opposites (III.2.16.34–58). The multiplicity of beings brings opposition in life, an opposition presented harmoniously in the plot of a drama, the drama of life (III.2.16.36–37). As the dramatic story relates the conflict to a kind of harmonious concordance by composing the complete story of the hero in conflict, in the same way in the universe the harmonious melody derives from the conflicting sounds in the rational proportions of musical scales (III.2.16.41–45; IV.4.41.6–9). Thus, Plotinus' conception of πόλεμος reflect Heraclitus' theory of the harmony of opposites expressed in frs 51 and 54: fragment 54 echoes at *Ennead* I.6.3.28–29, while fr. 51 to *Enneads* III.2.16.48, and IV.4.41.

In addition, for Heraclitus, the necessary interaction of the opposites requires *movement* and results in "change" (μεταβολή); even the "sacred barley drink" (κυκεών) has to be stirred, otherwise its dry ingredients settle and the potion as such loses its character and efficiency (fr. 125).[133] So change is actually "exchange" (ἀνταμοιβή) of fire—the standard for exchange like goods for gold and gold for goods (fr. 90). Thus, everything within the cosmic generation and destruction pays the price of its life and existence like the gains of *thumos* (fr. 85). Within the context of fr. 60, "the way-up and the way-down are one and the same": the "way" (ὁδός) signifies the *logos* as the linking path between the opposites and "up and down" (ἄνω κάτω) the two opposite sides of the cosmic unitary pattern. Heraclitus' fragment 60 has been interpreted in two ways: (1) by a psychological-elemental interpretation, and (2) by a physical-literal interpretation,[134] so that the image of ἄνω κάτω is a perfect example of the unity of the opposites. For Heraclitus, "living" and "dead," "waking" and "sleeping," "young" and "old," "day" and "night," "winter" and "summer," "war" and "peace," "satiety" and "hunger" (fr. 67) are opposite sides of the same *logos*. And *logos* also accounts for opposite predicates bringing opposite results: the sea water is good for fishes but harmful for humans (fr. 61); day in the presence of the sun but night its absence (fr. 57); gold is rubbish for donkeys but valuable for humans (fr. 9); mud is clean for pigs but dirty for humans (frs 13, 37).

In *Ennead* IV.8, Plotinus is undoubtedly aware of Heraclitus' fr. 60.[135] For Plotinus, the generation of life at each ontological level is a combination of two metaphysical moments: Procession (πρόοδος) and Return (ἐπιστροφή). The former is described as a downward-descending activity (κάτω) and the latter as an upward-ascending activity (ἄνω), a pattern that strongly reflects the Heraclitean one. Indeed, throughout the *Enneads*, the pattern of ἄνω κάτω is a common metaphor of generation between the different realities of Being: ἄνω represents the higher realm of the intelligible world and κάτω the lower realm of the perceptible world.[136]

Particularly in *Ennead* IV.8, the Soul is defined as a twofold nature, partly intelligible and partly perceptible (IV.8.7.1–2). As Plotinus clearly puts it in IV.8.8.11–13, every Soul has a part in "what is below" towards the direction of the corporeal body (κάτω πρὸς σῶμα), and a part in "what is above" towards the direction of the incorporeal intellect (ἄνω πρὸς νοῦν). It is the middle-path (ὁδός) that links the intelligible and perceptible worlds like an amphibious nature (ἀμφίβιος), which participates at the same time in both realities (8.4.31–35). While the Soul illuminates the heavens with its higher intelligible part, at the same time it illuminates the perceptible world with the lower light of its perceptible part (IV.3.3.17.8). The "great light" of the divine Intellect abides and shines and its radiance goes out through the world in accordance with *logos* and proportion (IV.3.17.12–18; VI.4.9.25–6). Thus, every soul has a power directed to the upper intelligible world and a power suited to administration in the lower world. As Plotinus vividly describes, it is like the light attracted upwards to the sun, but not grudging its administration to what lies below (IV.3.4.3–6).

So the beauty of the perceptible world is a manifestation of the noblest intelligible beauty (IV.3.6.23–25). But while the intelligibles are beautiful in themselves, the perceptibles receive their beauty by participation in the intelligibles, imitating intelligible beauty (6.25–28). Consequently, in the Plotinian universe, everything is animated by the vital agency of Soul.

> And the sun also is a god because it is ensouled, and the other heavenly bodies, and we, if we are in any way divine, are so for this reason: for "corpses are more throwable away than dung." [V.1.2.40–42; trans. Armstrong]

The latter phrase (νέκυες γὰρ κοπρίων ἐκβλητότεροι) is a direct quotation of Heraclitus' fr. 96.[137] Plotinus is a main source for this fragment, but he does not offer any particular interpretation, other than using Heraclitus' words to highlight the necessary vitality of the whole universe driven by the life of Soul.

Plotinus follows the same method throughout the *Enneads*. In I.6.5.43–45, he paraphrases Heraclitus' fragment 5, in II.3.13.13–17, fragment 11, in

I.6.6.1–6, fragment 13, in VI.3.11.22–25 frs 82 and 83. In all the above, Plotinus borrows a phrase from Heraclitus to stress the meaning of his own theory but without any further reference to a context for the fragment.[138] Particularly, in *Ennead* I.6 *On Beauty*, Plotinus refers twice to Heraclitus: to fr. 5 at I.6.5.43–45,[139] and to fr. 13 at I.6.6.1–6.[140] In the former case, fr. 5 is used to criticize the impurity and moral ugliness arising from the admixture of the Soul with body, while in the latter, fr.13 is used to stress the need for the Soul's purification from bodily impurity in order to ascend to true beauty and perfection. Here Plotinus refers, in all probability, to Heraclitus with the phrase "the ancient account" (ὁ παλαιὸς λόγος) in the first line of the passage, but his context is the elaboration of "purification" as self-control, courage, virtue, and wisdom, whereas for Heraclitus "washing in mud" for pigs is an example of a paradoxical opposite.

Likewise in *Ennead* II.3.13.13–17, Plotinus uses Heraclitus' fr. 11 to stress that only rational and living beings are self-controlled.[141] On the one hand, "soul-less things" (ἄψυχα) have unlimited movement and are controlled with an external power outside themselves, on the other hand, "ensouled beings" (ἔμψυχα) are either irrational animals controlled by others where someone "controls them with the whip," or rational animals controlled by themselves. Whereas for Plotinus the latter case is preferable, all living entities contribute to the perfection and harmony of the whole. Thus, again Plotinus recalls Heraclitus' fr. 11 out of its original context.

Finally, in *Ennead* VI.3, Plotinus refers successively at 11.22–26 to Heraclitus' fr. 82 (lines 22–24), and fr. 83 (lines 25–26),[142] where Heraclitus is the subject of φησίν in line 24. Plotinus is discussing the nature of true beauty compared to relative beauty. For Plotinus true beauty is beauty in itself, and, when we say that X is "more beautiful" than Y, we give a relative account of beauty and not beauty itself. Heraclitus' words in fr. 82 about the beauty of man compared with God and fr. 83 that a man, in his turn, is beautiful compared to a monkey are relative accounts of beauty and not true definitions of beauty. So again Plotinus' discussion quotes Heraclitus out of context. Heraclitus' words are used as apophthegms by Plotinus in a creative way that does not further the interpretation of Heraclitus but fits perfectly with Plotinus' own style of writing and expression.

Plotinus therefore throughout the *Enneads* shows a sound knowledge of Heraclitus' fragments on the nature of Soul. This suggests that he probably had access to the original text. Plotinus generally takes Heraclitus' words out of their original context in a philosophy of nature and cites them for his own metaphysical purposes. This conclusion shows that Plotinus does not have any intention of providing extant references to Heraclitean theory, but it does highlight the importance that Heraclitus had in this later period of Greek philosophical tradition. The work of Plotinus ensured Heraclitus' survival, in using quotations creatively as inspiring material that expresses philosophical truth. The truth of Heraclitus gives validity to the words of Plotinus and the latter needs this validity to justify his theories as a continuation rather than an interruption of Greek philosophical tradition. There is a similar aim in Plotinus' reference to Empedocles' *daimōn*.

5.3.3 The daimōn *in Empedocles*

In IV.8.1.17–23, Plotinus' refers directly to Empedocles' account of the descent of δαίμων and the Pythagorean concept of the embodied soul:

> *Ἐμπεδοκλῆς* τε εἰπὼν ἁμαρτανούσαις νόμον εἶναι ταῖς ψυχαῖς πεσεῖν ἐνταῦθα καὶ αὐτὸς φυγὰς θεόθεν γενόμενος ἥκειν πίσυνος μαινομένῳ νείκει τοσοῦτον παρεγύμνου, ὅσον καὶ *Πυθαγόρας*, οἶμαι, *καὶ οἱ ἀπ' ἐκείνου* ᾐνίττοντο περί τε τούτου περί τε πολλῶν ἄλλων. Τῷ δὲ παρῆν καὶ διὰ ποίησιν οὐ σαφεῖ εἶναι.
> And Empedocles, when he said that it is a law that sinful souls should fall into this world, and that he himself has come here as "an exile from god" who "puts his trust in raving strife," he reveals just as much as the riddling statements of Pythagoras and his followers about the descent of the soul and many other matters. But he is unclear because of his poetic language. [trans. Armstrong modified]

The above passage connects Empedocles with the early Pythagoreans. The relationship is not new in the Greek philosophical tradition; many ancient sources link Empedocles to the Pythagoreans and especially with their doctrine of the soul's reincarnations.[143]

Plotinus, in this passage, finds that both Empedocles and the Pythagoreans are obscure in their account of the descent of the Soul, but Empedocles is obscure not so much because of his theory as the ambiguity of his poetic language. Plotinus tends to accept the Empedoclean approach over the Pythagorean, and it is evident that in IV.8, he prefers to discuss Empedocles' doctrine of the soul rather than the Pythagorean one. As Armstrong observes, the impatience with which the Pythagoreans are treated is significant since for Middle-Platonists such as Numenius and the later Neoplatonists Pythagoras was a traditional and respected authority. The most striking example of Plotinus' criticism appears at *Ennead* IV.7.8[4].3–28 where Plotinus dismisses the Pythagorean doctrine of the soul as musical accord.[144]

Likewise in *Ennead* IV.8, the Pythagorean doctrine of the soul-body is given scant attention, whereas Empedocles' doctrine of the falling δαίμων is present throughout the treatise. In particular at 1.17–23, Plotinus' alludes to fr. 115 of the *Katharmoi* and especially Empedocles' account of the soul as a soul spirit which descends into the material world, passing through a number of lives, and born in all elements as different kinds of mortal beings.[145] Indirectly, with the law of the sinful souls (ἁμαρτανούσαις νόμον) in 1.18 Plotinus alludes to the first four lines of fr. 115 (1–4) about the divine "decree of necessity" (ἀνάγκης χρῆμα) and the eternal and sealed "broad oaths" (πλατέεσσι ὅρκοις) that govern the descent of the faulty soul (ἁμαρτήσας ἐπομόσσηι) in its continuous embodiments. With "an exile from god" (φυγὰς θεόθεν) in 1.19 and "puts his trust in raving strife" (πίσυνος μαινομένῳ νείκει) in 1.20, Plotinus quotes directly part of the last two lines of fr. 115 (13–14: φυγὰς θεόθεν καὶ ἀλήτης, νείκει μαινομένωι πίσυνος). For the latter lines, Plotinus, along with Philoponus, Asclepius, and Hierocles, is a recognized source.[146] Moreover, it is significant that the last two lines of fr. 115 have been used as an independent quotation by these ancient authors with particular reference to the nature of Soul and its embodiment. Philoponus characterizes theses lines as the "well-known" (τὸ πολυθρύλητον) account about the soul (*in Physica* 24.18–22). Based on these considerations, we can suppose that Plotinus wants to focus on the last lines and not the whole of Empedocles' fragment.

Empedocles' account of the descent of the faulty soul into the material world in fr. 115 reflects the "den" (ὑπ' ἄντρον ὑπόστεγον) of fr. 120 reported by Porphyry, the most eminent pupil of Plotinus, in the relevant work *De Antro Nympharum* 8.14. Plotinus himself quotes fr. 120 some lines later in the same chapter (1.33–34: ὥσπερ *Ἐμπεδοκλεῖ* τὸ ἄντρον), drawing an analogy between the Platonic "cave" (τὸ σπήλαιον) in the *Republic* and the "den" (τὸἄντρον) of Empedocles. Finally, a summary of Empedocles' fr. 115 and fr. 120 can be found in IV.8.5.5–6. In this passage, Plotinus clearly echoes Empedocles' fr. 115 and by extension fr. 120. In his aim to reconcile all the ancient accounts about the descent of the Soul into bodies, Plotinus denies the pessimistic idea of an erring Soul that "falls" into the body and replaces it with a optimistic one considering the descent of Soul as a kind of spiritual mission.

With regard to the context of fr. 115, there are contradictory interpretations about the cause of the descent of the δαίμων. On the one hand, an eschatological interpretation of the fragment finds Empedocles speaking pessimistically about himself as a fallen soul who is a murderer, punished with exile and a wanderer from the gods.[147] On the other hand, another interpretation suggests that Empedocles speaks metaphorically about the cosmic cycles without any intention of attributing to the life of the soul any sinful action that deserves punishment.[148] The former interpretation follows H. Diels in changing the text to "murder" (φόνῳ) in line 3, while the latter keeps the original reading "fear" (φόβῳ), and so removes the idea of sinful murder and blood-guilt from the fragment.

On this controversy, Plotinus enlightens us with his account. Initially, in *Ennead* IV.8, he is aware that the poetic language of Empedocles brings with it difficulties and uncertainties. But even if Plotinus has not quoted the third line exactly, it is relevant to his positive views of the Soul's descent in *Ennead* IV.8. The descent of the Soul into the body is not a "decline" nor a "fall," but an illumination of intelligible perfection (II.9.10–11). Likewise, the works of Soul are not evil or sinful, but an eternal manifestation of the divine goodness (II.9.12).

The concept of body as alien to the Soul and "punishing" it appears in some early Pythagorean doctrines,[149] where "body" (σῶμα) is equated with the "tomb" (σῆμα), or "prison" (φρουρᾷ) of the Soul. The more striking early evidence of both concepts appears in Philolaus' frs 14 and 15, the former cited by Clement in *Stromateis* 3.17, the latter by Athenagoras in *Legation* 6, and Plato in *Phaedo* 61d6–10. Whereas Philolaus' fragments are usually regarded as spurious, they provide an example of the soul-body Pythagorean doctrine which is echoed later in Plato's *Gorgias* 493a1–3, and *Cratylus* 400c1–7 as well as in Aristotle (fr. 60), Athenaeus 4.157c, and some Neopythagorean sources.[150] The common element in all the above sources is the "penalty" (τιμωρία) paid by the embodied soul.

Plotinus' theory is not in agreement with the Pythagorean τιμωρία. As he explains in *Ennead* IV.8, there are two cases for the Soul's descent to a worse condition: (1) *the unwilling* (τὸ ἀκούσιον): assigned by divine necessity for the purpose of the perfection of the whole; (2) *the willing* (τὸ ἑκούσιον): caused by the Soul's own motion which makes the Soul suffer by the experience of evil (5.8–16).[151] Within this framework, Plotinus' states that the fault (ἁμαρτία) of Soul can refer to two things: (1) to the motive of the Soul's descent, and (2) to the evil actions the Soul does in this world (5.16–24). Moreover, in IV.8.5.17–24, Plotinus' definition of "judgment" (δίκη) as "divine ordinance" (θεσμὸς θεῖος), the supervision of the chastising spirits and, more significantly, the conception of the Greek term ἁμαρτία in its original notion as the "fault" of the Soul and not as "sin," echo Empedocles' concept of the embodied Soul as δαίμων in fr. 115. It is, in all probability, this difference between the Empedoclean and the Pythagorean approaches to the embodied soul that influenced Plotinus in selecting the former as the more appropriate one.

In somewhat the same way as Empedocles in fr. 115 describes himself as an exiled soul that belongs to a divine nature, Plotinus in IV.8.1 describes himself as an inhabitant of a higher divine realm.[152] As for Empedocles, so for Plotinus, the descent of the Soul follows the divine law of necessity (IV.8.5). For the Soul it is necessary by the eternal law of nature (5.11) to experience its descent and the life of the material world, in order to recognize the perfection of the intelligible world and ascend to the higher divine realm. The Soul would not have knowledge of its powers if these powers were not actualized through its descent (5.25 ff.). The Souls' actuality reveals the hidden potency of nature by producing the varied splendor of the perceptible world. This splendor is a manifestation of divine beauty and the justification of Soul's intelligible origin.

For Plotinus, the error lies in the attitude of the Soul in the bodies and not in the nature of the material world. The material world, as a work of divine providence, is the best possible reflection of the intelligible world.[153] The ensouled body is neither in bitter and miserable durance, nor vulnerable to troubles, desires, fears, and evils, nor is the body its prison or tomb, nor the cosmos its cave or cavern (IV.8.3.1–6). Since the Soul remains impassive and primarily intelligible, the reason for its descent could be miserable and pessimistic, but the reason is intellection (3.6–30). The Soul experiences the world of the senses and, through the beauty of the perceptibles, understands the higher beauty of the intelligibles (IV.3.30). As Sara Rappe states, the process of the Soul's self-knowledge is based on a hierarchical increasing self-awareness, beginning from sense-perception, and ending with intellectual self-knowledge.[154] Indeed the Soul compares the lesser images of senses with the pure originals of intellection and discovers in its self the truth of the Forms (IV.7.20.14–20; IV.8.1.1–7).

For Plotinus, the real fault of the individual soul is its individuality, its inner desire to lose the immunity of the intelligible world. The descent into bodies is the consequence of this fault. As Plotinus vividly puts it in the beginning lines of *Ennead* V.1:

> Whatever is it, then, that has caused souls to forget God their father, and, although sharing in that world and belonging completely to him, to be ignorant both of themselves and of him? The beginning of their wickedness was their audacity, their birth, the first "otherness" and the wish to belong to themselves. When they had appeared in this world, they took pleasure in their free will and made much use of their self-movement. They ran along the opposite path and put a great distance between themselves and the God. [V.1.1.1–8; trans. Atkinson]

According to this passage, the main reason for the Soul's descent is "audacity" (τόλμα). Audacity brings the coming-to-birth, the first otherness and consequently the desire for individuality and self-isolation.[155] Thus, the beginning of evil does not lie in the material world but in the audacity of Soul.

Originally, τόλμα was the Pythagorean name for the Indefinite Dyad because it separated itself from the One.[156] Lydus (*De Mensibus* II.7.24 = DK 7B14) regards Pherecydes as the philosopher who introduced "audacity" into the Pythagorean tradition and identified it with the Dyad. According to H. S. Schibli, "the only use of these passages in Plotinus and Lydus which name Pherecydes is to serve as yet further illustrations of the continuing influence of the tradition that made Pherecydes the teacher of Pythagoras."[157] But the importance of τόλμα in Plotinus is much more significant since it is related to the self-individuality of the Soul. As Armstrong observes, Plotinus frequently in the *Enneads* takes up Pythagorean τόλμα to explain the cause of multiplicity: "that is of all reality other than and inferior to the One or good, in an audacious act of self-assertion, a will to independent existence."[158]

Plotinus describes Intellect's generation from the One as an act of audacity. This passage clearly echoes the Pythagorean τόλμα.[159]

> . . . Intellect is not dispersed in itself but is in reality all together with itself and its nearness after the One has kept it from dividing itself, thought it did somehow dare to stand away from the One . . . [VI.9.5.27–30 trans. Armstrong]

Thus, by comparing the descent of Soul in IV.8, and the audacity of Soul in V.1, an interesting relationship seems to be found for Plotinus between Empedocles' "flight" (φυγή), the Pythagorean "audacity" (τόλμα), and by extension Pherecydes to whom the term is attributed.

The Plotinian Soul includes an inner unquiet power which is responsible for its self-isolation and by extension for its descent. As Plotinus says in a parallel passage of *Ennead* III.7.11.15–20, the Soul includes an "officious nature" (φύσις πολυπράγμονος), an "unquiet power" (δύναμις οὐχ ἥσυχος), which continually wishes to produce something more than it possesses. This officious and unquiet nature of III.7 has to be identified with audacity; the self-inclination power described in IV.8.5.26 as the cause of Soul's descent into the corporeal world. In III.7.11, the officious nature of Soul drives the Soul to transfer continually what it sees in the intelligible world to something else, without wanting to be present altogether in the intelligible realm. Consequently, the Soul moves from the sameness and the self-identity of Intellect to the otherness of the cosmos. This description of the Soul's officious nature in III.7.11.15 corresponds closely to the description of the Soul's descent in IV.8.4.14–17, where the Soul becomes isolated. Again the unquiet nature of IV.8.4, as in III.7.11, misleads the Soul to focus only on the body, and thus to be separated from the wholeness of the intelligible world, flying away (IV.8.4.17) from the totality of Intellect to the partiality of the individual body. Thus, the cause of the Soul's descent is this spontaneous power to fly away from Intellect to the direction and ordering of the universal body (IV.8.5.24–27).

This "flight" from Intellect is for Plotinus the "flight" from God of Empedocles' fr. 115.[160] But for the Neoplatonist the same "flight" can be reversed upwards, return the Soul back to its divine origins (IV.8.5.27; I.8.6.10) and so escape multiplicity and partiality (VI.9.5.46) by transcending first to Intellect and then to the quiet unity and loneliness of the One (VI.9.11.51: φυγὴ μόνου πρὸς μόνον). The Soul has a desire to return to its source, and this return of the Soul to the intelligible world is an upward movement through which the Soul exercises the innermost transcendent element: the intelligible seed of *logos* (III.6.7.18; IV.8.4.31, 8.18). The Soul that exercises this contemplative power experiences the eternal life of intelligible unity and intellection, and not the life of bodily partiality, corporeal opposition and perceptible multiplicity (IV.8.4.28 ff.). When the Soul transcends to the divine realm of Intellect it becomes a fully actualized member of the intelligible world without perceptible distinctions and imperfections.[161]

Thus, the end of the Soul's journey is the ascent to the perfection of Intellect and the attendance on the One's absolute unity (VI.9.9). The ascended Soul contemplates the beauty of the eternal realm, filled with the love of the Good and drunk with the nectar of Intellect (VI. 7.35.33–4). The Soul that returns to the Intellect and contemplates the beauty of the Forms (IV.8.1.3) knows that this intelligible beauty is the aim of the philosopher's quest (V.5.1.2), as in Plato's *Symposium* (211a), it is the end of the lover's quest. Hence, Plotinus concludes in IV.8.5.1–8:

> Οὐ τοίνυν διαφωνεῖ ἀλλήλοις ἥ τε εἰς γένεσιν σπορὰ ἥ τε εἰς τελείωσιν κάθοδος τοῦ παντός, ἥ τε δίκη τό τε σπήλαιον, ἥ τε ἀνάγκητό τε ἑκούσιον, ἐπείπερ ἔχει τὸ ἑκούσιον ἡ ἀνάγκη, καὶ τὸ ἐν κακῷ τῷ σώματι εἶναι οὐδ' ἡ *'Εμπεδοκλέους* φυγὴ ἀπὸ τοῦ θεοῦ καὶ πλάνη οὐδ' ἡ ἁμαρτία, ἐφ' ᾗ ἡ δίκη, οὐδ' ἡ *'Ηρακλείτου* ἀνάπαυλα ἐν τῇ φυγῇ, οὐδ' ὅλως τὸ ἑκούσιον τῆς καθόδου καὶ τὸ ἀκούσιον αὖ.
>
> There is no contradiction between the sowing in birth and the descent for the perfection of the All, and the judgment and the cave, and necessity and free-will—since necessity contains free-will—and the being in the body as an evil. Nor is there is anything inconsistent about Empedocles' flight from god and wandering nor the fault upon which judgment comes, nor Heraclitus' rest on the flight, nor in general the willingness and also the unwillingness of the descent. [trans. Armstrong modified]

This conclusion reinstates Presocratic theories of the embodied soul and incorporates them into Plotinus' theory of the ensouled body. This reconciliation again shows the importance of Presocratic theory in Plotinus' thought.

Chapter 6

Conclusion

Plotinus belongs to a philosophical tradition originating with Presocratic thought. In using the Presocratics frequently in the *Enneads*, Plotinus' aim is to show that his philosophy is not an innovation, but that the fundamental principles of his system were rooted in the teaching of the ancients. Since key Presocratic theories were first stated before Plato and the Platonic adaptation of them, they have value, validity, and importance in their own right, and deserve to be regarded as the beginnings of Greek philosophy. The Presocratics may be obscure or inaccurate as they struggle with new ways of thinking and a more primitive terminology, but they are not necessarily erroneous. They were tackling philosophically interesting questions with an intelligent approach to their exploration.

Most of Plotinus' references to the Presocratics are concentrated on *Enneads* II.1 [40], *On Heaven*, II.4 [12], *On Matter*, III.7 [45], *On Eternity and Time*, IV.8 [6], *On the Descent of the Soul into the Bodies*, V.1 [10], *On the Three Primary Hypostases*, and VI.6 [34], *On Numbers*. According to Porphyry's chronological order of the *Enneads*, three of the above treatises belong to the first period of Plotinus' writings, but even so he was then of a mature age with many years of philosophical study behind him. During this time, he would have been working on the development of his fundamental philosophical ideas, and for this reason felt the need to return to his predecessors.

Whenever Plotinus refers to the Presocratics by name, he regards them not within the general classification of the modern term "Pre-Socratics," but more as "Preplatonists." Whereas Plato is the supreme philosopher, for Plotinus the Presocratics are the originators of the main lines of Greek philosophy. In his view, the fundamental philosophical ideas have been inaugurated by the Presocratics and developed further with more accuracy by Plato. On the other hand, Plotinus does not treat the Presocratics just as forerunners of Plato. Whenever Plotinus cites the Presocratics directly, he takes them seriously, in some cases harmonizing the Platonic and the Presocratic accounts, and showing more sympathy to the Presocratics than appears in Plato's negative or ironic attitude. Plotinus' interpretation indicates a much closer acquaintance with Presocratic texts and a better understanding of their ways of thinking than does Plato (and indeed Aristotle).

Plotinus therefore regards the Presocratics as eminent, autonomous, and original philosophical figures. He quotes almost all the leading Presocratics in his *Ennead* V.1, a treatise which is fundamental to his philosophical system of the Three Hypostases as well as to the interpretation of Plotinian thought as a whole. The Presocratics are treated with the same respect, and liable to be similarly criticized, as the most famous in the whole Greek philosophical tradition. Heraclitus, Parmenides, Empedocles, and Anaxagoras are of central importance in Plotinus' thought and for this reason he refers to them by name. Additionally, other Presocratics such as Pherecydes, the Milesians, the Pythagoreans, and the Atomists are treated with more caution in the *Enneads* and frequently criticized for their conclusions. Besides Plotinus' recognition of the Pythagorean concept of the supreme Monad and τόλμα as the cause of the Soul's descent, he clearly refutes the Pythagorean soul-harmony theory and the identification of time with the motion of the cosmic sphere. The Pythagoreans are undoubtedly less significant for him than they were for the later Neoplatonists. The Atomists are totally rejected for their theory of atoms as well as the atomic ideas of accidence and chance as necessary causes of the material world.

With regard to Heraclitus, Plotinus seems to be fully aware of his philosophical language and appears to be even more sympathetic towards him than Plato was. Plotinus adapts the words of some well-known Heraclitean fragments to his own flow of thought as apothegms but without connecting them to their original context. Yet Plotinus recognizes and accepts Heraclitean monism and regards Heraclitus as one of the Presocratics who foreshadowed the concept of the One. Plotinus also recognizes the everlasting flux of the heavenly bodies in Heraclitus' harmony of opposites and accepts and uses Heraclitus' image of cosmic *polemos*. Additionally, Heraclitus was one of the philosophers who aimed at self-knowledge and this would be for Plotinus the initial aim of the Soul, hence, the *logos* of the Plotinian Soul corresponds metaphysically to the *logos* of the Heraclitean Soul. Heraclitus' theory of soul leads Plotinus to understand that the descent of the Soul into bodies is not a fall or punishment, but an action of self-knowledge according to the law of divine necessity.

With regard to Parmenides, Plotinus is aware of the predicates of Eleatic Being and he applies them as metaphysical properties of the Intellect, the Second Hypostasis of Being. Consequently Plotinian Being, like Parmenidean Being, is one, continuous, indestructible, imperturbable, changeless, and timeless. On the other hand, Plotinus rejects Parmenides' assumption of immobility and oneness for Being. Since for Plotinus Intellect is the sum of its intelligibles, Being is not an unqualified and immovable "one" but the perfect unity-in-plurality of the Forms, so that Parmenides can here be regarded as the forerunner of Plato. Within this framework, Plotinus amalgamates the Platonic theory of Forms with Parmenides' theory of Being. Likewise, Plotinus' timeless eternity is a concept developed in contradistinction to the perpetual duration of time, synthesizing the tenseless atemporality of Parmenides' Being with the vital notion of cosmic everlastingness found in Heraclitus and Empedocles. These influences lead Plotinus to clarify for the first time within the metaphysical framework the non-durational life of Platonic Form and, by extension, the timeless eternal life of Intellect. Finally, Plotinus recognizes in Parmenides the first ontological connection between 'thinking' and 'being', but since Plotinus is influenced by his Platonic background, he develops this idea to give a metaphysical identification of Intelligence and Being, intelligible subject and intelligible object at the level of Intellect. This identification played a significant role in the history of philosophy and the development of Western metaphysics.

As far as Empedocles is concerned, Plotinus focuses mainly on his theory of soul. For Plotinus, it is erroneous to consider the exile of Empedocles' *daimōn* literally as a punishment for the Soul, but more as a poetic description of psychic embodiment. Moreover, he is well aware of Empedocles' natural philosophy of the four elements and the motive forces of Love and Strife, but, whereas he criticizes Empedocles' theory of the four elements, he accepts the forces of Love and Strife as the true powers that produce the beauty and perfection of the perceptible world. More significantly, Plotinus adapts the concept of *Philia* to represent the One and the unity of being.

For Plotinus, the concept of the One and the unity of being is present in Anaxagoras' nature of Nous, and especially in its purity and simplicity. In addition, Anaxagoras is respected for expressing successfully the simultaneous all-togetherness of Intellect in the *dictum* ὁμοῦ πάντα, and Plotinus prefers this expression to the ὁμοῦ πᾶν of Parmenides. Furthermore, Plotinus uses the other well-known Anaxagorean *dictum* πᾶν ἐν παντὶ, but for him the meaning of Anaxagoras' words should be applied at the level of Intellect and not at the level of Matter. Plotinus criticizes the whole theory of Anaxagoras' Matter and directs his criticism against its alleged ontological simultaneity with Nous. Plotinus' theory of Matter is more closely related to Anaximander's indefinite *apeiron*.

So Plotinus sees himself as continuing the Greek philosophical tradition started by the Presocratics. He is clearly aware of and influenced by Presocratic theories and terminology. His references to the Presocratics are both direct and indirect, and result in an amalgamation of their terminology with his own theoretical background. Their initiation of fundamental philosophical questions as well as their theoretical originality is incorporated into the Neoplatonic philosophy of the *Enneads*. Plotinus has a sound knowledge not only of Presocratic texts, but also of their contribution to the history of Greek philosophy. Presocratic concepts are often integral to the flow of his thought even where there is not a literal quotation, and their terms are used as appropriate for the philosophical needs of his own metaphysical discussion.

Thus, the considerable number of references and allusions to the Presocratics in the *Enneads* counters modern opinions of a negligible and superficial use of their fragments. Plotinus conceives Greek philosophy as an organic unity, starting and continuing within the classical philosophical tradition. This philosophical tradition is Plotinus' heritage and for this reason he reexamines and clarifies earlier views, and adapts them to his own philosophical system by integrating Presocratic hylozoism to his metaphysics. Presocratic theories and terminology can be found embedded in Plotinus' system of the Three Hypostases and the fundamental theories of the One and the unity of being, Intellect and the structure of being, eternity, and time, the formation of matter and the nature of the ensouled bodies. It is in these philosophical theories that Plotinus finds the Presocratic origins of his thought and establishes early Greek philosophical positions as the foundation of his theoretical principles.

Appendix: Text of Presocratic Fragments in Plotinus' *Enneads*

DIRECT REFERENCES

Anaxagoras

II.4.7.2–6:
Ἀναξαγόρας δὲ τὸ μίγμα ὕλην ποιῶν, οὐκ ἐπιτηδειότητα πρὸς πάντα, ἀλλὰ πάντα ἐνεργείᾳ ἔχειν λέγων ὃν εἰσάγει νοῦν ἀναιρεῖ οὐκ αὐτὸν τὴν μορφὴν καὶ τὸ εἶδος διδόντα ποιῶν οὐδὲ πρότερον τῆς ὕλης ἀλλ' ἅμα.

V.1.9.1–2:
Ἀναξαγόρας δὲ νοῦν καθαρὸν καὶ ἀμιγῆ λέγων ἁπλοῦν καὶ αὐτὸς τίθεται τὸ πρῶτον καὶ χωριστὸν τὸ ἕν

Empedocles

II.4.7.1–2:
Ἐμπεδοκλῆς δὲ τὰ στοιχεῖα ἐν ὕλῃ θέμενος ἀντιμαρτυροῦσαν ἔχει τὴν φθορὰν αὐτῶν.

IV.8.1.17–20:
Ἐμπεδοκλῆς τε εἰπὼν ἁμαρτανούσαις νόμον εἶναι ταῖς ψυχαῖς πεσεῖν ἐνταῦθα καὶ αὐτὸς φυγὰς θεόθεν γενόμενος ἥκειν πίσυνος μαινομένῳ νείκει τοσοῦτον παρεγύμνου

IV.8.1.33–34:
καὶ τὸ σπήλαιον αὐτῷ, ὥσπερ ***Ἐμπεδοκλεῖ*** τὸ ἄντρον

IV.8.5.5–6:
οὐδ' ἡ ***Ἐμπεδοκλέους*** φυγὴ ἀπὸ τοῦ θεοῦ καὶ πλάνη οὐδ' ἡ ἁμαρτία, ἐφ' ᾗ ἡ δίκη

V.1.9.5–9:
Τῷ δὲ ***Ἐμπεδοκλεῖ*** τὸ νεῖκος μὲν διαιρεῖ, ἡ δὲ φιλία τὸ ἕν-ἀσώματον δὲ καὶ αὐτὸς τοῦ το-τὰ δὲ στοιχεῖα ὡς ὕλη

Heraclitus

II.1.2.10–12:
Συγχωρῶν καὶ ἐπὶ τούτων δηλονότι ***τῷ Ἡρακλείτῳ***, ὃς ἔφη ἀεὶ καὶ τὸν ἥλιον γίνεσθαι.

IV.8.1.11–17:
Ὁ μὲν γὰρ ***Ἡράκλειτος***, ὃς ἡμῖν παρακελεύεται ζητεῖν τοῦτο, ἀμοιβάς τε ἀναγκαίας τιθέμενος ἐκ τῶν ἐναντίων, ὁδόν τε ἄνω κάτω εἰπὼν καὶ μεταβάλλον ἀναπαύεται καὶ κάματός ἐστι τοῖς αὐτοῖς μοχθεῖν καὶ ἄρχεσθαι εἰκάζειν ἔδωκεν ἀμελήσας σαφῆ ἡμῖν ποιῆσαι τὸν λόγον, ὡς δέον ἴσως παρ' αὐτῷ ζητεῖν, ὥσπερ καὶ αὐτὸς ζητήσας εὗρεν.

IV.8.5.6–7:
οὐδ' ἡ ***Ἡρακλείτου*** ἀνάπαυλα ἐν τῇ φυγῇ

V.1.9.3–5:
Καὶ ***Ἡράκλειτος*** δὲ τὸ ἓν οἶδεν ἀίδιον καὶ νοητόν· τὰ γὰρ σώματα γίγνεται ἀεὶ καὶ ῥέοντα

Parmenides

V.1.8.14–23:
Ἥπτετο μὲν οὖν καὶ ***Παρμενίδης*** πρότερον τῆς τοιαύτης δόξης καθόσον εἰς ταὐτὸ συνῆγεν ὂν καὶ νοῦν, καὶ τὸ ὂν οὐκ ἐν τοῖς αἰσθητοῖς ἐτίθετο τὸ γὰρ αὐτὸ νοεῖν ἐστί τε καὶ εἶναι λέγων. Καὶ ἀκίνητον δὲ λέγει τοῦτο—καίτοι προστιθεὶς τὸ νοεῖν—σωματικὴν πᾶσαν κίνησιν ἐξαίρων ἀπ' αὐτοῦ, ἵνα μένῃ ὡσαύτως, καὶ ὄγκῳ σφαίρας ἀπεικάζων, ὅτι πάντα ἔχει περιειλημμένα καὶ ὅτι τὸ νοεῖν οὐκ ἔξω, ἀλλ' ἐν ἑαυτῷ. Ἓν δὲ λέγων ἐν τοῖς ἑαυτοῦ συγγράμμασιν αἰτίαν εἶχεν ὡς τοῦ ἑνὸς τούτου πολλὰ εὑρισκομένου.

VI.6.18.42–44:
ὥστε ταύτῃ ***Παρμενίδης*** ὀρθῶς ἓν εἰπὼν τὸ ὄν· καὶ οὐ δι' ἐρημίαν ἄλλου ἀπαθές, ἀλλ' ὅτι ὄν· μόνῳ γὰρ τούτῳ παρ' αὐτοῦ ἐστιν εἶναι.

Pythagoras, Pythagoreans and Pherecydes

IV.7.8[4].3–5:
Τοῦτο γὰρ ἁρμονίαν τῶν ἀμφὶ ***Πυθαγόραν*** λεγόντων ἕτερον τρόπον ᾠήθησαν αὐτὸ τοιοῦτόν τι εἶναι οἷον καὶ ἡ περὶ χορδὰς ἁρμονία.

IV.8.1.20–22:
ὅσον καὶ ***Πυθαγόρας***, οἶμαι, καὶ οἱ ἀπ' ἐκείνου ᾐνίττοντο περί τε τούτου περί τε πολλῶν ἄλλων.

V.1.9.27–32:
Ὥστε τῶν ἀρχαίων οἱ μάλιστα συνταssόμενοι αὖ τοῖς ***Πυθαγόρου*** καὶ τῶν μετ' αὐτὸν καὶ ***Φερεκύδους*** δὲ περὶ ταύτην μὲν ἔσχον τὴν φύσιν· ἀλλ' οἱ μὲν ἐξειργάσαντο ἐν αὐτοῖς αὐτῶν λόγοις, οἱ δὲ οὐκ ἐν λόγοις, ἀλλ' ἐν ἀγράφοις ἐδείκνυον συνουσίαις ἢ ὅλως ἀφεῖσαν.

V.5.6.26–30:
Τάχα δὲ καὶ τὸ 'ἕν' ὄνομα τοῦτο ἄρσιν ἔχει πρὸς τὰ πολλά. Ὅθεν καὶ Ἀπόλλωνα *οἱ* ***Πυθαγορικοὶ*** συμβολικῶς πρὸς ἀλλήλους ἐσήμαινον ἀποφάσει τῶν πολλῶν. Εἰ δὲ θέσις τις τὸ ἕν, τό τε ὄνομα τό τε δηλούμενον, ἀσαφέστερον ἂν γίνοιτο τοῦ εἰ μή τις ὄνομα ἔλεγεν αὐτοῦ·

INDIRECT REFERENCE AND ALLUSIONS

General

Ennead VI.1.1.1–4:
Περὶ τῶν ὄντων πόσα καὶ τίνα ἐζήτησαν μὲν καὶ *οἱ* ***πάνυ παλαιοί,*** ἕν, οἱ δὲ ὡρισμένα, οἱ δὲ ἄπειρα εἰπόντες, καὶ τούτων ἕκαστοι οἱ μὲν ἄλλο οἱ δὲ ἄλλο τὸ ἕν, οἱ δὲ τὰ πεπερασμένα καὶ αὖ τὰ ἄπειρα εἰπόντες·

Anaxagoras

Fragment 1.1: ***ὁμοῦ πάντα*** χρήματα ἦν
Fragment 4.13: ***πάντων ὁμοῦ*** ἐόντων
Fragment 6.7: νῦν ***πάντα ὁμοῦ***

Enneads

I.1.8.6–8:
Ἔχομεν οὖν καὶ τὰ εἴδη διχῶς, ἐν μὲν ψυχῇ οἷον ἀνειλιγμένα καὶ οἷον κεχωρισμένα, ***ἐν δὲ νῷ ὁμοῦ τὰ πάντα.***

II.6.1.8–12:
Ἢ ἐκεῖ, ὅτι ἕν πάντα, ἐνθάδε δὲ διαληφθέντων τῶν εἰδώλων τὸ μὲν ἄλλο, τὸ δὲ ἄλλο· ὥσπερ ***ἐν μὲν τῷ σπέρματι ὁμοῦ πάντα*** καὶ ἕκαστον πάντα καὶ οὐ χεὶρ χωρὶς καὶ χωρὶς κεφαλή, ἔνθα δὲ χωρίζεται ἀλλήλων·

III.2.2.18–19:
Ὥσπερ δὲ ἐν λόγῳ ***τῷ ἐν σπέρματι ὁμοῦ πάντων***

III.3.7.8–9:
Τὸ μὲν γὰρ εἰς ἕν πάντα ἀρχή, ἐν ᾗ ***ὁμοῦ πάντα*** καὶ ὅλον πάντα.

III.6.6.21–23:
Δεῖ δ' αὐτὸ πάντη ὂν εἶναι· ἥκειν οὖν δεῖ παρ' αὐτοῦ πάντα ἔχον εἰς τὸ εἶναι· καὶ ***ὁμοῦ πάντα*** καὶ ἕν πάντα.

III.6.17.18 and 36:
. . . ***ὁμοῦ πάντα*** ἐφαίνετο ἐκ παντὸς τοῦ εἴδους . . . ἡ δὲ ὕλη, ἐφ' ἧς ἀναγκάζεται συνθεῖν, ***ὁμοῦ πᾶσα*** καὶ πανταχοῦ παρέχει ἑαυτήν·

III.6.18.24–26:
αὐτὴ (v. ψυχὴ) ***ὁμοῦ πάντα*** ἔχει καὶ τοῦ εἴδους ἑκάστου ὁμοῦ ὄντος αὐτῷ

III.6.18.35–36:
ἥ τε ὕλη ***πάντα ὁμοῦ*** ὥσπερ ἡ ψυχὴ οὐ δύναται εἰσοικίσασθαι·

III.7.3.19:
οἷον ἐν σημείῳ ***ὁμοῦ πάντων*** ὄντων καὶ οὔποτε εἰς ῥύσιν προιόντων (v. ὁ αἰών)

III.7.3.37:
ζωὴ ***ὁμοῦ πᾶσα***

III.7.11.13:
ὁμοῦ πᾶσαν καὶ ἄπειρον ἤδη ζωὴν

III.8.9.44–54:
Εἰ δέ τις οἴοιτο αὐτὸ τὸ ἓν καὶ τὰ πάντα εἶναι, ἤτοι καθ' ἓν ἕκαστον τῶν πάντων ἐκεῖνο ἔσται ἢ ***ὁμοῦ πάντα***. Εἰ μὲν οὖν ***ὁμοῦ πάντα*** συνηθροισμένα, ὕστερον ἔσται τῶν πάντων· εἰ δὲ πρότερον τῶν πάντων, ἄλλα μὲν τὰ πάντα, ἄλλο δὲ αὐτὸ ἔσται τῶν πάντων· εἰ δὲ ἅμα καὶ αὐτὸ καὶ τὰ πάντα, οὐκ ἀρχὴ ἔσται. Δεῖ δὲ αὐτὸ ἀρχὴν εἶναι καὶ εἶναι πρὸ πάντων, ἵνα ᾖ μετ' αὐτὸ καὶ τὰ πάντα. Τὸ δὲ καθ' ἕκαστον τῶν πάντων πρῶτον μὲν τὸ αὐτὸ ἔσται ὁτιοῦν ὁτῳοῦν, ἔπειτα ὁμοῦ πάντα, καὶ οὐδὲν διακρινεῖ. Καὶ οὕτως οὐδὲν τῶν πάντων, ἀλλὰ πρὸ τῶν πάντων.

IV.2.1.5–7:
Ἐκεῖ δὲ ***ὁμοῦ μὲν νοῦς πᾶς*** καὶ οὐ διακεκριμένον οὐδὲ μεμερισμένον, ***ὁμοῦ δὲ πᾶσαι ψυχαὶ*** ἐν αἰῶνι τῷ κόσμῳ, οὐκ ἐν διαστάσει τοπικῇ.

IV.2.2.42–44:
Εἰ γὰρ τοῦτο μὴ παραδεχοίμεθα, ἡ τὰ πάντα συνέχουσα καὶ διοικοῦσα φύσις οὐκ ἔσται, ἥτισ ***ὁμοῦ τε πάντα*** περιλαβοῦσα ἔχει καὶ μετὰ φρονήσεως ἄγει πλῆθος μὲν οὖσα, ἐπείπερ πολλὰ τὰ ὄντα, μία δέ, ἵν' ᾖ ἓν τὸ συνέχον, τῷ μὲν πολλῷ αὐτῆς ἑνὶ ζωὴν χορηγοῦσα τοῖς μέρεσι πᾶσι, τῷ δὲ ἀμερίστῳ ἑνὶ φρονίμως ἄγουσα.

IV.3.10.1–9:
Οὕτω δὴ ἀκούσαντας χρὴ πάλιν ἐπὶ τὸ ἀεὶ οὕτως ἐλθόντας ***ὁμοῦ λαβεῖν πάντα ὄντα***· οἷον τὸν ἀέρα, τὸ φῶς, τὸν ἥλιον, ἢ τὴν σελήνην καὶ τὸ φῶς καὶ πάλιν τὸν ἥλιον *ὁμοῦ* ***πάντα***, τάξιν δὲ πρώτων καὶ δευτέρων καὶ τρίτων ἔχοντα, καὶ ἐνταῦθα ψυχὴν ἀεὶ ἑστῶσαν ἢ τὰ πρῶτα καὶ τὰ ἐφεξῆς ὡς πυρὸς ἔσχατα, εἰς ὕστερον τοῦ πρώτου ἐκ τοῦ ἐσχάτου νοουμένου πυρὸς σκιᾶς, εἶτα ἐπιφωτιζομένου ἅμα καὶ τούτου, ὥστε οἷον εἶδος ἐπιθεῖν τῷ ἐπιβληθέντι πρώτῳ γενομένῳ παντάπασιν ἀμυδρῷ.

IV.4.2.10–11:
Εἰ δέ ἐστιν αὐτὸς τοιοῦτος οἷος πάντα εἶναι, ὅταν αὐτὸν νοῇ, ***πάντα ὁμοῦ νοεῖ***·

IV.4.11.17–28:
Πολλὰ γὰρ καὶ ἐφ' ἑνὸς ἑκάστου ζῴου τὰ γινόμενα κατὰ φύσιν καὶ οὐχ ***ὁμοῦ πάντα*** . . . Καὶ δὴ τὴν αὐτὴν φρόνησιν ἄξιον περιθεῖναι καὶ ταύτην καθόλου εἶναι οἷον κόσμου φρόνησιν ἑστῶσαν, πολλὴν μὲν καὶ ποικίλην καὶ αὖ ἁπλῆν ζῴου ἑνὸς μεγίστου, οὐ τῷ πολλῷ ἀλλοιουμένην, ἀλλὰ ἕνα λόγον καὶ ***ὁμοῦ πάντα***· εἰ γὰρ μὴ πάντα, οὐκ ἐκείνη, ἀλλὰ τῶν ὑστέρων καὶ μερῶν ἡ φρόνησις.

V.3.15.18–23:
Ἐπεὶ δὲ τὸ μετ᾽ αὐτὸ καὶ ὅτι μετ᾽ αὐτὸ δῆλον ποιεῖ τῷ τὸ πλῆθος αὐτοῦ ἓν πανταχοῦ εἶναι· καὶ γὰρ πλῆθος ὂν ὅμως ἐν τῷ αὐτῷ καὶ διακρῖναι οὐκ ἂν ἔχοις, ὅτι ***ὁμοῦ πάντα*** ἐπεὶ καὶ ἕκαστον τῶν ἐξ αὐτοῦ, ἕως ζωῆς μετέχει, ἓν πολλά· ἀδυνατεῖ γὰρ δεῖξαι αὐτὸ ἓν πάντα.

V.3.17.9–10:
Τί οὖν τὸ οὗ μετέχει, ὃ ποιεῖ αὐτὸ καὶ εἶναι καὶ ***ὁμοῦ τὰ πάντα***;

V.8.9.1–7:
Τοῦτον τοίνυν τὸν κόσμον, ἑκάστου τῶν μερῶν μένοντος ὅ ἐστι καὶ μὴ συγχεομένου, λάβωμεν τῇ διανοίᾳ, εἰς ***ἕν ὁμοῦ πάντα,*** ὡς οἷόν τε, ὥστε ἑνὸς ὁτουοῦν προφαινομένου, οἷον τῆς ἔξω σφαίρας οὔσης, ἀκολουθεῖν εὐθὺς καὶ τὴν ἡλίου καὶ ὁμοῦ τῶν ἄλλων ἄστρων τὴν φαντασίαν, καὶ γῆν καὶ θάλασσαν καὶ πάντα τὰ ζῷα ὁρᾶσθαι, οἷον ἐπὶ σφαίρας διαφανοῦς καὶ ἔργῳ ἂν γένοιτο πάντα ἐνορᾶσθαι.

V.8.11.5–6:
μηκέτι σχίσας ***ἓν ὁμοῦ πάντα*** ἐστὶ μετ᾽ ἐκείνου τοῦ θεοῦ ἀψοφητὶ παρόντος

V.9.6.3–11:
Νοῦς μὲν δὴ ἔστω τὰ ὄντα, καὶ πάντα ἐν αὑτῷ οὐχ ὡς ἐν τόπῳ ἔχων, ἀλλ᾽ ὡς αὑτὸν ἔχων καὶ ἓν ὢν αὐτοῖς. ***Πάντα δὲ ὁμοῦ*** ἐκεῖ καὶ οὐδὲν ἧττον διακεκριμένα. Ἐπεὶ καὶ ψυχὴ ὁμοῦ ἔχουσα πολλὰς ἐπιστήμας ἐν ἑαυτῇ οὐδὲν ἔχει συγκεχυμένον, καὶ ἑκάστη πράττει τὸ αὑτῆς, ὅταν δέῃ, οὐ συνεφέλκουσα τὰς ἄλλας, νόημα δὲ ἕκαστον καθαρὸν ἐνεργεῖ ἐκ τῶν ἔνδον αὖ νοημάτων κειμένων. Οὕτως οὖν καὶ πολὺ μᾶλλον ***ὁ νοῦς ἐστιν 'ὁμοῦ πάντα'*** καὶ αὖ οὐχ ὁμοῦ, ὅτι ἕκαστον δύναμις ἰδία.

V.9.7.11–12:
ἀλλ᾽ ἕστηκεν ἐν αὑτῷ ***ὁμοῦ πάντα*** ὤν

VI.3.1.17:
ὁμοῦ πάντα τὰ φανέντα εἰς ἓν ἦν ἀνάγειν

VI.4.9.3–5:
Εἶτα ταῦτα τὰ πολλὰ πρῶτα τί ἂν εἴη τὸ διεῖργον, ὥστε μὴ ***ἓν ὁμοῦ πάντα εἶναι***;

VI.4.14.4–6:
Καὶ γὰρ ἕν ἐστι καὶ ἄπειρον αὖ καὶ ***πάντα ὁμοῦ*** καὶ ἕκαστον ἔχει διακεκριμένον καὶ αὖ οὐ διακριθὲν χωρίς. Πῶς γὰρ ἂν καὶ ἄπειρον ἢ

οὕτω λέγοιτο, ὅτι ***ὁμοῦ πάντα*** ἔχει, πᾶσαν ζωὴν καὶ πᾶσαν ψυχὴν καὶ νοῦν ἅπαντα;

VI.5.5.3–4:
Δεῖ δὲ τηροῦντας ***ὁμοῦ πάντα*** τὰ λεγόμενα πολλὰ γεγονέναι λέγειν, ὡς κἀκεῖ ἐπὶ τοῦ κύκλου οὐκ οὔσας γραμμὰς ἀφωρισμένας ἔστι λαμβάνειν· ἐπίπεδον γὰρ ἕν.

VI.5.6.1–4:
Πολλὰ γὰρ ὄντα τὰ νοητὰ ἕν ἐστι, καὶ ἓν ὄντα τῇ ἀπείρῳ φύσει πολλά ἐστι, καὶ πολλὰ ἐν ἑνὶ καὶ ἓν ἐπὶ πολλοῖς καὶ ***ὁμοῦ πάντα,*** καὶ ἐνεργεῖ πρὸς τὸ ὅλον μετὰ τοῦ ὅλου, καὶ ἐνεργεῖ πρὸς τὸ μέρος αὖ μετὰ τοῦ ὅλου.

VI.6.7.1–4:
Ὅλως γὰρ δεῖ νοῆσαι τὰ πράγματα ἐν μιᾷ φύσει καὶ μίαν φύσιν πάντα ἔχουσαν καὶ οἷον περιλαβοῦσαν, οὐχ ὡς ἐν τοῖς αἰσθητοῖς ἕκαστον χωρίς, ἀλλαχοῦ ἥλιος καὶ ἄλλο ἄλλοθι, ἀλλ' ***ὁμοῦ ἐν ἑνὶ πάντα·*** αὕτη γὰρ νοῦ φύσις·

VI.7.33.7–14:
Ἐπειδὴ ὁ νοῦς ἴδιόν τι νοεῖ, ἠλάττωται, κἂν ***ὁμοῦ πάντα*** λάβῃ ὅσα ἐν τῷ νοητῷ· κἂν ἕκαστον, μίαν μορφὴν νοητὴν ἔχει· *ὁμοῦ* ***δὲ πάντα*** οἷον ποικίλην τινά, ἔτι ἐν δεήσει, οἷον δεῖ θεάσασθαι ὂν ὑπὲρ ἐκεῖνο τὸ πάγκαλον καὶ ποικίλον καὶ οὐ ποικίλον, οὗ ὀρέγεται μὲν ψυχὴ οὐ λέγουσα διὰ τί τοιοῦτον ποθεῖ, ὁ δὲ λόγος λέγει, ὅτι τοῦτο τὸ ὄντως, εἴπερ ἐν τῷ πάντη ἀνειδέῳ ἡ τοῦ ἀρίστου φύσις καὶ ἡ τοῦ ἐρασμιωτάτου.

Fragment 12.1–3:
νοῦς δέ ἐστιν ἄπειρον καὶ αὐτοκρατὲς καὶ ***μέμεικται οὐδενὶ χρήματι,*** ἀλλὰ μόνος αὐτὸς ἐπ' ἑωυτοῦ ἐστιν.

Fragment 12.12–13:
ἔστι γὰρ λεπτότατόν τε πάντων χρημάτων καὶ ***καθαρώτατον***

Enneads

I.8.2.15–19:
Οὐ δὴ ἐκεῖνος ὁ νοῦς τοιοῦτος, ἀλλ' ἔχει πάντα καὶ ἔστι πάντα καὶ σύνεστιν αὐτῷ συνὼν καὶ ἔχει πάντα οὐκ ἔχων. Οὐ γὰρ ἄλλα, ὁ δὲ ἄλλος· οὐδὲ χωρὶς ἕκαστον τῶν ἐν αὐτῷ· ὅλον τε γάρ ἐστιν ἕκαστον καὶ πανταχῇ πᾶν· καὶ ***οὐ συγκέχυται,*** ἀλλὰ αὖ χωρίς.

V.3.3.21–22 and 39–45:
Ἀλλ' αἴσθησις μὲν αἰεὶ ἡμέτερον δοκεῖ συγκεχωρημένον-ἀεὶ γὰρ αἰσθανόμεθα-νοῦς δὲ ἀμφισβητεῖται, καὶ ὅτι μὴ αὐτῷ ἀεὶ καὶ ὅτι ***χωριστός· χωριστὸς δὲ τῷ μὴ προσνεύειν αὐτόν, ἀλλ' ἡμᾶς μᾶλλον πρὸς αὐτὸν εἰς τὸ ἄνω βλέποντας.***

V.3.6.10–12:
Ζητοῦμεν δή, ὡς ἔοικεν, ἡμεῖς πεισθῆναι μᾶλλον ἢ ***νῷ καθαρῷ*** θεᾶσθαι τὸ ἀληθές.

V.3.14.14–15:
ὅταν ***νοῦν καθαρὸν*** ἔχωμεν, χρώμενοι, ὡς οὗτός ἐστιν ὁ ἔνδον νοῦς.

V.8.3.24–28:
Οὐ γὰρ δὴ ποτὲ μὲν φρονοῦσι, ποτὲ δὲ ἀφραίνουσιν, ἀλλ' ἀεὶ φρονοῦσιν ἐν ἀπαθεῖ τῷ νῷ καὶ στασίμῳ καὶ ***καθαρῷ*** καὶ ἴσασι πάντα καὶ γινώσκουσιν οὐ τὰ ἀνθρώπεια, ἀλλὰ τὰ ἑαυτῶν τὰ θεῖα, καὶ ὅσα νοῦς ὁρᾷ.

VI.2.8.5–7:
Ἴδε δὲ ***νοῦν καὶ καθαρὸν*** καὶ βλέψον εἰς αὐτὸν ἀτενίσας, μὴ ὄμμασι τούτοις δεδορκώς.

VI.8.5.1–2:
Ἆρ' οὖν ἐν νῷ μόνῳ νοοῦντι τὸ αὐτεξούσιον καὶ τὸ ἐπ' αὐτῷ καὶ ***ἐν νῷ τῷ καθαρῷ*** ἢ καὶ ἐν ψυχῇ κατὰ νοῦν ἐνεργούσῃ καὶ κατὰ ἀρετὴν πραττούσῃ;

VI.9.3.26–27:
ἀλλὰ ***καθαρῷ τῷ νῷ τὸ καθαρώτατον θεᾶσθαι*** καὶ τοῦ νοῦ τῷ πρώτῳ.

V.3.2.22:
νοῦς ὁ ἄκρατος.

V.3.12.14–5:
Ἀλλ' ἐξ ἑνὸς τοῦ ***νοῦ ἁπλοῦ ὄντος*** φήσουσι τὰς ἐνεργείας προελθεῖν· ἤδη μέν τι ἁπλοῦν τὸ πρὸ τῶν ἐνεργειῶν τίθενται.

Anaximander

Fragment 1:
τῶν ὄντων ***τὸ ἄπειρον*** . . . . ἐξ ὧν δὲ ἡ γένεσίς ἐστι τοῖς οὖσι, καὶ τὴν φθορὰν εἰς ταῦτα γίνεσθαι κατὰ τὸ χρεών· διδόναι γὰρ αὐτὰ δίκην καὶ τίσιν ἀλλήλοις τῆς ἀδικίας κατὰ τὴν τοῦ χρόνου τάξιν

Ennead

II.4.7.13–20:
Ὁ δὲ τὸ ἄπειρον ὑποθεὶς τί ποτε τοῦτο λεγέτω. Καὶ εἰ οὕτως ἄπειρον, ὡς ἀδιεξίτητον, ὡς οὐκ ἔστι τοιοῦτόν τι ἐν τοῖς οὖσιν· οὔτε αὐτοάπειρον οὔτε ἐπ' ἄλλῃ φύσει ὡς συμβεβηκὸς σώματί τινι, τὸ μὲν αὐτοάπειρον, ὅτι καὶ τὸ μέρος αὐτοῦ ἐξ ἀνάγκης ἄπειρον, τὸ δὲ ὡς συμβεβηκός, ὅτι τὸ ᾧ συμβέβηκεν ἐκεῖνο οὐκ ἂν καθ' ἑαυτὸ ἄπειρον εἴη οὐδὲ ἁπλοῦν οὐδὲ ὕλη ἔτι, δῆλον.

Democritus

Fragment 9:
νόμῳ χροιή, νόμῳ γλυκύ, νόμῳ πικρόν, ἐτεῇ δ' ἄτομα καὶ κενόν

Enneads

III.6.12.22–24:
Εἴ τις οὖν ἐνταῦθα ***τὸ νόμῳ χροιὴ*** καὶ τὰ ἄλλα ***νόμῳ*** λέγοι τῷ τὴν φύσιν τὴν ὑποκειμένην μηδὲν οὕτως ἔχειν, ὡς νομίζεται, οὐκ ἂν ἄτοπος εἴη τοῦ λόγου.

IV.4.29.31–33:
Εἰ μή τις λέγοι ***νόμῳ ὁρᾶν,*** καὶ τὰς λεγομένας ποιότητας μὴ ἐν τοῖς ὑποκειμένοις εἶναι.

Fragment 164:
καὶ γὰρ ζῷα ὁμογενέσι ζῴοις συναγελάζεται ὡς περιστεραὶ περιστεραῖς καὶ γέρανοι γεράνοις καὶ ἐπὶ τῶν ἄλλων ἀλόγων ὡσαύτως. ὣς δε καὶ ἐπὶ τῶν ἀψύχων, καθάπερ ὁρᾶν πάρεστιν ἐτί τε τῶν κοσκινευομένων σπερμάτων καὶ ἐπὶ τῶν παρὰ ταῖς κυματωγαῖς ψηφίδων· ὅπου μὲν γὰρ κατὰ τὸν τοῦ κοσκίνου δῖνον διακριτικῶς φακοὶ μετὰ φακῶν τάσσονται καὶ κριθαὶ μετὰ κριθῶν καὶ πυροὶ μετὰ πυρῶν, ὅπου δὲ κατὰ τὴν τοῦ κύματος κίνησιν αἱ μὲν ἐπιμήκαις ψηφῖδες εἰς τὸν αὐτὸν τόπον ταῖς ἐπιμήκεσιν ὠθοῦνται, αἱ δὲ περιφερεῖς ταῖς περιφερέσιν ὡς ἂν συναγωγόν τι ἐχούσης τῶν πραγμάτων τῆς ***ἐν τούτοις ὁμοιότητος.***

Enneads

II.4.10.3:
εἰ γὰρ ***τῷ ὁμοίῳ τὸ ὅμοιον***

VI.9.11.32:
ἀρχὴν ὁρᾷ καὶ συγγίνεται καὶ ***τῷ ὁμοίῳ τὸ ὅμοιον***

Empedocles

Fragments 17.7–8 and 26.5–6:
ἄλλοτε μὲν ***Φιλότητι*** συνερχόμεν' εἰς ἕν ἅπαντα,
ἄλλοτε δ' αὖ δίχ' ἕκαστα φορεύμενα ***Νείκεος*** ἔχθει.

Enneads

III.2.2.1–7:
Ὑφίσταται γοῦν ἐκ τοῦ κόσμου τοῦ ἀληθινοῦ ἐκείνου καὶ ἑνὸς κόσμος οὗτος οὐχ εἷς ἀληθῶς· πολὺς γοῦν καὶ εἰς πλῆθος μεμερισμένος καὶ ἄλλο ἀπ' ἄλλου ἀφεστηκὸς καὶ ἀλλότριον γεγενημένον καὶ ***οὐκέτι φιλία μόνον, ἀλλὰ καὶ ἔχθρα*** τῇ διαστάσει καὶ ἐν τῇ ἐλλείψει ἐξ ἀνάγκης πολέμιον ἄλλο ἄλλῳ.

IV.4.40.1–9:
Τὰς δὲ γοητείας πῶς; Ἢ τῇ συμπαθείᾳ, καὶ τῷ πεφυκέναι συμφωνίαν εἶναι ὁμοίων καὶ ἐναντίωσιν ἀνομοίων, καὶ τῇ τῶν δυνάμεων τῶν πολλῶν ποικιλίᾳ εἰς ἕν ζῷον συντελούντων. Καὶ γὰρ μηδενὸς μηχανωμένου ἄλλου πολλὰ ἕλκεται καὶ γοητεύεται· καὶ ***ἡ ἀληθινὴ μαγεία ἡ ἐν τῷ παντὶ φιλία καὶ τὸ νεῖκος αὖ***. Καὶ ὁ γόης ὁ πρῶτος καὶ φαρμακεὺς ὅτός ἐστιν, ὃν κατανοήσαντες ἄνθρωποι ἐπ' ἀλλήλοις χρῶνται αὐτοῦ τοῖς φαρμάκοις καὶ τοῖς γοητεύμασι.

VI.7.14.18–23:
Ἡ δὲ διαίρεσις ἔγκειται οὐ συγκεχυμένων, καίτοι εἰς ἕν ὄντων, ἀλλ' ἔστιν ἡ λεγομένη ***ἐν τῷ παντὶ φιλία*** τοῦτο, οὐχ ἡ ἐν τῷδε τῷ παντί· μιμεῖται γὰρ αὕτη ἐκ διεστηκότων οὖσα φίλη· ἡ δὲ ἀληθὴς πάντα ἕν εἶναι καὶ μήποτε διακριθῆναι. Διακρίνεσθαι δέ φησι τὸ ἐν τῷδε τῷ οὐρανῷ.

Fragment 84.3–4:
ἅψας παντοίων ***ἀνέμων λαμπτῆρας*** ἀμοργους, οἵ τ' ἀνέμων μὲν πνεῦμα διασκιδνᾶσιν ἀέντων

Ennead I.4.8.2–5:
Καὶ οὐκ ἐλεεινὸς ἔσται ἐν τῷ ἀλγεῖν, ἀλλὰ τὸ αὐτοῦ καίει [τῷ] ἔνδον φέγγος, ***οἷον ἐν λαμπτῆρι φῶς πολλοῦ ἔξωθεν πνέοντος ἐν πολλῇ ζάλῃ ἀνέμων καὶ χειμῶνι.***

Fragment 112.4:
χαίρετ᾽ ἐγὼ δ᾽ ὑμῖν θεὸς ἄμβροτος, οὐκέτι θνητός

Ennead IV.7.10.38–40:
πᾶσιν ἐπιλάμπει τοῖς νοητοῖς ἀλήθειαν· ὡς πολλάκις αὐτῷ δόξαι τοῦ το δὴ καλῶς εἰρῆσθαι· ***χαίρετ᾽, ἐγὼ δ᾽ ὑμῖν θεὸς ἄμβροτος*** πρὸς τὸ θεῖον ἀναβὰς καὶ τὴν πρὸς αὐτὸ ὁμοιότητα ἀτενίσας.

Fragment 120:
τόδ᾽ ὑπ᾽ ***ἄντρον*** ὑπόστεγον

Ennead IV.8.3.4–5:
καὶ ὁ κόσμος αὐτῇ σπήλαιον καὶ ***ἄντρον***

Heraclitus

Fragment 5:
καθαίρονται δ᾽ ἄλλωι αἵματι μιαινόμενοι οἷον εἴ τις ***εἰς πηλὸν ἐμβὰς πηλῶι ἀπονίζοιτο.***

Ennead I.6.5.43–45:
οἷον εἴ τις δὺς εἰς πηλὸν ἢ βόρβορον τὸ μὲν ὅπερ εἶχε κάλλος μηκέτι προφαίνοι, τοῦτο δὲ ὁρῷτο, ὃ παρὰ τοῦ πηλοῦ ἢ βορβόρου ἀπεμάξατο·

Fragment 8:
τὸ ἀντίξουν συμφέρον καὶ ἐκ τῶν διαφερόντων καλλίστην ***ἁρμονίαν*** καὶ πάντα κατ᾽ ἔριν γίνεσθαι

Enneads

III.2.16.40:
Τὸ μὲν οὖν δρᾶμα τὰ μεμαχημένα οἷον ***εἰς μίαν ἁρμονίαν*** ἄγει σύμφωνον οἷον διήγησιν τὴν πᾶσαν τῶν μαχομένων ποιούμενος· ἐκεῖ δὲ ἐξ ἑνὸς λόγου ἡ τῶν διαστατῶν μάχη· ὥστε μᾶλλον ἄν τις τῇ ἁρμονίᾳ τῇ ἐκ μαχομένων εἰκάσειε, καὶ ζητήσει διὰ τί τὰ μαχόμενα ἐν τοῖς λόγοις.

IV.4.41.8:
μία ἁρμονία, κἂν ***ἐξ ἐναντίων*** ᾖ

Fragment 10:
ἐκ πάντων ἓν καὶ ἐξ ἑνὸς πάντα

Fragment 50:
ἕν πάντα εἶναι

Enneads

II.3.16.53–54:
ὥστε ***ἓν ἐκ πάντων*** ἄλλως ἑκατέρως γινομένων καὶ ἄλλως αὖ ἐν τοῖς λόγοις.

II.6.1.8–9:
Ἦ ἐκεῖ, ὅτι ***ἓν πάντα***, ἐνθάδε δὲ διαληφθέντων τῶν εἰδώλων τὸ μὲν ἄλλο, τὸ δὲ ἄλλο·

III.1.4.17–20:
ἐπὶ τοῦ παντὸς ***ἓν ἔσται τὸ πᾶν*** ποιοῦν καὶ πάσχον καὶ οὐκ ἄλλο παρ᾽ ἄλλου κατ᾽ αἰτίας τὴν ἀναγωγὴν ἀεὶ ἐφ᾽ ἕτερον ἐχούσας, οὐ δὴ ἀληθὲς κατ᾽ αἰτίας τὰ πάντα γίγνεσθαι, ἀλλ᾽ ***ἓν ἔσται τὰ πάντα***.

III.3.1.9–12:
Ἐκ γὰρ ἑνός τινος ὁρμηθέντα πάντα εἰς ἓν συνέρχεται φύσεως ἀνάγκῃ, ὥστε καὶ διάφορα ἐκφύντα *καὶ ἐναντία γενόμενα τῷ ἐξ ἑνὸς εἶναι συνέλκεται* ὅμως εἰς σύνταξιν μίαν·

III.8.9.45:
αὐτὸ ***τὸ ἓν καὶ τὰ πάντα εἶναι***, ἤτοι καθ᾽ ἓν ἕκαστον

IV.4.38.17–19:
Πάντα δ᾽ ὅμως ***εἰς ἓν συμπλέκεται*** καὶ θαυμαστὴν τὴν συμφωνίαν ἔχει καὶ ἀπ᾽ ἄλλων ἄλλα, κἂν ἀπ᾽ ἐναντίων ἴῃ· ***πάντα γὰρ ἑνός***.

V.2.1.1–3:
Τὸ ἓν πάντα καὶ οὐδὲ ἕν· ἀρχὴ γὰρ πάντων, οὐ πάντα, ἀλλ᾽ ἐκείνως πάντα· ἐκεῖ γὰρ οἷον ἐνέδραμε· μᾶλλον δὲ οὔπω ἐστίν, ἀλλ᾽ ἔσται.

VI.5.1.24–26:
Εἰ δὲ ὂν καὶ ἐν τῷ ὄντι ἐκεῖνο, ἐν ἑαυτῷ ἂν εἴη ἑκάστῳ. Οὐκ ἀπέστημεν ἄρα τοῦ ὄντος, ἀλλ᾽ ἐσμὲν ἐν αὐτῷ, οὐδ᾽ αὖ ἐκεῖνο ἡμῶν· ***ἓν ἄρα πάντα τὰ ὄντα***.

Fragment 11:
πᾶν ἑρπετὸν πληγῇ νέμεται

Ennead II.3.13.13–17:
Τὰ μὲν οὖν ἄψυχα τῶν ἐν αὐτῷ πάντη ὄργανα καὶ οἷον ὠθούμενα ἔξω εἰς τὸ ποιεῖν· τὰ δὲ ἔμψυχα, τὰ μὲν τὸ κινεῖσθαι ἀορίστως ἔχει, ὡς ὑφ' ἅρμασιν ἵπποι πρὶν τὸν ἡνίοχον ἀφορίσαι αὐτοῖς τὸν δρόμον, ἅτε δὴ ***πληγῇ νεμόμενα***·

Fragment 13:
ὕες βορβόρωι ἥδονται μᾶλλον ἢ καθαρῶι ὕδατι

Ennead I.6.6.1–6:
Ἔστι γὰρ δή, ὡς ὁ παλαιὸς λόγος, καὶ ἡ σωφροσύνη καὶ ἡ ἀνδρία καὶ πᾶσα ἀρετὴ κάθαρσις καὶ ἡ φρόνησις αὐτή. Διὸ καὶ αἱ τελεταὶ ὀρθῶς αἰνίττονται τὸν μὴ κεκαθαρμένον καὶ εἰς Ἅιδου κείσεσθαι ***ἐν βορβόρῳ***, ὅτι τὸ μὴ καθαρὸν βορβόρῳ διὰ κάκην φίλον· οἷα δὴ καὶ ***ὕες***, οὐ καθαραὶ τὸ σῶμα, ***χαίρουσι*** τῷ τοιούτῳ.

Fragment. 45:
ψυχῆς πείρατα ἰὼν οὐκ ἂν ***ἐξεύροιο***, πᾶσαν ἐπιπορευόμενος ὁδόν· οὕτω ***βαθὺν λόγον ἔχει***.

Ennead III.6.15.14–15:
ἀλλ' ***εἴ ποτε ἐξεύροι αὐτὴν λόγος βαθύς*** τις ἐξ ἄλλων ὄντων

Fragment 51:
οὐ ξυνιᾶσιν ὅκως ***διαφερόμενον ἑωυτῷ ὁμολογέει***· παλίντονος ἁρμονίη ὅκωσπερ τόξου καὶ λύρης

Ennead III.2.16.47–48:
καὶ ***τὸ πᾶν ὁμολογεῖ ἑαυτῷ*** τῶν μερῶν πολλαχοῦ μαχομένων

Fragment 53:
Πόλεμος πάντων μὲν πατήρ ἐστι, πάντων δὲ βασιλεύς, καὶ τοὺς μὲν θεοὺς ἔδειξε τοὺς δὲ ἀνθρώπους, τοὺς μὲν δούλους ἐποίησε τοὺς δὲ ἐλευθέρους.

Fragment 80:
τὸν ***πόλεμον ἐόντα ξυνόν***, καὶ δίκην ἔριν, καὶ γινόμενα πάντα κατ' ἔριν καὶ χρεών

Enneads

III 2.15.5:
καὶ ὅτι ***πόλεμος ἀεὶ καὶ οὐ μήποτε παῦλαν οὐδ' ἂν ἀνοχὴν λάβοι***

III.2.16.36–37:
πολέμιον οὕτως ἕν ἐστι καὶ φίλον, ὥσπερ ἂν εἰ ***δράματος λόγος***

Fragment 54:
ἁρμονίη ἀφανὴς φανερῆς κρείσσων

Ennead I.6.2.28–31:
Αἱ δὲ ἁρμονίαι αἱ ἐν ταῖς φωναῖς ***αἱ ἀφανεῖς τὰς φανερὰς*** ποιήσασαι καὶ ταύτῃ τὴν ψυχὴν σύνεσιν καλοῦ λαβεῖν ἐποίησαν, ἐν ἄλλῳ τὸ αὐτὸ δείξασαι.

Fragment 82:
πιθήκων ὁ κάλλιστος αἰσχρὸς ἀνθρώπων γένει συμβάλλειν.

Ennead VI.3.11.24–25:
πιθήκων, φησίν, ***ὁ κάλλιστος αἰσχρὸς συμβάλλειν ἑτέρῳ γένει***

Fragment 83:
ἀνθρώπων ὁ σοφώτατος πρὸς θεὸν πίθηκος φανεῖται καὶ σοφίαι καὶ κάλλει καὶ τοῖς ἄλλοις πᾶσιν.

Ennead VI.3.11.22–24:
μὲν καθ' ἑαυτὸ καὶ ποιόν, κάλλιον δὲ τῶν πρός τι· καίτοι καὶ καλὸν λεγόμενον φανείη ἂν πρὸς ἄλλο αἰσχρόν, οἷον ***ἀνθρώπου κάλλος πρὸς θεόν***·

Fragment 92:
Σίβυλλα δὲ ***μαινομένωι στόματα*** ἀγέλαστα καὶ ἀκαλλώπιστα καὶ ἀμύριστα φθεγγομένη

Ennead II.9.18.20:
ἀπαξιοῦσιν ἀδελφοὺς λέγειν οὐδὲ τὴν κόσμου ψυχὴν ***στόματι μαινομένῳ***

Fragment 96:
νέκυες γὰρ κοπρίων ἐκβλητότεροι

Ennead V.1.2.40–42:
θεός ἐστι διὰ ταύτην ὁ κόσμος ὅδε. Ἔστι δὲ καὶ ἥλιος θεός, ὅτι ἔμψυχος, καὶ τὰ ἄλλα ἄστρα, καὶ ἡμεῖς, εἴπερ τι, διὰ τοῦτο· ***νέκυες γὰρ κοπρίων ἐκβλητότεροι***.

Fragment 101:
ἐδιζησάμην ἐμεωυτόν

Ennead V.9.5.31:
τὸ ἐμαυτὸν ἐδιζησάμην ὡς ἕν τῶν ὄντων

Fragment 113:
ξυνόν ἐστι πᾶσι τὸ φρονέειν

Ennead VI.5.10.12:
Καὶ γὰρ καὶ τὸ φρονεῖν πᾶσιν ὅλον· διὸ καὶ ***ξυνὸν τὸ φρονεῖν***, οὐ τὸ μὲν ὧδε, τὸ δὲ ὡδὶ ὄν· γελοῖον γάρ, καὶ τόπου δεόμενον τὸ φρονεῖν ἔσται.

Fragment 115:
ψυχῆς ἐστι ***λόγος ἑαυτὸν αὔξων***

Ennead VI.5.9.13–14:
Διὸ καὶ οἱ μὲν ἀριθμὸν ἔλεγον, οἱ δὲ ***λόγον αὐτὸν αὔξοντα τὴν φύσιν αὐτῆς***

Parmenides

Fragment 3:
τὸ γὰρ αὐτὸ νοεῖν ἐστίν τε καὶ εἶναι

Enneads

I.4.10.5–6:
Δεῖ γὰρ ὁ πρὸ ἀντιλήψεως ἐνέργημα εἶναι, εἴπερ ***τὸ αὐτὸ τὸ νοεῖν καὶ εἶναι***.

III.5.7.50–51:
. . . ***ὁμοῦ τὸ νοεῖν καὶ τὸ νοητὸν καὶ τὸ εἶναι*** . . .

III.8.8.6–8:
ἐπὶ τούτου δηλονότι ἤδη ἕν ἄμφω οὐκ οἰκειώσει, ὥσπερ ἐπὶ τῆς ψυχῆς τῆς ἀρίστης, ἀλλ' οὐσίᾳ καὶ τῷ ***ταὐτὸν τὸ εἶναι καὶ τὸ νοεῖν*** εἶναι.

V.1.4.31–33:
. . . δύο ὄντα τοῦτο τὸ ***ἕν ὁμοῦ νοῦς καὶ ὂν*** καὶ νοοῦν καὶ νοούμενον, ὁ μὲν νοῦς κατὰ τὸ νοεῖν, τὸ δὲ ὂν κατὰ τὸ νοούμενον.

V.2.1.13:
ὁμοῦ νοῦς γίγνεται καὶ ὂν

V.3.5.26–28:
Ἓν ἄρα οὕτω νοῦς καὶ τὸ νοητὸν καὶ τὸ ὂν καὶ πρῶτον ὄν τοῦτο καὶ δὴ καὶ πρῶτος νοῦς τὰ ὄντα ἔχων, μᾶλλον δὲ ὁ αὐτὸς τοῖς οὖσιν.

V.3.5.43:
ἕν ἅμα πάντα ἔσται, νοῦς, νόησις, τὸ νοητόν

V.3.6.7:
νοῦς γὰρ καὶ νόησις ἕν

V.3.8.38:
τὸ ἀληθῶς νοητόν, *καὶ νοοῦν καὶ νοούμενον, καὶ ἑαυτῷ*

V.4.2.43:
Τὸ γὰρ ὄν οὐ νεκρὸν οὐδὲ οὐ ζωὴ οὐδὲ οὐ νοοῦν· *νοῦς δὴ καὶ ὂν ταὐτόν*.

V.6.6.21–23:
ʻΟμοῦ ἄρα τὸ νοεῖν, τὸ ζῆν, τὸ εἶναι ἐν τῷ ὄντι. *Εἰ ἄρα ὄν, καὶ νοῦς, καὶ εἰ νοῦς, καὶ ὄν, καὶ τὸ νοεῖν ὁμοῦ μετὰ τοῦ εἶναι*.

V.9.5.30–32:
ʼΟρθῶς ἄρα *τὸ γὰρ αὐτὸ νοεῖν ἐστί τε καὶ εἶναι* καὶ ἡ τῶν ἄνευ ὕλης ἐπιστήμη ταὐτὸν τῷ πράγματι καὶ τὸ ἐμαυτὸν ἐδιζησάμην ὥς ἕν τῶν ὄντων· καὶ αἱ ἀναμνήσεις δέ·

VI.7.41.17–19:
Ἡμῖν μὲν γὰρ ἡ νόησις καλόν, τι ψυχὴ δεῖται νοῦν ἔχειν, *καὶ νῷ, ὅτι τὸ εἶναι αὐτῷ ταὐτόν, καὶ ἡ νόησις πεποίηκεν αὐτόν*·

Fragment 8.3:
ὡς *ἀγένητον* ἐὸν καὶ *ἀνώλεθρόν*

Fragment 8.19:
πῶς δʼ ἂν ἔπειτʼ *ἀπόλοιτο* ἐόν; πῶς δʼ ἄν κε *γένοιτο*;

Enneads

IV.3.5.5–8:
Ἢ *ἀπολεῖται* οὐδὲν τῶν ὄντων· ἐπεὶ κἀκεῖ οἱ νόες *οὐκ ἀπολοῦνται*, ὅτι μή εἰσι σωματικῶς μεμερισμένοι, εἰς ἕν, ἀλλὰ μένει ἕκαστον ἐν ἑτερότητι ἔχον τὸ αὐτὸ ὅ ἐστιν εἶναι.

IV.7.9.9–19:
Οὐ γὰρ δὴ πάντα ἐπακτῷ ζωῇ χρῆται· ἢ εἰς ἄπειρον εἶσιν· ἀλλὰ δεῖ τινα φύσιν πρώτως ζῶσαν εἶναι, ἣν ***ἀνώλεθρον*** καὶ ἀθάνατον εἶναι δεῖ ἐξ ἀνάγκης, ἅτε ἀρχὴν ζωῆς καὶ τοῖς ἄλλοις οὖσαν. Ἔνθα δὴ καὶ τὸ θεῖον ἅπαν καὶ τὸ μακάριον ἱδρῦσθαι δεῖ ζῶν παρ' αὐτοῦ καὶ ὂν παρ' αὐτοῦ, πρώτως ὂν καὶ ζῶν πρώτως, μεταβολῆς κατ' οὐσίαν ἄμοιρον, οὔτε γινόμενον οὔτε ἀπολλύμενον. Πόθεν γὰρ ἂν καὶ ***γένοιτο***, ἢ εἰς τί ***ἀπόλοιτο***; Καὶ εἰ δεῖ ἐπαληθεύειν τὴν τοῦ ὄντος προσηγορίαν, αὐτὸ οὐ ποτὲ μὲν εἶναι, ποτὲ δὲ οὐκ εἶναι δεήσει.

Fragment 1.29:
ἠμὲν Ἀληθείης εὐκυκλέος ***ἀτρεμὲς*** ἦτορ

Fragment 8.4:
ἔστι γὰρ μουνογενές τε καὶ ***ἀτρεμὲς*** ἠδέ τελεῖον.

Enneads

III.7.5.18–22:
Ὅθεν σεμνὸν ὁ αἰών, καὶ ταὐτὸν τῷ θεῷ ἡ ἔννοια λέγει· λέγει δὲ τούτῳ τῷ θεῷ. Καὶ καλῶς ἂν λέγοιτο ὁ αἰὼν θεὸς ἐμφαίνων καὶ προφαίνων ἑαυτὸν οἷός ἐστι, τὸ εἶναι ὡς ***ἀτρεμὲς*** καὶ ταὐτὸν καὶ οὕτως καὶ τὸ βεβαίως ἐν ζωῇ.

III.7.11.1–5:
Δεῖ δὴ ἀναγαγεῖν ἡμᾶς αὐτοὺς πάλιν εἰς ἐκείνην τὴν διάθεσιν ἣν ἐπὶ τοῦ αἰῶνος ἐλέγομεν εἶναι, τὴν ***ἀτρεμῆ*** ἐκείνην καὶ ὁμοῦ πᾶσαν καὶ ἄπειρον ἤδη ζωὴν καὶ ἀκλινῆ πάντη καὶ ἐν ἑνὶ καὶ πρὸς ἓν ἑστῶσαν.

I.1.9.23:
Ἀτρεμήσει οὖν οὐδὲν ἧττον ἡ ψυχὴ πρὸς ἑαυτὴν καὶ ἐν ἑαυτῇ

I.6.5.15:
ἐν ***ἀτρεμεῖ*** καὶ ἀκύμονι καὶ ἀπαθεῖ διαθέσει

III.2.2.16:
Νοῦς τοίνυν δούς τι ἑαυτοῦ εἰς ὕλην ***ἀτρεμὴς*** καὶ ἥσυχος τὰ πάντα εἰργάζετο·

III.2.4.15:
Ἔδει δὲ κίνησιν ἐξ ἀκινησίας εἶναι καὶ ἐκ τῆς ἐν αὐτῇ ζωῆς τὴν ἐξ αὐτῆς γεγονέναι ἄλλην, οἷον ἐμπνέουσαν καὶ οὐκ ***ἀτρεμοῦσαν*** ζωὴν ἀναπνοὴν τῆς ἠρεμούσης οὖσαν.

V.1.11.20:
ἄλλη γὰρ ἐκεῖ δύναμις καὶ ὑγίεια, καθ' ἣν ***ἀτρεμῆ*** πάντα καὶ ἱκανά

VI.9.5.14:
νοῦν ἥσυχον καὶ ***ἀτρεμῆ*** κίνησιν φατέον πάντα ἔχοντα ἐν αὑτῷ

VI.9.11.14:
ἡσυχῇ ἐν ἐρήμῳ καὶ καταστάσει γεγένηται ***ἀτρεμεῖ***

Fragment 8.5–6:
οὐδέ ποτ' ἦν οὐδ' ἔσται, ἐπεὶ νῦν ἔστιν ***ὁμοῦ πᾶν, ἕν, συνεχές***·

Fragment 8.25:
τῶι ξυνεχὲς πᾶν ἐστιν· ***ἐὸν γὰρ ἐόντι πελάζει***

Ennead III.7.11.53–54:
τὸ ***ἐν συνεχείᾳ ἕν***

Ennead VI.4.4.24–6:
Ὁμοῦ γὰρ πᾶν *τὸ ὄν*, κἂν πολὺ οὕτως ᾖ· ***ἐὸν γὰρ ἐόντι πελάζει***, καὶ ***πᾶν ὁμοῦ***, καὶ νοῦς πολὺς ἑτερότητι, οὐ τόπῳ, ***ὁμοῦ δὲ πᾶς***.

Ennead VI.6.18.6–8:
Ἀλλ' ὅς ἐστι, ***πᾶς ἐστιν ἓν ὢν καὶ ὁμοῦ*** καὶ ὅλος δὴ καὶ οὐ περιειλημμένος πέρατί τινι, ἀλλ' ἑαυτῷ ὢν ὅς ἐστι

Fragment 8.26:
αὐτὰρ ***ἀκίνητον*** μεγάλων ἐν πείρασι δεσμῶν

Ennead III.2.4.12–13:
ζωὴ γὰρ ἐνταῦθα κινουμένη, ἐκεῖ δὲ ἐκεῖ δὲ ***ἀκίνητος***

Ennead III.8.2.15–20:
Οὐ γὰρ δὴ δεῖται τῶν μὲν ὡς μενόντων, τῶν δὲ ὡς κινουμένων-ἡ γὰρ ὕλη τὸ κινούμενον, αὐτῆς δὲ οὐδὲν κινούμενον-ἢ ἐκεῖνο οὐκ ἔσται τὸ κινοῦν πρώτως, οὐδὲ ἡ φύσις τοῦτο, ἀλλὰ ***τὸ ἀκίνητον τὸ ἐν τῷ ὅλῳ***.

Ennead IV.4.16.23–25:
Εἰ δὲ τἀγαθόν τις κατὰ κέντρον τάξειε, *τὸν νοῦν* ***κατὰ κύκλον ἀκίνητον***, ψυχὴν δὲ κατὰ κύκλον κινούμενον ἂν τάξειε, κινούμενον δὲ τῇ ἐφέσει.

Ennead V.1.6.25–27:
Δεῖ οὖν ***ἀκινήτου ὄντος***, εἴ τι δεύτερον μετ' αὐτό, οὐ προσνεύσαντος οὐδὲ βουληθέντος οὐδὲ ὅλως κινηθέντος ὑποστῆναι αὐτό.

Ennead VI.3.27.8–14:
Εἰ δ' ἕτερον ἠρεμίαν στάσεως λέγοιμεν τῷ τὴν μὲν στάσιν περὶ ***τὸ ἀκίνητον παντελῶς εἶναι***, τὴν δὲ ἠρεμίαν περὶ τὸ ἑστώς, πεφυκὸς δὲ κινεῖσθαι, ὅταν μὴ κινῆται, εἰ μὲν τὸ ἠρεμίζεσθαι λέγοι τὸ ἠρεμεῖν, κίνησιν οὔπω παυσαμένην, ἀλλ' ἐνεστῶσαν· εἰ δὲ τὴν οὐκέτι περὶ τὸ κινούμενον οὖσαν, πρῶτον μὲν ζητητέον, εἴ τί ἐστι μὴ κινούμενον ἐνταῦθα.

Ennead VI.6.18.31–35:
Τὴν δὲ οὐσίαν ἐν αὐτοῖς διαβᾶσαν, ***ἀκίνητον εἰς μεταβολὴν*** παρέχουσαν αὐτοῖς τὴν ζωήν, καὶ τὴν φρόνησιν καὶ τὴν ἐν αὐτοῖς σοφίαν καὶ ἐπιστήμην θεασάμενος τὴν κάτω φύσιν ἅπασαν γελάσει τῆς εἰς οὐσίαν προσποιήσεφς.

Pherecydes

Fragment 14:
τόλμαν δὲ καὶ οἱ περὶ Φερεκύδην ἐκάλεσαν τὴν δυάδα καὶ ὁρμὴν καὶ δόξαν καλοῦσιν, ὅτι τὸ ἀληθὲς καὶ ψευδὲς ἐν δόξηι ἐστί.

Enneads

V.1.1.3–5:
'Αρχὴ μὲν οὖν αὐταῖς τοῦ κακοῦ ***ἡ τόλμα*** καὶ ἡ γένεσις καὶ ἡ πρώτη ἑτερότης καὶ τὸ βουληθῆναι δὲ ἑαυτῶν εἶναι.

Notes

CHAPTER 1. THE ORIGINS OF PLOTINUS' PHILOSOPHY

1. *Les Sources de Plotin* (1960) includes a series of influential papers on Plotinus' debt to earlier philosophy. On the philosophical sources of Neoplatonism in general a collection of papers appears in *Le Néoplatonism* (1971); cf. also Wallis (1995), pp. 16–36. With regard to Platonic influence in Plotinus cf. Dodds (1928); Charrue (1978); Gatti (1996); on Plato and Aristotle in Plotinus cf. Slezák (1979); on Stoics and Plotinus cf. Graeser (1972). For a complete bibliography on the Neoplatonic philosophical sources cf. Gerson' updated bibliography in Wallis (1995), pp. 187–188 and Dufour (2001).
2. Cf. Wallis (1995), p. viii.
3. Henry and Schwyzer (HS2) in their *Index Fontium* devote fifty pages of Plotinus' direct and indirect citations and allusions to his predecessors and contemporaries in the *Enneads*.
4. Cf. Gatti (1996), p. 10.
5. Not to be confused with his contemporary, the Christian Origen.
6. He had the nickname Saccas, connected with "sack," and perhaps having a reference to his poverty; for Ammonius as a source of Plotinus cf. Dodds (1960) *passim*.
7. Cf. Gatti (1996), p.16.
8. Cf. Gatti, *ibid.*, p. 21.
9. Cf. Wallis (1995), pp. 41–42.
10. See Shroeder (1996), p. 351.
11. This metaphor is also found in *Enneads* I.7.1; IV.2.1.24–9; V.1.12; VI.9.8.
12. See Armstrong's note in *Ennead* V.1, vol. V, p. 50, n. 1; for a complete account on the subject cf. also Armstrong (1967a), Part II, ch. 15, pp. 239–41.
13. Cf. Strange (1994), pp. 23–51; this introduction to Plotinus' philosophical method follows the detailed analysis of Slezák (1979) *passim.*
14. Cf. Strange, *ibid.,* pp. 23–24.
15. Cf. *Enneads* II.9.6.53: τὰ εἰρημένα τοῖς παλαιοῖς; I.6.6.1; I.3.3.5; II.9.15.31: ὁ παλαιὸς λόγος; III.6.2.7; V.1.8.3: δόξας παλαιάς; III.7.1.9: παλαιῶν ἀποφάσεις; II.9.10.13; II.9.15.31; III.6.2.7: τὰ τῶν παλαιῶν

καὶ θείων ἀνδρῶν; III.7.1.14: τῶν ἀρχαίων καὶ μακαρίων φιλοσόφων τὸ ἀληθές; VI.4.16.4: πάλαι πεφιλοσοφηκότων.

16. Cf. *Enneads* VI.1.1.2; VI.8.19.14; IV.3.25.33; V.8.5.24; VI.8.19.14: οἱ πάνυ παλαιοί; III 6.19.25; IV.3.11.1; V.1.6.4: οἱ πάλαι σοφοί; II.9.6.36: τοὺς θείους ἄνδρας; II.9.6.28: τῶν μακαρίων ἀνδρῶν.

17. Cf. Strange (1994), pp. 24–25.

18. See *Enneads* III.5.1.6; IV.8.1.23.

19. See Wallis (1995), p. 48.

20. Cf. Dörrie (1974), pp. 195–201.

21. Cf. Gatti (1996), p. 18.

22. Cf. *Enneads* I.2.3.5; I.3.4.12; I.4.16.10; II.1.2.7, 5.2, 6.7, 7.1, 7.31; II.2.2.24; II.3.9.2, 15.1; II.4.10.11; II.9.6.10, 6.23, 6.42, 17.2; III.5.1.6, 2.2, 5.6, 7.1, 8.7; III.6.11.1, 12.1; III.7.6.5, 13.19; III.9.3.3; IV.3.1.23, 22.8; IV.4.22.7, 22.12; IV.8.1.23, 4.35; V.1.8.1, 8.9, 8.14, 8.24, 9.12, 10.10; V.8.4.52, 8.7; V.9.9.8; VI.2.1.5, 1.14, 1.23, 22.1, 22.13; VI.3.1.2, 16.23; VI.6.4.11; VI.7.5.23, 6.33, 11.44, 7.25.1, 37.24, 39.29; VI.8.18.44.

23. For Plotinus' role as an interpreter of Plato cf. Atkinson (1983), p. 191–192.

24. Plotinus finds the threefold concept of reality in the *Second Platonic Epistle* 312e1–4 with also a reference to *Sixth Platonic Epistle* 323d2–5, and *Timaeus* 34b and 41d. Apart from *Ennead* V.1, Plotinus refers to the above Platonic accounts in *Enneads* III.5.8; I.8.2, and VI.7.42. Cf. also Armstrong, vol. V. p. 40 n.1.

25. Cf. Beierwaltes (1991) *passim*; Dodds' study (1928) on the *Parmenides* of Plato and the origins of the Neoplatonic One is the first serious survey of Plotinus and the Platonic concept of the One.

26. Cf. Findlay (1975) on the Neoplatonism of Plato, and, on the following affirmations of Plato's *Parmenides* in Plotinus' system, cf. Wallis (1995), p. 21.

27. On Plotinus One and the first hypothesis of Plato's *Parmenides* cf. Boussoulas (1976).

28. For Plotinus' systematization of Parmenides' hypotheses cf. Wallis (1995), p. 21.

29. Cf. Proclus, *Platonic Theology* I.33.16, and *in Parmenidem* 630.37 ff.; cf. Wallis, *ibid.*

30. Cf. Dodds (1928), p. 133.

31. See particularly *Ennead* V.1.8.8.

32. On Plato's unwritten doctrines cf. the study of Slezák (1993).

33. Cf. Krämer (1982), pp. 234–8.

34. Cf. Gerson's forward in Wallis (1995), p. ix.

35. For this debate cf. Gatti (1996), pp. 17–22.

36. Cf. Faggin (1992), pp. xix–xx.

37. Cf. Arnou (1935), col. 2260; cf. also Blum (1989), pp. 977–80.

38. Cf. Charrue (1978), p. 17.

39. Cf. *Enneads* IV.8.1.23 ff., and IV.4.22.11 ff.
40. Cf. Wallis (1995), p. 17.
41. Cf. Kalligas (1991), pp. 138–9.
42. Cf. Wallis, *ibid.*, p. 23 ff.
43. For Aristotle in Plotinus cf. Wallis, *ibid.*, pp. 23–25.
44. Cf. Graeser (1972) *passim.*
45. For Stoic influence in Plotinus cf. Gatti (1996), pp. 11–12, and Wallis (1995), p. 25.
46. Cf. Dodds (1928), p. 131.
47. Cf. Dodds, *ibid.*
48. Cf. Armstrong's note on this passage, p. 40, n. 1; cf. also Kalligas (1991), pp. 139–142.
49. For these Middle-Platonists cf. the relevant study of Dillon (1977).
50. On the discussion of these Middle-Platonists in Plotinus cf. Wallis (1995), pp. 30–32.
51. Some ancient sources attribute *Didaskalikos* to Alcinous; cf. Dillon (1985) *passim.* Göransson (1995) maintains the view that *Didaskalikos* was actually written by the Middle-Platonist Albinus, the student of Gauis, and not by Alcinous.
52. Cf. Wallis, *ibid.*, pp. 30–31.
53. Cf. Gatti (1996), p. 13.
54. Cf. Wallis (1995), p. 33.
55. For this passage cf. Smith (1993), pp. 255–257 (=236F).
56. Cf. Dodds (1965), p. 4.
57. Cf. Gatti (1996), p. 12.
58. Cf. Wallis, *ibid.*, p. 32.
59. Cf. Gatti, *ibid.*, p. 13.
60. For Plotinus and Alexander of Aphrodisias cf. Rist (1966) *passim.*
61. Cf. Emilsson (1996), p. 238.
62. Cf. Kalligas (1991), pp. 146–152.
63. Cf. Puech (1960) *passim.*
64. Cf. Armstrong' introductory note on *Ennead* II.9; cf. also Wallis (1995), pp. 12–3.
65. For Plotinus and Indian thought cf. Gregorios (2002).
66. See West (1971) *passim.*
67. See Wallis (1995), p. 14.
68. According to this story, Damascius, Simplicius, and other philosophers of the Academy migrated to Persia and joined the court of the new king Chosroes. Unfortunately, they were quickly disappointed and so returned to Athens, enjoying freedom from persecution after a treaty that was concluded between Chosroes and the Emperor Justinian.
69. It is significant that there is only one paper concerning Plotinus and the whole Presocratic tradition—Gelzer's (1982) "Plotins Interesse an der

Vorsokratiken," and some limited studies focusing on the role of some individual Presocratics in Plotinus: Roussos (1968), Lebedev (1987–1988), and Romano (1983) on Heraclitus; Burkert (1975) on Heraclitus and Empedocles; Edwards (1990) on Empedocles; Cilento (1964), Guérard (1987), O'Brien (1993), and Ousager (1995) on Parmenides; Shaw (1999) on the Pythagoreans.

70. See Armstrong' comments in vol. V, p. 42, n. 1; vol. IV, p. 398, n. 1; vol. II, p. 118, n. 1.

71. See Rist (1967), p. 178.

72. See Kahn (1979), p. 169.

73. Cf. Mansfeld (1999), p. 37; cf. also Mansfield (1992), pp. 300–307.

74. See *Enneads* IV.8.1–2; II.1.2, 4.7–11; V.1.9, 8–11.

75. Cf. Gelzer (1982), pp. 102–24.

76. Anaxagoras' fr. 1: I.1.8.8; III.6.6.23; IV.2.2.44; IV.4.11.27; V.3.15.21, 17.10; V.8.9.3; V.9.6.3, 6.8, 7.11–12; VI.4.14.4, 14.6; VI.5.5.3–4, 6.3; VI.6.7.4; VI.7.33.8; fr. 12: I.8.2.19; II.1.6.23–4; V.1.8.4–5, 9.1; V.3.3.21–2, 3.45, 6.11–12, 14.14; V.5.10.3; V.8.3.25–6; VI.2.8.6; VI.8.5.2; VI.9.3.26; A15: V.3.2.22; A20b: IV.4.30.19; A41: II.1.6.23–4; A54: II.7.1.4–6; A55: V.3.12.15; A107: III.6.19.21–2; Aëtius apud Stobaeus *Antologium* I.20: VI.3.25.1–5; Aristotle *Metaphysics* 984a: VI.1.1.2.

77. Anaximander's fr. 1: II.4.7.13, 15.10; A11, and A26: VI.6.3.25–6.

78. Democritus' fr. 9 and fr. 125: III.6.12.22, IV.4.29.32; fr. 164: II.4.10.3, VI.9.11.32; A1: V.9.3.15; A37: VI.1.1.2; A64: II.7.1.4–6, IV.7.3.3; A105: IV.7.3.1–2; Aëtius apud Stobaeus *Antologium* I.20: VI.3.25.1–5; Aristotle *De Caelo* 403b–404a: IV.7.3.1–2.

79. Empedocles' frs 17.7–8, 26.5–6: III.2.2.4–5, IV.4.40.6, VI.7.14.20; fr. 75: VI.3.25.25–7; fr. 84.3–4: I.4.8.4–5; fr. 109: I.6.9.29, II.4.10.3, VI.9.11.32; fr. 112.4: IV.7.10.38–9; fr. 120: IV.8.3.5; A52: VI.7.14.23; Stobaeus *Anth.* I.20: VI.3.25.1–5; Aristotle *Metaph.* 984a: VI.1.1.2.

80. Heraclitus' fr. 5: I.6.5.43–4; fr. 8: III.2.16.40, IV.4.41.8; fr. 10: II.3.16.42–43, 45, 53, III.3.1.9, IV.4.32.36–37, 38.17–19, VI.2.11.26; fr. 11: II.3.13.17; fr. 13: I.6.6.5–6; fr. 50: II.6.1.9–9, III.1.4.20, V.2.1.1, VI.5.1.26; fr. 51: II.3.16.45, III.2.16.34–35, 48, VI.7.2.52; fr. 54: I.6.3.28–9; fr. 82: VI.3.11.24–6; fr. 92: II.9.18.20; fr. 96: V.1.2.42; fr. 101: IV.8.1.17, V.9.5.31; fr. 112: III.6.2.31; fr. 113: VI.5.10.12; fr. 115: III.6.1.31, III.8.6.25, V.1.6.45, VI.5.9.14; A8: III.1.2.35; A9: III.5.6.17; Aristotle *Metaphysics* 984a: VI.1.1.2.

81. Leucippus' testimony A6: VI.3.25.34.

82. Parmenides' fr. 3: I.4.10.6, III.5.7.51, III.8.8.8, V.1.4.31–32, V.2.1.13, V.3.5.26–28, 43, V.3.6.7, V.3.8.38, V.4.2.43–44, V.6.6.21–3, V.9.5.26–20, VI.7.41.19–20; fr. 8.3: IV.7.9.11; fr. 8.4: III.7.5.21; fr. 8.4–6: III.7.11.3–4, 34; fr. 8.5: VI.4.4.25; fr. 8.5–6: VI.6.18.7, 42; fr. 8.6: III.7.11.53–4, V.1.8.22; fr. 8.19: IV.3.5.5–6, IV.7.9.16–17; fr. 8.25: VI.4.3.16, 4.24–5.

83. Philolaus' testimony A29: II.4.10.3, VI.9.11.32.

84. Pherecydes' fr. 14: V.1.1.4, 9.29; A7: V.1.6.52, 9.29.

85. Aristotle *Metaphysics* 985b: VI.6.5.10–12, Aristotle *Metaphysics* 986a: III.5.1.21–3; Aristoxenus fr. 35: VI.7.20.4; *Doxogr. Gr.* p. 282.8–11: VI.4.5.5–6, VI.6.9.38–9; *ibid.*, p. 318b4: III.7.7.25; *ibid.*, p. 386b8: III.6.1.31, V.1.5.9, VI.5.9.14, VI.6.16.45; Plutarch *De Isidorus* 75.381 ff., and Proclus *In Alcibiadem* 132.14: V.1.1.4, 9.29; Simplicius *in Physica* 700.19–20: III.7.2.4, 7.25.

86. See Aristotle *Metaphysics* 983b: VI.1.1.2.

87. Xenophanes' fr. 25: V.8.7.25–31.

88. See Rist (1967), pp. 177–8.

89. See Atkinson (1983), p. 186.

90. Cf. Atkinson (1983), p. 186.

91. Cf. Armstrong' notes in *Ennead* II.4, p. 118, n. 1; *Ennead* IV.8, p. 398, n. 1.

92. Cf. Roussos (1968), pp. 3–4.

93. σπάνια δὲ τὰ τῶν πρὸ τοῦ Πλάτωνος γεγονότων βιβλία.

CHAPTER 2. ONE AND UNITY

1. For a general introduction to Plotinus' theory of the One cf. Bales (1982), pp. 40–50; O'Meara (1993), pp. 44–78; Bussanich (1987), (1988), and (1996); Sumi (1993); Greogry (1999), pp. 24–38; Wallis (1995), pp. 57–61.

2. For *Ennead* VI.9 cf. the study of Meijer (1992), and the article of Miller (1977).

3. Cf. Bussanich (1988), p. 2.

4. Cf. *Enneads* V.4.1; V.5.6.

5. Cf. Blumenthal (1996), pp. 94–95.

6. Cf. Emilsson (2003), p. 363–64.

7. Cf. *Enneads* V.3.13; VI.7.17.4 ff.

8. Cf. O'Meara (1993), pp. 44–49.

9. As Wallis (1995) notes (p. 60, n. 2), Plotinus' definition of the One as δύναμις should not be translated and understood as "potentiality," since this interpretation falsely implies the Aristotelian sense of the term and so can erroneously lead to the conclusion that the One's by-products are more perfect than the One itself.

10. Cf. Lovejoy (1964), pp. 52–63.

11. Plotinus is influenced by Plato's *Philebus* (21d–22a and 61b–d), and the *Symposium*.

12. Cf. Armstrong, vol. VI, p. 12, n. 1. This is also followed by the *Index Fontium* of Henry and Schwyzer.

13. Cf. Atkinson's introduction and synopsis (1983); cf. also Armstrong, vol. V, pp. 7–8.

14. On this cf. Dodds (1960), p. 1 ff.
15. Cf. Atkinson, *ibid.*
16. Cf. Armstrong, *ibid.,* p. 42, n. 1.
17. Cf. *Enneads* III.5.1.6, and IV.8.1.23.
18. Cf. Meijer (1992), p. 23.
19. Plotinus' account of *Ennead* II.9.6 is a polemic account directed against the Gnostic misinterpretations of Greek philosophy. On this cf. also Kalligas (1997), pp. 354–356.
20. Cf. Meijer, *ibid.*, p. 21.
21. See Graeser (1972), p. 1.
22. Besides the criticism in V.1.9, and VI.7.37.3 on Aristotle's priority of the self-thinking and the plurality of "movers," Plotinus criticizes Aristotle's theory of time in III.7.9, Aristotle's theory of soul as an entelechy of body in IV.7.8[5], and the Categories in VI.1, and VI.3.
23. See Atkinson (1983), p. 185.
24. Atkinson (1983), p. 202 correctly observes that Plotinus' criticism of Aristotle is on a different level from the treatment of the Presocratics. For Atkinson and for Armstrong (*Ennead* V, p. 44, n. 1), Plotinus' criticism of Aristotle's Unmoved Movers looks like a Platonic development of Theophrastus in *Metaphysics* 5a14 ff., but this claim cannot be justified since we do not know how far Plotinus had Theophrastus in mind. A detailed analysis of Plotinus' argument against Aristotle is provided by Jaeger (1948), pp. 351–352.
25. On the Ideal Numbers cf. Armstrong's introductory note of *Ennead* VI.6, pp. 6–7.
26. Cf. Harder (1936) *passim.*; cf. also Rollof (1970) for a later development and justification of Harder's position.
27. Cf. also Armstrong's introductory note to V.5, pp. 152–53.
28. For this passage cf. below, ch. 3.2.
29. On Parmenides' One cf. Conche (1996), p. 138 and the relevant discussion of Tarán (1965), pp. 188–189. Barnes (1979) argues against the Parmenidean monism in his article "Parmenides and the Eleatic One." But this reading of Parmenides seems to be outside the textual evidence, especially of fr. 8.6 as well as of the ancient allusions to the fragment, especially of Plotinus' testimony in VI.6.18.40. Cf. also my discussion below, ch. 3.3.1.
30. Cf. Palmer (1999), pp. 91–92, and 166–173.
31. With the phrase τὸ πρῶτον ἕν, Plotinus refers to Plato's *Parmenides* 137c–142a. Another allusion to Plato's critique of Parmenides in the *Sophist* and the *Parmenides* appears also in *Ennead* VI.2.1.14–15 where Plotinus recognizes that Plato maintained the plurality of Being.
32. For Intellect as ἓν πολλά cf. *Enneads* V.3.15.10–11, 15.22; VI.2.9.11–12, 15.11–18, 17.22–25; VI.6.13.51–55; VI.7.14.11–12.
33. Cf. *Enneads* IV.2.2.52–55, and VI.2.6.13–14.

34. Cf. Atkinson (1983), pp. 196–198.
35. Cf. Atkinson (1983), p. 196.
36. Cf. Atkinson, *ibid.*
37. Cf. Coxon (1986), p. 34–35; cf. also *Ennead* III.7.11.
38. Cf. Armstrong, vol. VII, p. 75, n.1.
39. Cf. Roussos (1974), p. 463.
40. Cf. Atkinson (1983), p. 193.
41. The Eleatic Visitor in the *Sophist* names Parmenides as the "great" philosopher (237a4–5), and Socrates in the *Theaetetus* (183e ff.) describes Parmenides as "revered" and "awe-inspiring." In the same dialogue, Plato differentiates Parmenides from the other ancients for his denial of the process of coming-to-be (152e2), and recognizes the Eleatic opposition to the Heraclitean view of becoming (180e ff.); cf. also Plato's *Sophist* 237a ff. According to Plato, Parmenides, and Melissus are the philosophers who "insist that all things are One, and that this One stands still, itself within itself, having no place in which to move" (180e3–4).
42. For this rationale Plotinus seems to be based on Plato's *Republic* 509b; the first hypothesis of *Parmenides* 142a, and *Epistole* VII.341c5; cf. *Enneads* V.3.12.45–13.8; V.5.6.12; VI.9.4–5.
43. Cf. *Enneads* II.9.1.1–8; V.5.6.26–30; VI.7.38.1–2; VI.9.5.30–35.
44. Cf. Wallis (1995), p. 59.
45. Cf. Bussanich (1996), p. 42.
46. See Schroeder (1996), p. 336.
47. Cf. Wallis, *ibid.*, p. 59.
48. See *Enneads* II.9.1.7–12, and VI.7.38.4–9.
49. This view is followed by Armstrong (1977), Sells (1985), and Bussanich (1996).
50. See *Enneads* V.3.10.42; V.3.13; VI.9.5.30–46.
51. See *Enneads* VI.7.17.40, 32.9 ff.; VI.9.3; II.4.4.17–20.
52. See *Enneads* V.3.10.42; VI.7.9; VI.9.6.43–57.
53. See *Enneads* VI.9.5.30; V.5.4.15 ff.
54. See *Ennead* VI.8.17.22–27.
55. See *Enneads* V.5.10.19–21, 11.1; VI.7.32.15; VI.9.6.10.
56. On the apophatism of the One cf. Kordig (1982), pp. 114–121.
57. On the ἄπειρον of Anaximander cf. Kahn (1960), pp. 231–239; after an etymological analysis of the word ἄπειρον Kahn translates it as "boundless." But the translation "unlimited" is preferable as referring to lack of limit in space and time, and closer to the Greek negative prefix un- /α-; "boundless" obviously does not mean "no bound," but almost "no boundary," and this meaning denotes spatiality. Cf. also my analysis below, ch. 5.2.1.
58. Cf. Aristotle *Physics* 203b: ἀγένητον καὶ ἄφθαρτον ὡς ἀρχή τις οὖσα.

59. Throughout the *Enneads* whenever Plotinus mentions the Pythagoreans he refers to the Presocratic Pythagoreans and not the Neo-Pythagoreans.

60. Cf. Wallis (1995), p. 59.

61. Cf. Gezler (1982), pp. 129–130.

62. Cf. Kalligas (1991), p. 160.

63. Cf. Wallis (1995), p. 48.

64. Cf. Wallis, *ibid.*, pp. 32–33.

65. Cf. Wallis, *ibid.*, pp. 88–90.

66. Plutarch seems to receive the above information from the Egyptian tradition, and significantly Plotinus' origins were Egyptian.

67. Cf. Burkert (1972), pp. 141 ff.

68. Cf. Burkert, *ibid.*, p. 34 ff.

69. Cf. Wright (1981), p. 18.

70. For this account cf. DK testimony 31A23.

71. Cf. Wright, *ibid.*, pp. 253–255.

72. Cf. Empedocles' frs 11, 14, 15, 16.

73. Cf. Xenophanes' frs 23, 25, 26, 24; on Xenophanes' God cf. Lesher (1992), pp. 78–119.

74. Cf. Wright (1981), p. 255.

75. Cf. *Enneads* VI.4.7–8; V.3.9.7–20.

76. On the analogy of the sun in Plotinus cf. Wallis (1995), pp. 60–61, n.1.

77. Cf. *Enneads* III.6.15.1–6; IV.5.6.23–25; V.1.6.28–40; V.3.9.7–20, 12.39–40; V.5.7; VI.9.9.

78. See Aristoxenus in *Stobeus Ecl. I Proem*; on the One in Pythagorean Cosmogony cf. Philip (1966), pp. 48 ff.

79. Cf. Cornford (1974), pp. 148–149.

80. For the authenticity of this fragment cf. Huffman (1993), pp. 345–346.

81. For the authenticity and commentary of this fragment cf. Huffman, *ibid.*, pp. 276–230.

82. Cf. also *Enneads* VI.6.4.7 ff.; VI.3.13.19.

83. See Atkinson (1983), p. 210.

84. Cf. Atkinson, *ibid.,* p. 211. Atkinson is based on the authority of Philoponus (*in Physica* 515.30), and Simplicius (*in Physica* 542.9–12).

85. Armstrong (V.1, p. 45 n.1) is based on the authority of Longinus in Porphyry's *Life* 20.

86. On this discussion cf. Burkert (1972), pp. 218 ff.

87. Cf. KRS, p. 216, n. 1, 2.

88. Cf. Burkert, *ibid.*, pp. 223–225.

89. For this reference cf. DK testimony 7A7a.

90. The *Index Fontium* (HS2) gives *Ennead* V.1.6.52, but the correct reference is V.1.6.5.

91. For Pherecydes and the Pythagorean One cf. Schibli (1990), pp. 34–38.

92. For this position and discussion cf. Schibli, *ibid.*, p. 15.

93. Armstrong strangely regards that Plotinus' reference goes to Pherecydes' DK 7A29. But, there is not such a testimony in the DK edition.

94. For this position cf. HS2; Atkinson (1983), 209–210; Armstrong's comment at V.1.9.

95. For the relationship between Pherecydes and Pythagoras cf. Schibli, *ibid.*, pp. 11–13.

96. For these source cf. Schibli, *ibid.*, p. 11, n. 24.

97. Cf. Atkinson, *ibid.*, p. 210.

98. Cf. Shibli, *ibid.*, p. 15, n. 5.

99. Cf. below, ch. 5.3.3 for Pherecydes and the Pythagorean τόλμα.

100. See Atkinson (1983), p. 199.

101. Cf. Armstrong V.1, n. 2, p. 43.

102. Cf. Roussos (1968), pp. 38 ff.

103. Cf. Atkinson (1983), p. 201.

104. Cf. HS2, p. 343.

105. Cf. Kahn (1979), p. 131.

106. Cf. Kahn, *ibid.*, p. 132.

107. Cf. Marcovich (1967), pp. 116–117.

108. Cf. Roussos (1968), p. 38. Roussos devotes a whole chapter on the concept of unity and the One in Plotinus and Heraclitus (ch. 3); cf. especially notes 1 and 2 on the discussion of Plotinus' pantheism in connection to Heraclitus.

109. Cf. Roussos (1968), p. 39.

110. Armstrong claims without justification that the expression τὸ ἓν πάντα καὶ οὐδὲ ἕν of V.2.1.1–2 is an allusion to Plato's *Parmenides* 160b2–3.

111. Cf. *Enneads* IV.5.7.16–17; V.5.9.33 ff; VI.4.2.3–5; VI.5.1.25–26.

112. Cf. *Ennead* III.9.4: 1–2: the One is everywhere, for there is nowhere it is not and also VI.7.32.12–14; on this cf. Bussanich (1996), pp. 57–63.

113. D'Ancona Costa (1996), pp. 362–363.

114. Cf. *Enneads* V.3.15.27–31; V.4.2.16; VI.7.32.14; VI.8.21.24–5; cf. also Bussanich, *ibid.*

115. Cf. *Enneads* IV.9.5.11; II.3.16.53–54; IV.9.3.18.

116. See *Enneads* VI.2.5.4; V.9.4.13; VI.2.5.4; VI.7.15.20; II.3.16.53–54; II.6.1.8–9; III.1.4.17ff.; VI.2.2.36; VI.2.8.36; VI.5.1.24–26; VI.6.17.42; VI.7.14.22; VI.2.11.26; cf. Kalligas (1997), pp. 247–249.

117. See *Enneads* II.3.6.45; IV.4.38.17–19; III.2.16.39; III.3.1.11; I.8.6.54; IV.8.2.10.

118. Cf. Roussos (1968), pp. 41–43.

119. Cf. Porphyry, *Sentence* 27.12–13.

120. Cf. Kalligas (1997), p. 297.

121. Cf. D' Ancona Costa, *ibid.*, p. 363.

122. Cf. also Empedocles' frs 16, 19, 20, 21, 22, 35, 36.

123. Cf. also frs 6, 26, 37; Empedocles' theory of Matter is discussed below, ch. 5.2.2.

124. Cf. Armstrong, V.1, n. 2, p. 43.

125. Cf. Atkinson (1983), p. 201–202.

126. The same attitude is followed by Aristotle in *Metaphysics* 985a.

127. Cf. Aristotle's *Metaphysics* 1001a.

128. On the four roots cf. Wright's (1981) introductory section, pp. 22–30, and on Love and Strife, pp. 30–35; cf. also Inwood (2001), pp. 34–42.

129. On fr. 17 cf. Wright (1981), pp. 166–172, and on fr. 26 cf. 181–184; cf. also Inwood (2001), pp. 96–101, and for the role of Love and Strife, pp. 49–55; on Empedocles' cosmic periods cf. Minar (1963) and Trépanier (2003).

130. Cf. Atkinson (1983), p. 202.

131. Cf. Wright (1981), p. 193.

132. Cf. Dodds (1951), Appendix II; Merlan (1953) *passim.*; cf. Armstrong's (1955) response to Merlan; cf. also Armstrong (1967b), pp. 207–210, and Wallis (1995), pp. 70–72.

133. Cf. Kingsley (1995), p. 300; on this Kingsley follows Burkert (1962).

134. Cf. Armstrong, vol. IV, p. 260, n. 1.

135. Cf. *Enneads* III.1.5.8; IV.3.8.2; IV.5.1–2.

136. Cf. Wallis (1995), pp. 70–72. The connection of magic with the organic unity and sympathy of the universe relates Plotinus to the *Hermetica* (XVI), cf. Copenhaver (1992), p. 203 ff.

137. Cf. *Enneads* I.4.9.2, and IV.4.26.3, 43.22.

138. Cf. *Ennead* I.4.9.1 ff.

139. Cf. also Heraclitus' fr. 48.

140. Cf. my discussion below, ch. 5.3.2.

141. See Wallis (1995), p. 72.

142. Cf. *Enneads* II.3.9–10; III.3.6; IV.3.7.20–30.

143. For Empedocles' fr. 84 cf. the comment of Wright (1985), pp. 240–243.

144. Armstrong (vol. I, p. 193, n. 4) states that Plotinus' use of ἀντᾴδων καὶ ἀντεπᾴδων may have its source in Plato's metaphorical uses of ἐπῳδή in the *Charmides*, 156–7. In fact, Plotinus uses ἐπῳδή in this way of the highest sort of philosophy at V.3.17.18–20.

145. Cf. Kalligas (1994), p. 240.

146. Cf. Armstrong vol. IV, p. 268 n. 1; cf. also Armstrong (1967b), p. 208.

147. Cf. Wallis (1995), p. 72.

148. Cf. Edwards (1990), p. 153.

149. For Kalligas (1997), p. 375 the relationship of magical purification practices to medicine was assumed at the time of Plotinus and can found in the magical papyri which include various spells on the healing of body and soul. Plotinus may refer to *Katharmoi* where Empedocles demonstrates his expertise in medicine. Indeed, Plotinus relates magic to medicine at II.9.14.17, IV.4.43, and in IV.4.40 where γόης is also named φαρμακεὺς.

150. For the significance of Empedocles in Plotinus' theory of Soul cf. below, ch. 5.3.3.

151. For Anaxagoras' Mind cf. von Fritz (1964), Laks (1993), and Graham (1999), p. 162 ff.

152. Cf. Atkinson (1983), p. 199.

153. Cf. Armstrong, vol. V, p. 43, n. 2.

154. I prefer Atkinson's translation of χωριστὸν as "transcendent" and not as "separate" (see Armstrong's translation), because this translation fits better with Plotinus' interpretation of Anaxagoras' Mind in connection with the transcendent One.

155. Cf. KRS, p. 365.

156. Cf. McDiarmid (1953), pp. 85–96.

157. For Anaxagoras' fr. 11 cf. Sider (1981), p. 91; cf. also Wright (1985), pp. 128–129.

158. For Anaxagoras' fr. 12 cf. Sider *ibid.*, pp. 92–108; cf. also Wright (1985), pp. 129–131.

159. Cf. Wright's description, (1985), pp. xxix–xxx.

160. This is probably the reason for Simplicius (quoting Alexander, *in Physica* 300.27,—the context of fr. 13), noting that Aristotle did not mention Anaxagoras since Anaxagoras' Nous was not form but merely the cause of dissociation and subsequent arrangement of the cosmos, and so had nothing in common with the self-thinking Aristotelian Mind.

161. Cf. Plato's *Phaedo* 97b–99c.

162. Cf. Aristotle's *De Anima* 405a15–17.

163. See Atkinson (1983), p. 199.

164. *Enneads* V.3.6.10–12; V.3.14.14–15; V.8.3.24–28; VI.2.8.5–7; VI.8.5.1–2; VI.9.3.22–27.

165. Cf. also Anaxagoras' testimonies A45 (= Aristotle, *Phys* 203a19); A46 (= Aristotle, *GC.* 314a18); A60 (= Aristotle, *Metaphysics* 1056b28); A61 (= Aristotle, *Met* 1069b19). For some paraphrases cf. A1 (= Diogenes Laertius *VP* II 6–15); A42 (Hippolytus, *RH* I.8, 1ff.); A52 (= Aristotle, *Physics* 187a26).

166. Cf. Teodorsson (1982), p. 24.

167. Cf. *Enneads* I.1.8.8; IV.2.1.5–7; IV.4.2.10–11; V.8.9.3; V.8.11.5–6; V.9.6.4–10; V.9.7.11–12; VI.4.9.3–5; VI.6.7.1–4; VI.5.6.1–4; VI.7.33.7–14;

I.8.2.20, II.4.5.1; III.3.7.8–9; III.5.7.51; III.6.6.21–23; IV.1.2.42–44; IV.3.10.1–9; IV.4.11.17–28; V.3.15.18–23; V.3.17.9–10; VI.2.21.55; VI.3.1.17; VI.4.14.4–6;VI.5.7.7.

168. Cf. *Enneads* III.8.9.44–54, and VI.5.5.3–4.

169. Cf. *Enneads* III.7.3.19; III.7.3.37; III.7.11.13.

170. Cf. *Ennead* III.6.18.24–25.

171. Cf. *Ennead* II.6.1.8–12.

172. Cf. *Enneads* III.6.17.18, 36, and 18.35.

173. Plotinus may be reading Anaxagoras in the light of Plato's *Phaedrus* (67c5 ff.) where purification is connected to the separation from material objects.

174. Cf. also *Enneads* I.8.2.15–19; V.3.3.21–22, 39–45, 12.14–5.

CHAPTER 3. INTELLECT AND BEING

1. For Plotinus' theory of Intellect cf. Wallis (1995), pp. 67–70; Gerson (1994), p. 42–57; O'Meara (1993), pp. 22–33; Blumenthal (1996) *passim*; Gregory (1999), pp. 39–53.

2. For the influence of Numenius (fr. 25, 26, 30) and Albinus (*Eisagoge* ch. 10) in Plotinus' conception of Intellect cf. Armstrong, *ibid.*, pp. 9–13, and 49.

3. See Armstrong (1967a), p. 49.

4. Cf. Wallis (1995), p. 54.

5. See Blumenthal (1996), p. 94.

6. Cf. *Ennead* VI.7.8.30–2 with Wallis, *ibid.*, p. 55, and Gerson (1994), pp. 44–45.

7. On this discussion cf. Blumenthal, *ibid.*, p. 93.

8. On the influence of this passage as well of that in *Metaphysics* cf. Gerson, *ibid.*, p. 53.

9. Cf. Emilsson (1996), p. 238.

10. Cf. Gerson (1994), p. 53.

11. On Plotinus' Indefinite Dyad and Intelligible Matter cf. Rist (1962), and Nikulin (1998).

12. Cf. Armstrong (1967a), pp. 65–66.

13. See *Enneads* VI.7.15.10–24; V.3.11; V.7.15.

14. Cf. *Enneads* V.1.8.26; V.3.15.22; VI.2.9.11–12, 15.14–16, 17.25; VI.6.13.52–3; VI.7.14.11–12; cf. also Gerson (1994), pp. 44–45.

15. Cf. also *Ennead* V.9.8.4 ff.; cf. Wallis (1995), p. 55.

16. On this analysis cf. Wallis, *ibid.*, p. 67.

17. Cf. Wallis (1995), pp. 106, 124–5, 130–3, 149–156.

18. See *Enneads* III.8.8.17–19, and V.5.1.35.

19. Cf. *Enneads* III.7.11.36 ff.; V.3.6.15 ff.

20. See *Ennead* VI.9.5. Thomas Aquinas in *Summa Theologia* 14.7 seems to reflect Plotinus in stating that there are two forms of discursive thinking: (1) involving reasoning from premises to conclusion, and (2) involving a transition from one object to another.

21. On this analysis cf. also Wallis (1995), p. 52.

22. On the two modes of discursive alterity cf. Rappe (1996), p. 255.

23. Cf. *Enneads* V.3.5, and IV.4.1.

24. Cf. *Enneads* V.1.4.2 ff.; V.2.10.8–14; V.6.1. For Plotinus' criticism on discursive thinking and the importance of non-discursive thinking in the *Enneads* cf. Rappe (2000), pp. 23–67.

25. Cf. Lloyd (1969) *passim.*; (1986) *passim.*; (1990), pp. 164–6.

26. Cf. Sorabji (1980), pp. 217–19; (1982), pp. 310–14; (1983), pp. 152–6.

27. Cf. also Emilsson (1996), pp. 241–242.

28. See *Enneads* V.5.1.38–42, and V.8.5.5–6.

29. Cf. above, ch. 2.3.

30. Cf. above, ch. 2.5.3.

31. Parmenides' ἐόν denotes in ontological terms "whatever there is," and thus is translated here by the noun Being. This translation is used by Coxon (1986); on the meaning, cf. below, ch. 3.3.1.

32. Diels-Kranz (= 28B8.4) suggest ἔστι γὰρ οὐλομελές. Gallop (1984, p. 64) suggests οὖλον μουνογελές. But, as Owen (1960) showed, the appropriate reading should be ἔστι γὰρ μουνογενές, and this reading is followed by Táran (1965), and Coxon (1986).

33. Diels-Kranz, *ibid.*, and Coxon *ibid.*, suggest ἠδ' ἀτέλεστον; while Táran (1965), and Gallop (1984, p. 64) read ἠδέ τελεστόν. On the completeness of Being, I have followed Owen's (1960), p. 102 correction ἠδὲ τελεῖον rather than the traditional ἠδ' ἀτέλεστον preserved by Simplicius and followed by Diels and Kranz as well as the majority of modern scholars. Diels translates ἀτέλεστον as "endless," "without temporal limits." But ἀτέλεστον denotes "imperfection," "incompleteness," "without spatial or temporal end," notions that are incompatible with Parmenidean Being (cf. fr. 8.32: οὐκ ἀτελεύτητον τὸ ἐὸν; 8.42: τετελεσμένον ἐστί). Simplicius' misreading of ἀτέλεστον as it implies "unlimited temporality" derives propably from his Neoplatonic misinterpretation of Parmenides' Being as ἄπειρον (cf. *in Physica* 30.4, and 29.22 in connection with Melissus' argument in fr. 2: if Being were the result of a process, it would have an end but since it is not the result of a process, it does not have an end; on this cf. Tarán (1965), p. 93. Thus, Owen's correction ἠδὲ τελεῖον is in all probability the original reading of Parmenides' words. This reading is followed by Coxon (1986), p. 196, and Wright (1985), p. 82. For other variants of fr. 8.4 cf. Tarán (1965): ἠδε τελεστόν; Preler: ἠδ' ἀτάλαντον. For a complete discussion on the subject

cf. Tarán (1965), pp. 93–95; Coxon (1986), pp. 195–196; Conche (1996), pp. 133–134. Cf. also Gallop (1984), p. 64.

34. Based on the aforementioned analysis, fr. 8.4 is reconstructed as ἔστι γὰρ μουνογενές τε καὶ ἀτρεμές ἠδέ τελεῖον. For a complete discussion on the different views of the textual reconstruction cf. Gallop, *ibid.*, p. 64.

35. For this analysis cf. Wright (1985), pp. 82–87.

36. Cf. Owen (1960) *passim*. According to Curd (1997), p. 9, n.1, Owen's interpretation is the most influential account of Parmenides.

37. Cf. Owen, *ibid.*, pp. 14–6.

38. Cf. Barnes (1982), vol. I, pp. 163–4.

39. Cf. Barnes, *ibid.*, pp. 170–1; cf. also the discussion of Burnyeat (1982).

40. See Gallop (1984), p. 32 n.23.

41. See Coxon (1986), p. 194.

42. Cf. Broadie (1999), pp. 209–212.

43. For Parmenides' monism cf. my discussion above, ch. 2.3.

44. Cf. Coxon (1986), pp. 194 ff.

45. On Parmenides' influence on Plato's theory of Forms cf. Coxon, *ibid.*, pp. 26–8.

46. Cf. Parmenides' frs 8.40, and 6.8.

47. Cf. Parmenides' frs 2.5–9, 6.2–3, 8.15–18.

48. For Parmenides' rejection of nonbeing cf. Mourelatos (1970), ch. 3, and Austin (1986), pp. 11–43.

49. See Mourelatos, *ibid.*, p. 75.

50. On this position cf. Verdenius (1942), p. 237.

51. Cf. Coxon, *ibid.*, p. 33.

52. For the latter reference cf. above, ch. 2.3.

53. For a complete discussion of this passage and the influence of the Platonic dialogues on Plotinus' establishment of the theory of Three Hypostases cf. Atkinson (1983), pp. 186–192; cf. also Armstrong vol. V, p. 40–1, n.1, and 2.

54. See frs 2.2, 3, 6.1, 8.8, 8.34, 8.36.

55. For this analysis cf. Gallop, *ibid.*, p. 43.

56. See frs 7.2, 8.34, 8.50, 16.4.

57. See frs 4.1, 6.6, 16.3.

58. Cf. Gallop, *ibid.*, p. 44.

59. See Wright (1997), p. 11: "the potential range of νόημα identifies with its actual object."

60. Cf. Tarán (1965), pp. 41–44, Gallop (1984), pp. 56–57, and Conche (1996), pp. 87–90.

61. Cf. Gallop, *ibid.*, p. 57; Gallop also gives various translations of the fragment.

62. Cf. Wright (1985), p. 79.

63. Following Diels, Calogero (1932) suggests that the fragment has to be joined to fr. 2 with the phrase ὅσσα νοεῖς φάσθαι, translating as "for to think is the same as to say that that which you think exists," p. 19; cf. the rejection by Tarán (1965), p. 42.

64. Cf. Tarán (1965), p. 41 ff.

65. See Bauch (1910), p. 44, and Vlastos (1953), p. 168 notes 1, and 2.

66. See Tarán, *ibid.*, p. 41.

67. See Zeller (1882), p. 687, n. 1; this reading is followed by Burnet (1892); Cornford (1939); Tarán (1965), and Wright (1985).

68. For further interpretations of the fragment cf. Calogero (1932), and O'Brien-Frère (1987).

69. Cf. Gallop (1984), p. 87.

70. Cf. Gallop, *ibid.*, p. 43.

71. Cf. Snell (1924), p. 53; Friedländer (1958), p. 376, n. 6; I owe the references to Tarán (1965), pp. 41–42; cf. also the rejection of Snell's view by Vlastos (1953), p. 168.

72. In the same context, Untersteiner (1958), Beaufret (1984), Cordero (1984), Heitsch (1991), Reale-Ruggiu (1991), and Collobert (1993) understand: "because the same one is to think and to be"; cf. the analysis of this discussion by Conche (1996), pp. 87–90.

73. See Conche, *ibid.*, p. 90.

74. Cf. Phillips (1955), p. 16 ff.

75. Cf. Coxon (1986), p. 179.

76. This reference is not included in DK 28B3, but it is restored in the editions of Mansfeld (1964), p. 77, Coxon (1986), p. 54, and Conche (1996), p. 87. Tarán (1965), p. 194 seems to follow Diels' position and regards Proclus' quotation more as a paraphrase of fr. 8.34 than of fr. 3. On this cf. Conche, *ibid.*, p. 87, n. 1. In my view, Proclus' second quotation of fr. 3 in the *Platonic Theology* I.66.3–5 testifies to his direct knowledge of Parmenides.

77. Cf. Morrow-Dillon (1987), p. 387 ff.

78. The reference is given in Coxon, *ibid.*, p. 54.

79. See Phillips, *ibid.*; Atkinson (1983), pp. 92–3, and pp. 193–194; Gallop (1984), p. 31, n. 22; Coxon (1986), p. 34–5.

80. Cf. LSJ s.v. ἅπτω III, and Thucydides 1.97 'τούτων (i.e., Athenian history between the Persian and Peloponnesian Wars) δὲ ὅσπερ καὶ ἥψατο ἐν τῇ 'Αττικῇ ξυγγραφῇ 'Ελλάνικος, βραχέως τε καὶ τοῖς χρόνοις οὐκ ἀκριβῶς ἐπεμνήσθη.

81. Cf. Atkinson (1983), p. 193: "ἥπτετο does not imply superficiality but rather suggests lack of clarity or completeness."

82. εἰ γὰρ καὶ μὴ διακριβοῦσιν, ἀλλ' *ἅπτονταί* γέ πῃ τῆς ἀληθείας

83. Cf. Atkinson (1983) on the reading of the paragogic ἐστίν in line 17 as necessary for the scansion of Parmenides' quotation.

84. Cf. Atkinson (1983), pp. 92–3.

85. Cf. Roussos (1974), p. 463.

86. Cf. *Enneads* I.4.10.6; III.5.7.51; III.8.8.8; V.1.4.31–32; V.1.8.17–18; V.2.1.13; V.3.5.26–32; and 43, V.3.6.7; V.3.8.38; V.4.2.43–44; V.6.6.22–3; V.9.5.29–30; and VI.7.41.18.

87. Cf. Conche (1996), p. 87.

88. Cf. Coxon (1986), p. 54.

89. Cf. Atkinson (1983), p. 92.

90. Cf. *Enneads* III.5.7.51; V.1.4.31–32; V.2.1.13; V.3.5.26–32, and 43; V.3.6.7; V.3.8.38; V.4.2.43–44; V.6.6.22–3, and VI.7.41.18.

91. Cf. Plato's *Phaedo* 72e5–6, *Meno* 80 c–d, *Phaedrus* 250 a–b.

92. Cf. Aristotle's *De Anima* 430a3–4, and 431a1–2.

93. Cf. my discussion below, ch. 5.3.2.

94. See Armstrong vol. V, p. 298, n. 4.

95. Cf. also *Ennead* VI.6.18.40.

96. In IV.8.1.17, Plotinus writes: ὁ 'Ηράκλειτος . . . ὥσπερ καὶ αὐτὸς ζητήσας εὗρεν, and in V.8.4.53: ὁ Πλάτων . . . εἴασε ζητεῖν καὶ ἀνευρίσκειν.

97. Cf. below, ch. 4.6.2.

98. Cf. Armstrong vol. V, p. 298, n. 3; for Armstrong, the name νομοθέτης is probably taken by Numenius' Second God.

99. See Armstrong, vol. III, p. 384, n. 1.

100. Cf. Armstrong, vol. I, p. 198, n. 1.

101. Cf. Kalligas (1994), p. 243.

102. For this analysis cf. Wallis (1995), p. 67.

103. Cf. Atkinson (1983), p. 194.

104. Cf. *Enneads* V.3.5.43; cf. V.5.2.1, and VI.7.41.12.

105. On the Platonic Genera in Plotinus cf. Atkinson's comment, *ibid.*, pp. 94–95.

106. See my discussion above, ch. 2.3.

107. Parmenides' ἀγένητον echoes later in Plato's *Phaedrus* 245d1.

108. Cf. also DK testimonies 28A7, A8, A22, A23, A25, A28, A36. The fragment has no textual difficulties and, as Coxon notes in his commentary (1986; 194–195), ἀγένητον here is the earliest genuine occurrence of the term, while ἀνώλεθρον can be found in Anaximander's fr. 3 and Homer's *Iliad* N 761.

109. For a further analysis of this argument cf. Gallop (1984), pp. 15–16.

110. Cf. Roussos (1974), p. 463.

111. It is noteworthy that here Plotinus also echoes Plato's *Phaedrus* 245d1 concerning the "ungenerated source" of Being. Plato's aim is to show the Forms as the ultimate source without beginning or end in space and time, but his argument again is reminiscent of Parmenides' train of thought. Plotinus'

discussion on the immortality of the intelligibles in *Enneads* II.4.5.24–29; III.5.9.24–29, and V.4.1.18–19 clearly alludes also to Plato's *Phaedrus*.

112. For Parmenides' fr. 8.25 cf. Coxon (1986), pp. 203–205, and Conche (1996), pp. 150–152.

113. Cf. Roussos (1974), p. 463.

114. Cf. Armstrong, vol. VI, p. 286, n. 1.

115. Cf. Gallop (1984), pp. 16–17.

116. Cf. Wright (1985), p. 84.

117. I translate ἀτρεμές as "immutable," or "unshaken" in the case of Parmenides and as "imperturbable" in the case of Plotinus, since the latter gives a metaphysical and sometimes mystical context to the word.

118. The word ἀτρεμές is alternatively translated as "unshaken" and/or "unmoved" by Táran (1965); Coxon (1986), and Wright (1985), "steadfast" by Gallop (1984), "unwavering" by Jonathan Barnes (1987), "qui ne temble pas," and "immobile" by Conche (1996). But any translation which connotes "lack of motion" is not an accurate interpretation of ἀτρεμές. The word denotes "lack of tremble" (ἀ-τρεμές) and not "lack of motion." Parmenides states clearly the "immobility" of Being with the term ἀκίνητος in fr. 8.26, and 8.38. Thus, ἀτρεμές could be better understood and translated as "unshaken," "immutable," and "changeless" including somehow the idea of the "calmness of being" in its context.

119. The phrase 'Αληθείης εὐκυκλέος of fr. 1.29 prefigures the εὐκύκλου σφαίρης of fragment 8.43. However, the reading of both εὐκυκλέος and ἀτρεμές in fr. 1.29 is queried by some modern scholars because of some variation in the ancient sources. Whereas εὐκυκλέος is given only by Simplicius (*in De Caelo* 557.26), Diogenes Laertius (*Vitae Philosophorum* 9.22), Sextus Empiricus (*Adversus Mathematicos* 7.111, and 114), Plutarch (*Adversus Colotem*, 114d–e), and Clemens (*Stromateis* V.59) give εὐπειθέος "well-persuasive," while Proclus (*In Timaeus* I.345) has εὐφεγγέος "well-bright." Simplicius' εὐκυκλέος was first defended by Diels (1897; cf. also DK 28B1), and later followed by Burnet (1930); Untersteiner (1958); Vuia (1961); Táran (1965); Riezler (1970); Cordero (1984); Kirk; Raven and Schofield (1983); Wright (1985); Couloubaritis (1990), and Reale-Ruggiu (1991); the εὐπειθέος reading of Diogenes, Sextus, Plutarch, and Clemens was defended by Karsten (1835); Riaux (1840); Stein (1867); Jackson (1908); Jameson (1958); Deichgräber (1959); Fränkel (1962); Mourelatos (1970); Townsley (1975); Mansfeld (1983); Gallop (1984); Coxon (1986); Austin (1986); Barnes (1987); O'Brien-Frère (1987); Heitsch (1991); Collobert (1993); Conche (1996), and Roussos (2002); Proclus' εὐφεγγέος reading is rejected by all modern scholars as a Neoplatonic misinterpretation of Parmenides' verse. On this Táran (1965) notes that Proclus' reading is based

upon the Neoplatonic conception of the "intelligible light" found initially in Plotinus *Enneads* V.5.7, and VI.7.36 (cf. also *Ennead* V.3.12.40 ff.: ὡς ἀπὸ ἡλίου φῶς νοῦν θησόμεθα). It seems to me that, from the above variants, Simplicius' εὐκυκλέος fits better in the context of fragment 1.29, since a "well-rounded" Truth expresses more accurately the "well-rounded" sphere of Being in fr. 8.43 as well as the "intelligible discourse" of Truth in fr. 5. However, according to Coxon's criticism, "the most serious objection to εὐκυκλέος is that it goes beyond the climax of 'Αλήθεια in asserting that reality is not simply 'like a sphere' (fr. 8.43) but is circular." But the "circularity" of Being is a poetic simile in Parmenides, and so can be applied to Truth. Thus, while most of the ancient sources and modern scholars follow the reading of εὐπειθέος instead of εὐκυκλέος, the latter is preferable as *lectio difficilior*, and, as Táran (1965), p. 17 notes, Simplicius is the best authority for Parmenides' text and thus it should be preferred.

120. For fr. 1.29 (DK) cf. the following commentaries: Táran (1965), pp. 16–17, and chapter II; Gallop (1984), p. 53, and p. 36 n.55; Wright (1985), p. 78; Coxon (1986), pp. 168–9; Conche (1996), pp. 61–63; Roussos (2002), pp. 61–63.

121. Most of the ancient sources agree in this reading. Only Plutarch quotes ἀτρεκές (precise, certain) instead of ἀτρεμές; Sextus in *Adversus Mathematicos* 7.114 quotes ἀτρεμές, but some lines before, at 7.111, gives the erroneous ἀτρεκές. Hence, most modern scholars follow the same interpretative line in reading ἀτρεμές in fr. 1.29 with the sole notable exception of Fränkel (1962, p. 402, n. 11) who keeps Plutarch's ἀτρεκές. It has to be noted that the misplacement of ἀτρεκές in fr. 1.29 could be also derived from the wrong attribution of the epithet to ἀλήθεια and not to ἦτορ since the meaning of ἀτρεκές commonly refers to the "certainty of Truth," and the "propriety of Mind" (cf. Pindar fr. 213.4: νόος ἀτρέκειαν), as well as the personification of "Strict Justice" in the name of 'Ατρέκεια (Pindar, *Olympias* 10.13, and Euripides fr. 91). However, as Coxon (1986, p. 168) maintains, wherever Parmenides uses the word ἀλήθεια (frs 3, 4, 8.51), the context is not Truth in logical or linguistic terms, but Truth in ontological terms: "it is not the truth as an attribute of thought or language but as objective reality." Finally, the correctness of ἀτρεμές can also be justified by the attribution of ἀτρεμές to Being in fr. 8.4. It is worth noting that Simplicius, who is the most reliable source for fr. 8, quotes both frs 1.29 and 8.4 closely together within the same discussion, a fact which supports the correctness of ἀτρεμές (cf. *In De Caelo* 557, *passim*).

122. As Conche puts it (1996), p. 63: "Il désigne ici la parfaite égalité de l'être à soi-même."

123. Parmenides' use of ἀτρεμές reminds us of the calmness of the sea in Semonides fr. 7.37–8: ὥσπερ θάλασσα πολλάκις ἀτρεμὴς ἕστηκ', ἀπήμων, χάρμα ναύτῃσιν μέγα.

124. See Coxon (1986), p. 169.

125. This can be clearly observed in *Enneads* III.7.5.18–22, III.7.11. 1–5, I.1.9.23, I.6.5.15, III.2.2.16, III.2.4.15, V.9.11.20, VI.9.5.14, and VI.9.11.14.

126. Surprisingly Henry and Schwyzer omit the ἀτρεμές of fr. 1.29 and refer only to fr. 8.4.

127. Cf. McGuire-Strange (1988), note 54. The authors regard ἀτρεμές at 5.21 as an allusion only to Parmenides' fr. 1.29 and not also to 8.4.

128. Cf. Roussos (1974), p. 463.

129. Cf. the comment of Kalligas (1994) on 9.23–26; he refers to the ἀτρεμές of Parmenides' ἐόν only in fr. 8.4, and not fr. 1.29.

130. Cf. also *Ennead* IV.3.5.5–8.

131. See VI.9.5.14: νοῦν ἥσυχον; III.9.6.4: νόησις ἥσυχος; V.3.7.14: ἡσυχία τοῦ νοῦ. On the quietness of *Nous* cf. II.9.1.15–27, III.7.11.6, and 12.11; V.9.8.7–8.

132. On the θόρυβος of the bodies cf. *Enneads* IV.3.29.32–36; IV.8.8.4 ff.; VI.4.15.18–23.

133. See *Phaedo* 66d and *Timaeus* 43b.

134. See Armstrong, vol. I, p. 114, n. 1.

135. Cf. Kalligas (1994), p. 179 on I.1.9.23–26.

136. Cf. *Enneads* III.8.3.3–14, and 6.9 ff.; IV.3.18.19–24; V.1.4.38 ff.; VI.7.34.28–32.

137. The smooth and bright tranquility of the mirror is related to Intellect's self-thinking identity of Being, which looks back to Parmenides' fr. 3; cf. Kalligas, *ibid.*, pp. 242–243.

138. Armstrong vol. I, p. 245, n.3 correctly notes that the "inward beauty" of the soul refers to Socrates' prayer at *Phaedrus* 279b9, while in the same dialogue 247c6, Plato describes the world of Forms as "without color and shape."

139. Cf. *Enneads* IV.4.2.23–32; IV.7.10.28–37; V.1.5.1–4; V.3.4.10–141 VI.5.12.16–25; VI.7.35.4; on the intellectualized soul cf. Bussanich (1996), p. 56.

140. On the return to the One cf. Wallis (1995), pp. 82–90, and (1976) *passim.*; O'Meara (1993), pp. 103–106; Bussanich (1996), pp. 55–57.

141. For Mysticism in Plotinus and later Neoplatonism cf. Rist (1964) *passim.*

142. Cf. Bussanich (1996), p. 56; Bussanich's remark is based on Wallis (1976).

143. For the "end of the journey" cf. Plato's *Republic* 532e3. See also Plotinus' description of the Soul's return in *Ennead* I.6.8.16–27.

144. For Plotinus' formula "alone to the alone" cf. also *Enneads* I.6.7.8, and VI.7.34.7.

CHAPTER 4. ETERNITY AND TIME

1. *Ennead* III.7 can be also supplemented by other relevant passages throughout the *Enneads*. On χρόνος cf. especially *Ennead* I.4 *On Well-Being*; cf. the classification of the passages on χρόνος in the *Enneads* by S. H. Sleeman (1980) in the *Lexicon Plotinianum* according to their context. On Plotinus' theory of αἰών cf. also *Enneads* I.5.7.15 ff., II.5.3.8 ff., IV.1.6, IV.3.25.15, IV.4.1.12 ff., IV.4.15.2 ff., V.1.4.17–18, VI.2.21.54, VI.5.11.16 ff., VI.6.18.36 ff.

2. In modern scholarship the nature and importance of *Ennead* III.7 have attracted the research interest of many scholars. Cf. the recent commentary in modern Greek by Kalligas (2004), pp. 515–576; cf. also the studies of Strange (1994); Clark (1944); Jonas (1962); Manchester (1978); Graeser (1987), and Smith (1996 and 1998); cf. also Sorabji (1983), chs 8–11; Callahan (1948), ch. 3; Turetzky (1998), ch. 5; and Gerson (1994), ch. VI. 3.

3. The latter argument seems to be originally Plotinian, while the former derives from Plato in the *Parmenides* (138b2–3) that "a container is distinct from what it contains" and Aristotle's rejection in the *Physics* (218a30–b20) that "time" cannot be related to any kind of physical motion or be subject to motion; cf. Strange (1994), p. 41.

4. Plotinus' radical philosophical position on the concepts of time and eternity seems to have had a great influence not only on later Neoplatonists such as Iamblichus, Proclus, and Damascius, but also on early Christian, Medieval and Arabic thought. For instance, St. Augustine in the *Confessions* clearly reflects Plotinus' concept of time (cf. XI. 14–28), and especially his mysticism (cf. VII, IX, and X), while Boethius' definition of αἰών in *De Consolatione Philosophiae* (V. Prosa 6) as *interminabilis vitae tota simul et perfecta possessio* echoes Plotinus' definition of αἰών as the life of the intelligible world, cf. Sorabji (1983), ch.11; McGuire and Strange (1988), p. 251; cf. Wallis (1995), pp. 167 ff.

5. Cf. Armstrong vol. III, p. 293.

6. Cf. Sorabji (1983), pp. 197–99.

7. Plotinus, as a determined Platonist, develops his thesis on the foundation of the traditional Platonic definition of time given at *Timaeus* 37c6–d7. Henry and Schwyzer in their *Index Fontium* locate more than fifteen allusions just to *Timaeus* 37c–39e in this particular *Ennead*. Kalfas' commentary on the *Timaeus* (1995), n. 132–134 offers interesting observations on the passage of time and presents the different viewpoints of the subject derived from Robinson (1986); Whittaker (1968); O'Brien (1985), and Tarán (1979). On Plato's theory of time cf. also Callahan (1948), pp. 3–37; Leyden (1964) *passim*; Sorabji (1983), pp. 108–112; Mohr (1986), *passim.*; the most complete philosophical comparison between the Plato's view of time in the dialogues

mentioned is in Goldin (1998). Plato's theory of time are not of course limited to the *Timaeus* but can be also to be found in the Myth of the *Politicus* (268e–274e), where he speaks of "backward running time," and in some of the central aporetic questions in the *Parmenides* (e.g. 140e–141a, 152a), where he establishes the metaphysics of the One by using the idea of time and progress. But even if Plotinus was aware of these passages, in *Ennead* III.7, he only makes use of the *Timaeus'* passage on time.

8. On *Timaeus* 37d cf. ; cf. III.7.1.19–20, 2.12–13, 11.20, and 46–47, 13.24; cf. also *Enneads* I.5.7.15, V.1.4.18, V.8.1.27, V.9.2.27, VI.5.11.16.

9. Cf. *Ennead* III.7.12.22–33, 13.19–24.

10. Cf. *Ennead* III.7.2.35, 6.6.

11. On *Timaeus* 29e cf. III.7.6.50; cf. also *Enneads* II.9.17.16–17, and V.4.1.35.

12. On *Timaeus* 35a cf. *Ennead* III.7.6.28; cf. also *Enneads* I.1.8.10–12, III.4.6.34–5, III.9.1.34–7, IV.1.10–15, IV.2.2.49–52, IV.3.4.13, 19.1–8, and 28–31, IV.9.2.26–8, VI.4.1.2–3, and 27, VI.7.13.20–1.

13. Cf. Strange (1994), p. 41.

14. Strato (*apud* Sextus Empiricus *Adversus Mathematicos* X 177) uses the word μονή instead of στάσις, but this does not change the philosophical meaning of the definition. For Plotinus the two terms seem to have equal meaning, especially at the level of Intellect.

15. Using this analysis, Plotinus refers indirectly to the ancient accounts given by Aristotle, the Stoics, the Epicureans, and the Pythagoreans. According to Strange, *ibid.*, pp. 42–43 n. 55, and n. 58., Plotinus worked on *Physics* IV.11–14 with material and arguments drawn from the Peripatetic commentaries of the *Physics* and especially with Alexander of Aphrodisias' lost commentary *in Physica*, which is actually the main source of Simplicius' commentary on time *in Physica*, and the only source for the pre-Alexandrian tradition. As Strange suggests, Plotinus' phrase "to him who says [time] is the measure of the motion of the all" (πρὸς τὸν λέγοντα μέτρον κινήσεως τοῦ παντὸς) at III.7.10.12–13, refers indirectly to Alexander. So probably Plotinus uses Alexander's commentary as a main source but takes the original position directly from Aristotle.

16. Cf. Callahan (1948), pp. 94–98; McGuire and Strange (1988), p. 268, n. 73; Strange (1994), pp. 41–47.

17. On Aristotle's theory of time cf. Callahan (1948), pp. 38–87; Annas (1975) *passim*; Bostock (1980) *passim*; Sorabji (1983), pp. 7–12, 84–9, 214–218; Bolotin (1997) *passim.*

18. Cf. Strange (1994), p. 43, n. 56.

19. Cf. Armstrong vol. III, p. 320, n. 3, and p. 326, n.1; even so, if Plotinus' echoes Strato's insight on the kinetic problems of the Aristotelian definition, it is still debatable whether Plotinus is aware of this view.

20. Strato of Lampsacus (*apud* Simplicius *in Physica* 789.2–9); see Strange, *ibid.*, p. 43, n. 56.

21. See Sambursky (1959), p. 101.

22. Cf. *SVF* II 509–521, and I 93. On the Stoic theory of Time cf. Sambursky, *ibid.*, pp. 98–109; Rist (1969), pp. 273–288; Sorabji (1983), pp. 21–27.

23. Cf. Armstrong vol. III, p. 320, n. 5.

24. Cf. Graeser (1972), pp. 15–16, and 40.

25. *Letter to Herodotus*, Bailey (1928), pp. 72–73; Epicurus fr. 294 *apud* Sextus Empiricus *Adversus Mathematicos* X 219; Stobaeus *Anthologium* I.8.40b.11; Lucretius i. 459–463.

26. Simplicius *in Physica* IV.10, 700.19–20; cf. Aristotle *Physics* 218b1, and also Stobaeus *Anthologium* I.8.40b.2, who attributes to Pythagoras the definition of time as τὴν σφαῖραν τοῦ περιέχοντος.

27. On Epicurus' theory of time cf. Bailey (1928), pp. 241–242; Sorabji (1983), p. 95; on the Epicurean theory of Time-Atoms cf. Turetzky (1998), pp. 34–37; Sorabji (1983), pp. 370, and 375–7. Plotinus seems not be aware of the later theory but mainly criticizes the Epicurean view of time as relating accidentally to motion.

28. See Bailey, *ibid.*, p. 241.

29. σύμπτωμα συμπτωμάτων, τοῦτο δ' ἐστὶ παρακολούθημα κινήσεων.

30. HS2 apparatus (7.26) associate the Epicurean παρακολούθημα with Chrysippus' definition of time as τὸ παρακολουθοῦν διάστημα τῇ τοῦ κόσμου κινήσει, but Chrysippus' definition focuses more on the concept of διάστημα than τὸ παρακολουθοῦν. Plotinus' reference would therefore be closer to the Epicureans than the Stoics but still subject to the general criticism of definitions of time related to motion.

31. I am following Jonas (1962), p. 297, n.3, and McGuire-Strange (1988), p. 266, n. 11, that the words ἀίδιος and αἰώνιος in *Ennead* III.7 are synonymous. Since Plotinus denies any duration for αἰών, it is erroneous to translate the word ἀίδιος as "everlasting" (*contra* Armstrong).

32. See *Ennead* IV.4.15.2: αἰὼν μὲν περὶ νοῦν, χρόνος δὲ περὶ ψυχήν.

33. See McGuire and Strange (1988), p. 265, n. 1.

34. Cf. McGuire and Strange, *ibid.*

35. Cf. Sorabji (1983), p. 138.

36. Cf. Sorabji, *ibid.*

37. Cf. LSJ, pp. 2008–9.

38. Cf. LSJ, p. 45.

39. Cf. LSJ, p. 36.

40. For αἰών personified cf. LSJ, p. 45.

41. Epiphanius *Adversus Haereses* 51.22–3: ἡ Κόρη ἐγέννησε τὸν Αἰῶνα.

42. Suda 522.6–7: τὸ ἄρρητον ἄγαλμα τοῦ Αἰῶνος.

43. For αἰών associated with ψυχή cf. Onians (1954), ch. VI, and Claus (1981), pp. 11–13. For the early Greek concept of ψυχή cf. Benveniste, E. (1932), and Bremmer (1983).

44. See *Iliad* 16.453; 19.27; 22.58; *Odyssey* 7.224.

45. Cf. Benveniste (1937), p. 104 ff.; Claus (1981), p. 12; Wright (1995), p. 130.

46. Cf. *Iliad* 17.302; 9.415; 24.725.

47. Cf. *Odyssey* 5.152; 5.160; 18.204.

48. Cf. Claus (1981), pp. 11–12.

49. Cf. Claus, *ibid.,* p. 12, n. 8.

50. Cf. Onians (1954), pp. 208–209.

51. See Onians, *ibid.*

52. Cf. the *Hymn to Hephaestus* 6–7: αἰῶνα τελεσφόρον εἰς ἐνιαυτὸν εὔκηλοι διάγουσιν, and Aeschylus *Suppliants* 574: δι' αἰῶνος κρέων ἀπαύστου; cf. Wright (1995), p. 130.

53. *De Caelo* 279a25–28: αἰὼν ἀπὸ τοῦ αἰεὶ εἶναι τὴν ἐπωνυμίαν εἰληφώς.

54. The tables include *only* the extant Presocratic fragments since the extant fragments are more likely to include the original linguistic form of the phrase. As the testimonies usually reflect the style of later philosophic sources and are not to be trusted as reliable reports of the original usage, the quotations here are restricted to the DK B fragments; the main A testimonies are listed below in the next pages of this chapter.

55. Cf. DK testimonies of Anaximander (A10), Anaximenes (A6), Democritus (A49), Heraclitus (A1), while ἀΐδιος in Anaximander (A9; A10; A11; A12; A17), Anaximenes (A5), Xenophanes (A36), Parmenides (A7; A22; A23; A34; A37), Pherecydes (A7), Empedocles (A1; A5), Anaxagoras (A43), Democritus (A37; A71), Xenophanes (A1; A28; A33; A37), Heraclitus (A6; A8), Melissus (A37), and Alcmaeon (A1).

56. Cf. DK testimonies of Thales (A1), Anaximander (A11; A15), Heraclitus (A5; A10), Zeno (A25; A27; A28), Anaxagoras (A1; A45), and Democritus (A39; A71).

57. Cf. Kalfas (1995), p. 382 n. 133.

58. Cf. Strange (1994), p. 33.

59. Cf. my discussion above, ch. 2.5.1.

60. αἰών ἐστιν, ἀπὸ τοῦ αἰεὶ εἶναι τὴν ἐπωνυμίαν εἰληφώς, ἀθάνατος καὶ θεῖος.

61. Cf. Armstrong, vol. III, p. 309; cf. also McGuire-Strange (1988), n. 49.

62. On this passage cf. Kalfas (1995), n. 133–138.

63. Cf. Robinson (1986), pp. 143–4; cf. also Kalfas (1995), p. 383.

64. Φιλόλαος δέ φησιν ἀριθμὸν εἶναι τῆς τῶν κοσμικῶν αἰωνίας διαμονῆς . . .

65. For Philolaus' fr. 23 cf. Huffman (1993), pp. 354–355.

66. Cf. Huffman, *ibid.*, p. 355.

67. Cf. also line 14: τὸ κινέον ἐξ αἰῶνος ἐς αἰῶνα περιπολεῖ.

68. Cf. Huffman, *ibid.*, pp. 341–344.

69. Cf. Huffman, *ibid.*, p. 355.

70. περὶ δὲ φύσιος καὶ ἁρμονίας . . . τῶν πραγμάτων ἀίδιος ἔσσα.

71. See the testimony of Philo *De opificio mundi* 100; cf. also Philolaus' fr. 20.

72. ἡγεμὼν καὶ ἄρχων ἁπάντων, θεός, εἷς, ἀεὶ ὤν, μόνιμος, ἀκίνητος, αὐτὸς ἑαυτῶι ὅμοιος, ἕτερος τῶν ἄλλων; on this cf. Huffman (1993), pp. 334–339.

73. Cf. Diogenes Laertius *Lives of Eminent Philosophers* 3.6.7.

74. Cf. Tarán (1979), pp. 44–45; Tarán's conclusion is based on Plato's clear denial of special terminology in other dialogues (*Meno* 87bc; *Republic* 533d–e; *Theaetetus* 184b–c; *Statesman* 261e; *Laws* 864a–b), as well as on the ambiguous usage of αἰώνιος in *Timaeus* 37d; cf. also Kalfas (1995), p. 384.

75. Cf. Robinson (1986), p. 149.

76. Cf. Cherniss (1962), pp. 211 ff., and 420 n. 351. Cherniss maintains that Plato uses ἀεί with two meanings: the one related to the sensible becoming and implying temporal duration, the second related to the True Being of the Forms and implying non-durational eternity. Cherniss' support for his thesis is based on a Neoplatonic passage taken from Proclus (*In Timaeum* I.239.2–6). In this passage, Proclus distinguishes clearly the temporal ἀεί from the eternal ἀεί: ἄλλο γὰρ τὸ ἀεὶ τὸ χρονικὸν καὶ ἄλλο τὸ αἰώνιον. The χρονικὸν ἀεί refers to the ever-generated, divisible and incomplete being of temporal becoming, while the αἰώνιον ἀεί refers to ungenerated, indivisible, infinite, and complete intelligible being. Following this line of interpretation, Vlastos (1965), p. 408, n. 3, points out that Plato was probably the first who "glimpsed" the notion of "timeless eternity," or more clearly "timelessness in contradiction to perceptual duration."

77. Cf. Cornford (1937), p. 98, n.1, and p. 102.

78. Cf. Whittaker (1968), p. 131–136. Whittaker, following Cornford, argues that Cherniss' non-durational interpretation rests upon an insecure basis. Interpreting Plato in the Neoplatonic light of Proclus is anachronistic, in the framework of a later Platonic system. Whittaker maintains that nowhere in the Platonic *corpus* does the word ἀεί indicate an extra-durational sense (cf. for instance *Parmenides* 135B5–C3; *Sophist* 248A10–12; *Politicus* D5–7). And he notes that "the notion of non-durational eternity is an accepted feature of Neoplatonic doctrine from Plotinus onwards." This argument is also followed by O'Brien (1985), who maintains that the view of non-durational eternity

cannot be found in Plato nor earlier in Parmenides nor later in Aristotle, but it is a thesis developed by Plotinus in *Ennead* III.7, and attributed anachronistically to Plato's *Timaeus*.

79. Cf. above, ch. 3.3.1.

80. For A-series flowing time (past, present, future), and B-series static time (earlier, simultaneously, later) see McTaggart (1908).

81. Parmenidean Monism therefore is clearly contrasted with Heraclitean Pluralism. The polemic attitude of the Eleatic towards the Ephesian is more obvious in fragment 6. In this fragment, according to Parmenides, alongside the clear justification of ἔστιν and the rejection of οὐκ ἔστιν there is the contradiction of ἔστιν and οὐκ ἔστιν together. Parmenides argues against this contradictory thesis, and against those people (including philosophers) who do not distinguish *is* from *is not*, but they want to have both at once *temporally* (now but not then or later) and *spatially* (here but not there). As Parmenides puts it, these are people without judgment (ἄκριτα φῦλα), deaf (κωφοὶ), and blind (τυφλοί) with a two-headed contradictory mind (δίκρανοι) (cf. fr. 6.5). They are unthinking mortals whose beliefs have no genuine conviction (οὐκ ἔνι πίστις ἀληθής) (fr. 1.30). This strong Parmenidean criticism is general, but in all probability has a particular target in Heraclitus. The phrase "for all whom their journey turns backwards again" (πάντων δὲ παλίντροπός ἐστι κέλευθος) in fragment 6.16 echoes clearly the "backward attunement" (παλίντροπος ἁρμονίη) of Heraclitus' fragment 51. This assumption can also be supported by the use of the word "two-headed mind" (δίκρανος) in fragment 6.5. Whereas for Heraclitus one opposite *presupposes* the other, for Parmenides the one opposite would *exclude* the other. But further, any one perceptible opposite is unacceptable, and any plurality, even the minimum of two, is impossible. Plurality can be found only in the "many" opinions of mortals (βροτῶν δόξαι) who are deceived by their sense and never in the "one" Way of Truth (πίστις ἀληθής) (fr. 1.30).

82. Simplicius *in Physics* IX.30.3; IX.78.14; IX.143.13; IX.145.5; cf. Barnes (1987), p. 134; Gallop (1984), p. 65; cf. also KRS, p. 249.

83. Cf. Tarán (1965), p. 85; Coxon (1986), p. 62; Conche (1996), p. 127.

84. For this view cf. Owen (1960) and (1966); cf. also Sorabji (1983), p. 99, n. 3.

85. Cf. Barnes (1979), vol. 1, p. 163; Cf. Sorabji, *ibid.*

86. Sorabji (1983), collects, along with his own, eight different interpretations of Parmenides' fr. 8.5–6, cf. chapter 8 and especially pp. 98–108.

87. Cf. Fränkel (1970), p. 191, n. 1.

88. Cf. Tarán (1965), pp. 175–88.

89. Cf. Gallop (1984), pp.13–14.

90. Cf. Schofield (1970), *passim.*

91. Cf. O'Brien (1980), *passim.*

92. Cf. Gallop, *ibid.*, p. 14.

93. Sorabji, *ibid.* uses the terminology of McTaggart (1908) to formulate the second interpretation of fr. 8.5–6.

94. Cf. Sorabji (1983), pp. 128–30.

95. Cf. Owen (1966), *passim.*

96. Cf. Barnes, *ibid.* pp. 193–4.

97. See Sorabji's analysis p. 100, n. 10. Sorabji offers a translation of the passage in p. 262.

98. Cf. Whittaker (1968); (1969); (1970), pp. 25 ff. Sorabji offers Whittaker's interpretation in pp. 105–107.

99. Cf. Whittaker, *ibid.*

100. Cf. Sorabji, *ibid.*, p. 107.

101. See Whittaker, *ibid.*

102. Cf. Kneale (1960), pp. 90–2.

103. For Parmenides' argument cf. Gallop (1984), pp. 15–16, and Coxon (1986), p. 197.

104. Parmenides' question is an interesting application of what came to be known as the Principle of Sufficient Reason first introduced as such by the French scholastic philosopher Abelard and later developed by Leibniz: *nothing can be so without there being a reason why it is so*. Furthermore, Gallop, *ibid.*, states that Parmenides' argument is also parallel to the antithesis to Kant's First Antinomy: *Being could not have arisen at a given point in time, unless there had been sufficient reason for its doing so.*

105. Cf. KRS, p. 250.

106. For the text of this passage, I adopt the Greek suggested by Coxon and Conche which is closely based on Simplicius' original *in Physica* IX.149.6: οὐδ' εἰ χρόνος ἐστὶν ἢ ἔσται; IX.86.31: οὐδὲν γὰρ ἔστιν ἢ ἔσται; cf. Coxon (1986), p. 76, and his comment at pp. 210–211; Conche (1996), p. 126, and pp. 165–167.

107. Cf. Coxon, *ibid.*, and Conche, *ibid.*

108. Cf. DK, p. 238; Tarán (1965), p. 83, and pp. 128–129; Gallop (1984), p. 70.

109. Cf. DK, *ibid.*

110. Cf. Tarán, *ibid.*, and Gallop, *ibid.*

111. See Conche, *ibid.*, p. 165.

112. See Coxon, *ibid.*, p. 210.

113. See frs 1; 2; 3; 7.17; 8.13.

114. See frs 4.3; 7.3.

115. Cf. also Melissus' fr. 2.3. Simplicius understands the ἀεὶ ἄπειρον of fr. 3 as an explicit (σαφὲς πεποίηκεν) early reference to the ἀεὶ ὂν infinitum (*in Physica* 109.30 ff: τὸ ἀεὶ ὂν ἄπειρον λέγει).

116. This contraposition between the two Presocratics has been already observed by Simplicius himself in quoting fr. 6 (*De Caelo* 557.16: Μέλισσος μὲν . . . Παρμενίδης δὲ . . .). Indeed, Parmenides argues for a finite sphere-like Being which is utterly unchanging, complete on every side, all continuous, equal to itself on every side, resting uniformly in its limits (fr. 8.42–49). On the other hand, Melissus' Being is similarly unchanging, complete, immobile, lacking emptiness, pain, or variation in density, but with no defined limit or boundary (fr. 7). In fragments 5 and 6, Melissus argues from Parmenides' premise against spatial limit. Melissus states that since limit presupposes two points to be defined (δύο εἴη) and Being has to be one (ἓν), then Being has to be without limits (ἄπειρον).

117. Cf. Tarán (1965), pp. 180 ff.

118. Cf. Sorabji (1983), p. 112.

119. Cf. Strange (1994), p. 40.

120. This discussion of αἰών in *Ennead* III.7 can also be supplemented with other parallel passages throughout the *Enneads*: in the discussion of well-being and time in *Ennead* I.5.7; in the denial of the divine memory in IV.3.25, IV.4.1.15; concerning the nature of intelligible life at VI.6.18, and in the discussion of the eternal nature of intelligible beings in II.5.3, IV.1, V.1.4, VI.2.21, and VI.5.11. According to these passages eternity is used (1) to stress the difference between the eternal and sensible realm as well as, (2) to maintain the timelessness of intelligible nature.

121. According to this dialogue the five Genera (or the Categories) that illustrate Plato's intelligible world of being and its metaphysical structure are: Being (τό ὂν αὐτὸ), Rest (στάσις), Motion (κίνησις), Sameness (ταὐτόν), and Otherness (θάτερον). Plotinus evaluates in detail the "genera of being" mainly in three successive *Enneads* VI.2, VI. 3, and VI. 4 *On the Genera of Being* (numbers 42–44 in Porphyry's chronological order). In *Ennead* III. 7 the μέγιστα γένη of the *Sophist* seem to play a central role in the investigation of αἰὼν and its properties. Plotinus systematizes in the second chapter of III.7 the γένη of Motion, Rest, and Sameness and through this systematization proceeds to the identification (1) of Motion with the Life (or the Activity) of Intellect (or the intelligible substance); (2) of Rest with the stability and the changeless perfection of the intelligible world; and (3) of Sameness with the unextended nature of the intelligible realm. Cf. McGuire and Strange (1988) at the introduction in *Ennead* III. 7. See also III.7.2.20–36.

122. In this case [eternity = στάσις ἁπλῶς] (2.24–28), first, the term στάσις should not be applied to αἰώνιον for eternity cannot be named αἰώνιον, since the αἰώνιον is τὸ μετέχον αἰῶνος, and not eternity itself. As McGuire and Strange (1988), n. 25 observe, this argument denies the assumption of self-predication. Likewise, quantity itself is not a quantity (II.4.9.5–6),

and intelligible shapes do not themselves have shapes (VI.6.17.25–26). Second, if Rest is eternal, then how could Motion have the same property? For if Motion is eternal in terms of Rest, Motion will paradoxically exist in Rest, and that leads to an absurd conclusion. Third, Rest does not includes the notion of "always" which is a fundamental presupposition for eternity, especially the "always" that signifies the eternal state of Being and not the "always" of time.

123. In this case [eternity = στάσις περὶ τὴν οὐσίαν] (2.29–31), if eternity is allied with Rest which belongs to the intelligible substance, the other genera of being will be excluded from eternity, particularly that of Motion, which fundamentally relates eternity to Life and the Activity of Intellect. In general, as Plotinus finally argues, it is erroneous to limit our understanding of eternity to the concept of Rest, for Rest does not include unity and lack of extension. Eternity undoubtedly participates in Rest, but it is not Rest itself (2.35–36). The notion of eternity must equally imply: (1) unity, (2) development, and (3) lack of extension.

124. See *Ennead* III.7.4.5–12; cf. also V.5.2.18 ff., and V.3.5.23–26.

125. Cf. McGuire and Strange (1988), n. 43.

126. Cf. my discussion at ch. 3.4.3.

127. Cf. Kalligas (1994), pp. 254–5.

128. For fr. 52 cf. the commentaries of Marcovich (1967), pp. 490–495; Kahn (1979), pp.227–229; Wright (1985), p. 73; Roussos (2000a), p. 200.

129. See frs 121, 114, 125a; the connection between fr. 52 and political criticism is echoed in Diogenes Laertius' testimony of Heraclitus' misanthropy (*Lives* IX.3). According to Diogenes, Heraclitus become misanthropic, withdrew from the city of Ephesus and lived at the temple of Artemis where he preferred to play draughts with children than to establish laws for the Ephesians (εἰς τὸ ἱερὸν τῆς 'Αρτέμιδος μετὰ τῶν παίδων ἠστραγάλιζεν). But Diogenes' story is probably fictitious, based more on fr. 52 than a reliable historic source.

130. See frs 1, 5, 14, 20, 34, 87; Cf. KRS, pp. 181–183.

131. Lucian relates fr. 52 to fr. 25: Παῖς παίζων, πεσσεύων, διαφερόμενος, συμφερόμενος.

132. For these ancient sources cf. Marcovich, *ibid.,* pp. 490–493.

133. Cf. Marcovich, *ibid.*, p. 493.

134. For Empedocles and meaning of the clepsydra cf. Furley (1975).

135. The most important later double personification is of Mandulis αἰών worshipped at the Roman garrison town of Talmis in two forms, as a full-grown man and as a child, cf. Nock (1972), pp. 357–358. The two shapes of Mandulis Aion appeared side by side representing probably a solar deity associated with Isis.

136. Cf. Kahn (1979), pp.227–229; Wright (1985), p. 73; Roussos (2000a), p. 200.

137. As far as the ancient game of *pesseia* is concerned, the nature of the game was probably that of a board game where an individual moves pieces on a board; cf. Wright, *ibid.*, p. 73. The individual tries to win by using skill and/or chance, as in backgammon or modern Greek *tavli*. Plato at *Theaetetus* 146a describes a children's ball game (οἱ παῖδες οἱ σφαιρίζοντες) where the winner becomes a king. Marcovich also suggests that the game could mean "play draughts," a game called πόλις, an interpretation which is linked to the political context of the fragment; cf. Marcovich, *ibid.*, p. 494, and Kahn, *ibid.*, p. 494. In fact, we do not know how far the *pesseia* was really a children's game. On the contrary, Homer in the *Iliad* I.106 ff. presents the insolent suitors sitting in front of the palace door and playing *pesseia* (πεσσοῖσι). If we bear in mind Heraclitus' view of children's immaturity (cf. frs 56, 79117, 79) then we can assume, as Marcovich interprets fr. 52, that a "mature or aged man is just as foolish as a child, in any respect and especially for the political wisdom or insight: a king on the throne behaves like a child."

138. The continuous process is shown by the present continuous tense of παίζων and πεσσεύων in the fragment.

139. Cf. Kahn, *ibid.*, p. 228.

140. See frs 16.2; 17.11; 26.10; 110.3; 129.6.

141. See fr. 115.2.

142. See frs 17.29, 110.8; 30.2; 115.7.

143. See frs 12.3; 17.13, 35; 26.92; 35.12; 108.1.

144. See frs 21.12; 23.8.

145. See fr. 115.5.

146. Cf. frs 12, 13, 17.

147. ἔ<στ>ι γὰρ καὶ πάρος ἦν τε καὶ ἔσσεται, οὐδέ ποτ', οἴω; on the text of fr. 6, I have followed Wright's correction, suggested, and explained in p. 174 of her edition.

148. Cf. frs 17.13, 26.12.

149. The connection of recurring χρόνος with fr. 26 can also be justified by the same usage of περιπλομένοιο with χρόνος in frs 17.29 and 110.8 in the genitive absolute: περιπλομένοιο χρόνοιο.

150. Cf. Wright (1981), pp. 187–192.

151. Cf. Wright, *ibid.*, p. 254.

152. Cf. Empedocles' frs 17, and 110.

153. Cf. especially fr. 105, and frs 106–110.

154. Cf. Wright's, *ibid.* commentary on the fragment pp. 270–275.

155. Fr. 115.5: δαίμονες οἵτε μακραίωνος λελάχασι βίοιο the μακραίωνες δαίμονες here are probably to be identified with the δολιχαίωνες θεοί in fragments 21.12 and 23.3.

156. Cf. Wright, *ibid.*, p. 273.

157. On this distinction between ζωή and βίος cf. LSJ, p. 316; LSJ use the Plotinian passage as an original example of the distinction.

158. *Ennead* III.7.13.43: τῆς ψυχῆς κίνησιν τὴν ἐν αὐτῇ ἐν διεξόδῳ; cf. also *Enneads* IV.3.12.28, and IV.4.1.

159. See Strange, *ibid.*, p. 49.

160. Cf. *Ennead* II.2 *passim.*

161. Cf. *Enneads* VI.1.14.19–24: τὸ ἐν χρόνῳ ἄλλο … ἄλλο παρὰ χρόνον; for the distinction between ἐν χρόνῳ and χρόνον cf. also *Enneads* III.2.15.19, IV.3.13.13, IV.4.15.12–13, VI.4.14.17, VI.5.11.14, VI.9.3.43.

162. See *Enneads* IV.7.13.3–5; IV.8.3.23 ff.; V.1.1.1–22; VI.8.2.30–33; cf. Strange (1994), p. 48; McGuire and Strange (1998), n. 101; Jonas (1962), pp. 314–320.

163. Cf. Jonas (1962), p. 309, n. 16; Manchester (1978), pp. 121–123.

164. Cf. McGuire and Strange (1988), n. 98.

165. Cf. Strange (1994), p. 47.

166. Cf. Wallis (1995), pp. 30–32, and 102–103.

167. On the *Timaeus* as mythical science cf. Wright (2000), pp. 1–22.

168. Pherecydes' Χρόνος should not be regarded as an abstract entity but more as a radical mythical personification of divine Time with, for the first time, a first philosophical coloration. In Pherecydes there is an etymological connection between Κρόνος and Χρόνος, since Χρόνος probably derives from χραίνω and Κρόνος from κραίνω which originally express what someone experiences by a gentle touch. Shibli (1990), pp. 27–28 effectively maintains that this allegorical play between Χρόνος and Κρόνος may well have originated with Pherecydes, introducing Χρόνος in a more philosophical and abstract sense, as a self-creative cosmic principle beyond temporal becoming. In support of Shibli's interpretation, there is Hermias' testimony that Pherecydes named Χρόνος for Κρόνος (A9: Κρόνον δὲ τὸν χρόνον cf. also fr. 4). According to Plutarch, the allegorical connection between Κρόνος and Χρόνος was common among the Greeks (*De Iside et Osiride* 363d: Ἕλληνες Κρόνον ἀλληγοροῦσι τὸν χρόνον). It is this allegorical connection between Κρόνος and Χρόνος that leads Plato in the *Cratylus* (401e) to connect Κρόνος with his wife Ῥέα, and to support the well-known Heraclitean image of "time in flux" (402a ff.).

169. Diogenes Laertius preserves Pherecydes' words as follows, fr. 1: Ζὰς μὲν καὶ Χρόνος ἦσαν ἀεὶ καὶ Χθονίη· Χθονίηι δὲ ὄνομα ἐγένετο Γῆ, ἐπειδὴ αὐτῆι Ζὰς γῆν γέρας διδοῖ.

170. On Pherecydes' Χρόνος cf. Shibli, *ibid.*, ch. 2, part B. Shibli shows that Pherecydes' Χρόνος as a divine deity is not far removed from the traditional images of χρόνος as the "all-seeing," "all-revealing," "all-creative," and "all-destructive" deity found in Greek poetry and tragedy. For instance, Semonides

names Χρόνος as πανδαμάτωρ (531.5); Sophocles as εὐμαρὴς θεός (*Electra*, 179), as μακρὸς κἀναρίθμητος (*Ajax*, 646); as ὁ μέγας who both blights all things (*Ajax*, 713), and is the preserver of all (*Ajax* 933: ἄρχων χρόνος). This universal nature of time echoed the description of χρόνος attributed to Thales as "the wisest" (DK 11A1: σοφώτατος χρόνος), and Xenophanes' epistemological account in fr. 18 on human understanding according to the process of time: searching in time brings to humans greater understanding and reveals discoveries which had not been intimated by the gods at the beginning (χρόνῳ ζητοῦντες ἐφευρίσκουσιν ἄμεινον); cf. Lesher (1992), pp. 149–155.

171. The idea of everlastingness in Pherecydes, with a slight textual difference, is also preserved by the Neoplatonic philosopher Damascius. See DK 7A8: Φερεκύδης δὲ ὁ Σύριος Ζάντα μὲν εἶναι ἀεὶ καὶ Χρόνον καὶ Χθονίαν τὰς τρεῖς πρώταςἀρχάς. For both Damascius and Diogenes Laertius, χρόνος appears to have an everlasting nature existing before any cosmogonical event. In all probability, the passage in Diogenes passage is a more accurate source for the cosmogonical context of Pherecydes, while Damascius gives a Neoplatonic reading in his own words.

172. See DK 7A8: τὸν δὲ Χρόνον ποιῆσαι ἐκ τοῦ γόνου ἑαυτοῦ πῦρ καὶ πνεῦμα καὶ ὕδωρ. These three elements are distributed in different mixtures into five nooks and from these arise a second generation of numerous gods (A8: ἐξ ὧν ἐν πέντε μυχοῖς διῃρημένων πολλὴν ἄλλην γενεὰν συστῆναι θεῶν). Furthermore, Χρόνος as a self-creative nature can be found in Crtitias' fr. 18: ἀκάμας χρόνος περί τ' ἀενάῳ ῥεύματι πλήρης φοιτᾷ τίκτων αὐτὸς ἑαυτόν, and generally as a creative principle in Pindar, *Ol.* 2.17: Χρόνος ὁ πάντων πατὴρ, as well as in Euripides' *Heraclidae* 900 where χρόνος, along with αἰών, is personified as Destiny's parents: Μοῖρα τελεσσιδώτειρ' Αἰών τε Χρόνου παῖς. This verse can be traced back to Heraclitus' enigmatic fragment 52, where αἰών is personified as a child that plays; cf. my discussion above, ch. 4.51.

173. Cf. Shibli (1990), p. 29.

174. Cf. Kahn (1964), pp. 231–239; for the nature of ἄπειρον cf. below, ch. 5.2.1.

175. *Refutatio* I.6.1–2 = DK 12A11.

176. It is unlikely that plural or innumerable worlds (κόσμοι) can be attributed to Anaximander. The idea of innumerable worlds starts with the Atomists when there is unlimited time and material. For Anaximander, according to Hippolytus, κόσμοι might be "arrangements," or perhaps temporally successive worlds from and into the ἄπειρον.

177. See DK 12A10: ἀπεφήνατο δὲ τὴν φθορὰν γίνεσθαι καὶ πολὺ πρότερον τὴν γένεσιν ἐξ ἀπείρου αἰῶνος ἀνακυκλουμένων πάντων αὐτῶν.

178. On ἀίδιος κίνησις in Anaximander cf. Kahn, *ibid.*, pp. 39–42; cf. also KRS, pp. 126–128; cf. also Aristotle in *Physics* 250b11, and *De Caelo* 295a7.

179. See DK 13A5: κίνησιν δὲ καὶ οὗτος ἀίδιον ποιεῖ.

180. See DK 13A7: κινεῖσθαι ἀεί.

181. See DK 67A8: ἀεὶ κινούμενα ὑπέθετο στοιχεῖα τὰς ἀτόμους; cf. also 67A10; cf. also Kahn, *ibid.*, p. 40, and note 2 in p. 235.

182. See DK 13A6: κίνησιν ἐξ αἰῶνος ὑπάρχειν.

183. For this discussion cf. Kahn (1964), p. 235. While generation and destruction come and go in a recurring process, Anaximander's ἄπειρον cannot be clearly justified as a sphere. In mathematical terms, a "boundless," or "infinite" nature which lacks "limits" cannot have a particular "limited" shape to describe it, even metaphorically. But, a sphere does have uniformity of surface with no distinctive point/limit/radius.

184. For the "assessment of time" cf. KRS, pp. 120–121; these scholars offer an interesting comparison between Anaximander's χρόνος and the trial conducted by χρόνος in Solon fr. 24.

185. Cf. Wright (1985), pp. xi–xiii.

186. On the relationship between Anaximander's χρόνος and Pherecydes' χρόνος cf. Shibli (1990), pp. 29–32.

187. It is likely that Anaximander's radical conception of the everlasting ἄπειρον differentiated from χρόνος (= DK 12A15), which influenced the idea of Time, deriving from the ἄπειρον, which is found in the Pythagoreans (fr.30: οὐρανὸν εἶναι ἕνα, ἐπεισάγεσθαι δὲ ἐκ τοῦ ἀπείρου χρόνον τε καὶ πνοὴν καὶ τὸ κενόν) as well as the concept of ἄπειρος χρόνος found later in Zeno (29A25), Anaxagoras (59A45) and Democritus (68A39).

188. For Heraclitus flux of becoming cf. the article of Wiggins (1982); cf. also Osborne (1997), pp. 99–102.

189. For an introduction of *Ennead* II.1 cf. Armstrong's introduction pp. 6–7, as well as Kalligas (1997), pp. 185–190.

190. See Roussos (1968), p. 8 and pp. 10–11.

191. II.11.24–25: ῥεούσης ἀεὶ τῆς φύσεως τοῦ ὑποκειμένου; 2.5–6: τῆς φύσεως τοῦ σώματος ῥεούσης ἀεί; 3.1–3: Πῶς οὖν ἡ ὕλη καὶ τὸ σῶμα τοῦ παντὸς . . . ἀεὶ ῥέον; . . . ῥεῖ ἐν αὑτῷ· ῥεῖ γὰρ οὐκ ἔξω; 4.29: Καὶ εἰ μεταβάλλει ἀεί, τὸ πᾶν μένει; 8.23: ἀεὶ ῥέοντα.

192. Cf. for instance I.8.4.5; IV.3.26; IV.5.7.4; IV.7.3.19, 8.45; V.1.9.5; V.6.6.16; VI.3.2.3; VI.4.10.25; for the term ῥεῖν in the *Enneads* cf. Sleeman (1980), pp. 930–931.

193. Cf. Roussos, *ibid.*, p. 10.

194. Cf. Aristotle *Metaphysics* 987a, and 1078b. In *Physics* 253b, he speaks again about the everlasting mobility of all things having in mind primarily Heraclitus.

195. Cf. Kalligas (1997), p. 193.

196. See Armstrong vol. II, p. 6.

197. See *Ennead* II.2.5; cf. also IV.3.12.13–17.

198. Cf. Kirk (1954), pp. 264–279.

199. *apud* Diogenes Laertius VIII: γίνεσθαί τε πάντα κατ' ἐναντιότητα καὶ ῥεῖν τὰ ὅλα ποταμοῦ δίκην; cf. Marcovich (1967), pp. 316–317 and 329–335; cf. KRS, p. 201.

200. Cf. Roussos (1968), pp. 14–17; Armstrong, *ibid.*, Kalligas (1997), p. 193.

201. Cf. Roussos, *ibid.*, pp. 14–15, and Armstrong, *ibid.*

202. Cf. Roussos (1968), pp. 16–17.

203. See Heraclitus' position in frs 6, 12; 36, 76, 77.

204. It is also significant that for the Greeks the clepsydra measures time with the flow of water. For Heraclitus, the river-image represents the original meaning of everlasting change, observed as a natural phenomenon. Even if the waters are ever-flowing, the river as a whole remains the same, so that an analogy is drawn between the flux of the river and the flux of time. As Sorabji (1983) puts it p. 42, n. 40, Heraclitus admittedly "is not talking of time, so much as things in time, when he says that nothing stays put and that you cannot step into the same river twice."

205. οἱ μὲν γὰρ τὴν τοῦ ὅλου κίνησιν εἶναί φασιν, οἱ δὲ τὴν σφαῖραν αὐτήν; cf. also DK 58B33; 31B29; 44A12.

206. οἱ δὲ τὴν σφαῖραν αὐτὴν τοῦ οὐρανοῦ, ὡς τοὺς Πυθαγορείους ἱστοροῦσι λέγειν.

207. Stobaeus *in Anthologium* I.8.40b.2 attributes to Pythagoras the definition of Time as ἡ σφαῖρα τοῦ περιέχοντος as does pseudo-Plutarch in *Placita* 884b Πυθαγόρας τὸν χρόνον τὴν σφαῖραν τοῦ περιέχοντος εἶναι.

208. Cf. Armstrong, vol. III, p. 298, n. 2; Armstrong recognizes only passage III.7.2.1–4.

209. Cf. McGuire and Strange (1988), n. 17.

210. On the Neoplatonic accounts of Orphic Cosmogonies cf. KRS, pp. 22–26. cf. Laks and Most (1997), pp. 159–165, *Chronos* in Column XII.

211. Cf. fr. 12: ἀντὶ μὲν τῆς μιᾶς τῶν ὅλων ἀρχῆς τὸν Χρόνον τιθέντες and fr. 13: Χρόνος ἀγήραος.

212. This cosmogonical figure of Orphic Χρόνος is probably influenced by the Iranian god Zuran Akarana: "the unending time." For the possible Oriental influences in the Orphic accounts cf. KRS, p. 22, n. 1.

213. Cf. Burkert (1972), pp. 75–77; for the association of the Pythagoreans with the Orphic cult cf. Clement *Stromateis* I.131, and Herodotus II.81; cf. also KRS, pp. 220–222.

214. Cf. Burkert, *ibid.*

215. *Republic* 616b ff.

216. fr. 34 = B.III fr. 51: ἀριθμός = χρόνος.

217. Cf. Aristotle, *Metaphysics* 985b30.

218. fr. 37 DK: ἄστρον δὲ τὴν γῆν ἔλεγον ὡς ὄργανον καὶ αὐτὴν χρόνου.

219. Cf. Wright (1995), pp. 142–144.

220. Cf. Wright, *ibid.*

221. But, it has to be noted, that the circularity of the natural phenomena was a traditional Greek view since it related to spherical celestial bodies. For the early Greeks the surface of the earth was conceived as round like the circle of horizon and covered by the dome of Ouranos. In Homer, the correlative and generative source of everything is the life-fluid of the cosmic river Okeanos which encircles the surface of the Earth (*Iliad* XIV, 244; cf. 201, 302); in the *Iliad* (XVII, 607f), Homer describes the well-made shield of Achilles as round, putting Okeanos along its outer rim. Hesiod similarly describes the round "Shield of Hercules" (*Theogony*, 141).

222. For the Stoic view of the "continuous time" cf. Turetzky (1998), pp. 38–42.

223. See Wright (1995), p. 144; cf. also Sambursky (1959), pp. 200–201.

224. *On Human Nature* 38, *SVF* 2.625.

225. Cf. Simplicius' comment on Aristotle's *Physics* 250b23.

226. It is this Stoic theory of eternal recurrence which strongly influences Nietzsche's philosophical theory of "eternal return," cf. Turetzky (1998), pp. 109–116; for the whole concept of eternal return and its significance in the history of ideas cf. Eliade (1949) *passim.*

227. See DK 18A1.

228. Cf. Burkert (1962), p. 35, n. 35.

229. For *Ennead* II.2 cf. Kalligas (1997), pp. 208–219.

230. On the circular motion of the heaven Plotinus follows Plato's *Timaeus* where the circular motion of the heaven is the bodily manifestation of the Soul (34a–b; 36e–37a); cf. Kalligas, *ibid.,* p. 208–209. As Armstrong, *ibid.*, observes, by following the Platonic theory, Plotinus denies both the Aristotelian conception of movement by the unmoved mover (*De Caelo* 285a and *De Anima* 407b), and the materialistic exegesis of the Stoics. Plato in the *Laws* 897c maintains that the circular movement of the heaven is the best and most reasonable movement corresponding to a better soul; cf. also Cornford (1937), p. 56.

231. ὡς αἱ τρεῖς μόναι γραμμαὶ ὁμοιομερεῖς εἰσιν, ἡ εὐθεῖα, ἡ κυκλικὴ καὶ ἡ κυλινδρικὴ ἕλιξ.

232. ἡ μὲν εὐθεῖα λέγεται, ἡ δὲ περιφερής, ἡ δὲ μικτή, ὡς ἡ ἕλιξ; cf. also 127.22 where Damascius testifies to an Egyptian derivation.

233. ἡ ἕλιξ ἑνοειδῶς περιέχει τὸ εὐθὺ καὶ περιφερές; cf. also Alexander Aphrodiseas *in Aristotelis Topicorum* 328.2.

234. Cf. Kalfas (2000), pp. 392–393; cf. also Mourelatos (1980), *passim.*

235. See DK12A10.

236. Cf. KRS, pp. 126–128.

237. See frs 17, 22, 24, 26, 27, 31; Cf. Wright (1981), pp. 206–207; cf. also KRS, pp. 296–299. Empedocles speaks again of δίνη in fr. 115 with reference to the eddies of the air (l. 11: αἰθέρος ἔμβαλε δίναις).

238. Cf. Aristotle's criticism of Empedocles' vortex in *De Caelo* 295a29; Simplicius *in Caelo*, 528, and the different interpretations of Guthrie (1960), v. 2, p. 179.

239. DK 59A1: ὅλος ὁ οὐρανὸς ἐκ λίθων συγκέοιτο· τῇ σφοδρᾷ δὲ περιδινήσει συνεστάναι καὶ ἀνεθέντα κατενεχθήσεσθαι.

240. Cf. KRS, pp. 419–420.

241. Cf. Simplicius *in Physica* 327.24; on this theory cf. below, ch. 5.2.4.

CHAPTER 5. MATTER AND SOUL

1. Cf. Plotinus *Enneads* II.4 *On Matter* and III.6 *On Impassibility*. Additionally, there are observations on the nature of ὕλη in *Ennead* II.5 *On What Exists Potentially and What Actually*.

2. For Plotinus' theory of ὕλη cf. Wallis (1995), pp. 48–51; Gerson (1994), pp. 108–115; O'Brien (1996) *passim.* Plotinus' conception of ὕλη has attracted the interest of many modern scholars and especially in comparison not only with ancient thinkers such as Plato, Aristotle, Alexander of Aphrodisias, St. Augustine, and St. Gregory of Nyssa cf. Jevons (1964), Hetzler (1982), Raiger (1990), and Corrigan (1996), but also with later philosophers such as Berkeley and Bergson cf. May (1970), Corrigan (1994), as well as Arabic and Indian thought cf. Evangeliou (2002) *passim.*

3. See *Enneads* II.5.4–5; III.6.7; V.9.16.27; cf. also Wallis (1995), p. 49.

4. Cf. Gerson (1994), pp. 108–110.

5. For matter and evil cf. O'Brien (1996) pp. 171–172; cf. also Rist (1961), *passim.*

6. See Wallis, *ibid.*

7. Cf. Kalligas (1997), p. 397.

8. See *Enneads* II.4.1.14, 9.4; II.7.2.30; III.6.6.3, 7.4.

9. See *Enneads* III.6.6.6, 7.3, 7.41, 9.42, 11.45, 13.16–30.

10. See *Enneads* I.8.9.10; II.4.2.2–4, 10.4.

11. See *Enneads* I.6.3.11; I.8.8.22; II.4.2.3–4, 3.2, 4.17, 10.23; V.9.3.20.

12. See *Enneads* II.4.12.23; III.6.7.14.

13. See *Ennead* II.5.5.34.

14. See *Enneads* I.8.3.13–31; II.4.7.13–19; II.4.15–16; VI.6.3.32.

15. See *Enneads* I.8.10.1, 2.10–11; II.4.7.11, 8.1–2, 10.2, 13.7, 14.29; IV7.3.8; VI.1.26.10; VI.9.7.12.

16. Cf. Gerson (1984), p. 110.
17. Cf. Armstrong vol. II, p. 163.
18. For the phrase, cf. Plato, *Republic* 382a4.
19. For his phrase, cf. Plato, *Sophist* 254d1.
20. Cf. Gerson, *ibid.*, p. 112.
21. Cf. *Ennead* IV.2.1.31–41; Paul Kalligas (1997), p. 398.
22. Cf. O'Brien (1996), pp. 187–189.
23. Cf. Kalligas (1997), p. 400.
24. For body and soul in Plotinus cf. Clark (1996) and Kalligas (2000).
25. Cf. Kalligas, *ibid.*, p. 166.
26. Cf. Roussos (1974), p. 463.
27. Cf. Kalligas (1997), pp. 266–267.
28. See *Physics* 187a; *Metaphysics* 988a and 1069b.
29. Cf. Armstrong vol, II, p. 118, n. 1; cf. also Kalligas (1997), follows the same view that Plotinus' criticism of the Presocratic in *Ennead* II.4.7 has Aristotelian origins, pp. 266–267. The same interpretative line is followed by Henry and Schwyzer in the *Index Fontium* only in the case of Empedocles.
30. Cf. Kalligas, *ibid.*, p. 267.
31. Cf. Aristotle, *Metaphysics* 1069b20–23.
32. In II.4.7.13–20 ἄπειρον signifies the indefiniteness of Matter and not unlimitedness as in Anaximander. For this reason, ἄπειρον is going to be translated as the "indefinite."
33. For Anaximander's ἄπειρον cf. Kahn (1964), pp. 231–239; Barnes (1982), pp. 28–37; Hussey (1972), p. 17 ff.; KRS, pp. 105–117; Schofield (1997), pp. 60–64.
34. See Kahn, *ibid.*, p. 233.
35. See Schofield, *ibid.*, p. 60.
36. The last three sources appear to come directly from the summary of Anaximander from Theophrastus' lost work Φυσικῶν Δοξαί. For the introduction on the doxographical material of Anaximander cf. Kahn, *ibid.*, pp. 11–24; for Kahn, Simplicius seems to be a more accurate source for Theophrastus' account on Anaximander.
37. See Armstrong vol. II, p. 120, n. 2.
38. Cf. Kalligas, *ibid.*, p. 267.
39. The term ἀδιεξίτητον in connection with ἄπειρον has Aristotelian origins cf. *Physics* 204a14 and 207b27–29; cf. also Galen, *Quod Qualitates Incorporeae Sint* 473.5, and Alexander of Aphrodisias *in Metaphysics* 396.18. Simplicius *in De Caelo* 204.12 and 205.23, *in Physica* 76.22, 174.14, 470–471, 474.16, 513.24, 847.20, 946.6, 947.16, 1178.18, 1314; Philoponus *in Analytica Posteriora* 45.21, 225.8, 249.19, 256.12 and so forth.
40. Cf. also *Enneads* V.7.1; VI.6.21.10.
41. Cf. also *Enneads* III.6.7.7–9; VI.5.12.8; VI.6.1–3.

42. Cf. also *Enneads* I.8.3; III.6.7; VI.6.3.30 ff.

43. Cf. Empedocles' frs 6, 26, 35, 37. On the nature of the four Empedoclean roots cf. Wright (1981), pp. 22–30 and (1997b), pp. 178–184; Barnes (1982), pp. 308–315; Inwood (2001), pp. 76, 77, 84, 88–96; for some general observations on the four-elements theory and the cosmic cycle in Empedocles cf. Hussey (1972), pp. 130–132; Ring (1987), pp. 138–139; KRS, pp. 284–294; McKirahan (1994), pp. 259–266; Kahn (1974), pp. 432–433 and 440–443; Burnet (1930), p. 229 ff.; Vamvakas (2001), pp. 356–358; Kingsley (1994), *passim*.

44. In fr. 6 Zeus corresponds to fire, Hera to air, Nestis to water and Aidoneus to earth. For the terms used by Empedocles on the four roots cf. Wright (1981), p. 23.

45. Cf. Wright (1997b), p. 179; Hussey (1972), p. 130.

46. For Parmenides and Empedocles cf. Wright (1997b), pp. 179–180.

47. For Empedocles' cosmic cycle and the elements cf. Barnes (1982), pp. 308–310.

48. See DK 31A88.

49. Cf. Inwood (2001), p. 203.

50. Cf. also *Metaphysics* 988a and *On Generation and Corruption* 328b33–329b5. On these passages cf. Henry and Schwyzer *Index Fontium* p. 341; Armstrong vol. II, p. 120, note 1; Kalligas (1996), p. 266. Moreover, the identification of Matter with the four elements in Empedocles is also testified at Aëtius I.7.28 (= DK 31A32) and I.52 (= DK 31A47), as well as Theophrastus *De Causis Plantarum* I.12.5 (*apud* Aëtius V.26.4 = DK 31A70).

51. Cf. O' Brien (1996), pp. 175–177.

52. ὕλην Steinhart, Henry and Schwyzer: ὕδωρ codd.

53. Cf. Kalligas (1997), p. 266.

54. This can be also justified by the synonymic trace of μῖγμα in the σύμμιξις of fragment 4.

55. See Armstrong, *ibid.*, p. 120, n. 1.

56. Cf. Roussos (1974), p. 163.

57. Henry and Schwyzer in the *Index Fontium* erroneously quote Anaxagoras' reference as line 4 instead of line 2.

58. See Armstrong, *ibid.*

59. Cf. Wright (1985), pp. xxix–xxx.

60. For an introduction to Anaxagoras' theory of matter cf. Taylor (1997), pp. 209–216.

61. Teodorsson (1982), collects the most important modern interpretation of Anaxagoras' theory of matter including: (1) the studies of Tannery (1887); Burnet (1930); Capelle (1919); Cornford (1975), and Peck (1926), and (1931), for the nature of ὁμοιομερῆ and the opposites; (2) the studies of Bailey (1928); Zafiropulo (1948); Cleve (1965); Vlastos (1974); Strang (1975); Stokes

(1965); Schwabe (1975), and Schofield (1980), for the nature of σπέρματα (pp. 45–63). For Anaxagoras and the concept of matter before Aristotle cf. the relevant article of Kerferd (1974).

62. Cf. Kerferd (1974), pp. 490–491.

63. Cf. Bailey (1928), p. 546; Zafiropulo (1948) pp. 278–279, and Cleve (1965), pp. 173–174.

64. Cf. Strang (1963), pp. 104–105; cf. also the reply of Stokes (1965), pp. 9–10.

65. See Taylor (1997), p. 210.

66. Cf. Vlastos (1975), pp. 461–467.

67. Cf. Schofield (1980), p. 124.

68. See *Metaphysics* 984a11, and *De Caelo* 302a28.

69. See DK 59A43; cf. also *Physics* 203a19 ff.; *On Generation and Corruption* 314a18; cf. also Barnes (1982), correctly doubts Aristotle's reading of Anaxagoras' principles as homegenous materials, p. 321. Cf. also the criticism of Cornford (1975), and the reply of Kerferd (1974), p. 499 ff.

70. Cf. Robinson (1968), p. 176; Kerferd (1974), pp. 494–496.

71. For Empedocles' elements and Anaxagoras' theory of Matter cf. Kerferd (1974), p. 494 ff.; Teodorsson (1982), pp. 43–44; Taylor (1997), pp. 210–211. Cf. also Zeller (1882), pp. 1210–1211; Gomperz (1922), p. 175; Burnet (1930), pp. 265–266; Cornford (1975), p. 314; Peck (1926), pp. 66–70, and Raven (1954), pp. 132–133 as quoted in Teodorsson (1982), p. 44, n. 108.

72. Cf. Teodorsson, *ibid.*

73. Cf. *Enneads* I.6.2.24; II.7.1.6; IV.2.3.14; IV.9.4.11; V.3.5.4; VI.7.13.10.

74. Cf. *Enneads* IV.9.5.11; II.3.16.53–54; IV.9.3.18.

75. See III.6.6.22–23: *καὶ* ὁμοῦ πάντα *καὶ* ἓν πάντα.

76. Cf. the discussion of Taylor (1997), p. 211.

77. Cf. Taylor, *ibid.*

78. Cf. *Enneads* II.6.1.1–11; III.3.3.34–38; III.7.4.8–11; V.3.6.12–15, 15.22; V.6.6.12; VI.3.8.29; VI.4.7.22–25.

79. Cf. Armstrong, vol. IV, pp. 336–337.

80. For ὁμοπάθεια cf. also *Enneads* I.2.3.13–16; IV.2.1.51; IV.5.1.12; IV.9.1–2; VI.4.1.22.

81. Cf. Armstrong, vol III, pp. 6–7.

82. Cf. the introductory notes of Bréhier and Harder on *Ennead* III.1.

83. Cf. Kalligas (1997), p. 307, and his introduction of *Ennead* II.7.

84. See Armstrong, vol. II, p. 194, n. 1.

85. Cf. DK 68A43.

86. Cf. also Leucippus' testimonia DK 67A1, A7, 24, and Democritus' testimonia DK 68A1, A37, A39, A46a, A47, A48b, A60, A66, A69, A82, A83, A112, A132, A135.

87. Cf. Armstrong, vol. III, p. 42 n. 1.

88. Cf. *Enneads* IV.3.13.8; IV.4.39.17.

89. For an introduction to the Atomic theory cf. Guthrie (1960), vol. I, pp. 389–399; Brumbaugh (1964), pp. 78–92; Hussey (1972), pp. 141–148; KRS (1983), pp. 402–433; Wright (1985), pp. xxxi–xxxii; Ring (1987), pp. 149–157; McKirahan (1994), ch. 16; Sandywell (1996), pp. 378–382; Taylor (1997), pp. 220–228, and (1999), pp. 160–184.

90. Barnes (1982), pp. 44–69 mentions that Democritus (and probable Leucippus) uses in frs 9 and 125 the plural ἄτομα and not the adjective ἄτομος as the doxography testifies in frs 141, 167, and A57.

91. For the reply of the Atomists to the Eleatics cf. the relevant article of Furley (1974); cf. also See KRS, p. 408; Sandywell, *ibid.*, p. 378.

92. Cf. Simplicius *in Physica* 28.15 = DK 68A38; Hippolytus, *Refutatio* I.13 = DK 68A40.

93. See *Index Fontium*, and Armstrong's notes on both passages.

94. This reference has been observed by the *Index Fontium* of Henry and Schwyzer, and Kalligas (1997), p. 382; Armstrong vol. II, p. 298, and Roussos (1967), p. 77.

95. Cf. Rist (1967), p. 112.

96. The same positive position appears in III.4.1, II.3.17, and I.8.7. On the other hand, in some later treatises such as II.4 and I.8, Plotinus follows a pessimistic view of matter described as the main source of evil. Plotinus' contradictory position about the material world echoes somehow Plato's contradictory viewpoints about the perceptible world. Cf. Armstrong vol. IV, pp. 394–395.

97. See Armstrong, vol. IV, p. 398, n. 1.

98. In this passage, I am following the reading of παρ' αὐτῶν maintained by Harder (1956), v. I, p. 444, and Roussos (1968), p. 17, n. 4 instead of παρ' αὐτῷ maintained by Henry and Schwyzer in the OCT.

99. See Heraclitus' frs 51, 67, 84, 88, 90, 102, 126; the similarity between the terms ἀμοιβάς in line 12, and ἀνταμοιβή of fr. 90 is noteworthy.

100. For these allusions cf. my discussion above, ch. 3.3.3.

101. Cf. Kirk (1954), pp. 250–254.

102. Cf. Marcovich (1967), pp. 300–306.

103. Cf. Roussos (1968), pp. 17–27.

104. Cf. Kahn (1979), pp. 169–170.

105. For this references of Heraclitus' frs 84a–b cf. Marcovich (1967), p. 302.

106. Iamblichus' *De Anima* (*apud.* Stobaeus *Anthologium* I.49.39.40–44): [Ἡράκλειτος] μὲν γὰρ ἀμοιβὰς ἀναγκαίας τίθεται ἐκ τῶν ἐναντίων, ὁδόν τε ἄνω καὶ κάτω διαπορεύεσθαι τὰς ψυχὰς ὑπείληφε καὶ τὸ μὲν τοῖςαὐτοῖς ἐπιμένειν κάμα τον εἶναι, τὸ δὲ μεταβάλλειν φέρειν ἀνάπαυσιν.

107. Cf. Kirk (1954), p. 250.
108. Cf. Roussos (1968), p. 19.
109. See Kirk, *ibid.*
110. Cf. Roussos, *ibid.*, p. 22.
111. Cf. Burkert (1975), pp. 137–139.
112. See Marcovich (1967), pp. 301–302.
113. Cf. also Harder (1956), pp. 440–443.
114. See Kahn (1979), p. 169.
115. Cf. Bywater (1877), p. 34.
116. Cf. Gilbert (1909), p. 168.
117. Cf. Gigon (1935), p. 94.
118. Cf. Guthrie (1960), p. 445
119. Cf. Kirk (1954), pp. 250–254.
120. Cf. Burnet (1930), p. 154.
121. Cf. Marcovich, *ibid.*
122. Cf. Roussos (1968), pp. 19–20.
123. Cf. Kahn (1979), p. 169.
124. Cf. Marcovich (1967), pp. 301–302.
125. See Roussos (1968), pp. 23–25.
126. See Heraclitus' frs 20, 30, 64, 90, 94.
127. Cf. Wright (1985), pp. 72–73.
128. Cf. Kahn (1979), p. 243.
129. Whereas in this the words ἐξεύροι, λόγος, βαθύς, reflect clearly Heraclitus' fr. 45, the passage has not been recognized by modern scholarship.
130. Marcovich (1967), p. 568–569 regards fr. 115 as spurious and suggests that "a measure which increases itself" is not in accordance with the thought of Heraclitus; and that the textual attestation is weak. On the other hand, Wright (1985), p. 72 replies that the increasing nature of the soul explains why *logos* is so deep and consequently how the "human intellect has an inexhaustible capacity to extend the range of its understanding." Along similar lines Kahn (1979), p. 237 accepts the authenticity of fr. 115 and further relates it to (1) the deep *logos* of soul in fr. 45, and the exhalation of heated vapor in fr. 12, and (2) the Homeric concept of the soul as the wrath "which increases like smoke within the breasts of men" (*Iliad* XVIII.10), and (3) the notion attested in Hippocratic writing that the soul feeds itself with the body.
131. Cf. Roussos (1968), p. 34–37; Roussos and the *Index Fontium* point out as an allusion to fr. 115 also III.6.1.31, but nothing in the Plotinian text justifies this reference.
132. Cf. Kirk (1949) *passim*, and Hussey (1991) *passim.*
133. Cf. Wright (1985), p. 65, and Kirk (1951) *passim.*
134. For both interpretations cf. Kahn (1979), pp. 240–241.
135. For Heraclitus' fr. 60 in Plotinus cf. Roussos (1968), pp. 37–31.

136. Cf. *Enneads* V.3.3.37; VI.1.14.1; V.2.22.80; III.2.16.13; II.9.10.19.

137. For Heraclitus' fr. 96 in Plotinus cf. Roussos, *ibid.*, pp. 69–71.

138. See Roussos (1968), p. 65 on Plotinus' use of Heraclitus' fragment to support his own aesthetic and psychological positions.

139. For this reference cf. Roussos, *ibid.*, pp. 72–73.

140. Cf. Roussos, *ibid.*, pp. 66–69. Armstrong erroneously notes that this reference goes to Plato's *Phaedo* 69c1–6, vol. I, p. 249, n. 1. Armstrong's position is followed by Kalligas (1994), pp. 271–272.

141. For fr. 11 in the *Enneads* cf. Roussos pp. 71–72; cf. also Kalligas (1997), p. 244.

142. Cf. Roussos, *ibid.*, pp. 73–76.

143. Cf. Burkert (1972), p. 111, n. 7, and p. 133 ff.

144. Plotinus criticism in IV.7.8^4.3–28 follows Plato's *Phaedo* 85e ff.

145. Fragment 115 is for the most part a combination of Plutarch's *De Exilio* 607c and Hippolytus' *Refutatio* VII.29. For Empedocles as δαίμων cf. Wright (1981), pp. 69–76; cf. also Inwood (2001), pp. 86–90.

146. For the sources of fr. 115 cf. Wright (1981), p. 136, and pp. 270–272.

147. Cf. Long (1948), p. 105–110; Zuntz (1971), ch. 2; Inwood (2000), p. 277.

148. Cf. Wright (1981), p. 69 ff.

149. Cf. Burkert (1972), pp. 247–248.

150. Cf. Huffman (1993), pp. 402–410, and Burkert, *ibid.*

151. Cf. Rist (1967), p. 126, and Leroux (1996), p. 296.

152. Cf. Dillon (1996), pp. 316–317.

153. For divine providence in Plotinus cf. *Enneads* III.2; III 3.6–7; VI.8.17.4–10.

154. Cf. Rappe (1996), p. 254.

155. See Armstrong, vol V, p. 10, n. 1.

156. On audacity cf. Armstrong vol. V, p. 10, n.1.

157. See Schibli (1990), p. 16, n. 5.

158. See Armstrong, *ibid.*

159. Other allusion of the Pythagorean audacity are in I.8.9.18–19, and III.8.8.32–6.

160. On this discussion cf. also *Enneads* I.2.13; IV.4.20.12; VI.9.9.24.

161. Cf. *Enneads* IV.4.2.23–32; IV.7.10.28–37, V.1.5.1–4, VI.5.12.16–25, VI.7.35.4; cf. also Bussanich (1996), p. 56.

Bibliography

A. PRIMARY SOURCES

(i) Plotinus

Armstrong = Armstrong, A. H. (1966–1988), *Plotinus*, Greek text with English translation in 7 vols., Cambridge/Mass.: Heinemann.

Atkinson, M. (1983), *Plotinus: Ennead V.1 On the Three Principal Hypostases*, Oxford: Oxford University Press.

Beirewaltes, W. (1995), *Eternità e tempo. Plotino*, Enneade *III, 7*, Milano: Pubblicazioni des Centro di ricerche di metafisica, temi metafisici e problemi del pensiero antico.

Bréhier, É. (1997–1999), *Plotin, Texte établi et traduit*, in 7 vol., Paris: Les Belles Lettres.

Harder, R. (1956–60), *Plotins Schriften*, in 5 vol. continued by R. Beutler and W. Theiler, Hamburg: Felix Meiner.

HS1 = Henry, P., and H. R. Schwyzer (1951, 1959, 1973), *Plotini Opera* 3 vols. (*editio maior*) (v.1, Bruxelles: Edition Universelle, *Enneads* I–III); (v.2, Bruxelles: Editions Universelle and Paris: Declee de Brouwer, *Enneads* IV–V; (v.3, Paris: Desclee de Brouwer and Leiden: E. J. Brill, *Ennead* VI).

HS2 = Henry, P., and H. R. Schwyzer (1964, 1976, 1982), *Plotini Opera* 3 vols. (*editio minor*) Oxford: Clarendon Press (v.1, *Enneads* I–III); (v.2, *Enneads* IV–V); (V.3, *Ennead* VI).

Kalligas, P. (1991), *Porphyry's Life of Plotinus* [in modern Greek], Athens, Centre of Edition of Ancient Greek Authors, Athens Academy.

———, (1994), *Plotinus' Ennead I: Ancient Greek text, translation and commentary* [in modern Greek], Athens, Centre of Edition of Ancient Greek Authors, Athens Academy.

———, (1997), *Plotinus' Ennead II: Ancient Greek text, translation and commentary* [in modern Greek], Athens, Centre of Edition of Ancient Greek Authors, Athens Academy.

———, (2004), *Plotinus' Ennead III: Ancient Greek text, translation and commentary* [in modern Greek], Athens, Centre of Edition of Ancient Greek Authors, Athens Academy.

MacKenna, S. (1969), *The Enneads*, 4th edn, rev. by B. S. Page, London: Faber and Faber.

McGuire, J. E., and Strange, J. E. (1988), 'An annotated translation of Plotinus *Ennead* III.7: *On eternity and time*', *Ancient Philosophy* 8: 251–271.

Life = *Porphyrii Vita Plotini* text with English translation in Armstrong vol. 1.

Sleeman, J. H. (1980), *Lexicon Plotiniaum*, Leiden: E. J. Brill.

(ii) Presocratics

Barnes, J. (1979), *The Presocratic Philosophers*, in 2 vols., London: Routledge and Kegan Paul.

———, (1987), *Early Greek Philosophy*, Harmondsworth: Penguin.

Beaufret, J. (1984), *Parménide: Le Poème*, La Clayetter: Michel Chandeigne.

Bollack, J. (1969), *Empédocle*, Paris: Les éditions de minuit.

Burnet, J. (1930), *Early Greek Philosophy*, London: Adam and Charles Black.

Bywater, J. (1877) *Heracliti Ephesi Reliquiae*, Oxford.

Conche, M. (1996), *Parménide: Le Poème Fragments*, Paris: Presses Universitaires de France.

Copenhaver, B. (1992), *Hermetica*, Cambridge: Cambridge University Press.

Coxon, A. H. (1986), *The Fragments of Parmenides*, Assen: Van Gorcum.

DK = Diels, H. (1951–2), *Die Fragmente der Vorsokratiker*, 6th edn. Revised with additions and index by W. Kranz, Berlin: Weidmann.

Gallop, D. (1984), *Parmenides of Elea: Text and Translation with Introduction*, University of Toronto Press.

Gigon, O. (1935), Untersuchungen zu Heraklit, Basel dissertation, Leipzig.

Gilbert, O. (1909), 'Heraklits Schrift περὶ φύσιος' *Neue Jahrbücher für klassische Alterum*, 23: 161–179.

Heitsch, E. (1991), *Parmenides: Die Fragmente*, München and Zürich: Artemis Verlag.

Huffman, C. A. (1993), *Philolaus of Croton: Pythagorean and Presocratic*, Cambridge: Cambridge University Press.

Inwood, B. (1992), *The Poem of Empedocles: A Text with an Introduction*, University of Toronto Press.

Kahn, C. H. (1979), *The Art and Thought of Heraclitus*, Cambridge: Cambridge University Press.

Karsten, S. (1835), *Parmenidis eleatae carminis reliquiae*, Amsterdam: Amstelodami.

Lassale, F. (1858), *Dle Philosophie Herakleitos'des Dunklen von Ephesos*, Berlin.

Leroux, G. (1996), 'Human freedom in the thought of Plotinus' in Gerson, pp. 292–314.

Lesher, J. (1992), *Xenophanes of Colophon, Fragments: a Text and Translation with a Commentary*, Toronto/Buffalo/London: University of Toronto Press.

Marcovich, M. (1967), *Heraclitus: Greek Text with a short Commentary*, Los Andes University Press.

Martin, A., and Primavesi (1998), *L' Empédocle de Strasbourg*, Berlin/NY: Walter de Gruyter.

McKirahan, R. D. Jr. (1994), *Philosophy Before Socrates*, Indianapolis/Cambridge: Hackett.

O'Brien D., and Frère J. (1987), *Le Poème de Parménide*, Paris/Brussels: Vrin et Ousia.

Reale-Ruggiu, G. (1991), *Parmenide: Poema Sulla Natura*, Milan: Rusconi.

Robinson, T. M. (1987), *Heraclitus, Fragments: A text and Translation with a Commentary*, University of Toronto Press.

Roussos, E. N. (2000a), *ΗΡΑΚΛΕΙΤΟΣ*, vol. 2, Athens: Stigmi.

———, (2000b), *ΠΑΡΜΕΝΙΔΗΣ*, vol. 2, Athens: Stigmi.

Schibli, H. S. (1990), *Pherecydes of Syros*, Oxford: Clarendon Press.

Sider, D. (1981), *The Fragments of Anaxagoras*, Meisenheim, Hain Verlag, (Beiträge zur klassischen Philologie 118).

Tarán, L. (1965), *Parmenides: A Text with Translation, Commentary and Critical Essays*, Princeton: Princeton University Press.

Taylor C. C. W. (1999), *The Atomists: Leucippus and Democritus, A Text and Translation with a commentary*, University of Toronto Press.

Untersteiner, M. (1958), *Parmenide: Testimonianze e frammenti*, Firenze: La 'Nuova Italia'.

Wright, M. R. (1981), *Empedocles: The Extant Fragments*, New Haven: Yale University Press.

———, (1985), *The Presocratics*, Bristol: Bristol Classical Press.

Zafiropulo, J. (1948), *Anaxagore de Clazomène*, Paris: Les Belles Lettres.

(iii) Plato and Aristotle

Barnes, J. (1983), *The Complete Works of Aristotle*, Princeton: Princeton University Press.

Burnet, J. (1900–1907), *Plato: Opera*, in 5 vols. Oxford: Clarendon Press.

Cooper, J. M. (1997), *Plato: Complete Works*, Indianapolis/Cambridge: Hackett.

Kalfas, V. (1995), *Plato's Timaeus*, [in modern Greek] Athens: Polis.

Lulofs, H. J. (1965), *Aristotle: Physics*, Oxford: Clarendon Press.

Ross, W. D. (1936), *Aristotle: Metaphysics*, 2 vols. Oxford: Clarendon Press.

———, (1953), *Aristotle: Metaphysics*, 2 vols. Oxford: Clarendon Press.

———, (1961), *Aristotle: De Anima*, Oxford: Clarendon Press.

Stocks, J. L. (1922), *Aristotle: De Caelo*, Oxford: Clarendon Press.

Taylor, A. E. (1928), *A Commentary of Plato's Timaeus*, Oxford: Clarendon Press.

Zeyl, D. J. (2000), *Plato's Timaeus*, Indianapolis/Cambridge: Hackett.

B. SECONDARY SOURCES

Adamson, P. (2002), *The Arabic Plotinus: A Philosophical Study of the 'Theology of Aristotle'*, London: Duckworth.

Allen, R. E., and Furley, David J., eds. (1975), *Studies in Presocratic Philosophy*, London: Routledge and Kegan Paul.

Annas, J. (1975), 'Aristotle, Number and Time', *Philosophical Quarterly* 25: 97–113.

Armstrong, A. H. (1955), 'Was Plotinus a magician?', *Phronesis* 1, 1: 73–79.

———, (1967a), *The Architecture of the Intelligible Universe in the Philosophy of Plotinus*, Amsterdam: Adolf Hakkert.

———, (1967b), 'Plotinus' in *The Cambridge history of later Greek and early medieval philosophy*, ed. by A. H. Armstrong, Cambridge: Cambridge University Press.

———, (1971), 'Eternity, life and movement in Plotinus' account of νοῦς', in *Le Néoplatonism*, pp. 67–76.

———, (1977), 'Negative Theology', *Downside Review* 95: 176–189.

SVF = Arnim, J. V. (1903), *Stoicorum Veterum Fragmenta*, Leipzig: Teubner.

Arnou, R. (1935), 'Platonisme des Pères', in *Dictionnaire de théologie catholique* XII.2, coll. 2258–92, Paris: Librairie Letouzey et Ané.

Aubenque, P. (1987), 'Syntaxe et sémantique de l'être dans le poème de Parménide', in *Études sur Parménide*, Paris/Brussels: Vrin et Ousia.

Austin, S. (1986), *Parmenides: Being, Bounds and Logic*, Yale University Press.

Bailey, C. (1928), *The Greek Atomists and Epicurus*, Oxford: Clarendon Press.

Bales, E. F. (1982), 'Plotinus' theory of the One', in Harris, pp. 40–50.

Barnes, J. (1979), 'Parmenides and the Eleatic One', *Archiv für Philosophie* 61:1–21.

———, (1982), *The Presocratic Philosophers*, London: Routledge and Kegan Paul.

Bauch, B. (1910), *Geschichtphilosophie: eine kriegsvorlesung*, Berlin: Reuther & Reichard.

Beierwaltes, W. (1991), *Pensare l'Uno: Studi sulla filosofia neoplatonica e sulla storiadei suoi influssi*, Milano: Vita e Pensiero.

Benveniste, E. (1932), 'Grec ψυχή', *Bulletin de la Société de Linguistique de Paris* 33: 165–8.

———, (1937), 'Expressions indoeuropéenes de l'éternité', *Bulletin de la Société de inguistique de Paris* 38: 102–112.

Berkeley, G. (1998) *A Treatise Concerning the Principles of Human Knowledge*, edited by Dancy J., Oxford: Oxford University Press.

Blum, P. R. (1989), 'Platonismus', *Historisches Wörterbuch der Philosophie* 7: 977–985.

Blumenthal, H. J. (1971), *Plotinus' Psychology*, The Hague: Martinus Nijhorf

———, (1996), 'On Soul and Intellect' in Gerson, pp. 82–104.

Bolotin, D. (1997), 'Aristotle's Discussion of Time', *Ancient Philosophy* 14: 47–62.

Bostock, D. (1980), 'Aristotle's Account of Time', *Phronesis* 25: 148–169.

Boussoulas, N. I. (1976), 'Le thème de la liberté-créativité dans la pensée préplatonicienne, platonicienne et néoplatonicienne', *Diotima* 4: 69–77.

Bremmer, J. (1983), The *Early Greek Concept of Soul*, Princeton: Princeton University Press.

Broadie S. (1999), 'Rational Theology' in Long, pp. 205–224.

Brumbauch, R. S. (1964), *The Philosophers of Greece*, New York: Crowell.

Burkert, W. (1972), *Lore and Science in Ancient Pythagorianism*, Cambridge: Cambridge University Press.

———, (1962), 'ΓΟΗΣ Zum griechischen "Schamanismus"', *Reinisches Museum* 105: 36–55.

Burkert, W. (1975), 'Plotin, Plutarch und die Platonisierende interpretation von Heraclit und Empedokles', in Mansfeld and Rijk, pp.137–146.

Burnet, J. (1892), *Early Greek Philosophy*, London: Adam and Charles Black.

Burnyeat, M. F. (1982), 'Idealism and Greek Philosophy: What Descartes saw and Berkeley missed', *The Philosophical Review* 91: 3–40.

Bussanich, J. R. (1987), 'Plotinus on the inner life of the One', *Ancient Philosophy* 7: 163–189.

———, (1988), *The One and its relation to Intellect in Plotinus*, Leiden: Brill.

———, (1996), 'Plotinus' metaphysics of the One' in Gerson, pp. 38–65.

Callahan, J. F. (1948), *Four Views of Time in Ancient Philosophy*, NY: Greenwood Press.

Calogero G. (1932), *Studi sull' eleatismo*, Roma: Tipografia del senato.

Capelle, W. (1919), 'Anaxagoras', *Neue Jahrbücher für das klassische Alterum* 43: 81–102.

Charrue, J–M. (1978), *Plotin, lecteur de Platon*, Paris: Les Belles Lettres.

Cherniss H. (1962), *Aristotle's Criticism of Plato and the Academy*, NY: Russell & Russell.

Cilento, V. (1964), 'Parmenide in Plotino', *Gior. critico della filosofia Iitaliana* 43, 2: 194–203.

Clark, G. H. (1944), 'The Theory of Time in Plotinus', *Philosophical Review* LIII: 337–358.

Clark, S. R. L. (1996), 'Plotinus: Body and Soul' in Gerson, pp. 275–291.

Claus, D. (1981), *Towards the Soul*, New Haven/London: Yale University Press.

Cleve, F. (1965), *The Giants of Pre-Sophistic Greek Philosophy*, v. I, The Hague: M. Nijhoff.

Cockburn, D. (1997), *Other Times: Philosophical perspectives on past, present and future*, Cambridge: Cambridge University Press.

Collobert, C. (1993), L'être de Parménide ou le refus du temps, Paris: Éd. Kimé.

Cordero N–L (1984), *Les deux chemins de Parménide*, Paris/Brussels: Vrin et Ousia.

Cornford, F. M. (1937), *Plato's Cosmology*, London: Routledge & Kegan Paul.

———, (1939), *Plato and Parmenides*, London: Routlege & Kegan Paul.

———, (1974), 'Mysticism and Science in the Pythagorean tradition' in Mourelatos, pp. 135–160.

———, (1975), 'Anaxagoras' theory of matter' in Allen and Furley, pp. 275–322.

Corrigan, K. (1982), 'Plotinus and St. Gregory of Nyssa: Can matter have a positive function?' in Livingston, pp. 14–20.

———, (1994), 'Berkeley and Plotinus on the non-existence of matter', *Hermathena* 157: 67–85.

———, (1996), *Plotinus' theory of matter-evil and question of substance: Plato, Aristotle, and Alexander of Aphrodisias*, Leuven: Peeters.

Couloubaritis, L. (1990), *Mythe et philosophie chez Parménide*, 2nd edn., Bruxelles: Ousia.

Curd, P. K. (1991), 'Knowledge and unity in Heraclitus', *The Monist* 74: 531–49.

———, (1997), *The Legacy of Parmenides: Eleatic Monism and later Presocratic Thought*, Princeton: Princeton University Press.

D'Ancona Costa (1996), 'Plotinus and later Platonic philosophers on the causality of the First Principle' in Gerson, pp. 356–385.

Deichgräber, K. (1959), *Parmenides' Auffahrt zur Göttin des Rechts*, Wiesbaden.

Dillon, J. (1977), *The Middle Platonist*, London: Duckworth.

———, (1985), *Alcinous: the Handbook of Platonism*, Oxford: Oxford University Press.

———, (1987), *Proclus' Commentary On Plato's Parmenides*, trans. G. Morrow and J. M. Dillon, Princeton: Princeton University Press.

———, (1996), 'An ethic in late antique sage' in Gerson, pp. 315–335.

Dillon, J., and Gerson, L. P. (2004), *Neoplatonic Philosophy: Introductory Readings*, Indianapolis/Cambridge: Hackett.

Dodds, E. R. (1928), 'The Parmenides of Plato and the Origin of the Neoplatonic One', *Classical Quarterly* 22: 129–42.

———, (1951), *The Greeks and the Irrational*, Berkley/Los Angeles: University of California Press.

———, (1960), 'Numénius et Ammonius' in *Les Sources de Plotin*, 1–61.

———, (1965), *Pagan and Christian in an Age of Anxiety*, Cambridge: Cambridge University Press.

Dörrie, H. (1974), 'Plotino: Tradizionalista o innovatore?' in *Plotino e il Neoplatonismo in Oriente e in Occidente*, Att del Convengo internazionale dell' Accademia Nazionale dei Lincei, Rome: Academia Nazionale del Lincei.

Dufour, R. (2001), 'Plotinus: A Bibliography 1950–2001', *Phronesis* vol. XLVI no. 3.

Edwards, J. (1990), 'A late use of Empedocles: the Oracle on Plotinus', *Mnemosyne* 43: 151–5.

Eliade, M. (1949), *Le Myth De L'Eternel Retour*, Gallimard.

Emilsson, E. K. (1996), 'Cognition and its object', in Gerson, pp. 217–249.

———, (2003), 'Plotinus', in Furley, pp. 363–387.

Evangeliou, C. (2002), 'Plotinus' Criticism of Materialism', in Gregorios, pp. 199–210.

Faggin, G. (1992), *Plotino Enneadi, Porfirio Vita di Plotino*, Milano: Rusconi.

Findlay, J. N. (1975), 'The three hypostases of Plotinism', *Rev. of Metaphysics* 28, 4: 660–680.

Fränkel, H. (1962), *Dichtung und Philosophie des früben Griechentums*, München: Beck.

———, (1970), *Wege und Formen frühgriechischen Denkens*, München: Beck.

Friedländer, P. (1958), *Plato I: An Introduction*, trans. by. H. Meyerhof, NY: Harper & Row.

Fritz, K. von (1964), 'Der ΝΟΥΣ des Anaxagoras', *Archiv für begriffsgeschichte* 9: 87–102.

Furley, D. (2003), *Routledge History of Philosophy: From Aristotle to Augustine*, vol. 2, London/New York: Routledge and Kegan Paul.

———, (1974), 'The atomists' reply to the Eleatics', in Mourelatos, pp. 504–526.

———, (1975), 'Empedocles and the clepsydra', in Allen and Furley, pp. 265–74.

Gatti, M. L. (1996), 'Plotinus: the Platonic tradition and the foundation of Neoplatonism', in Gerson, pp. 10–37.

Gelzer, T. (1982), 'Plotins Interesse an den Vorsokratiken,', *Museum Helveticum* 39: 101–31.

Gerson, L. P. (1994), *Plotinus*, London/New York: Routledge and Kegan Paul.

———, (ed.) (1996) *Cambridge Companion to Plotinus*, Cambridge: Cambridge University Press.

Gifford, E. H. (1903), *Eusebii Praeparatio Evangelica*, Oxford: Clarendon Press.

Gill, M. L. (1987), 'Matter and Flux in Plato's *Timaeus*', *Phronesis* 32: 34–53.

Goldin, O. (1998), 'Plato and the Arrow of Time', *Ancient Philosophy* 18: 125–143.

Gomperz, T. (1922), *Griechische Denker*, Berlin-Leipzig: Veit &Comp.

Göransson, T. (1995), *Albinus, Alcinous, Arius Didymus*, Göteborg: Ekblad & Co.

Graeser, A. (1972), *Plotinus and the Stoics: A preliminary study*, Leiden: E. J. Brill.

———, (1987), 'Zeitlichkeit und Zeitlosigkeit: Bemerkungen zu Plotins Unterscheidung zweier 'immer' (III, 7)', *Philosophisches Jahrbuch* 94, 1: 142–148.

Graham, D. W. (1999), 'Empedocles and Anaxagoras: Responses to Parmenides', in Long, pp. 159–180.

Gregorios, P., ed. (2002), *Neoplatonism and Indian Philosophy*, State University of New York Press.

Gregory, J. (1999), *The Neoplatonists*, London/New Cork: Routledge and Kegan Paul.

Guérard, C. (1987), 'Parménide d'Élée chez les néoplatoniciens', in *Études sur Parménide II: Problèmes d'interprétation*, publ. Sous la dir. De P. Aubenque, Bibli. d' hist. de la philos, Paris, Vrin, vol. 2, 294–313.

Guthrie, W. K. C. (1960), *The Greek Philosophers: From Thales to Aristotle*, Harper & Row.

Harder, R. (1936), 'Eine neue Schrift Plotins', *Hermes* 71: 1–10.

Harris, R. B., ed. (1976), *The Significance of Neoplatonism*, Virginia: ISNS.

———, ed. (1982), *The Structure of Being*, Albany: State University of New York Press.

Heidel, W. A. (1913), 'On certain Fragments of the Presocratics: critical notes and elucidations', *Proceedings in American Academy of Arts and Sciences*, 48: 681–734.

Hetzler, F. M. (1982), 'Matter and spirit: The ultimate artistic realities', *Diotima* 10: 26–34.

Hussey, E. (1972), *The Presocratics*, London: Duckworth.

———, (1982), 'Epistemology and Meaning in Heraclitus', in Schofield and Nussbaum, 1–32.

———, (1991), 'Heraclitus on living and dying', *The Monist* 74: 517–30.

Jackson, D. (1908), 'On Parmenides fr. 1.28-32', *Proceedings of the Cambridge Philological Society* 4: 4–20.

Jameson, G. (1958), 'Well-rounded truth and circular thought in Parmenides', *Phronesis* 3: 15–30.

Jevons, F. R. (1964), 'Dequantitation in Plotinus' cosmology, I', *Phronesis* 9, 1: 64–71.

Jonas, H. (1962), 'Plotin über Ewigkeit und Zeit', *Politische Ordnung unmd Menschliches Existenz, München*, pp. 295–319.

Kahn, C. (1960), *Anaximander and the origins of Greek cosmology*, Columbia University Press.

———, (1974), 'Religion and natural philosophy in Empedocles' doctrine of the soul', in Mourelatos, pp. 426–456.

Kalligas, P. (1997), '*Logos* and the Sensible Object in Plotinus', *Ancient Philosophy* 17: 397–410.

———, (2000), 'Living Body, Soul, and Virtue in the philosophy of Plotinus', *Dionysius* 18:25–38.

Kerferd, G. B. (1974), 'Anaxagoras and the concept of matter before Aristotle', in Mourelatos, pp. 489–503.

Kingsley, P. (1994), 'Empedocles and his interpreters: the four-element doxography', *Phronesis* 39: 235–254.

———, (1995), *Ancient Philosophy, Mystery, and Magic: Empedocles and the Pythagorean Tradition*, Oxford: Oxford University Press.

Kirk, G. S. (1949), 'Heraclitus and death in battle', *American Jour. of Philology* 70: 384–393.

———, (1951), 'Natural change in Heraclitus', *Mind* 60: 384–93.

———, (1954), *Heraclitus: The Cosmic Fragments*, Cambridge: Cambridge University Press.

KRS = Kirk, G. S., Raven, J. E., and Schofield, M. (1983), *The Presocratic Philosophers*, 2nd edn, Cambridge: Cambridge University Press.

Kneale, W. (1960), 'Time and eternity in theology', *Proceedings of the Aristotelian Society* 61: 87–108.

Kordig, C. (1982), 'The mathematics of mysticism: Plotinus and Proclus', in Harris, pp. 114–121.

Krämer, H. J. (1982), *Platone e fondamenti della metafisica*, Milano: Vita e Pensiero.

Laks, A. (1993), 'Mind's crisis: on Anaxagoras' nous', *Southern Jour. of Phil.* 31: 19–38.

Laks A., and Most G. (eds.) (1997), *Studies on the Derveni Papyrus*, Oxford: Clarendon Press.

Lebedev, A. (1987–1988), 'The imagery of lampadedromia in Heraclitus and the quotes of Heraclitus in Plotinus IV.8', *Philosophia* 17–18: 233–257, Athens: Research Centre of Greek Philosophy at the Academy of Athens.

Leyden, W. (1964), 'Time, number and eternity in Plato and Aristotle', *Philosophical Quarterly* 14: 35–53.

Livingston, E. A. (ed.) (1982), *Studia Patristica XVII*, Oxford: Pergamon Press.

Lloyd, A. C. (1969), 'Non-Discursive Thought: An Enigma of Greek Philosophy', *Proceedings of the Aristotelian Society* 70: 261–74.

———, (1986), 'Non-Propositional Thought in Plotinus', *Phronesis* 31: 258–65.

———, (1990), *The Anatomy of Neoplatonism*, Oxford: Oxford University Press.

Long, A. A. (1999), *The Cambridge Companion to Early Greek Philosophy*, Cambridge: Cambridge University Press.

Long, H. S. (1948), *A Study of the Doctrine of Metepsychosis in Greece from Pythagoras to Plato*, Phd. D. diss., Princeton University Press.

Lovejoy, A. O. (1964), *The Great Chain of Being*, Harvard University Press.

McTaggart, J. M. E. (1908), 'The unreality of time', *Mind* 17: 457–474.

Malin, S. (2001), *Nature Loves to Hide*, Oxford: Oxford University Press.

Manchester, P. (1978), 'Time and Soul in Plotinus III, 7 [45], 11', *Dionysius* 2: 101–136.

Mansfeld, J. (1964), *Die Offenbarung des Parmenides und die menschliche Welt*. Assen: Van Gorcum.

———, (1983), *Die Vorsokratiker I*, Stuttgart: Reclam.

———, (1992), *Heresiography in Context: Hippolytus' Elenchos as a Source for Greek Philosophy*, Leiden/New York/Cologne: Brill.

———, (1999), 'Sources' in Long, pp. 22–44.

Mansfeld, J., and De Rijk, L. M. (1975), *Kephalion: Studies in Greek Philosophy and its Continuation Offered to Professor C. J. de Vogel*, Assen: Van Gorcum.

May, W. E. (1970), 'The reality of matter in the metaphysics of Bergson', *International Philosophical Quarterly* 10: 611–722.

McDiarmid, J. B. (1953), 'Theophratus on the Presocratic Causes', *Harvard Studies in Classical Philology* 61: 85–156.

McTaggart, J. (1908), 'The unreality of time', *Mind*, 18: 457–84.

Meijer, P. A. (1992), *Plotinus on the Good or the One (Ennead VI, 9): an analytical commentary*, Amsterdam: Gieben.

———, (1997), *Parmenides Beyond the Gates: the divine revelation on Being, Thinking and doxa*, Amsterdam: Gieben.

Merlan, P. (1953), 'Plotinus and magic', *Isis* 44: 341–348.

Miller, C. L. (1977), 'Union with the One, Ennead VI, 9, 8–11', *The New Scholasticism* 51, 2: 182–195.

Minar, L. (1963), 'Cosmic Periods in the Philosophy of Empedocles', *Phronesis* 8: 127–145.

Mohr, R. D. (1986), 'Plato on time and eternity', *Ancient Philosophy* 6: 39–46.

Morewedge, P. (ed.) (1992), *Neoplatonism and Islamic Thought*, SUNY Press.

Mourelatos, A. P. D. (1970), *The Route of Parmenides*, Yale University Press.

———, (ed.) (1974), *The Pre-Socratics: A Collection of Critical Essays*, NY: Anchor Doubleday.

———, (1980), 'Plato's real astronomy: Republic VII.527D–531D' in Anton (ed.), *Science and the Sciences* in Plato, New York.

Le Néoplatonism (1971), Colloque de Royaumont, 9–13 juin 1969, Paris: Centre Nationale de la Recherche Scientifique.

Nikulin, D. (1998), 'Intelligible matter in Plotinus', *Dionysius* 16: 85–113.

Nock, A. D. (1972), *Essays on Religion and the Ancient World*, Oxford: Clarendon Press.

Nussbaum, M. C. (1972), 'ψυχή in Heraclitus', *Phronesis* 17: 1–16, 153–170.

O'Brien, D. (1980), 'Temps et intermporalité chez Parménide', *Les Études Philosophiques*, pp. 257–272.

———, (1985), 'Temps et éternité dans la philosophie grecque' in *Mythes et representations du temps*, pp. 59–85.

———, (1993), 'Le non-être dans la philosophie grecque: Parménide, Platon, Plotin' in *Études sur le Sophiste de Platon*, pp. 317–364.

———, (1996), 'Plotinus on matter and evil', in Gerson, pp. 171–195.

O'Meara, D. J. (1993), *Plotinus: An Introduction to the Enneads*, Oxford: Oxford University Press.

Onians, R. B. (1954), *The Origins of European Thought*, Cambridge: Cambridge University Press.

Osborne, C. (1997), 'Heraclitus' in Taylor, pp. 88–127.

Ousager, A. (1995), 'Plotinus on motion and personal identity in time and space [Part I]' in *Classica et mediaevalia* 46: 113–144.

Owen, G. E. L. (1960), 'Eleatic Questions', *Classical Quarterly* 10: 84–102.

———, (1966), 'Plato and Parmenides on the timeless present', *The Monist* 50: 317–340.

Palmer, J. A. (1999), *Plato's reception of Parmenides*, Oxford: Oxford University Press.

Peck, A. L. (1926), 'Anaxagoras and the parts', *Classical Quarterly* 20:57–71.

———, (1931), 'Anaxagoras: Predication as a problem of physics', *Classical Quarterly* 25:27–37; 112–120.

Philip, J. A. (1966), *Pythagoras and Early Pythagorianism*, Toronto: University of Toronto Press.

Phillips, E. D. (1955), 'Parmenides on Thought and Being', *Philosophical Review* 64: 15–29.

Puech, H.-Ch., 'Plotin et les Gnostiques' in *Les sources de Plotin*, pp. 159–190.

Raiger, M. (1990), 'Plotinus on matter', *Lyceum* 2, 2: 37–51.

Rangos, S. (1999), 'Between Physics and Nous: Logos as Principle of Meditation in Plotinus', *Journal of Neoplatonic Studies* 7, 2: 1–42.

Rappe, Sara (1996), 'Self-knowledge and subjectivity in the *Enneads*' in Gerson, pp. 250–274.

———, (2000), *Reading Neoplatonism: Non-Discursive Thinking in the Texts of Plotinus, Proclus and Damascius*, Cambridge: Cambridge University Press.

Raven, J. E. (1954), 'The basis of Anaxagoras' cosmology', *Classical Quarterly* 4: 123–137.

Riaux, F. (1840), *Essai sur Parménide d'Élée*, Paris.

Riezler, K. (1970), *Parmenides: Text, Ubersetzung und Interpretation*, 2nd ed. Avec Nachwort de Hans-Georg Gadamer.

Ring, M. (1987), *Beginning with the Presocratics*, California: Mayfield Pub.

Rist, J. M. (1961), 'Plotinus on matter and evil', *Phronesis* 6: 154–166.

———, (1962), 'The Indefinite Dyad and Intelligible Matter in Plotinus', *CQ* 13: 223–31.

———, (1964), 'Mysticism and transcendence in later Neoplatonism', *Hermes* 92: 213–225.

———, (1966), 'On tracking Alexander of Aphrodisias', *Archiv für Gesschichte der Philosophie* 48: 89–90.

———, (1967), *Plotinus: The Road to Reality*, Cambridge: Cambridge University Press.

———, (1969), *Stoic Philosophy*, Cambridge: Cambridge University Press.

Robinson, J. M. (1968), *An Introduction to Early Greek Philosophy*, Cambridge: Cambridge University Press.

———, (1986), 'The Timaues on types of duration', *Illinois Classical Studies* 11:134–151.

Roloff, F. (1970), *Plotin Die Grosschrift III, 8; V, 8; V, 5; II, 9*, Berlin: de Gruyter.

Romano, F. (1983), 'Plotino, interprete de Eraclito', *Studi e ricerche sul neoplatonismo*, Naples, Guida editori, pp. 27–34.

Roussos, E. N. (1968), *Ο ΗΡΑΚΛΕΙΤΟΣ ΣΤΙΣ ΕΝΝΕΑΔΕΣ ΤΟΥ ΠΛΩΤΙΝΟΥ*, Athens.

———, (1974), Roussos, 'ΒΙΒΛΙΟΚΡΙΣΙΑΙ *of Plotini Opera* Tomi III. Eds. P. Henry et H.R. Schwyzer: Paris / Bruxelles / Leiden, De Brouwer / 1951–1973', *Philosophia* 4: 459–465, Athens: Research Centre of Greek Philosophy the Academy of Athens.

Sambursky, S. (1959), *Physics of the Stoics*, London: Routledge.

———, (1956), *The Physical World of the Greeks*, trans. Merton Dagut. New York: Macmillan Co.

Sandywell, B. (1996), *Presocratic Reflexivity: The Construction of Philosophical Discourse*, London/New York: Routledge.

Schofield, M. (1970), 'Did Parmenides discover eternity?', *Archiv für Geschichte der Philosophie* 52: 113–135.

———, (1980), *An Essay of Anaxagoras*, Cambridge: Cambridge University Press.

———, (1997), 'The Ionians' in Taylor, pp. 47–87.

Schofield, M., and Nussbaum, M. C. (eds.) (1982), *Language and Logos: Studies in Ancient Greek Philosophy*, Cambridge: Cambridge University Press.

Schroeder, F. M. (1996), 'Plotinus and Language' in Gerson (1996), pp. 336–355.

Schwabe, W. (1975), 'Welches sind die materiellen Elemente bei Anaxagoras?' *Phronesis* 20:1–10.

Sells, M. A. (1985), 'Apophasis in Plotinus: A critical approach', *Harvard Theological Review* 78, 1–2: 47–65.

Shaw, G. (1999), 'Eros and Arithmos: Pythagorean theurgy in Iamblichus and Plotinus', *Ancient Philosophy* 19,1: 121–143.

Slezák, T. (1979), *Platon und Aristoteles in der Nuslehre Plotins*, Basek/Stuttgart: Schwabe.

———, (1993), *Platon lessen*, Frommann-Holzboog: Stuttgart.

Smith, A. (ed.) (1993), *Porphyrii Philosophi Fragmenta*, Leipzig: Teubner.

———, (1996), 'Eternity and time' in Gerson, pp. 196–216.

———, (1998), 'Soul and time in Plotinus', in *Psukhe—Seele—anima: Festschrift für Karin Alt zum 7. Mai 1998*, hrsg. Von. J. Holzhausen, Stuttgart: Teubner, pp. 355–344.

———, (2004), *Philosophy in Late Antiquity*, London/New York: Routledge.

Snell, B. (1946), *Die Entdeckung des Geistes*, Hamburg.

Sorabji, R. (1980), *Necessity, Cause and Blame*, London: Duckworth.

———, (1982), 'Myths About Non-Propositional Thought' in Schofield and Nussbaum.

———, (1983), *Time, Creation and the Continuum: Theories in Antiquity and the Early Middle Ages*, London: Duckworth.

Les Sources de Plotin (1960), Geneva: Fondation Hardt.

Sparshott, F. E. (1972), *Looking for Philosophy*, Montreal and London: McGill-Queen's University Press.

Stein, H. (1867), 'Die Fragmente des Parmenides περὶ φύσεως', in *Symbola philologorum Bonnesium*, in honor of Friedrich Ritschl, vol. II, Leipzig: Teubner.

Strang, C. (1975), 'The physical theory of Anaxagoras', *Archiv für Gesschichte der Philosophie* 45: 101–118.

Strange, Steven (1994), 'Plotinus on the nature of eternity and time', in *Aristotle in Late Antiquity: Studies in philosophy and the history of philosophy*, Washington DC, The Catholic University of America Press.

Stokes, M. C. (1965), 'On Anaxagoras: Part I: Anaxagoras' theory of matter; Part II: The order of cosmogony', *Archiv für Gesschichte der Philosophie* 47:1–19; 217–250.

Suda = *Suidas Lexicographus*, edited by Bernhardy G., 1853, Halle.

Sumi, A. (1993), *The One's knowledge in Plotinus*, PhD thesis, Loyola University of Chicago.

Tannery, P. (1887), *Pour l'historie de la science hellène*, Paris.

Tarán, L. (1979), 'Perpetual duration and atemporal eternity in Parmenides and Plato', *The Monist* 62: 43–53.

Taylor C. C. W. (ed.) (1997), *Routledge History of Philosophy Volume 1: From the Beginning to Plato*, London/New York: Routledge.

Teodorsson, S. (1982), *Anaxagoras' Theory of Matter*, Göteborg: Acta Universitatis.

Townsley, A. L. (1976), 'Some comments on Parmenidean Eros', *Eos*, 64: 153–161.

Trépanier, S. (2003), 'Empedocles on the Ultimate Symmetry of the World', *Oxford Studies in Ancient Philosophy* 24: 1–58.

Tugwell, S. (1964), 'The Way of Truth', *Classical Quarterly* 14: 36–41.

Turetzky, P. (1998), *Time*, London/New York: Routledge.

Vamvakas, K. (2001), *ΟΙ ΘΕΜΕΛΙΩΤΕΣ ΤΗΣ ΔΥΤΙΚΗΣ ΣΚΕΨΗΣ*, University of Crete Press.

Verdenius, W. J. (1942), *Parmenides: some comments on his poem*, Groningen: J. B. Walters.

Vlastos, G. (1953), Review of J. Zafiropoulo L' École éléate (Paris 1950), *Gnomon* 25:166–9.

———, (1965), 'Creation in the Timaeus: Is it a fiction?', in *Studies in Plato's Metaphysics*, ed. Allen, pp. 401–419.

———, (1974), 'The physical theory of Anaxagoras' in Mourelatos, pp. 459–488.

Vuia, O. (1961), *Remontée aux sources de la pensée occidentale. Héraclite, Parménide, Anaxagore*, Paris: Les travaux du Centre Roumain de Recherches.

Wallis, R. T. (1976), 'ΝΟΥΣ as Experience', in Harris, pp. 121–153.

———, (1995), *Neoplatonism*, 2nd edn., London: Duckworth.

West, M. L. (1971), *Early Greek Philosophy and the Orient*, Oxford: Clarendon Press.

Whittaker, J. (1968), 'The eternity of the platonic forms', *Phronesis* 13: 131–144.

———, (1969), 'Ammonius on the Delphic E', *Classical Quarterly* 19: 185–192.

———, (1971), *God, Time, Being*, *in Symbolae Osloenses*, supp. vol. 23, 1–66.

Wiggins, D. (1982), 'Heraclitus' conceptions of flux, fire and material persistence', in Schofield and Nussbaum, pp. 1–32.

Wright, M. R. (1995), *Cosmology in Antiquity*, London/New York: Routledge.

———, (1997a), 'Philosophers Poets: Parmenides and Empedocles', in *Form and Content in DidacticPoetry*, ed. C. Atherton, Bari: Levanti Eidtori, 1–22.

———, (1997b), 'Empedocles', in Taylor, pp. 175–207.

———, (ed.) (2000), *Reason and Necessity: Essays on Plato's Timaeus*, London: Duckworth.

Zeller, E. (1882), *A History of Greek Philosophy from the Earliest Period to the Time of Socrates*, 2 vol, trans., in English by S. F. Alleyne, London: Longmans.

Zuntz, G. (1971), *Persephone: Three Essays on Religion and Thought in Magna Gaecia*, Oxford: Oxford University Press.

Index Fontium

References of Presocratic Fragments and Testimonies in the *Enneads*
The Presocratic references follow the numbering and arrangement of Diles-Kranz, *Fragmente der Vorsokratiker*.

Index